THE OLD FARMER'S ALMANAC

CALCULATED ON A NEW AND IMPROVED PLAN FOR THE YEAR OF OUR LORD

2021

Being the 1st after Leap Year and (until July 4) 245th year of American Independence

FITTED FOR BOSTON AND THE NEW ENGLAND STATES, WITH SPECIAL CORRECTIONS AND CALCULATIONS TO ANSWER FOR ALL THE UNITED STATES.

Containing, besides the large number of Astronomical Calculations and the Farmer's Calendar for every month in the year, a variety of NEW, USEFUL, & ENTERTAINING MATTER.

ESTABLISHED IN 1792
BY ROBERT B. THOMAS (1766–1846)

Knowledge is telling the past. Wisdom is predicting the future.
–W. Timothy Garvey, American endocrinologist and clinical investigator (b. 1951)

Cover design registered U.S. Trademark Office

Copyright © 2020 by Yankee Publishing Incorporated, An Employee-Owned Company
ISSN 0078-4516

Library of Congress Card No. 56-29681

Cover illustration by Steven Noble • Original wood engraving (above) by Randy Miller

The Old Farmer's Almanac • Almanac.com
P.O. Box 520, Dublin, NH 03444 • 603-563-8111

CONTENTS

10

24

2021 TRENDS
Facts to Ponder and Forecasts to Watch For 6

ABOUT THIS ALMANAC
Contact Us — 1, 98, 100
To Patrons — 4

AMUSEMENT
The Most Practiced Sport in the World — 188
How to Clean Your Chimney — 192
Essay Contest Winners — 248
Mind-Manglers — 250
Anecdotes & Pleasantries — 252

192

ASTROLOGY
Convincing Signs — 198
Secrets of the Zodiac — 224
Best Days for 2021 — 226

ASTRONOMY
Eclipses — 102
Bright Stars — 104
The Twilight Zone/ Meteor Showers — 106
The Visible Planets — 108
Astronomical Glossary — 110
Test Your Sky-Q — 154

154

CALENDAR
Three-Year Calendar — 114
How to Use This Almanac — 115
Calendar Pages — 120–147
Holidays and Observances — 148
Glossary of Almanac Oddities — 152
Tides — 235, 236
Time Corrections — 238

FOOD

Recipe Contest Winners	60
Make Room for Maple!	174

GARDENING

Small-Space Gardening 101	32
Growing Wild	40
How to Make a Field	178
Planting by the Moon's Phase	230
Frosts and Growing Seasons	232
Phenology: Nature's Calendar	233

GENEALOGY

Secret Symbols of Cemeteries	196

HOME REMEDIES

Time-Tested Tips for Fighting Colds and Flu	184

MISCELLANY

Gestation and Mating Tables	229
Table of Measures	234
A Reference Compendium	257

NATURE

Birds on the Wing	72
When Predators Come Calling	160
Best Fishing Days	228

PETS

How to Pick a Pet	168

ROMANCE

Love Lessons From Old Valentines	66

SPECIAL REPORT

Farming for Good	48

WEATHER

From Sea to Rising Sea	80
Winter/Summer Weather Maps	96
General Weather Forecast	97
How We Predict the Weather	202
How Accurate Was Our Forecast Last Winter?	204
Weather Regions Map	205
Forecasts by Region	206–223

TOGETHER!

Hello, friends! Thank you for your support! We're happy to be celebrating another year, *thanks to you: you,* the folks who buy the Almanac; *you,* the advertisers who believe in our brand; *you,* the merchants who display and sell the Almanac; *you,* the distributors and drivers who deliver the Almanac to stores or directly to readers; *you,* our printers; *you,* our circulation partners; *you,* our contributors and colleagues. We thank you!

For 229 years, through all kinds of literal and figurative weather, you have turned to us for advice, wisdom, and a reason to smile. Exceeding your expectations continues to be our purpose: Our dedication to being "useful, with a pleasant degree of humor" is unwavering, now and into the future.

Indeed, this Almanac, the oldest continuously published periodical in North America, is a sturdy thread sewing together more than two centuries of human experience.

Today this strand stitches the printed pages of this book to the limitless world of Almanac.com, where you can easily explore a tapestry of information on thousands of pages about gardening, astronomy, weather, nature, food and cooking, home remedies, pet care, puzzles, humor, and much, much more.

Peruse these digital pages, cycle through the seasons with our free e-newsletter, or connect with a question or comment at any time. Reach out to us on Facebook, Instagram, and Pinterest. We're here for you, with you, because of you.

Together, let us not lose sight of the wonders of the natural world, for we are forever linked to it and through it. Consider the words of the seventh editor of this Almanac, Horace Ware, in the 1919 edition:

"If the reader of this Almanac shall achieve the calmness of mind so often induced by a study of the heavens, with their vastness of time and space, or if, in contemplating the changing seasons, with their perpetual renewing of life, he shall be brought into closer contact with Mother Nature and a better realization of her healing processes . . . then we are content."

It is the eternal truth of these notions that continues to connect *us* with *you.*

–J. S., JUNE 2020

However, it is by our works and not our words that we would be judged. These, we hope, will sustain us in the humble though proud station we have so long held in the name of

Your obedient servant,

4

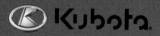

2021 TRENDS

WHAT'S COOKING?

"Plant-based eating will continue to expand. Consumers will have a range of options for protein, from traditional animal protein to plant-based to cell-based."

–Melanie Zanoza Bartelme, global food analyst, Mintel

RETHINKING RECYCLING

● Restaurants are using edible tableware (e.g., wheat bran plates, pasta straws).

● Companies are collecting food containers from restaurant customers, cleaning them, and then returning them to restaurants for reuse.

● People are carrying personal cutlery and

BUZZWORD
Reducetarians:
people who eat less meat

containers to avoid using disposables.

GOING SOLO
Brands are catering to the boom in single-person households with . . .

● packaged food sold in single-serving portions

● bread loaves in half-sizes

FOOD'S PAST
"Organic" isn't enough anymore: "Consumers want to know what else is being done to show that companies care about how their food is grown and produced."
–Laurie Demeritt, CEO, The Hartman Group

FOLLOW US:

FACTS TO PONDER AND FORECASTS TO WATCH FOR

Compiled by Stacey Kusterbeck

BY THE NUMBERS:
15% of U.S. restaurants serve meatless burgers

$3,459: amount average U.S. household spent dining out in 2018

Consumers want . . .
- crops grown using practices that are good for soil health

- animals spending time outdoors

- farm/factory workers treated fairly

FOOD'S PRESENT
- In home fridges, we're storing foods—especially fruit and vegetables—by color for visual appeal and to inspire healthy choices.

- We're growing "counter-to-table" food in the kitchen.

FOOD'S FUTURE
- Robot arms will help with cooking by lifting, pouring, and chopping.

- Refrigerators will alert us to spoiled food.

SMART MARKETS
- "Time-pressed shoppers are demanding quicker and more meaningful experiences."
–Phil Lempert, founder, SupermarketGuru.com

Some supermarkets will be . . .
- stocking plant-based items that promise to improve brain and bone health

- offering customers multiyear agreements to auto-replenish groceries

- giving farmers in-store floor space for growing produce

- selling food produced on farms practicing regenerative agriculture
(continued)

IN THE GARDEN

"People are coming together, on- and offline, to connect and share their love of plants"—e.g., at plant swaps, people are tagging cuttings with details of their plant's history.

–Katie Dubow, president, Garden Media Group

WE'RE GROWING . . .

- cover crops to control weeds and enrich soil

- mushrooms on inoculated logs

- many plants in small spaces using indoor aeroponics systems

FRUGAL GROWERS ARE

- making terrariums in discarded bottles

- propagating plant cuttings in dry/empty fish tanks

- composting food scraps overnight in electric composters

THE MOST PHOTOGENIC PLANTS . . .

- are chartreuse, pink, or purple

- are flowering tropicals

- have variegated foliage

COMPANION PLANTERS, UNITE!

- "People are gardening in the front yard to get to know their neighbors."
–Leslie Halleck, author, Plant Parenting (Timber Press, 2019)

THE FUTURE LOOKS ROSY

- "People are using roses as landscape shrubs rather than pampered specimens."
–Bob Osborn, author, Hardy Roses *(Firefly Books, 2020)*

MUST-HAVE HOUSEPLANTS

- plants in categories based on their lighting requirements

- plants packaged with specialty soils

(continued)

FOLLOW US:

9

• genetically modified plants that remove toxins from the air

HOUSEPLANTS ARE HOUSEWIDE

• in dark corners: low-light succulents

• in bedrooms: bromeliads

• in bathrooms: ferns

NEW LOOKS FOR LANDSCAPES

• "Native and prairie-like plantings are getting reimagined." Gardeners are creating "mini meadows" in side yards and on grass strips between streets and homes.
–Jennifer Smock, horticulturist, Missouri Botanical Garden

WE'RE GROWING UP . . .

• Outdoors: With trailing vines (English ivy, vinca vine,

'COOL WAVE' PANSIES

wandering Jew), flowering plants (bridal veil, 'Cool Wave' pansies), and tropical plants in pots on walls or fences to maximize small spaces
–Tim Pollak, outdoor floriculturist, Chicago Botanic Garden

• Indoors: In any room, with vertical hydroponics systems that produce fresh fruit and veggies for harvest

TOPS IN TINY TOMATOES

Dwarf-size varieties in pots are all the rage:
• Jennifer Smock likes 'Geranium Kiss', 'Little Bing', 'Micro Tom', and 'Patio Choice Yellow'.

'LITTLE BING' TOMATOES

• PanAmerican Seed suggests 'Tidy Rose' compact beefsteak and Kitchen Minis series 'Siam', an indoor cherry tomato.

FLORAL FAVES

• In vases: Bouquets overflow with billowy, blousy blooms—"The more ruffled, the more petals, the fuller, the better."

In gardens: "Old-fashioned flowers—dahlias, zinnias, and sweet peas—are making a comeback."
–Marc Hachadourian, director, Glasshouse Horticulture, New York Botanical Garden

DAHLIAS

FOR HEAVEN'S STAKES!

• We're cutting shrubs like willow, hazel, and smoke bush to ground level and using the stems as stakes or fencing material.
–Adam Dooling, curator, Outdoor Gardens and Herbaceous Collections, New York Botanical Garden

(continued)

FOLLOW US:

![Photo of a dog and two cats sharing a food bowl]

OUR ANIMAL FRIENDS

"Nutrient-dense insect- and plant-based pet foods are growing in popularity. Pet owners are seeking hypoallergenic diets that are also better for the environment."

–Glenn A. Polyn, editor in chief, Pet Age

PET TECH PAWS-IBILITIES

- collars that transmit a dog's vital signs to its vet

- cat litter that changes color if the animal is ill

- "more ways to track pet health, monitor needs, and stay in contact"
–Susan Dankert, communications director, Pet Industry Joint Advisory Council of Canada

- pet doors that can be opened/closed remotely by owners when not at home

BY THE NUMBERS

85% of cat owners say that their pet makes them healthier

92% of dog owners say that their pet makes them healthier

- onscreen games for dogs to play, with treats for prizes

PET PERKS ABOUND

"Pet boarding continues to set new standards, while cities and communities are converting unused public spaces into dog parks and pet-friendly areas," says Phillip Cooper, president, Pet Industry Expert. Plus, he reports . . .

Photo: chendongshan/Getty Images

FOLLOW US:

FIREWOOD ALERT!

You have the power to protect forests and trees!

BUY IT WHERE YOU BURN IT.

Pests like the invasive emerald ash borer can hitchhike in your firewood. You can prevent the spread of these damaging insects and diseases by following these firewood tips:

▶ Buy locally harvested firewood at or near your destination.

▶ Buy certified heat-treated firewood ahead of time, if available.

▶ Gather firewood on site when permitted.

What might be in your firewood?

GYPSY MOTH is a devastating pest of oaks and other trees. Female moths lay tan patches of eggs on firewood, campers, vehicles, patio furniture — anything outside! When these items are moved to new areas, this pest gets a free ride.

SPOTTED LANTERNFLY sucks sap from dozens of tree and plant species. This pest loves tree-of-heaven but will feed on black walnut, white oak, sycamore, and grape. Like the gypsy moth, this pest lays clusters of eggs on just about any dry surface, from landscaping stone to firewood!

ASIAN LONGHORNED BEETLE will tunnel through, and destroy, over 20 species of trees — especially maple trees. The larvae of this beetle bore into tree branches and trunks, making it an easy pest to accidentally transport in firewood.

EMERALD ASH BORER — the infamous killer of ash trees — is found in forests and city trees across much of the eastern and central United States. This insect is notoriously good at hitching rides in infested firewood. Don't give this tree-killing bug a ride to a new forest, or a new state!

DONTMOVE FIREWOOD.org

This graphic is for illustrative purposes only. Many of these pests will only infest certain types of trees, making it very unlikely for a single log to contain all species as shown.

Visit dontmovefirewood.org for more information.

• Gas stations, convenience stores, and laundromats are getting DIY dog washes and vending machines that offer pet treats.

• Pet "hotels" offer special diets, swimming pools, workout classes, play time, and video links for owners who wish to check on pets.

• Veterinary services are being offered in retail stores.

• Dogs and their owners are attending fitness classes together.

BUZZWORD
Fur-ternity leave: time off for workers to care for new pets

HEALTH CHECK

"More people will forgo indoor gyms for outdoor workouts and organized fitness classes in parks."

–Florence Williams, author, The Nature Fix
(W. W. Norton & Co., 2017)

NATURE NURTURES
• City dwellers with trees within walking distance of home are healthier than those without or with only green space.

COMING SOON . . .
• toilets that monitor blood pressure

• devices that get moisture from air and turn it into drinkable water

• floors that detect a person's fall, then call for help

DUTIFUL DOCTORS . . .
• write prescriptions for patients to be outdoors, with times and locations specified

• prescribe placebos for patients who take them knowingly

HEALTHY HABITS
• scheduling doctor house calls digitally

• joining workout classes in progress, viewed on home screens *(continued)*

BY THE NUMBERS
120 minutes per week: minimum time people need to spend outdoors in order to feel healthier

FOLLOW US:

BY THE NUMBERS

Percentage of Americans who think that their tax rate is . . .

- too high: **57%**
- just right: **34%**
- too low: **9%**

46% of Canadians say that major credit card debt would end a relationship

$12,615: amount of credit card debt that would end a relationship in the U.S.

24% of Canadians were debt-free as of January 2019

13% of Americans never plan to retire

77% of Canadian workers would accept less pay in exchange for improved well-being (e.g., child or elder care, more personal or mental health days, more lenient time-off policies)

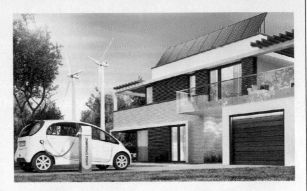

MONEY MATTERS

"Environmental issues will become even more important as Gen Z consumers gain more buying power."
–*Melanie Zanoza Bartelme, global food analyst, Mintel*

SMALL IS BIG

- Rural areas and smaller cities often have larger available talent pools and lower costs of living. As a result, "More entrepreneurs are staying in their hometowns, rather than clustering in San Francisco and New York."
–*Jason Feifer, editor in chief,* Entrepreneur

GROWTH OPPORTUNITIES

- "Thanks to a range of start-ups, the average person is now investing in shares of things they were never able to before— commercial real estate, antique cars, even fractional shares of expensive stocks like Apple," says Jason Feifer. As the value of the item rises, so does the value of the shares.

GOTTA HAVE IT NOW?

- Impulse buys will burgeon due to frictionless payments (tap to pay, apps to pay, etc.): "Paying for what you buy will get easier and easier."
–*Kit Yarrow, author,* Decoding the New Consumer Mind *(Jossey-Bass, 2014)*

(continued)

Photo: sl-f/Getty Images

FOLLOW US:

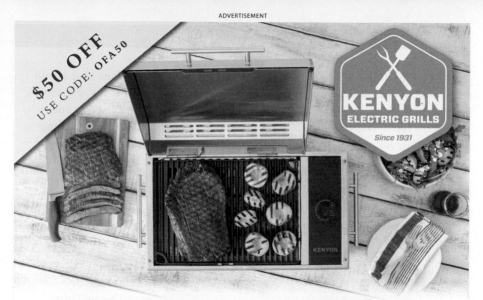

$50 OFF
USE CODE: OFA50

KENYON
ELECTRIC GRILLS
Since 1931

DISCOVER THE SECRET
TO PERFECTLY GRILLED FOOD

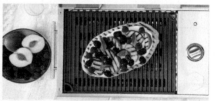

550°F+ IN UNDER
7 MINUTES

FLAMELESS AND
SMOKELESS

YEAR-ROUND
GRILLING

ENJOY HEALTHY
COOKING

PROUDLY HANDCRAFTED IN CONNECTICUT

COOKWITHKENYON.COM | 860.664.4906

PENNY-PINCHING
- "People are loading their phones with apps to tap friends and family for that $10 owed to them and to keep a closer eye on their stocks and spending."
–Quentin Fottrell, personal finance editor, MarketWatch

POCKET CHANGERS
- Workers are asking employers to allocate a portion of paychecks for goals other than retirement (e.g., travel funds, loan payments).

BUZZWORD
Circular economy: the practice of reusing existing products instead of making new ones

- "We're questioning the way things have always been done (e.g., celebrating with an expensive meal, buying a house) and becoming more comfortable with saying no to social obligations that strain our finances, choosing instead to save and spend on what brings us and our families the greatest meaning and benefit—such as traveling, going back to school, making other investments."
–Sandra E. Martin, editor in chief, MoneySense

- Businesses are "rounding up" purchases to the nearest dollar and putting the difference into our savings accounts.

COLLECTIBLES

"High-end objects (e.g., designer bags, watches, cars, wine, jewelry) have caught the interests of collectors and dealers."
–Kelly Juhasz, Toronto appraiser

U.S. INTERESTS
- "Anything related to the Apollo Moon missions and space in general has skyrocketed in value."
–Tony Drew, professor, Asheford Institute of Antiques

AUCTION ACTION
- A Babe Ruth NY Yankees shirt from 1928–30 sold for $5.64M.

- The first mid-engine 2020 Corvette Stingray, VIN 001, sold for $3M.

(continued)

FOLLOW US:

- The green Ford Mustang used in the 1968 film *Bullitt* sold for $3.4M.

- A letter dated July 6, 1776, signed by John Hancock and announcing the adoption of the Declaration of Independence sold for $1M.

- An 1870s copper and zinc weathervane depicting firefighters and a pair of horses hauling a steam fire engine sold for $437,500.

GOOD BETS TO BUY NOW

- factory-sealed vintage video games

- antique cast-iron skillets and vintage Pyrex and CorningWare bakeware

- game-worn jerseys (to be displayed on mannequins in man caves)

- Inuit sculptures made of soapstone

AROUND THE HOUSE

"Traditional decor—moldings, built-in shelving, ornate plasterwork—is back in a big way."

–Ana Cummings, president, Alberta chapter, Decorators and Designers Association of Canada

THIS YEAR'S COLORS

- in living rooms: sofas in dark gray or navy blue; throw pillows and rugs in red, yellow, blue

- in kitchens: dark green cabinets

- in bathrooms: black walls and vanities

- on walls, inside or out: olive green

HOME BUYERS SEEK . . .

- farmhouse exteriors (porches, large doors) and modern interiors

- car-free communities

- "jewel box houses"— small, with luxurious amenities

- accessory dwelling units (ADUs) for family or tenants

(continued)

FOLLOW US:

INTERIOR WISH LISTS

- hand-washing sinks in front vestibules
- mixed metals for bath fixtures
- large walk-in showers
- dual islands in kitchens, with one for socializing and one for cooking
- deep-soaking and claw-foot tubs

RETRO REBOUNDS

- "Home decor will remind us of our grandmothers' collections of china, needlepoint pillows, and decorative tchotchkes."

–Cate Geiger Kalus, style director, Country Living

HEADS UP!

"Designers are turning their attention to the fifth wall—the ceiling!," says Alessandra Wood, interior design expert at Modsy. We'll see ceilings . . .

- papered to match walls
- painted in patterns

HOME TECH TODAY

- faucets that change color with the water temperature
- ovens that cook food at different temperatures simultaneously

NATURE'S COMING IN

"Honest, real materials will be big," including . . .

- natural wood and raw stone
- textured wool blankets

–Kelly DeVore, interior design chair, Columbus College of Art & Design

- portable countertop dishwashers
- rooftop gardens on glass homes with hydraulics that lower them into the ground

COMING SOON . . .

- countertops that adjust their height automatically, based on facial and voice recognition
- faucets that dispense chilled, boiling, or carbonated water

SOLO OCCUPANTS SEEK

- mini appliances and small grill pans and Dutch ovens
- countertops that slide over cooktop surfaces   *(continued)*

BY THE NUMBERS

Home style preference in the U.S.:

54%:
contemporary

41%:
modern farmhouse

–The American Institute of Architects Home Design Trends Survey

FOLLOW US:

ON THE FARM

"Massive rooftop food gardens and farms are showing up around the world, from Thailand to France to Canada."

–Michael Levenston, executive director, City Farmer, Vancouver, Canada

FORWARD-LOOKING FARMERS ARE . . .

- creating conservation easements to protect agricultural land from development
- "rewilding" farmland to reintroduce native plants and attract birds, mammals, and other animals
- relying on GPS to maximize planting and harvesting efficiency

THE NEW FARM

- Online tools are connecting beginning farmers with like-minded land owners.
- Developers are converting vacant commercial buildings into indoor farms.
- Investors are buying conventional farmland and converting it to organic.

(continued)

BY THE NUMBERS: U.S.

25% of farmers are beginners (with 10 years of experience or less)

133,176 farms and ranches use renewable energy-producing systems (more than double those in 2012)

130,056 farms sell directly to consumers
–2017 Census of Agriculture, USDA

1,400: number of urban farms in Detroit, Michigan

8.3 million: acres of land certified for organic field crop production

18,155: farms certified to grow organically

45% of principal farm operators also have off-farm jobs

441 acres: average farm size

BY THE NUMBERS: CANADA

778 acres: average farm size

Photo: juliet514/Getty Images

FOLLOW US:

SoClean.

Fast and Easy Sleep Equipment Maintenance

- Saves time
- Easy to use
- 100% waterless
- Risk-free

Try SoClean Risk-Free for 30 Nights

Visit SoClean.com

Contraindications for Use: Persons with underlying lung diseases, such as asthma and COPD, and those with cardiovascular disease may be sensitive to ozone and should consult with their physician before using this product.

Choose Life
Grow Young with HGH

From the landmark book Grow Young with HGH comes the most powerful, over-the-counter health supplement in the history of man. Human growth hormone was first discovered in 1920 and has long been thought by the medical community to be necessary only to stimulate the body to full adult size and therefore unnecessary past the age of 20. Recent studies, however, have overturned this notion completely, discovering instead that the natural decline of Human Growth Hormone (HGH), from ages 21 to 61 (the average age at which there is only a trace left in the body) and is the main reason why the body ages and fails to regenerate itself to its 25 year-old biological age.

Like a picked flower cut from the source, we gradually wilt physically and mentally and become vulnerable to a host of degenerative diseases, that we simply weren't susceptible to in our early adult years.

Modern medical science now regards aging as a disease that is treatable and preventable and that "aging", the disease, is actually a compilation of various diseases and pathologies, from everything, like a rise in blood glucose and pressure to diabetes, skin wrinkling and so on. All of these aging symptoms can be stopped and rolled back by maintaining Growth Hormone levels in the blood at the same levels HGH existed in the blood when we were 25 years old.

There is a receptor site in almost every

New! Doctor Recommended

The Reverse Aging Miracle

RELEASE YOUR OWN GROWTH HORMONE AND ENJOY:

- Improved sleep & emotional stability
- Increased energy & exercise endurance
- Loss of body fat
- Increased bone density
- Improved memory & mental alertness
- Increased muscle strength & size
- Reverse baldness & color restored
- **Regenerates Immune System**

- Strengthened heart muscle
- Controlled cholesterol
- **Normalizes blood pressure**
- Controlled mood swings
- Wrinkle disappearance
- Reverse many degenerative disease symptoms
- Heightened five senses awareness
- Increased skin thickness & texture

All Natural Formula

This program will make a radical difference in your health, appearance and outlook. In fact we are so confident of the difference GHR can make in your life we offer a 100% refund on unopened containers.

1-877-849-4777
www.biehealth.us

A Product of Global Health Products

BIE Health Products
3840 East Robinson Road
Box 139
Amherst, NY 14228

GHR

DISCOVER   VISA   MasterCard

DIV 2037839 ON

cell in the human body for HGH, so its regenerative and healing effects are very comprehensive.

Growth Hormone, first synthesized in 1985 under the Reagan Orphan drug act, to treat dwarfism, was quickly recognized to stop aging in its tracks and reverse it to a remarkable degree. Since then, only the lucky and the rich have had access to it at the cost of $10,000 US per year.

The next big breakthrough was to come in 1997 when a group of doctors and scientists, developed an all-natural source product which would cause your own natural HGH to be released again and do all the remarkable things it did for you in your 20's. Now available to every adult for about the price of a coffee and donut a day.

GHR now available in America, just in time for the aging Baby Boomers and everyone else from age 30 to 90 who doesn't want to age rapidly but would rather stay young, beautiful and healthy all of the time.

The new HGH releasers are winning converts from the synthetic HGH users as well, since GHR is just as effective, is oral instead of self-injectable and is very affordable.

GHR is a natural releaser, has no known side effects, unlike the synthetic version and has no known drug interactions. Progressive doctors admit that this is the direction medicine is seeking to go, to get the body to heal itself instead of employing drugs. GHR is truly a revolutionary paradigm shift in medicine and, like any modern leap frog advance, many others will be left in the dust holding their limited, or useless drugs and remedies.

It is now thought that HGH is so comprehensive in its healing and regenerative powers that it is today, where the computer industry was twenty years ago, that it will displace so many prescription and non-prescription drugs and health remedies that it is staggering to think of.

The president of BIE Health Products stated in a recent interview, I've been waiting for these products since the 70's. We knew they would come, if only we could stay healthy and live long enough to see them! If you want to stay on top of your game, physically and mentally as you age, this product is a boon, especially for the highly skilled professionals who have made large investments in their education, and experience. Also with the failure of Congress to honor our seniors with pharmaceutical coverage policy, it's more important than ever to take pro-active steps to safeguard your health. Continued use of GHR will make a radical difference in your health, HGH is particularly helpful to the elderly who, given a choice, would rather stay independent in their own home, strong, healthy and alert enough to manage their own affairs, exercise and stay involved in their communities. Frank, age 85, walks two miles a day, plays golf, belongs to a dance club for seniors, had a girl friend again and doesn't need Viagra, passed his drivers test and is hardly ever home when we call - GHR delivers.

HGH is known to relieve symptoms of Asthma, Angina, Chronic Fatigue, Constipation, Lower back pain and Sciatica, Cataracts and Macular Degeneration, Menopause, Fibromyalgia, Regular and Diabetic Neuropathy, Hepatitis, helps Kidney Dialysis and Heart and Stroke recovery.

For more information or to order call
877-849-4777
www.biehealth.us

These statements have not been evaluated by the FDA. Copyright © 2000. Code OFA.

● Developers of apartment buildings have been adding rooftop farms to be maintained by residents or a designated "urban farmer."

● "Farm families are looking for other streams of revenue. There is a growing trend to diversify."
–*Mark O'Neill, spokesman, Pennsylvania Farm Bureau*

FOR HEALTHIER HERDS
Farmers are using . . .
● fitness trackers to count cows' steps

● microphones to hear how fast livestock chew their cud (slow chewing indicates not feeling well)

EXPERT OBSERVATIONS
● "More farmers are expanding their crop rotations with small-grain crops to buffer against ongoing low commodity crop prices and increasingly volatile weather."
–*Tamsyn Jones, outreach coordinator, Practical Farmers of Iowa*

● "Biotechnology is creating more reliable harvests."
–*Mike Tomko, communications director, American Farm Bureau Federation*

FARMERS' MARKETING TECHNIQUES
● setting up social media accounts for farm animals

● opening their operations to educate visitors or posting videos online to show that their practices are environmentally friendly and humane

CLOTHING UP CLOSE

"Trends are changing so fast that different silhouettes—wide legs, flare bottoms, and skinny jeans; full, slim, knee- and full-length skirts— are all in style during a single season."
–*Lynn Boorady, department head, design, housing, and merchandising, Oklahoma State University*

(continued)

FOLLOW US:

29

EVIDENCE THAT WE'RE ECO-FRIENDLY

- naturally colored cottons

- natural dyes in earth tones (green, orange, brown)

- textile made from the bark of cork oak trees

- use of raw wool from black sheep (no dyeing needed)

- "leather" made from pineapple leaves, sea kelp, or mushrooms

CLOTHING WITH A STORY

- People are selling used clothing with personal stories and photos of previous wearers in it.

- Scannable tags will reveal where and how a garment and/or its fabric was made.

SIZING UP SIZES

- "Body sizing technology is growing rapidly," says Lynn Boorady.

OCEAN WASTE WEAR

- Jackets fashioned from discarded fishing nets

- Sneakers made with recovered plastics

- Shorts made from plastic bottles

THE CIRCULAR CLOSET

- People are buying used luxury garments, wearing them, and then selling them.

WHAT WOMEN ARE WEARING . . .

- equestrian styles

- high necks, ruffle and feather details
–Suzanne Cotton, fashion design chair, Columbus College of Art & Design

- animal prints in bright yellow and orange

MEN ARE WEARING . . .

- shearling-lined shoes, sockless

- collarless jackets

- T-shirts made with seaweed fiber (to absorb moisture)

BROKEN-IN IS IN

- blazers with frayed hems

- sneakers bought already dirty

OLD IS GOLD

- "Designers have a thrifty mind-set, using found or reclaimed fabrics, off cuts (scraps), and old clothing with labor-intensive techniques to create garments to be worn and cherished."
–Lisa Z. Morgan, apparel design chair, Rhode Island School of Design ■

FOLLOW US:

SMALL-SPACE
GARDENING
101

**All you need to know to grow
food in an area of almost any size**

By making efficient use of
every inch of soil and sun-
shine, you can easily grow
plenty of produce in a small garden or
proper container. Intensive gardening
techniques have been used for centuries by many cultures to compensate
for limitations of climate, water,
labor, and arable land. Today, we can
employ these same practical ideas to
get a bountiful harvest from a small
space. What are you waiting for?

(continued)

Can't contain yourself over your big results
from small spaces? Share your pride with the
world on 📷 @theoldfarmersalmanac!

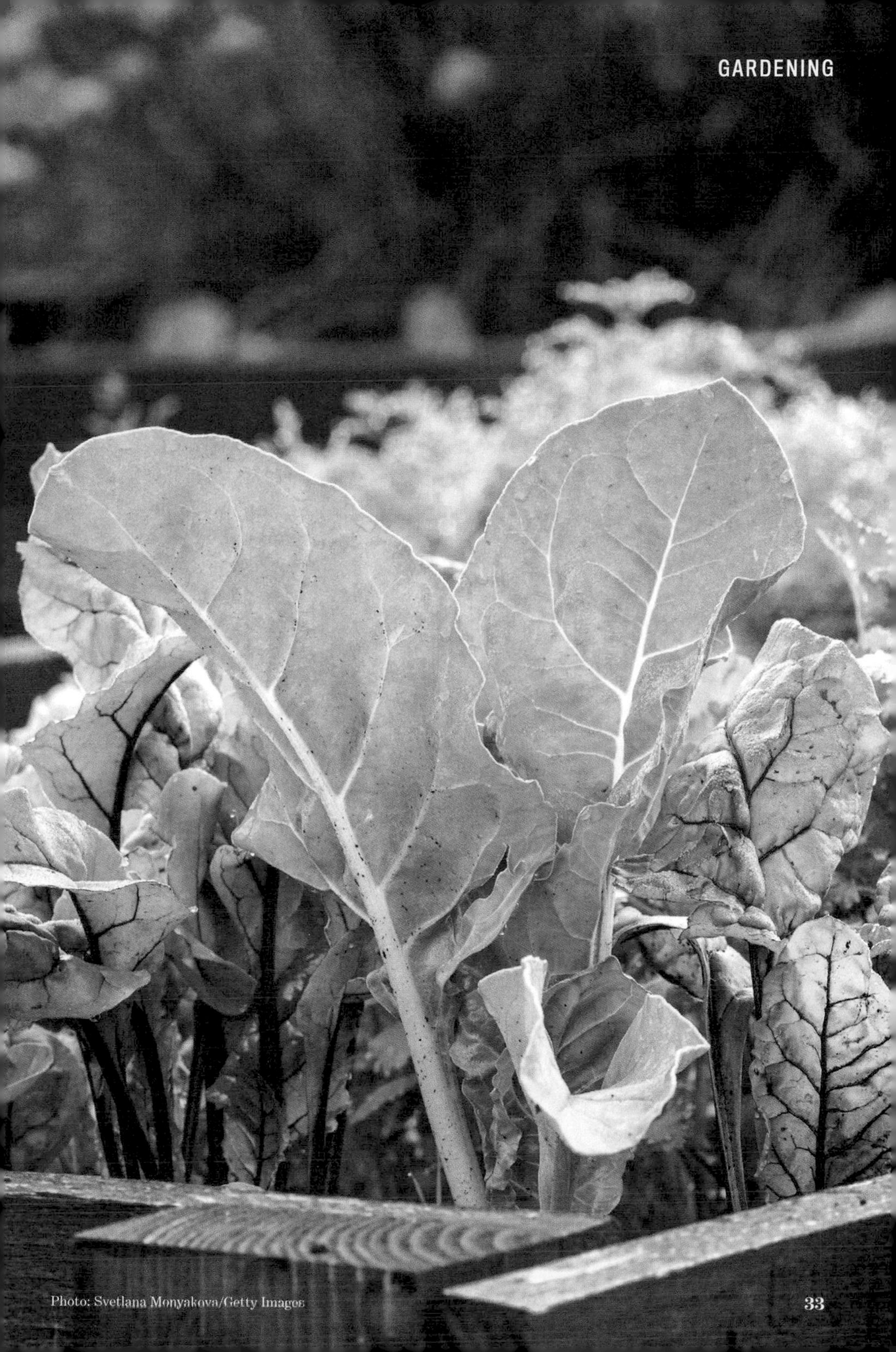

Photo: Svetlana Monyakova/Getty Images

RAISE A BED

A raised bed can yield up to 10 times as much produce as an in-ground garden of the same size with paths between rows. Raised beds allow you to concentrate your energy and time in a small area—working, watering, weeding, and fertilizing economically.

• Go to Almanac.com/raised-beds for guidance on building one.

• By utilizing season-extending devices such as cold frames, cloches, row covers, and plastic tunnels, you can make the most of the entire growing season.

SUN OR SHADE?

Either way, you've got it made: You can grow *something*. Although most vegetables need a minimum of 6 hours of sunlight per day (some need 8 hours), there are exceptions:

• Leafy greens (lettuce and spinach) grow well in partial shade.

• Beets, garlic, peas, and radishes can get by on 4 hours of sunlight per day.

SECOND THAT

Succession planting keeps the garden in continual production. Whenever one crop is harvested, you should have seedlings ready to transplant in its place. For best results, use quick-maturing varieties to fit several crops into one season. *(continued)*

Photos, clockwise from top: cjp/Getty Images; IlonaImagine/Getty Images; Nadezhda Nesterova/Getty Images

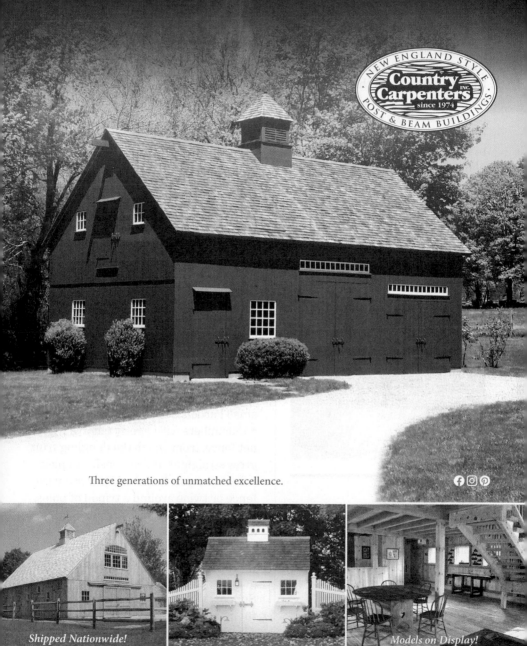

CLOSE IN

"Intercropping" means growing two or more crops together to save space. Plants should be placed close enough so that their leaves will touch, shading the ground between them when they are fully mature. This will keep weeds down and conserve moisture, eliminating the need to mulch and weed. As the plants begin to crowd out their neighbors, harvest the early-maturing ones, leaving room for the others to develop.

• Pair lettuce with longer-season vegetables such as broccoli, peppers, or tomatoes.

ROOT FOR PAIRS

Some intercropping partners thrive if their roots occupy a different depth of soil.

• Pair shallow-rooted vegetables, such as bush beans, with deeply rooted beets to make good use of space without creating root competition.

• Plant heavy feeders such as cabbage or cucumbers with light-feeding carrots or beans to reduce the competition for soil nutrients.

GROW UP

Lay out your garden plot (see Gardenplanner.almanac.com for a free trial of our software) or set out your pots with the fence, trellis, or wall on the north side. By planting the tallest plants there, you will avoid shading the smaller ones. Vining plants, if left to sprawl, take up valuable space in a small garden, so help them to grow up.

• Cucumbers will eagerly climb a nylon net fence, from which the dangling fruit grow straighter and are easier to pick.

• Peas and pole beans will cover a wire fence or twine around a tripod of poles.

• Some heavier plants, such as cantaloupes, melons, and winter squashes, may need help in climbing, so tie their vines to the structure to get them going in the right direction. Support the fruit with slings to keep them from tearing off the vine too soon.

• Tomatoes produce more fruit and ripen earlier if kept off the ground on a trellis or in a wire cage. *(continued)*

PLOT A POT FOR PICKING

When growing in a container, you can use just about anything that holds dirt and has drainage holes in the bottom.

• Hanging baskets work well for cherry tomatoes or strawberries.

• A 10-inch-wide pot is perfect for lettuce or radishes.

• Use a 5-gallon plastic bucket for a tomato or pepper plant.

• A 55-gallon food-grade plastic barrel, cut in half, will make two huge planters. Remember that adequate soil depth is important for developing a strong, healthy root system in a container.

• Lettuce, spinach, beans, and round beets need 6 inches of soil depth.

• Carrots, peas, and peppers need 8 inches.

• Eggplant, squash, and cucumbers need 10 inches.

• Tomatoes need 12 inches. ■

BASIC POTTING SOIL RECIPE

1 bucket (10 quarts) peat moss*
½ bucket (5 quarts) perlite
½ bucket (5 quarts) vermiculite
½ bucket (5 quarts) screened compost or
    composted cow manure
2 cups fine sand
2 cups pelleted time-release fertilizer
½ cup lime (to counter the acid of peat and keep
    the pH level near neutral)*

Mix thoroughly. Makes enough to fill two 14-inch tubs or four 12-inch hanging baskets. Double or triple the recipe for bigger containers.

*Because the use of peat can be considered non-environmentally friendly, you may wish to substitute coco coir for the peat moss, using roughly the same amount. If you use coco coir instead of peat, leave out the lime or your soil will be too basic. Coco coir has an almost-neutral pH, while peat is more acidic; lime is used to counter the peat.

HOW MUCH SOIL YOU NEED

CONTAINER	AMOUNT
POTS AND TUBS	
8-inch	3 quarts
10-inch	6 quarts
12-inch	8 quarts
14-inch	12 quarts
16-inch	20 quarts
20-inch	24 quarts
24-inch	28 quarts
30-inch	72 quarts
36-inch	96 quarts
HANGING BASKETS	
12-inch	6 quarts
16-inch	10 quarts

–Almanac editors

GROWING WILD

A tale of one man's attempts to tame a few of nature's beauties.

BY BOB SCAMMELL

Late one March, while walking to my truck, I was startled by bright-purple color emanating from the wild prairie crocus *(Anemone patens)* patch, snuggled up against the southwest-facing foundation of our house. This was the earliest blooming, by at least 2 weeks, of the latest addition to our wildflower garden.

By "wild flower garden," I do not mean the result of broadcasting packets of alleged wildflower seed collections into the landscape. No, our prairie crocus patch grew from seeds carefully collected out on Alberta's bald prairie by an avid wildflower gardener friend. We planted the seeds in the one place in our garden that emulates prairie conditions. Two decades later, they continue to be the first bloomer in the seasonal progression of color from the perennials in our wild garden.

In the wildflower garden at our former house, we used the same kind of hot, dry location to grow wild cacti—red-flower pincushion plant *(Coryphantha vivipara)* and yellow-blooming prickly pear *(Opuntia polyacantha)*—all of which we rescued from a prairie pipeline construction right-of-way and then transplanted.

Location is critical for wildflower gardening. We strive to duplicate in our garden the soil, moisture, and sun exposure conditions in which the plant thrived in the wild. Our most spectacular failure illustrates the importance of this point: We dug a

MARSH MARIGOLD

WILD PRAIRIE CROCUS

SASKATOON SERVICEBERRY

WESTERN WOOD LILY

41

Wild cacti such as red-flower pincushion *(above)* and yellow-blooming prickly pear *(below)* were rescued from a prairie pipeline construction right-of-way.

few early blue violets *(Viola adunca)* from an uncut corner of our hay field and carefully planted them in our sunny rose garden. The early blue transplants survived just long enough to bloom and set seed once, thereby ensuring the escape of their progeny. (The seedpods of the early blue explode, throwing the seed considerable distances.) In this case—probably abetted in their escape by ants—they made it 18 feet across our concrete driveway to a strip of lawn that our neighbor seldom mows. Now, every May, this strip of grass taunts us with its mass of early blues.

There will inevitably be failures in this kind of wild gardening. We have a fertile shade garden, which seems ideal for a ground cover of bunchberry *(Cornus canadensis)*. So, twice we have saved plants from the construction of a shed on our boreal forest–aspen parkland ranch and planted them in our shady garden back home. Both times, they thrived for a spell and then expired for no obvious reason. Likewise, we failed with giant red Indian paintbrush *(Castilleja miniata)*,

Pussy willow *(above)* was grown from clippings taken from a fellow gardener's tree, and wolf willow *(below)* was grown from clippings collected along a trout stream bank.

although we think that this was because the soil was too dry and lacking in decomposing wood.

Our wild garden lacks some favorite wild species because we know that we don't have the right environmental conditions. Plants like yellow water lily *(Nuphar lutea)* and marsh marigold *(Caltha palustris)* require a pond of cool, untreated water, which we can't provide in our urban setting.

Like many large gardens, ours has some low, perennially damp spots that are ideal for propagating certain wild plants from cuttings. We've had success with willow and willow relatives using this method and now have wolf willow *(Elaeagnus commutata)* from clippings collected along a trout stream bank, plus a magnificent pussy willow tree *(Salix discolor)* grown from clippings taken from a stately tree belonging to a friendly fellow wild gardener.

Some wild plants run amok in the civilized surroundings and relatively fertile soil of an urban garden. The wolf willow threatens to occupy our whole garden with its suckering habit! We keep it, though, and just hack it back because we love the spicy, musky scent of its flowers. We could not keep up with the wild chokecherry *(Prunus virginiana),* which we had grown from pits that we saved from the fruit of a favorite heavy-yielding, large-fruit shrub located in a sandpit that was being cleared. We were ruthless with its suckers and

Train at home to

Work at Home

Be a Medical Billing Specialist

WORK AT HOME!

✔ Be home for your family
✔ Be your own boss
✔ Choose your own hours

SAVE MONEY!

✔ No day care, commute, or office wardrobe/lunches
✔ Possible tax breaks
✔ Tuition discount for eligible military and their spouses
✔ Military education benefits & MyCAA approved

Earn up to $37,800 a year and more!*

Now you can train at home to work at home or in a doctor's office, hospital or clinic making great money...up to $37,800 a year and more as your experience and skills increase! It's no secret, healthcare providers need Medical Billing Specialists. In fact, the U.S. Department of Labor projects 10% growth from 2018 to 2028, for specialists doing medical billing.

10 Years	**10%**
5 Years	**Increase In Demand!****

Experts train you step by step...be ready to work in as little as four months!

With our Medical Billing program, you learn step by step with easy-to-understand instruction, plenty of examples, plus Toll-Free Hotline & E-mail Support. Graduate in as little as four months and be ready to step into this high-income career!

Get FREE Facts. Contact us today!

SENT FREE!

U.S. Career Institute®
2001 Lowe St., Dept. FMAB2A90
Fort Collins, CO 80525

1-800-388-8765
Dept. FMAB2A90
www.uscieducation.com/FMA90

YES! Rush me my free Medical Billing information package.

Name _____ Age ____

Address _____ Apt ____

City _____ State_____ Zip _____

E-mail _____ Phone _____

Accredited • Affordable • Approved
Celebrating over 35 years of education excellence!

✳DEAC
DISTANCE EDUCATION
ACCREDITING COMMISSION

BBB
ACCREDITED
BUSINESS
A+ Rating

CL396

*With experience, https://www.bls.gov/oes/current/oes433021.htm, 6/4/19
** https://www.bls.gov/ooh/office-and-administrative-support/financial-clerks.htm#tab-6, 10/3/19

45

Lady's slipper orchids *(above left)* and shooting stars *(above right)* were dug up and relocated to save them from being sprayed with 2,4-D herbicide.

completely eradicated the lot of them.

By contrast, our wild Saskatoon serviceberry *(Amelanchier alnifolia)* stays put, blossoms beautifully, and provides us with several arguably better-than-blueberry pies each year, with plenty of fruit left over for the birds.

Early in May, I noticed that our clump of yellow lady's slipper orchids *(Cypripedium calceolus)* was just starting to come up, while beside it, a companion clump of shooting stars *(Dodecatheon pulchellum)* was close to blooming. Forty-some-odd years ago, these two started as refugees from the then–commonly sprayed 2,4-D herbicide. We had advance warning and went out and dug our favorite clump of lady's slippers plus an unusually large-flower shooting star plant. Our western wood lilies *(Lilium philadelphicum)* came to our garden in the same way.

You need the best wild plant field guide for your region to know which wildflowers are so rare that you should never remove them from their environment. (Instead, try to protect them where they are.) This is the case with the half-dozen fairy slipper orchid plants

(*Calypso bulbosa*) left on our ranch. The species is rare and endangered because people cannot resist picking them, which kills the plants, and they can not be successfully transplanted because, like many wild orchids, they require a certain fungus in their native soil.

The yellow lady's slipper was becoming scarce in Alberta 40 years ago and was even being sold by scavengers to greenhouses, sometimes door-to-door. In 1917, the species was declared extinct in Britain, allegedly the victim of the Victorian mania for orchid collecting. But then, almost a decade ago, stories started appearing in newspapers that described the discovery of the last wild lady's slipper plant in Britain. Considerable efforts have been made in the UK to reintroduce lady's slipper back into the wild—probably grown from stock that was taken from the wild more than a century ago—and it has been flourishing in public and private wildflower gardens ever since.

Protecting the secret site of the last lady's slipper makes a good story. But a better story, the environmental miracle of restoring the species to its former habitats, could come, ironically, from the Victorian vice of wild orchid collecting and the culture that caused its virtual extinction. ∎

Some wildflowers, like the fairy slipper orchid *(above)*, are so rare that you should never remove them from their environment.

Bob Scammell was an avid gardener and sportswriter in Alberta. He was the author of *Good Old Guys, Alibis, and Outright Lies* (Johnson Gorman Publishing, 1996) and a member of the Alberta Sports Hall of Fame and Museum.

FARMING
for
GOOD

by Stacey Kusterbeck and Karen Davidson

FARMERS SHARE THEIR
STORIES, INSPIRATIONS,
DREAMS, AND ADVICE.

AYERS BROOK GOAT DAIRY
RANDOLPH, VERMONT

Farmers at Ayers Brook Goat Dairy have learned the hard way to goat-proof everything—light switches, doorknobs, the grain auger. "Goats are curious by nature. They can't resist the opportunity to fiddle with something. If you look away for 5 seconds, you will have a cleanup project on your hands that will consume your entire afternoon," says owner Miles Hooper.

A herd of 1,000 does produces milk for Vermont Creamery and a local producer of goat's milk caramel sauce, among other customers. "It's a marginal business. A lot of things have to go right for you to get paid," notes Hooper. Producing high-quality milk is a priority. "Our contribution to the industry is not the amount of milk that we put in the bulk tank, but the genetic work we do to create heathier, more efficient animals," Hooper explains. "The more protein—par-

ticularly casein—that we have in our goat's milk, the better the conversion factor from pounds of milk to cheese."

With a healthier profit margin, the farmers preserve both their livelihood and the environment. Recently, Hooper purchased a piece of land slated for development and preserved it for agriculture through a conservation easement with the Vermont Land Trust. In 2014, he added solar panels to a 14,000-square-foot barn, allowing the 266-acre farm to be run completely on solar electricity.

Years ago, Hooper visited goat farmers in rural France who somehow found time for an unrushed midday meal. Living by this example, Hooper intends to show his children that farming doesn't necessarily mean nonstop labor: "We are trying to keep the farm fun and lighthearted enough that they might actually be inclined to take it on." *(continued)*

Dosi Alvarez

ALVAREZ ORGANIC FARMS
LA UNION, NEW MEXICO

Dosi Alvarez farms land on the New Mexico–Texas border that his grandfather cleared with horses in 1910. After getting his degree in animal science, he worked for a beef selector and a packing company. "Then my dad was ready to retire—and I was ready to come home to the farm," he says.

Alvarez started out farming Pima cotton conventionally and continued until 1992, when his son was born. "I was sitting in the barn looking at buckets full of insecticides and herbicides and said, 'This is no place to raise a kid.'" At around the same time, a Swiss spinning mill in search of organic cotton contacted Alvarez's co-op. He saw an opportunity: "I had my dad, who was farming before chemicals, to fall back on for knowledge. We took the plunge, starting with 25 acres of organic cot-

ton." After 2 years of good crops, they decided to go all-in on organic. Today, all 1,100 acres (about half rented) are certified organic. Cotton is still the main crop (it is used in eco-conscious fashions and textiles), but he also grows wheat, alfalfa, and pecans. Alvarez's son, an integral part of the operation, hopes to take over the farm one day.

Alvarez, always ready to try something new, recently planted some colored cotton, which naturally produces brown and green fiber. His unsprayed fields, he says, are a refuge for beneficial insects: "Because of this, I don't have an insect problem to speak of." Conventional farmers in the area wonder aloud how he controls all of the weeds. "I tell them, 'I use that new organic herbicide, *Azadon*. That's Spanish for 'hoe,'" laughs Alvarez. *(continued)*

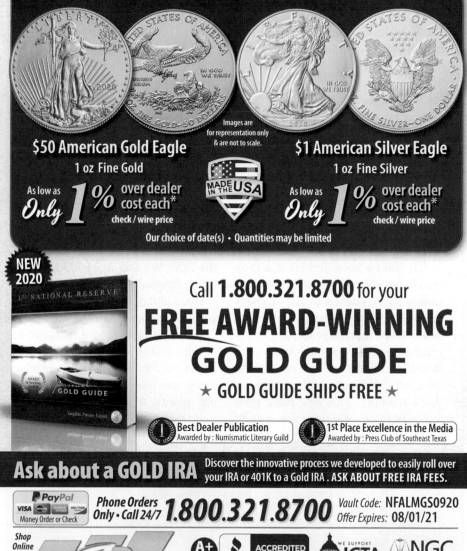
51

THE HOUWELING GROUP
DELTA, BRITISH COLUMBIA

Gone are the days when flake-like tomato seeds are planted in the nesting cavities of an egg carton—at least for professional growers like Ruben Houweling. He has fine-tuned a process that takes Dutch seeds to 20-inch transplants for commercial growers to buy in 6 weeks.

The Houweling Group, a precision greenhouse operation in Delta, British Columbia, produces seedling tomato plants for about half of the commercial greenhouses on the western coast of the U.S. and Canada. These plants produce the tomatoes that are sold in many grocery stores.

"To plant a seed and plant a crop is to believe in tomorrow," says Houweling, who started in the nursery that belonged to his grandfather Cornelius more than 35 years ago.

Each seed is deposited into a plug to settle in for 2 weeks. Then, workers graft a fruiting seedling to a rootstock seedling. This new plant goes into a humidity chamber for a week for the graft to fuse. The grafted seedling is then planted into a 4-inch cube of rock wool, an inert substrate.

One week later, these cubes are placed in a greenhouse nursery to be nurtured by frequent doses of fertilized water. When the first flowers appear, the transplants are shipped to the growers.

Despite the assistance of state-of-the-art lighting and irrigation, the greenhouse is in tune with each season's climatic variations. Says Houweling: "Especially through the fall, winter, and spring, we are aware of available light and the angle of the Sun. We still need to harvest as much free solar energy as possible."

Houweling reports that they plan to expand the seedling service in the near future, another example of the current high-density trend in agriculture to produce more on less land, while protecting plants from the harshest elements of weather. *(continued)*

Photo: The Houweling Group

LENNOX FARM
MELANCTHON, ONTARIO

The French family plants a winter garden like no other. Following a British tradition dating back to 1817, they "force" rhubarb to produce stalks in a dark hothouse, resulting in a crop that is more tender and less tart than their outside plants (which produce some 200,000 pounds annually).

Their "forced" rhubarb grows indoors on dirt floors, with the plants packed tightly together under three hothouses that total 10,000 square feet. In a good season, Lennox Farm will produce 10,000 to 12,000 pounds of winter rhubarb per hothouse.

That's a lot of rhubarb—and a lot of noise. Winter rhubarb makes an audible sound when the buds break open. Not unlike champagne being uncorked, this "pop" (similar to a tongue click) is music to their ears.

The principles of growing winter rhubarb have changed little over the centuries, according to parents Bill and Diane French. The perennial is grown in 3 acres of outdoor fields for 2 years. Every November, workers at Lennox Farm lift the rhubarb crowns (each can weigh between 80 and 100 pounds!) and transplant them to the hothouses.

Once nestled into their dirt rows, the crowns rest for 50 days with no light and little or no heat; temperatures are 3°C or lower. After winter solstice, the heat is turned to 10°C to activate new growth.

By Valentine's Day, the ruby-color stalks are ready for harvest, to become rhubarb crumble, strawberry-rhubarb pie, or preserves. Notably, these harbingers of spring require less sugar in cooking preparation than their field cousins.

Son Brian thinks that rhubarb might play a role in the burgeoning craft movement. Using a portable cider press, he makes juice from his outdoor rhubarb crop that local wineries and cideries find to be the perfect "pucker" ingredient.

While working as a student teacher in 2016, Kamal Bell noticed that some of his middle school students spent a lot of time in the school garden. He proposed starting an agricultural program so that students could work the small plot in summertime, but the principal said no. The idea was too big for Bell to ignore. He decided to buy a 12-acre lot and start his own farm. He named it "Sankofa" (a West African word meaning "to go back and get what might have been lost"—in this case, the students' African roots and agricultural heritage).

The land was rock-hard and covered with trash and trees. Using a rented bulldozer, he cleared 3 acres. Today, radishes, kale, peppers, watermelon, squash, okra, and cowpeas thrive there, as do the five teenagers in the farm's Agricultural Academy program. "It's their farm as well. They have a commitment and a responsibility," says Bell. "The farm is a great teacher. You learn how to be patient and that you don't control everything."

It's a community effort: At first, a local church served as a classroom; now all teaching takes place at the farm. There's no shortage of volunteers, thanks to social media and news coverage. "Now we've built our own brand. People are paying attention," Bell notes. The farm has diverse revenue sources, including online sales of honey, speaking engagements (mainly at museums and schools), and agritourism: A "Bees in the TRAP" (Teaching Responsible Apiary Practices) experience allows participants to suit up and learn the basics of beekeeping. Bell dreams of opening a "u-pick" operation to get healthy produce into local people's hands—and perhaps more: "We now know how to start a farm from a plot of land," he says. "We can go anywhere now and use this model." *(continued)*

Kamal Bell
(second from left)

SILVERTIP RANCH
BRIDGER, MONTANA

The Hergenrider family arrived in Montana's Clark's Fork Valley in 1916 and have been farming their land ever since. "My ancestors were pursuing opportunities offered by the Great Western Sugar Company, a company that we still grow sugar beets for today," says Rhonda Hergenrider, who manages the 700-acre farm with her father and sister. Her grandfather told stories of digging beets by hand, removing the tops with knives, and then shoveling them into horse-drawn wagons.

Nonetheless, change has been a constant. The family has raised hogs for years, but they now market the meat, too, selling direct-to-consumer through a local co-op, the Yellowstone Valley Food Hub. Selling direct "is a way to control your price," reports Hergenrider. "But 'value-added' also means 'work-added' and 'time-added'!" The farm also meets the growing demand for malt barley (used in craft beer, malted milk balls, and pizza crusts). About half of the land is now used for raising cattle. "As we move into the future, I see our cattle numbers increasing. I enjoy them," Hergenrider says.

Since childhood, Hergenrider had always planned to do something to help farmers. She did so off-farm for a decade after college, writing about agriculture and selling insurance to farmers and ranchers. But the farm girl missed the smell of freshly cut hay and tilled soil, working outdoors—and variety. "In farming, just when one thing gets old, the seasons change and it's time to do something else," observes Hergenrider. "But my biggest passion is, and always has

been, farming itself." Her school-age son and daughter love the lifestyle, too: "My kids express interest, but they are young," says Hergenrider. "We'll just navigate through it one day at a time." *(continued)*

Photo: Laura C. Nelson/www.lauracnelson.com

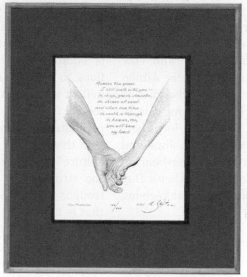

STRAWBERRY TYME FARMS
SIMCOE, ONTARIO

The Cooper brothers, Dalton, 23, and Mason, 21, are fourth-generation growers who vow that the sweetness of their Albion and San Andreas strawberries is as mouthwatering in fall as it is in spring. It used to be that local berries were available only in June and early July, but now ever-bearing berries produce from Mother's Day through to Canadian Thanksgiving in October.

Dalton (left) and Mason Cooper

"These berries have quite a bit of juice in them," says Mason.

Along with their parents, John and Diane, they are experimenting with a new growing system at Strawberry Tyme Farms near Simcoe, Ontario. Inspired by European growers and guided by owner manuals, they have built several 20-foot-high tunnels spanning 8 acres. Each is equipped with adjustable vinyl flaps to regulate temperatures and deflect wind. Even the bees are protected from the elements as they pollinate the berries.

In this practice of "precision agriculture" or "protected agriculture," the strawberries grow in elevated troughs holding a soilless substrate that is nursed by a dripper dispensing nutrient-rich water. Through the appropriate timing of light and food delivery, the flowering and fruiting cycles can be managed more precisely and predictably.

"At 42 inches above the ground, this system is much better for picking because you don't have to bend over," explains Dalton. "It takes half the time to pick berries."

Unlike field-grown fruit, these berries are safe from soilborne diseases such as verticillium wilt, and the troughs keep the plants free from any mud-splash that field berries would suffer from pelting rain.

The first season, in 2019, was so promising that the Cooper family plans to transition its 28 acres of field strawberries to protected covers and troughs over the next decade. ∎

The profiles of the U.S. farmers were written by **Stacey Kusterbeck,**
a regular contributor to the Almanac. **Karen Davidson,** editor of *The Grower,*
a leading Canadian horticultural magazine, and frequent contributor to
the Almanac, wrote the profiles of the Canadian farmers.

"APPETIZERS" RECIPE CONTEST WINNERS

Many thanks to the hundreds of you who submitted recipes!

STYLING AND PHOTOGRAPHY:
SAMANTHA JONES/QUINN BREIN COMMUNICATIONS

Our testers loved the combination of two classic appetizers in one phenomenal bite. Drizzling dressing over the eggs is the perfect way to top off these prize-winning apps.

FIRST PRIZE: $300
BUFFALO EGGS

12 eggs, hard-boiled and shelled
1 package (8 ounces) cream cheese, softened
½ cup cooked shredded chicken
¼ cup buffalo sauce
¼ cup shredded sharp cheddar cheese
2 tablespoons mayonnaise
2 tablespoons yellow mustard
2 tablespoons dill pickle relish
paprika, for sprinkling
sliced celery, for topping
ranch or blue cheese dressing, for drizzling

Preheat oven to 350°F.

Cut eggs in half and remove yolks to a bowl.

To the bowl, add cream cheese, chicken, buffalo sauce, cheddar, mayonnaise, mustard, and relish. Mix thoroughly and scrape into a baking dish. Bake for 15 minutes. Remove from oven and allow to cool for 10 minutes.

Spoon mixture into egg white halves and refrigerate. Before serving, sprinkle with paprika and top with celery. Serve with dressing.

Makes 12 servings.

–*Eric S. Trent, Frankfort, Kentucky*
(continued)

FOOD

ENTER THE 2021 RECIPE CONTEST:
FIVE OR FEWER INGREDIENTS

Got a great recipe that uses five or fewer ingredients
(excluding salt and pepper) and is loved by family and friends?
Send it in and it could win! See contest rules on page 251.

SECOND PRIZE: $200
STUFFED JALAPEÑOS

1 package (8 ounces) cream cheese, softened
2 cups shredded sharp cheddar cheese
1 clove garlic, minced
16 jalapeños, halved and seeded
crushed french-fried onions, for topping

Preheat oven to 350°F. Line a baking sheet
with parchment paper.

In a bowl, combine cream cheese, cheddar,
and garlic.

Fill pepper halves with cheese mixture and
place on prepared baking sheet. Top with
french-fried onions and bake for 15 minutes.

Makes 16 servings.

–Becky Powers, Charleston, South Carolina

HOW TO HANDLE JALAPEÑOS
Always use caution when cooking with chile peppers
such as jalapeños. Capsaicin, the oil-like compound that contains
their fiery heat, is concentrated in the membrane, or rib, of
a chile. If you can, wear gloves while handling them; afterward, wash
your gloved (or bare) hands thoroughly with soap and cool
water. Try not to touch your eyes or face for several hours after
working with chile peppers.

THIRD PRIZE: $100
SPICY MEXICAN SHRIMP BITES

½ pound cooked deveined
shrimp, diced
1½ cups frozen corn, thawed
3 scallions, sliced
2 Roma tomatoes, seeded and diced
1 jalapeño, seeded and diced
1 clove garlic, minced
5 tablespoons olive oil, divided
1 tablespoon chopped fresh cilantro
1½ teaspoons chili powder
1 teaspoon salt
zest and juice of 2 limes
1 loaf French bread

In a bowl, combine shrimp, corn,
scallions, tomatoes, jalapeño,
and garlic.

In a separate bowl, combine
3 tablespoons of olive oil, cilantro,
chili powder, salt, lime zest, and
lime juice. Pour over shrimp
mixture and stir to incorporate.
Refrigerate for 1 hour.

Preheat oven to 350°F.

Cut French bread into ½-inch
slices and lightly brush with
remaining 2 tablespoons of
olive oil. Bake for 5 minutes, or
until lightly browned. Remove
from oven and, using a slotted
spoon, top each toast round
with spicy shrimp salad.

Makes 12 servings.

–Donna Gribbins, Shelbyville, Kentucky

HONORABLE MENTION
ZIPPY POTATO BALLS

2 cups warm mashed potatoes
2 tablespoons (¼ stick) butter,
softened
2 tablespoons milk
½ cup Cheese & Chive Egg Creations
½ cup finely chopped green onion
½ cup finely chopped baby spinach
¼ cup finely chopped cremini
mushrooms
¼ cup finely chopped red bell pepper
½ teaspoon salt
½ teaspoon freshly ground black
pepper
⅛ teaspoon hot pepper sauce
⅛ teaspoon crushed red pepper flakes
1½ cups panko bread crumbs

Preheat oven to 400°F. Line
two baking sheets with parchment
paper.

In a bowl, combine mashed
potatoes, butter, and milk. Mash
until potatoes have absorbed butter
and milk. Set aside to cool.

In a separate bowl, combine
Egg Creations, onions, spinach,
mushrooms, bell peppers, salt, black
pepper, hot pepper sauce, and red
pepper flakes. Add potato mixture
and stir to combine. Form into
1½-inch balls and roll in panko bread
crumbs. Bake on prepared baking
sheets for 15 to 20 minutes, or until
crispy. Serve warm.

Makes 12 servings.

–Helen Humphreys, London, Ontario ■

Spicy Mexican Shrimp Bites

Love Lessons From
OLD VALENTINES

*When it comes to saying "I love you,"
sweet nothings from the past can provide
prescient pointers for the present.*

By Lisa Hix

From the ancient Romans' mid-February bacchanal called Lupercalia to the three saints named Valentine once recognized by the Catholic church, on up through *billets-doux* in the Victorian Age and ever since, lovers and admirers have been sending each other sweet missives on February 14.

We've mined the history of these cards for valuable hints on how to best woo your love—with paper or in person.

1. PAY ATTENTION TO DETAIL.

In the 15th century, nuns in Europe created devotional readings with delicate, knife-cut designs resembling lace. "We later see similar designs in valentines with lace borders," notes Nancy Rosin, president of the National Valentine Collectors Association.

Lesson: It's the little things that count.

(continued)

Photo, above: The Nancy Rosin Collection. Opposite: Diane Lambombarbe/Getty Images

2. FLOWERS. FLOWERS. FLOWERS.

The "language of flowers," or floriography, came to Europe from the Ottoman Empire in the early 1700s. The red rose is well known as the symbol of romantic love, but almost all flowers have their own meaning; for a list, go to Almanac.com/flower-meaning.

Lesson: Blooms always help your love to blossom.

3. FEEL FREE TO BE MYSTERIOUS.

Polite society in the 18th and 19th centuries demanded that men and women keep their passions to themselves, so Valentine's Day flourished. Anyone could reveal his/her true feelings without risking humiliation.

"Valentines were generally sent anonymously," Rosin says. "If they were marked, sometimes it was just the initials, or the name written backward, or it just said, 'From a serious admirer.'" Part of the game was identifying the sender, Rosin says.

Lesson: It's okay to be coy.

4. BE BOLD.

German-Americans in 18th-century Pennsylvania created "illuminated" valentines featuring Fraktur-font calligraphy and decorated borders, as well as cards with cutout silhouettes. By the early 19th century, more elaborate devices such as pull-out tabs and secret messages had become all the rage, as valentines evolved to become more embellished with artistic touches like gilding and embossing.

Lesson: Innovation is seductive.

5. PUT SOME EFFORT INTO IT!

By the early 19th century, valentine greetings had become everything from simple pulp cards embossed with sweet images to missives of fine paper made from the rags of linen, cotton, and hemp.

"Life was very different in those times," explains Rosin. She describes a besotted suitor working by candlelight to write, draw, cut, weave, or fold the perfect valentine using the then-luxury product known as paper.

Lesson: "Homemade" means straight from the heart.

LOVE NOTES

• "Emotionally, valentines were important because life was relatively short [a century or two ago]. Men and women wanted to get married, and they married young," says Rosin. A valentine might include paper gloves or a paper wedding band–a metal ring or real fabric gloves.

"If a woman received gloves for Valentine's Day and she accepted them and wore them on Easter Sunday, it was an acceptance of a marriage proposal," Rosin adds.

• The Civil War made love confessions urgent. Valentines from the period (1861-65) show sweethearts parting ways or a tent with flaps to pull back to reveal a soldier inside. The lovelorn would send one another locks of hair.

• In the 1800s, a woman gave the man she loved a delicate slip called a "watch paper" that was placed in his pocket watch to protect the glass. "Every time the man opened his watch to see the time, he would see this message from his beloved," reports Rosin.

• If a suitor lacked the skills to write verse in calligraphy on a piece of embossed paper stationery, he could hire a stationery store clerk with lovely handwriting to do it. Those unable to conceive an appropriately romantic rhyme could purchase a broadside or chapbook known as a Valentine Writer, which provided both declarations of love and poetic responses for a recipient to use.

(continued)

ESTHER, THE LOVE MERCHANT

One woman is credited with popularizing paper lace valentines in the the United States. Esther Howland, whose family owned the largest book and stationery store in Worcester, Massachusetts, received an intricate English valentine from one of her father's business associates in 1847. Enamored with the idea, the 19-year-old convinced her father to order lace paper and embellishments from London and New York City and set to work making valentines. When her brother took her samples on his sales trip, he returned with more than $5,000 ($160,000 in today's dollars) worth of orders. Howland brought in her friends to build the valentines in an assembly-line style.

"Esther Howland made valentines more readily available," says Rosin. "Her valentines had multiple layers of beautiful lace papers. The message would usually be deep inside."

6. THERE'S NO SUCH THING AS A BAD VALENTINE.

By the mid-1800s, technology was allowing the mass production of valentine cards. Hallmark's first card appeared in 1913. Expensive and time-consuming handmade paper confections were going out of fashion, and paramours no longer had an excuse for not showing their love.

Lesson: Be sure to give your valentine something—anything!

From the simplest of missives during the Great Depression to battleworn envelopes sent from overseas during World War II and other conflicts to classroom exchanges in the 1950s and '60s accompanied by little candy hearts, valentines have evolved into today's talking cards, e-cards, and video vows of devotion. Through it all, though, love has reigned supreme. ∎

Lisa Hix is the senior editor of CollectorsWeekly.com.

DO YOU SAVE VALENTINES?
Show us your favorites. Post pics at
@theoldfarmersalmanac

BIRDS ON THE
WING

Facts and fallacies
about avian migration

BY KATHERINE SWARTS

TAKE A GANDER AT THIS!
Show us your feathered
friends, whether in the wild or
at home. Post pics at
@theoldfarmersalmanac

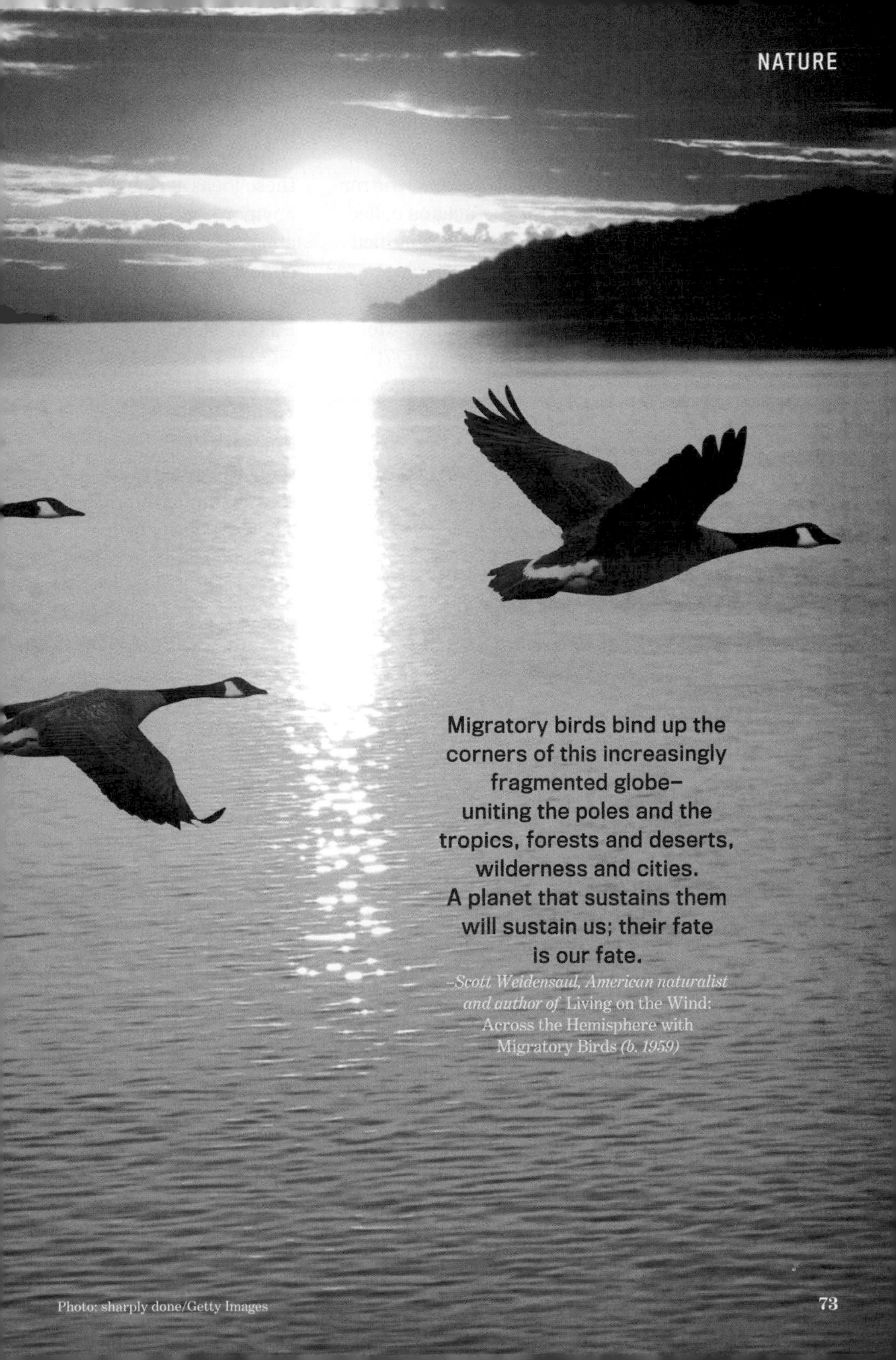

Migratory birds bind up the corners of this increasingly fragmented globe–uniting the poles and the tropics, forests and deserts, wilderness and cities. A planet that sustains them will sustain us; their fate is our fate.

–Scott Weidensaul, American naturalist and author of Living on the Wind: Across the Hemisphere with Migratory Birds *(b. 1959)*

Photo: sharply done/Getty Images

WINGING IT

The question of where songbirds and swallows go in winter puzzled humanity for millennia. Early observers came up with various theories—which were mostly wrong.

• Many people believed that birds hibernated.

grew underwater in crustacean shells before appearing each winter. (For this reason, the marine crustaceans called barnacles were named after the barnacle goose.)

• British minister and scientist Charles Morton wrote in the late 17th

ally start migrating long after hummingbirds do).

Although nobody takes these ideas seriously anymore, actual facts about migration can be almost as strange.

PREPARING FOR TAKEOFF

• Songbirds fatten up for migration, sometimes literally doubling their weight to guarantee maximum energy. They're helped by a hormonal change called hyperphagia, which drives them to eat more and store more body fat.

• Pre-migration, birds undergo other changes. Fresh new feathers grow in to maximize flight efficiency and endurance. Often, these feathers are less colorful than in summer, making the birds less conspicuous to predators.

• Hemoglobin in a bird's blood increases before migration, for maximum aerobic efficiency. Reproductive organs shrink, trimming unneeded weight.

THE BAR-TAILED GODWIT MAKES THE LONGEST KNOWN NONSTOP MIGRATION, FLYING 7,000 MILES IN 8 DAYS OVER THE OCEAN BETWEEN ALASKA AND NEW ZEALAND.

• Aristotle theorized that the redstarts that he saw in summer (thrushlike flycatchers, not to be confused with the American warblers also called redstarts) changed coloring and shape to become the European robins of winter.

• A 12th-century British theory held that geese

century that birds likely migrated into space on a 2-month flight: "Whither should these creatures go, unless it were to the Moon?"

• Well into the 20th century, many people believed that migrating hummingbirds rode on the backs of geese (although geese actu-

ALONG THE FLYWAY

• Many species that seem to stay all year are

75

in fact migratory: Only individual birds change. American robins that nest in Tennessee may head for Tex-Mex regions when days get shorter—to be replaced nock mountain in New Hampshire, Smith Point in southeast Texas, and Hawk Ridge in Duluth, Minnesota, are famous for their autumn "hawk watches," where

TINY HUMMINGBIRDS ARE MAJOR LONG-DISTANCE FLYERS. THE 3.1-INCH RUFOUS HUMMINGBIRD FLIES 3,900 MILES (NEARLY 78.5 MILLION TIMES ITS BODY LENGTH) FROM ALASKA TO MEXICO.

by robins that spent the summer in New England.

• Every avian order has long-distance migrants. The yellow-bellied sapsucker (a woodpecker), which spends summer in Canada and the northeastern United States, flies as far south as Panama for the winter.

• Raptors (birds of prey) migrate, too. Hawk Mountain in Pennsylvania, Pack Monad-

thousands of hawks (and kites, falcons, vultures, and eagles) pass overhead daily. In Canada, try Holiday Beach Migration Observatory in southwest Ontario.

A FLOCK OF FACTS

• If "migration" is defined as an annual journey of significant distance to and from the same geographical area, fewer than half of bird species actually migrate. Irregular "migrations," called "irruptions," occur when birds temporarily relocate due to changes in food supply or weather. If new conditions persist, irruption travelers may stay permanently.

• True migrants don't follow the food supply, at least not by conscious decision. They start south before any reduction in food (or bird feeders) becomes obvious, responding to subtle atmospheric and daylight differences.

• Songbirds are usually most active by day, but during migration, they do most of their long-distance travel at night. (One reason: There's less risk that hungry hawks and falcons will spot them crossing open areas.)

• Birds in zoos retain migration instincts. During travel seasons, they become restless and stay on whichever side of their cages matches the direction in which they "should" be flying.

• According to scientists, the number of birds in the United States and Canada has declined by

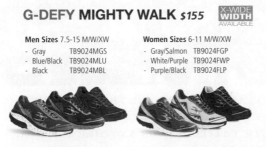

3 billion, or 29 percent, over the past 50 years.

BIRDS THAT GO THE DISTANCE

• Birds that fly the longest distances have the longest and most sharply pointed wings—the most aerodynamic design for lengthy flights.

• Ruby-throated hummingbirds, just 3½ inches long, can fly 1,245 miles without a break. Many take a straight line across the Gulf of Mexico to Central America.

• The blackpoll warbler, a 5½-inch songbird whose favorite breeding territory is the boreal forest covering much of Canada and Alaska, flies 2,300 miles to South America and the Caribbean.

• Migrating birds can fly high as well as far. Songbirds have been tracked at altitudes of 2,000 feet. Geese and raptors may go up to over 30,000 feet.

• For all of their endurance, migrating birds aren't above hitchhiking. Many have stopped on ships while crossing water, sometimes in huge numbers if the weather is bad.

• When the wind is contrary on long flights, the result is often a fallout—unusually large numbers of birds stopping in one place at the same time. Although fallouts are a thrill for bird watchers, the birds have a rough time, fighting first the weather and then avian crowds vying for food.

• One last, little-known fact: Whatever the time of year, there are always some birds on the move for migration. ■

Katherine Swarts lives in Houston, Texas, near the Central Flyway, a "superhighway" for migratory birds.

FOR ABSOLUTE DISTANCE, ARCTIC TERNS ARE THE MIGRATORY CHAMPIONS, NESTING IN THE ARCTIC EVERY SUMMER AND THEN FLYING TO ANTARCTIC LATITUDES FOR ANOTHER SUMMER. DEPENDING ON THE DIRECTNESS OF ITS ROUTES, ONE ARCTIC TERN MAY MAKE THE EQUIVALENT OF THREE ROUND TRIPS TO THE MOON OVER THE COURSE OF ITS 30-YEAR LIFETIME.

From Sea to Rising Sea

WITH OCEAN LEVELS RELENTLESSLY INCREASING, IT'S TIME TO UNDERSTAND WHY, HOW, AND *WHERE*.

by Brian Fagan

HIGH TIMES?
Are you seeing signs of higher
tides or water levels? Share images
on 📷 @theoldfarmersalmanac

Pigeon Point Lighthouse
stands sentinel over California's
rocky shore.

Ross Sea, Antarctica

The greatest sea level change will result from the continued melting of Antarctic ice sheets.

Twenty thousand years ago, the world was in a deep freeze. There had been so much water sucked up from the oceans and locked up in glacial ice that world sea levels were some 400 feet below modern ones. The Greenland ice sheet alone was 30 percent larger than it is today.

Global geography was also radically different. You could walk dry-shod across a low-lying land bridge from Siberia to Alaska—and early peoples did exactly that. Britain was part of the Continent; the Thames flowed through the English Channel. The North Sea was a low maze of rivers, marshes, and wetlands—a paradise for the several thousand hunters and fishers who lived there.

Then natural global warming set in some 15,000 years ago. Ice sheets retreated rapidly by geological standards, releasing at least four major surges of glacial meltwater from land. One such surge from melting North American ice sheets triggered a sea level rise of up to 50 feet that contributed to the inundation of the North Sea.

Today, the seas are rising again. According to NOAA, the global mean sea level has risen about 6.5 inches (16 centimeters) since 1880, nearly half of it since 1950. This is unevenly distributed, nationally and globally, but it is happening almost everywhere.

Generations of scientists have wrestled with the still only partially understood

causes of sea level rise, but knowledge about sea level change is improving every year. Today, scientists use data from satellites and other instruments to record sea level changes every 6 minutes. Here is some of what we know.

1. About two-thirds of global sea level rise comes from melting glacial ice. The greatest sea level change will result from the continued melting of Antarctic ice sheets. By 2100, that melting continent may increase global sea levels by up to 6 feet.

2. Thermal expansion due to warming ocean temperatures has caused about a third of all global sea level rise. As water temperatures increase, the ocean expands and sea levels climb. Today's ocean is 1.2 degrees Fahrenheit warmer than it was in 1950, and this has already caused more than 6 inches of additional sea level rise in San Francisco Bay, parts of arctic Canada, and possibly elsewhere.

Over the past decade, thermal expansion has increased and sea level rise has accelerated.

3. The gradual sinking of land, or subsidence, is an inexorable factor. Humans are responsible for about 80 percent of land subsidence in the United States. Our constant pumping of subsurface ground water for drinking and agriculture has caused the land to subside over wide areas.

4. Densely populated

Cape Hatteras Light

BEACONS OF SAFETY . . . OR SIGNS OF TROUBLE?

Lighthouses have long been an iconic symbol of the ocean and its power. Shifting sands and rising seas have made it necessary to relocate exposed towers inland. Cape Hatteras Light in North Carolina was moved more than a half-mile southwest in July 1999, with the aid of hydraulic jacks, beams, and sensors that kept track of vibration and wind strength. New erosion means that it may need to be moved again. Pistons prodded Martha's Vineyard's 400-ton Gay Head lighthouse 129 feet inland at the rate of 4 inches per minute. In Canada, a storm surge in 2004 so badly damaged the Cascumpec lighthouse at Alberton Harbor, Prince Edward Island, that it was removed 6 months later.

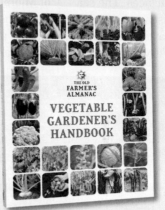

coastal cities, with their massive buildings, complex infrastructures, and road networks, compress the underlying and surrounding land surfaces. The sea level rises as a result, and seawater moves inland. Fifty-four percent of sea level rise around Norfolk, Virginia, is due to sinking land. Intense development and high-rise construction are causing large segments of Miami-Dade County in southern Florida to sink by as much as 2 inches annually.

5. The warm Gulf Stream compounds sea level problems in Florida and large portions of the U.S. east coast. The Stream flows northward off Florida's east coast, a giant "conveyor belt" that is affected by melting

Tuktoyaktuk, Northwest Territories, Canada

A CONCRETE SOLUTION

Rising sea levels are threatening not only dense population centers but also small, remote communities, close to or below sea level. Arctic peoples along the northern coastlines of the United States and Canada face serious risks. Their ancestors moved constantly, using temporary summer camps. Today, these transitory encampments are occupied year-round, many of them on low barrier islands. Once protected by permafrost and sea ice, they are now at risk from wave damage during storms and aggressively climbing sea levels.

Tuktoyaktuk is an Inuvialuit village on the Arctic Ocean in Canada's Northwest Territories. For generations, it has been a base for beluga whale and caribou hunting. Shrinking ice (by about 8 percent per year since the 1960s) and rising sea levels have increased the threat of storm surges. With the permafrost melting, the community is endangered. The inhabitants are moving buildings from vulnerable spots to safer ground and considering building up the island; one solution involves stacking concrete slabs on the beach.

glacial ice. Far up north, lighter-weight, cool, fresh meltwater enters the ocean and slows the Stream, causing sea levels to rise. Short-term slowing of the Stream has serious consequences in Florida. The temporary slowdowns can add between 1 and 3 feet to tides over a day or a week. More extreme Gulf Stream flooding can occur if there is also heavy rainfall that coincides with a high tide.

6. Along both coasts of Florida and the Gulf, hurricanes, with their violent sea surges, add another dimension. Super storms such as Katrina in Louisiana and Harvey in Texas barrel ashore into low-lying or even below–sea level areas with destructive winds and fast-rising sea surges, temporarily raising coastal sea levels several feet above even the highest tides.

7. Weather—but not simply precipitation—is also a factor in sea level rise. Scientists study the effects of global weather systems such as warm-water El Niño, which can raise

Along both coasts of Florida and the Gulf, hurricanes, with their violent sea surges, add another dimension.

sea levels for months at a time. Weather's most vulnerable target may be California, where over 25 million people are at risk. Sea levels in San Francisco Bay are now rising by about 1 inch every 10 years—much faster than in 1950, when the rate was basically stable. Adding to the threat, winter storms can elevate high tides as much as a foot. If the current accelerating rate of sea level rise continues, two-thirds of California's beaches will disappear by the year 2100.

Warming temperatures contribute to subsidence. As summers become hotter, wetlands become drier, the soil dries out and loses its density, and the land sinks.

We face a vulnerable future, partly because there are so many of us. Coastal Canadian and U.S. populations have risen to millions over the past 2,000 years. Almost 40 percent of the U.S. population lives in coastal areas that are prone to flooding shore erosion and storms. In Canada's Newfoundland and Yukon, sea levels are rising faster than normal.

If conditions continue on the current pathway, glacier and ice sheet melt will raise sea levels by 38 inches by 2100. The most dramatic effects occur in low-lying environments, where even a small rise can inundate a surprisingly large area—for example, about 77 percent of Charleston, South Carolina, could be under water if the sea level rose 12 feet. One in six homes in Boston could be inundated regularly by 2100. The Chesapeake Bay area, with its low shorelines, has persistent and widespread flooding problems; between 1900 and 2017, local sea levels rose about a foot and a half around the Bay.

T he situation for residents of South Florida is especially dire. Twelve thousand houses—at least $6.4 billion worth of property—in Miami are in danger of ceaseless flooding by 2050. One of every four people in the United States who will be affected by sea level incursions between 2020 and 2100 lives in Miami-Dade County.

We can expect more frequent high tide flooding, deadly storm surges, and contamination of freshwater aquifers that sustain us. The decisions that we make about living with higher sea levels over the next few years will affect everyone's future. ■

Brian Fagan is distinguished emeritus professor of anthropology at the University of California, Santa Barbara. He is the author of several books on ancient climate change, including *The Attacking Ocean* (Bloomsbury Press, 2014).

NOT IN MY BACKYARD?

Residents of communities located hundreds or even thousands of miles from the ocean might feel safe from rising coastal waters. But research suggests that many will feel the effects.

It is estimated that more than 13 million people in the United States could be displaced by ocean level rise by the end of the century. Their retreat and resettlement into both urban and rural locations could reshape communities in the heart of the country and result in land-use and trade-off conflicts, including, for example, possible sales of public lands for human settlement.

Many communities are unprepared for a coastal emigration. "Future migrants will need jobs, houses, and health care," says David Wrathall, an assistant professor in Oregon State University's College of Earth, Ocean, and Atmospheric Sciences and lead author of a policy paper published in *Nature Climate Change* in November 2019. "Their kids will need schools. The availability of these things will affect where coastal migrants go and their quality of life when they get there."

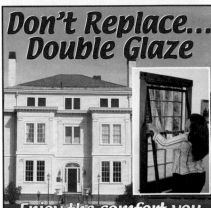

WINTER 2020–21

WET? YOU BET!

IT'S SNOW TIME!

MORE WET ...

SNOW DUMPS

IT'S SNOW TIME!

THAN WHITE

SNOW PELTING, THEN MELTING

SHEETS OF SLEET

COOL, DRY

NOT SO COLD, NOT TOO WET

MILD, WHITE N WET S

WARM, DRY

COOL, WET

GORGEOUS!

These weather maps correspond to the winter and summer predictions in the
General Weather Forecast (opposite) and on the regional forecast pages, 206–223.
To learn more about how we make our forecasts, turn to page 202.

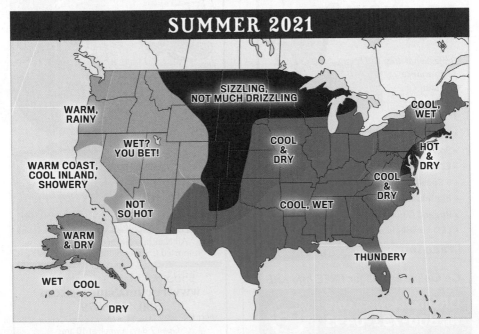

SUMMER 2021

WARM, RAINY

SIZZLING, NOT MUCH DRIZZLING

COOL, WET

WET? YOU BET!

COOL & DRY

HOT & DRY

WARM COAST, COOL INLAND, SHOWERY

COOL & DRY

NOT SO HOT

COOL, WET

WARM & DRY

THUNDERY

WET   COOL

DRY

Maps: AccuWeather, Inc.

THE GENERAL WEATHER REPORT AND FORECAST

FOR REGIONAL FORECASTS, SEE PAGES 206-223.

What's shaping the weather? We are currently transitioning from Solar Cycle 24 to Solar Cycle 25. Cycle 24 was the smallest in more than 100 years and possibly the smallest since the Dalton Minimum in the early 1800s, while Cycle 25 is expected to also bring very low solar activity. Although low levels of solar activity have historically been associated with cooler temperatures, on average, across Earth, we believe that recent warming trends will dominate in the eastern and northern parts of the United States in the coming winter, with below-normal average temperatures limited to the western portion of the nation.

WINTER will be colder than normal in Maine; the Intermountain, Desert Southwest, and Pacific Southwest regions; and eastern Hawaii and near or above normal elsewhere. Precipitation will be below normal from Delmarva into North Carolina; in the southern Appalachians, Georgia, and Florida; from the Ohio Valley westward to the Pacific and southward to the Gulf and Mexico; and in western Hawaii and above or near normal elsewhere. Snowfall will be greater than normal in the Northeast, Wisconsin, Upper Michigan, the High Plains, and northern Alaska and below normal in most other areas that receive snow.

SPRING will be warmer than normal in the northeastern corner of the country; from Iowa northward through the Upper Midwest and westward through the southern Intermountain region; and in the western Desert Southwest, Alaska, and western Hawaii and near or cooler than normal elsewhere. Rainfall will be above normal in the Northeast, Southeast, Florida, and eastern Great Lakes; from the High Plains into Oklahoma and Texas; and in the Desert Southwest and southern California and below or near normal elsewhere. Watch for a tropical storm threat in Florida in mid-May.

SUMMER will be hotter than normal in the Atlantic Corridor and western Great Lakes; from the Upper Midwest southwestward to the southern Intermountain region; and in the Pacific Northwest, coastal California, and Alaska and near or below normal elsewhere. Rainfall will be above normal in the Northeast and eastern Great Lakes; from the western Ohio Valley south- and westward to the Gulf of Mexico; from Washington southward through California; and in western Hawaii and near or below normal elsewhere.

The best chance for a major hurricane strike will occur from South Carolina to New England in early to mid-August. Expect tropical storm threats from Florida to southern New England in early to mid-September.

AUTUMN will be warmer than normal in the Intermountain, Pacific Northwest and Southwest regions, and Alaska and below normal elsewhere. Precipitation will be above normal in the Northeast and Delmarva; from the eastern Great Lakes southwestward to the Tennessee Valley; in southern Texas and the southern and central High Plains; and in the western Desert Southwest, Pacific Southwest, and southern Alaska and near or below normal elsewhere. ∎

TO GET A SUMMARY OF THE RESULTS OF OUR FORECAST FOR LAST WINTER, TURN TO PAGE 204.

THE OLD
FARMER'S ALMANAC

Established in 1792 and published every year thereafter
ROBERT B. THOMAS, *founder* (1766–1846)

YANKEE PUBLISHING INC.

EDITORIAL AND PUBLISHING OFFICES
P.O. Box 520, 1121 Main Street, Dublin, NH 03444
Phone: 603-563-8111 • Fax: 603-563-8252

EDITOR *(13th since 1792):* Janice Stillman
ART DIRECTOR: Colleen Quinnell
MANAGING EDITOR: Jack Burnett
SENIOR EDITORS: Sarah Perreault, Heidi Stonehill
EDITORIAL ASSISTANTS: Tim Clark,
Benjamin Kilbride
WEATHER GRAPHICS AND CONSULTATION:
AccuWeather, Inc.

V.P., NEW MEDIA AND PRODUCTION:
Paul Belliveau
PRODUCTION DIRECTOR: David Ziarnowski
PRODUCTION MANAGER: Brian Johnson
SENIOR PRODUCTION ARTISTS:
Jennifer Freeman, Janet Selle, Susan Shute

WEB SITE: ALMANAC.COM
SENIOR DIGITAL EDITOR: Catherine Boeckmann
ASSOCIATE DIGITAL EDITOR: Christopher Burnett
NEW MEDIA DESIGNERS: Amy O'Brien, Holly Sanderson
E-COMMERCE DIRECTOR: Alan Henning
PROGRAMMING: Peter Rukavina

CONTACT US
We welcome your questions and comments about articles in and topics for this Almanac. Mail all editorial correspondence to Editor, The Old Farmer's Almanac, P.O. Box 520, Dublin, NH 03444-0520; fax us at 603-563-8252; or contact us through Almanac.com/Feedback. *The Old Farmer's Almanac* can not accept responsibility for unsolicited manuscripts and will not acknowledge any hard-copy queries or manuscripts that do not include a stamped and addressed return envelope.

All printing inks used in this edition of *The Old Farmer's Almanac* are soy-based. This product is recyclable. Consult local recycling regulations for the right way to do it.

Thank you for buying this Almanac! We hope that you find it "useful, with a pleasant degree of humor." Thanks, too, to everyone who had a hand in it, including advertisers, distributors, printers, and sales and delivery people.

OUR CONTRIBUTORS

Bob Berman, our astronomy editor, is the director of Overlook Observatory in Woodstock and Storm King Observatory in Cornwall, both in New York.

Tim Clark, a retired English teacher from New Hampshire, has composed the weather doggerel on the Calendar Pages since 1980.

Bethany E. Cobb, our astronomer, is an Associate Professor of Honors and Physics at George Washington University. She conducts research on gamma-ray bursts and specializes in teaching astronomy and physics to non–science majoring students. When she is not scanning the sky, she enjoys rock climbing, figure skating, and reading science fiction.

Castle Freeman Jr. this year reprises his role as author of the Farmer's Calendar essays, which he composed for more than 25 years. The essays come out of his interest in wildlife, the outdoors, and rural New England life.

Celeste Longacre, our astrologer, often refers to astrology as "a study of timing, and timing is everything." A New Hampshire native, she has been a practicing astrologer for more than 25 years. Her book, *Celeste's Garden Delights* (2015), is available for sale on her Web site, www.celestelongacre.com.

Michael Steinberg, our meteorologist, has been forecasting weather for the Almanac since 1996. In addition to college degrees in atmospheric science and meteorology, he brings a lifetime of experience to the task: He began predicting weather when he attended the only high school in the world with weather Teletypes and radar.

THE OLD
FARMER'S ALMANAC

Established in 1792 and published every year thereafter

ROBERT B. THOMAS, *founder* (1766–1846)

YANKEE PUBLISHING INC.
P.O. Box 520, 1121 Main Street, Dublin, NH 03444
Phone: 603-563-8111 • Fax: 603-563-8252

PUBLISHER *(23rd since 1792):* Sherin Pierce
EDITOR IN CHIEF: Judson D. Hale Sr.

FOR DISPLAY ADVERTISING RATES
Go to Almanac.com/AdvertisingInfo or
call 800-895-9265, ext. 109

Stephanie Bernbach-Crowe • 914-827-0015
Steve Hall • 800-736-1100, ext. 320

FOR CLASSIFIED ADVERTISING
Cindy Levine, RJ Media • 212-986-0016

AD PRODUCTION COORDINATOR:
Janet Selle • 800-895-9265, ext. 168

PUBLIC RELATIONS
Quinn Brein • 206-842-8922
Ginger Vaughan • ginger@quinnbrein.com

CONSUMER MAIL ORDERS
Call 800-ALMANAC (800-256-2622)
or go to Almanac.com/Shop

RETAIL SALES
Stacey Korpi • 800-895-9265, ext. 160
Janice Edson, ext. 126

DISTRIBUTORS
NATIONAL: Comag Marketing Group
Smyrna, GA
BOOKSTORE: Houghton Mifflin Harcourt
Boston, MA
NEWSSTAND CONSULTANT: PSCS Consulting
Linda Ruth • 603-924-4407

Old Farmer's Almanac publications are available for sales promotions or premiums. Contact Beacon Promotions, info@beaconpromotions.com.

YANKEE PUBLISHING INCORPORATED
AN EMPLOYEE-OWNED COMPANY

Jamie Trowbridge, *President;* Paul Belliveau, Jody Bugbee, Ernesto Burden, Judson D. Hale Jr., Brook Holmberg, Sandra Lepple, Sherin Pierce, *Vice Presidents.*

PRINTED IN U.S.A.

ECLIPSES

There will be four eclipses in 2021, two of the Sun and two of the Moon. Solar eclipses are visible only in certain areas and require eye protection to be viewed safely. Lunar eclipses are technically visible from the entire night side of Earth, but during a penumbral eclipse, the dimming of the Moon's illumination is slight. See the **Astronomical Glossary, page 110,** for explanations of the different types of eclipses.

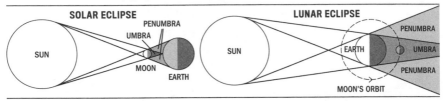

MAY 26: TOTAL ECLIPSE OF THE MOON. This eclipse is only partially visible from North America. The best views will be from western North America; and the eclipse also will be visible from Hawaii. The Moon will enter the penumbra at 4:46 A.M. EDT (1:46 A.M. PDT) and umbra at 5:45 A.M. EDT (2:45 A.M. PDT). It will leave the umbra at 8:53 A.M. EDT (5:53 A.M. PDT) and penumbra at 9:51 A.M. EDT (6:51 A.M. PDT).

JUNE 10: ANNULAR ECLIPSE OF THE SUN. This eclipse is visible from northern and northeastern North America, beginning at 4:12 A.M. EDT and ending at 9:11 A.M. EDT. The time of maximum eclipse varies by location. Note that this is an annular eclipse; the Moon will never fully obscure the visible surface of the Sun: At maximum eclipse, an "annulus" (ring) of full sunlight will still be visible. It is safe to view this eclipse only when using eye protection such as "eclipse glasses" or a solar filter.

NOVEMBER 18-19: PARTIAL ECLIPSE OF THE MOON. This eclipse is visible from North America and Hawaii. The Moon will enter the penumbra at 1:00 A.M. EST on November 19 (10:00 P.M. PST, November 18) and umbra at 2:18 A.M. EST on November 19 (11:18 P.M. PST, November 18). It will leave the umbra at 5:47 A.M. EST (2:47 A.M. PST) and penumbra at 7:06 A.M. EST (4:06 A.M. PST) on November 19.

DECEMBER 4: TOTAL ECLIPSE OF THE SUN. This eclipse is not visible from North America. (It will be visible from the Falkland Islands, the southern tip of Africa, Antarctica, and southeasternmost Australia.)

TRANSIT OF MERCURY. Because of Mercury's proximity to the Sun, the planet can be seen for only a few weeks before and after times of greatest elongation. It is observable near greatest eastern elongation during evening twilight and near greatest western elongation during morning twilight. In 2021, Mercury is best viewed from the Northern Hemisphere after sunset during the last 3 weeks of January and all of May. Look for a conjunction between Mercury and Jupiter on the morning of March 5, between Mercury and Venus on the evening of May 28, and between Mercury and Mars on the evening of August 18.

THE MOON'S PATH

The Moon's path across the sky changes with the seasons. Full Moons are very high in the sky (at midnight) between November and February and very low in the sky between May and July.

FULL-MOON DATES (ET)					
	2021	2022	2023	2024	2025
JAN.	28	17	6	25	13
FEB.	27	16	5	24	12
MAR.	28	18	7	25	14
APR.	26	16	6	23	12
MAY	26	16	5	23	12
JUNE	24	14	3	21	11
JULY	23	13	3	21	10
AUG.	22	11	1 & 30	19	9
SEPT.	20	10	29	17	7
OCT.	20	9	28	17	6
NOV.	19	8	27	15	5
DEC.	18	7	26	15	4

BRIGHT STARS

TRANSIT TIMES

This table shows the time (ET) and altitude of a star as it transits the meridian (i.e., reaches its highest elevation while passing over the horizon's south point) at Boston on the dates shown. The transit time on any other date differs from that of the nearest date listed by approximately 4 minutes per day. To find the time of a star's transit for your location, convert its time at Boston using Key Letter C **(see Time Corrections, page 238).**

STAR	CONSTELLATION	MAGNITUDE	TIME OF TRANSIT (ET) BOLD = P.M. LIGHT = A.M.						ALTITUDE (DEGREES)
			JAN. 1	MAR. 1	MAY 1	JULY 1	SEPT. 1	NOV. 1	
Altair	Aquila	0.8	**12:50**	8:58	5:58	1:58	**9:50**	**5:50**	56.3
Deneb	Cygnus	1.3	**1:40**	9:48	6:48	2:48	**10:40**	**6:41**	92.8
Fomalhaut	Psc. Aus.	1.2	**3:56**	**12:04**	9:04	5:04	1:01	**8:57**	17.8
Algol	Perseus	2.2	**8:06**	**4:14**	**1:14**	9:15	5:11	1:11	88.5
Aldebaran	Taurus	0.9	**9:34**	**5:42**	**2:42**	10:42	6:38	2:38	64.1
Rigel	Orion	0.1	**10:12**	**6:20**	**3:20**	11:20	7:16	3:17	39.4
Capella	Auriga	0.1	**10:15**	**6:23**	**3:23**	11:23	7:19	3:19	93.6
Bellatrix	Orion	1.6	**10:23**	**6:31**	**3:31**	11:31	7:27	3:27	54.0
Betelgeuse	Orion	var. 0.4	**10:52**	**7:01**	**4:01**	**12:01**	7:57	3:57	55.0
Sirius	Can. Maj.	-1.4	**11:42**	**7:50**	**4:50**	**12:50**	8:47	4:47	31.0
Procyon	Can. Min.	0.4	12:40	**8:44**	**5:44**	**1:45**	9:41	5:41	52.9
Pollux	Gemini	1.2	12:46	**8:51**	**5:51**	**1:51**	9:47	5:47	75.7
Regulus	Leo	1.4	3:09	**11:13**	**8:13**	**4:13**	**12:10**	8:10	59.7
Spica	Virgo	var. 1.0	6:25	2:33	**11:29**	**7:30**	**3:26**	11:26	36.6
Arcturus	Boötes	-0.1	7:15	3:23	12:24	**8:20**	**4:16**	**12:16**	66.9
Antares	Scorpius	var. 0.9	9:29	5:37	2:37	**10:33**	**6:30**	**2:30**	21.3
Vega	Lyra	0	11:36	7:44	4:44	12:44	**8:36**	**4:36**	86.4

RISE AND SET TIMES

To find the time of a star's rising at Boston on any date, subtract the interval shown at right from the star's transit time on that date; add the interval to find the star's setting time. To find the rising and setting times for your city, convert the Boston transit times above using the Key Letter shown at right before applying the interval **(see Time Corrections, page 238).** Deneb, Algol, Capella, and Vega are circumpolar stars—they never set but appear to circle the celestial north pole.

STAR	INTERVAL (H.M.)	RISING KEY	RISING DIR.*	SETTING KEY	SETTING DIR.*
Altair	6 36	B	EbN	E	WbN
Fomalhaut	3 59	E	SE	D	SW
Aldebaran	7 06	B	ENE	D	WNW
Rigel	5 33	D	EbS	B	WbS
Bellatrix	6 27	B	EbN	D	WbN
Betelgeuse	6 31	B	EbN	D	WbN
Sirius	5 00	D	ESE	B	WSW
Procyon	6 23	B	EbN	D	WbN
Pollux	8 01	A	NE	E	NW
Regulus	6 49	B	EbN	D	WbN
Spica	5 23	D	EbS	B	WbS
Arcturus	7 19	A	ENE	E	WNW
Antares	4 17	E	SEbE	A	SWbW

*b = "by"

New Bladder Control Pill Sales May Surpass Adult Diapers By 2022

Drug-free discovery works, say doctors. Many adults ditching diapers and pads for clinical strength pill that triggers day and night bladder support.

By J.K. Roberts
Interactive News Media

INM — Over 150,000 doses have shipped to bladder sufferers so far, and sales continue to climb every day for the 'diaper replacing' new pill called BladderMax.

"We knew we had a great product, but it's even exceeded our expectations," said Keith Graham, Manager of Call Center Operations for BladderMax.

"People just keep placing orders, it's pretty amazing," he said.

But a closer look at this new bladder control sensation suggests that maybe the company shouldn't have been caught off guard by its success.

There are very good reasons for BladderMax's surging popularity.

To begin with, clinical studies show BladderMax not only reduces embarrassing bladder leakages quickly, but also works to strengthen and calm the bladder for lasting relief.

Plus, at just $2 per daily dose, it's very affordable.

This may be another reason why American diaper companies are starting to panic over its release.

WHAT SCIENTISTS DISCOVERED

BladderMax contains a proprietary compound with a known ability to reduce stress, urgency, and overflow leakages in seniors suffering from overactive bladder.

This compound is not a drug. It is the active ingredient in BladderMax.

Studies show it naturally strengthens the bladder's muscle tone while relaxing the urination muscles resulting in a decrease in sudden urgency.

Many sufferers enjoy a reduction in bathroom trips both day and night. Others are able to get back to doing the things they love without worrying about embarrassing leakages.

"I couldn't sit through a movie without having to go to the bathroom 3-4 times," says Theresa Johnson of Duluth, GA. "but since using BladderMax I can not only sit through a movie, but I can drive on the freeway to another city without having to immediately go to the bathroom."

With so much positive feedback, it's easy to see why sales for this newly approved bladder pill continue to climb every day.

SLASHES EMBARRASSING LEAKAGES BY 79%

The 6 week clinical study was carried out by scientists in Japan. The results were published in the Journal of Medicine and Pharmaceutical Science in 2001.

The study involved seniors who suffered from frequent and embarrassing bladder leakages. They were not instructed to change their daily routines. They were only told to take BladderMax's active ingredient every day.

The results were incredible.

Taking BladderMax's active ingredient significantly reduced both sudden urges to go and embarrassing urine leakages compared to the placebo.

In fact, many experienced a 79% reduction in embarrassing accidents when coughing, sneezing, laughing or physical activity at 6 weeks.

HOW IT WORKS IS INCREDIBLE

Studies show that as many as one in six adults over age 40 suffers from an overactive bladder and embarrassing leakages.

"Losing control of when and how we go to the bathroom is just an indication of a weakening of the pelvic muscles caused by age-related hormonal changes," says Lewis.

"It happens in both men and women, and it is actually quite common."

The natural compound found in BladderMax contains the necessary

As new pill gains popularity, products like these will become unnecessary.

ingredients needed to help strengthen bladder muscles to relieve urgency, while reducing frequency.

Plus, it helps relax bladder muscles allowing for complete emptying of the bladder.

This proprietary compound is known as 'EFLA940'®.

And with over 17 years of medical use there have been no adverse side effects reported.

RECOMMENDED BY U.S. MEDICAL DOCTORS

"Many of my patients used to complain that coughing, sneezing or even getting up quickly from a chair results in wetting themselves and they fear becoming a social outcast," reports Dr. Clifford James M.D. "But BladderMax changes all that."

"BladderMax effectively treats urinary disorders, specifically overactive bladder," said Dr. Christie Wilkins, board certified doctor of natural medicine.

OLD FARMER'S ALMANAC READERS GET SPECIAL DISCOUNT SUPPLY

This is the official release of BladderMax and so for a limited time, the company is offering a special discount supply to our readers. An Order Hotline has been set up for our readers to call, but don't wait. The special offer will not last forever. All you have to do is call TOLL FREE 1-800-615-9302. The company will do the rest.

THE TWILIGHT ZONE/METEOR SHOWERS

Twilight is the time when the sky is partially illuminated preceding sunrise and again following sunset. The ranges of twilight are defined according to the Sun's position below the horizon. **Civil twilight** occurs when the Sun's center is between the horizon and 6 degrees below the horizon (visually, the horizon is clearly defined). **Nautical twilight** occurs when the center is between 6 and 12 degrees below the horizon (the horizon is distinct). **Astronomical twilight** occurs when the center is between 12 and 18 degrees below the horizon (sky illumination is imperceptible). When the center is at 18 degrees (**dawn** or **dark**) or below, there is no illumination.

LENGTH OF ASTRONOMICAL TWILIGHT (HOURS AND MINUTES)

LATITUDE	JAN. 1–APR. 10	APR. 11–MAY 2	MAY 3–MAY 14	MAY 15–MAY 25	MAY 26–JULY 22	JULY 23–AUG. 3	AUG. 4–AUG. 14	AUG. 15–SEPT. 5	SEPT. 6–DEC. 31
25°N to 30°N	1 20	1 23	1 26	1 29	1 32	1 29	1 26	1 23	1 20
31°N to 36°N	1 26	1 28	1 34	1 38	1 43	1 38	1 34	1 28	1 26
37°N to 42°N	1 33	1 39	1 47	1 52	1 59	1 52	1 47	1 39	1 33
43°N to 47°N	1 42	1 51	2 02	2 13	2 27	2 13	2 02	1 51	1 42
48°N to 49°N	1 50	2 04	2 22	2 42	–	2 42	2 22	2 04	1 50

TO DETERMINE THE LENGTH OF TWILIGHT: The length of twilight changes with latitude and the time of year. See the **Time Corrections, page 238,** to find the latitude of your city or the city nearest you. Use that figure in the chart above with the appropriate date to calculate the length of twilight in your area.

TO DETERMINE ARRIVAL OF DAWN OR DARK: Calculate the sunrise/sunset times for your locality using the instructions in **How to Use This Almanac, page 116.**

Subtract the length of twilight from the time of sunrise to determine when dawn breaks. Add the length of twilight to the time of sunset to determine when dark descends.

EXAMPLE:
BOSTON, MASS. (LATITUDE 42°22')

Sunrise, August 1	5:37 A.M. ET
Length of twilight	- 1 52
Dawn breaks	3:45 A.M.
Sunset, August 1	8:03 P.M. ET
Length of twilight	+1 52
Dark descends	9:55 P.M.

PRINCIPAL METEOR SHOWERS

SHOWER	BEST VIEWING	POINT OF ORIGIN	DATE OF MAXIMUM*	NO. PER HOUR**	ASSOCIATED COMET
Quadrantid	Predawn	N	Jan. 4	25	–
Lyrid	Predawn	S	Apr. 22	10	Thatcher
Eta Aquarid	Predawn	SE	May 4	10	Halley
Delta Aquarid	Predawn	S	July 30	10	–
Perseid	**Predawn**	**NE**	**Aug. 11–13**	**50**	**Swift-Tuttle**
Draconid	Late evening	NW	Oct. 9	6	Giacobini-Zinner
Orionid	Predawn	S	Oct. 21–22	15	Halley
Taurid	Late evening	S	Nov. 9	3	Encke
Leonid	Predawn	S	Nov. 17–18	10	Tempel-Tuttle
Andromedid	Late evening	S	Nov. 25–27	5	Biela
Geminid	**All night**	**NE**	**Dec. 13–14**	**75**	**–**
Ursid	Predawn	N	Dec. 22	5	Tuttle

*May vary by 1 or 2 days   **In a moonless, rural sky   **Bold** = most prominent

Fast-disappearing classics...

1935-1937 Set of Buffalo Nickels!

SAVE OVER 70%!

Get 3 Buffalo nickels from 1935-1937 for only $3.90! Struck over 80 years ago, these classic coins feature the most uniquely American design ever minted! The Indian/buffalo motif was a major change from traditional Liberty designs, and these coins have been cherished since their introduction in 1913. Produced in limited quantities, most Buffalo nickels wore out or were lost in circulation, or have disappeared into permanent collections. And those that remain in existence today are scarce and in great demand!

SAVE OVER 70% plus FREE GIFT!

Get a consecutive 3-year set of 1935-1937 Buffalo nickels now for ONLY $3.90 and **SAVE OVER 70%** off the regular price of $13.50, plus **Free Shipping**. Order by deadline and also get a **FREE** Lincoln Wheat cent, last issued over 60 years ago!

You'll also receive our fully illustrated catalog, plus other fascinating selections from our Free Examination Coins-on-Approval Service, from which you may purchase any or none of the coins – return balance in 15 days – with option to cancel at any time. **Order now and *SAVE!***

Order by deadline for a
FREE Gift!
Original 1909-1958
Lincoln Cent with the
Wheat Ears reverse
(Date our choice)

Mail coupon or order online today at
www.LittletonCoin.com/specials

Serving Collectors Since 1945

45-Day Money Back
Guarantee of Satisfaction

©2020 LCC, Inc.

Special Offer for New Customers Only

☑YES! Please send my consecutive 3-Year Set of 1935-1937 Buffalo Nickels for the special price of $3.90 – *regularly $13.50*, plus Free Shipping (limit 5 sets). Also send my FREE 1909-1958 Lincoln Wheat Cent (one per customer, please).

Order Deadline: 12:00 Midnight, August 31, 2021

Name _____
Please print clearly

Address _____ Apt#_____

City_____ State_____ Zip_____

E-Mail_____

Please send coupon to:
Littleton Coin Co.®, Dept. 5PX402
1309 Mt. Eustis Rd, Littleton NH 03561-3737

QTY	DESCRIPTION	PRICE	TOTAL
	3-Coin Buffalo Nickel Set Consecutive Dates *(limit 5 sets)*	$3.90	
	Custom Buffalo Nickel Display Folders **SPECIAL SAVINGS!** *–SAVE 36%* Made in USA (Reg. $3.95)	$2.50	
FREE Shipping!		**TOTAL $**	

☐ Check payable to Littleton Coin Co.
☐ VISA ☐ MasterCard ☐ American Express ☐ Discover

Card #: _____ Exp. Date ☐☐/☐☐

☐☐☐☐☐☐☐☐☐☐☐☐☐☐☐☐

THE VISIBLE PLANETS

Listed here for Boston are viewing suggestions for and the rise and set times (ET) of Venus, Mars, Jupiter, and Saturn on specific days each month, as well as when it is best to view Mercury. Approximate rise and set times for other days can be found by interpolation. Use the Key Letters at the right of each listing to convert the times for other localities **(see pages 116 and 238).**

FOR ALL PLANET RISE AND SET TIMES BY ZIP CODE, VISIT ALMANAC.COM/ASTRONOMY.

VENUS

Venus begins 2021 as an unremarkable morning star, neither high nor particularly bright but easily seen from the year's opening predawn hours until mid-February. It's then lost behind the Sun's glare through most of the spring, until it begins a long evening star apparition in May, low in the west after sunset. Venus brightens and slowly gets a bit higher up through the summer, but it doesn't become truly eye-catching until fall. It's at its best this year in December: During the final week of 2021, Venus has a brilliant, dazzling conjunction with Mercury in evening twilight.

Jan. 1	rise	5:45	E	Apr. 1	set	7:15	D	July 1	set	10:01	E	Oct. 1	set	8:06	A
Jan. 11	rise	6:03	E	Apr. 11	set	7:40	D	July 11	set	9:56	E	Oct. 11	set	7:59	A
Jan. 21	rise	6:16	E	Apr. 21	set	8:05	E	July 21	set	9:46	D	Oct. 21	set	7:55	A
Feb. 1	rise	6:23	E	May 1	set	8:31	E	Aug. 1	set	9:33	D	Nov. 1	set	7:56	A
Feb. 11	rise	6:23	E	May 11	set	8:56	E	Aug. 11	set	9:18	C	Nov. 11	set	6:59	A
Feb. 21	rise	6:19	D	May 21	set	9:19	E	Aug. 21	set	9:02	C	Nov. 21	set	7:01	A
Mar. 1	rise	6:13	D	June 1	set	9:40	E	Sept. 1	set	8:45	C	Dec. 1	set	6:58	A
Mar. 11	rise	6:03	D	June 11	set	9:53	E	Sept. 11	set	8:30	B	Dec. 11	set	6:46	A
Mar. 21	rise	6:51	C	June 21	set	10:00	E	Sept. 21	set	8:17	B	Dec. 21	set	6:18	A
												Dec. 31	set	5:32	B

MARS

This is a mediocre year for Mars, which has no opposition in 2021. It starts out in early January at its biggest and brightest—a dazzling magnitude 0.0 in Pisces, dominating the southern sky. Fading rapidly as winter progresses, Mars speeds through Aries and then Taurus before fading to a still-respectable magnitude 1 by the start of spring. The Red Planet then fades further and sinks lower as it crosses into Gemini in April, Cancer in June, and Leo in July, after which it's lost in the Sun's glare. It might be glimpsed, low and dim at magnitude 2, as a predawn morning star in Scorpius during the final few weeks of the year.

Jan. 1	set	1:26	D	Apr. 1	set	12:47	E	July 1	set	10:18	E	Oct. 1	set	6:32	C
Jan. 11	set	1:11	D	Apr. 11	set	12:36	E	July 11	set	9:55	E	Oct. 11	rise	6:47	D
Jan. 21	set	12:57	E	Apr. 21	set	12:24	E	July 21	set	9:32	D	Oct. 21	rise	6:42	D
Feb. 1	set	12:44	E	May 1	set	12:11	E	Aug. 1	set	9:05	D	Nov. 1	rise	6:37	D
Feb. 11	set	12:34	E	May 11	set	11:55	E	Aug. 11	set	8:41	D	Nov. 11	rise	5:33	D
Feb. 21	set	12:24	E	May 21	set	11:39	E	Aug. 21	set	8:16	D	Nov. 21	rise	5:29	D
Mar. 1	set	12:16	E	June 1	set	11:19	E	Sept. 1	set	7:48	C	Dec. 1	rise	5:25	E
Mar. 11	set	12:07	E	June 11	set	11:00	E	Sept. 11	set	7:22	C	Dec. 11	rise	5:21	E
Mar. 21	set	12:58	E	June 21	set	10:40	E	Sept. 21	set	6:57	C	Dec. 21	rise	5:18	E
												Dec. 31	rise	5:14	E

BOLD = P.M. LIGHT = A.M.

JUPITER

The solar system's largest planet opens 2021 still near Saturn as a low evening star. By mid-January, it's just too low to see. In late February, it emerges as a very bright predawn morning star. After this, it rises 2 hours earlier each month. It's up before midnight beginning in late June and visible all night when it comes to opposition on the night of August 19–20. It's well placed for viewing through the rest of the year but solely as an evening star after Thanksgiving.

Jan. 1	set	6:05	A	Apr. 1	rise	4:39	D	July 1	rise	11:00	D	Oct. 1	set	2:52	B
Jan. 11	set	5:37	B	Apr. 11	rise	4:04	D	July 11	rise	10:20	D	Oct. 11	set	2:11	B
Jan. 21	set	5:10	B	Apr. 21	rise	3:29	D	July 21	rise	9:39	D	Oct. 21	set	1:31	B
Feb. 1	rise	6:54	E	May 1	rise	2:54	D	Aug. 1	rise	8:53	D	Nov. 1	set	12:50	B
Feb. 11	rise	6:22	E	May 11	rise	2:18	D	Aug. 11	rise	8:11	D	Nov. 11	set	11:10	B
Feb. 21	rise	5:49	E	May 21	rise	1:42	D	Aug. 21	set	5:55	B	Nov. 21	set	10:36	B
Mar. 1	rise	5:23	D	June 1	rise	1:01	D	Sept. 1	set	5:05	B	Dec. 1	set	10:03	B
Mar. 11	rise	4:50	D	June 11	rise	12:23	D	Sept. 11	set	4:19	B	Dec. 11	set	9:31	B
Mar. 21	rise	5:16	D	June 21	rise	11:40	D	Sept. 21	set	3:35	B	Dec. 21	set	9:01	B
												Dec. 31	set	8:31	B

SATURN

As the year begins, the Ringed Planet, in Capricornus, is still visible as a low evening star beneath much brighter Jupiter. By mid-January, it's immersed in evening twilight. In late February, it begins its predawn morning star apparition. Steadily higher up at dawn through winter into early spring, Saturn rises before midnight beginning in June. Its best 2021 viewing begins about a month before its August 2 opposition, when it's out all night. It remains an easy target for the rest of the year, becoming strictly an evening sky object in late autumn. Its stunning rings, moderately "open" (in view), require at least 30x magnification.

Jan. 1	set	5:59	B	Apr. 1	rise	4:06	E	July 1	rise	10:08	E	Oct. 1	set	1:31	B
Jan. 11	set	5:25	B	Apr. 11	rise	3:28	E	July 11	rise	9:27	E	Oct. 11	set	12:51	B
Jan. 21	set	4:52	B	Apr. 21	rise	2:51	E	July 21	rise	8:45	E	Oct. 21	set	12:12	B
Feb. 1	rise	6:39	E	May 1	rise	2:13	E	Aug. 1	rise	8:00	E	Nov. 1	set	11:27	B
Feb. 11	rise	6:03	E	May 11	rise	1:34	E	Aug. 11	set	5:04	B	Nov. 11	set	9:50	B
Feb. 21	rise	5:28	E	May 21	rise	12:56	E	Aug. 21	set	4:21	B	Nov. 21	set	9:13	B
Mar. 1	rise	4:59	E	June 1	rise	12:12	E	Sept. 1	set	3:35	B	Dec. 1	set	8:38	B
Mar. 11	rise	4:23	E	June 11	rise	11:28	E	Sept. 11	set	2:53	B	Dec. 11	set	8:03	B
Mar. 21	rise	4:46	E	June 21	rise	10:48	E	Sept. 21	set	2:11	B	Dec. 21	set	7:28	B
												Dec. 31	set	6:55	B

MERCURY

The smallest planet is also the fastest, dashing around the Sun at 30 miles per second. For us to readily observe this world, it must be at least 5 degrees above the horizon 40 minutes after sunset or before sunrise, when its brightness exceeds magnitude 0.5. This year, such favorable conditions occur in twilight during the last 3 weeks of January and all of May. It's lower during September and the last 2 weeks of December. As a morning star, Mercury is best seen this year from the last half of March into early April, in mid-July, and in the first half of November.

DO NOT CONFUSE: • *Mercury with Saturn during their predawn conjunction from February 18 to 26. Mercury is much brighter and slightly orange.* • *Mars and the famous Scorpius star Antares when they meet before dawn in the final 6 days of this year. Although they are the same orange color, Antares is brighter.* • *Venus with Mercury when they meet low in evening twilight from December 27 to 29. Although Mercury is quite bright, Venus is even more luminous.*

ASTRONOMICAL GLOSSARY

APHELION (APH.): The point in a planet's orbit that is farthest from the Sun.

APOGEE (APO.): The point in the Moon's orbit that is farthest from Earth.

CELESTIAL EQUATOR (EQ.): The imaginary circle around the celestial sphere that can be thought of as the plane of Earth's equator projected out onto the sphere.

CELESTIAL SPHERE: An imaginary sphere projected into space that represents the entire sky, with an observer on Earth at its center. All celestial bodies other than Earth are imagined as being on its inside surface.

CIRCUMPOLAR: Always visible above the horizon, such as a circumpolar star.

CONJUNCTION: The time at which two or more celestial bodies appear closest in the sky. **Inferior (Inf.):** Mercury or Venus is between the Sun and Earth. **Superior (Sup.):** The Sun is between a planet and Earth. Actual dates for conjunctions are given on the **Right-Hand Calendar Pages, 121–147;** the best times for viewing the closely aligned bodies are given in **Sky Watch** on the **Left-Hand Calendar Pages, 120–146.**

DECLINATION: The celestial latitude of an object in the sky, measured in degrees north or south of the celestial equator; comparable to latitude on Earth. This Almanac gives the Sun's declination at noon.

ECLIPSE, LUNAR: The full Moon enters the shadow of Earth, which cuts off all or part of the sunlight reflected off the Moon. **Total:** The Moon passes completely through the umbra (central dark part) of Earth's shadow. **Partial:** Only part of the Moon passes through the umbra. **Penumbral:** The Moon passes through only the penumbra (area of partial darkness surrounding the umbra). See **page 102** for more information about eclipses.

ECLIPSE, SOLAR: Earth enters the shadow of the new Moon, which cuts off all or part of the Sun's light. **Total:** Earth passes through the umbra (central dark part) of the Moon's shadow, resulting in totality for observers within a narrow band on Earth. **Annular:** The Moon appears silhouetted against the Sun, with a ring of sunlight showing around it. **Partial:** The Moon blocks only part of the Sun.

ECLIPTIC: The apparent annual path of the Sun around the celestial sphere. The plane of the ecliptic is tipped 23½° from the celestial equator.

ELONGATION: The difference in degrees between the celestial longitudes of a planet and the Sun. **Greatest Elongation (Gr. Elong.):** The greatest apparent distance of a planet from the Sun, as seen from Earth.

EPACT: A number from 1 to 30 that indicates the Moon's age on January 1 at Greenwich, England; used in determining the date of Easter.

EQUINOX: When the Sun crosses the celestial equator. This event occurs two times each year: **Vernal** is around March 20 and **Autumnal** is around September 22.

EVENING STAR: A planet that is above the western horizon at sunset and less than 180° east of the Sun in right ascension.

GOLDEN NUMBER: A number in the 19-year Metonic cycle of the Moon, used in determining the date of Easter. See **page 149** for this year's Golden Number.

MAGNITUDE: A measure of a celestial object's brightness. **Apparent magnitude** measures the brightness of an object as seen from Earth. Objects with an apparent magnitude of 6 or less are observable to the naked eye. The lower the magnitude, the greater the brightness; an object with a magnitude of –1, e.g., is brighter than one with a magnitude of +1.

(continued)

Prep Your Garden the EASY Way with a
DR® Rototiller!

TOW-BEHIND...

...and WALK-BEHIND!

The **PRO XL DRT** has dual-rotating tines for both cultivating and sod-busting!

TOW-BEHINDS including models for ATVs and tractors.

WALK-BEHINDS including front- and rear-tine models.

CULTIVATORS for preparing small plots or weeding between rows.

1B22DA © 2020

FREE SHIPPING
6 MONTH TRIAL
SOME LIMITATIONS APPLY
Go online or call for details.

Go Online or Call for FREE Info Kit!
DRrototiller.com
TOLL FREE **800-731-0493**

DR
PROFESSIONAL POWER
DONE RIGHT

BURN SAFELY

with the Stainless Steel
BurnCage™

PERFECT FOR:
- **Sensitive financial documents**
- **All burnable household waste***
- **Old leaves & branches**

STAINLESS STEEL is light, durable, and portable (folds for easy storage).

PERFORATED CONSTRUCTION maximizes airflow and traps embers.

1600° TEMPERATURES mean more thorough burning with less ash.

Available in 3 Sizes!

MAX   XL   Original

1B22DB © 2020

No more **UNSAFE** and **UNSIGHTLY** rusty barrel!

* Always check local ordinances before burning.

Go Online or Call for FREE Info Kit!
BurnCage.com
TOLL FREE **800-731-0493**

DR
PROFESSIONAL POWER
DONE RIGHT

MIDNIGHT: Astronomically, the time when the Sun is opposite its highest point in the sky. Both 12 hours before and after noon (so, technically, both A.M. and P.M.), midnight in civil time is usually treated as the beginning of the day. It is displayed as 12:00 A.M. on 12-hour digital clocks. On a 24-hour cycle, 00:00, not 24:00, usually indicates midnight.

MOON ON EQUATOR: The Moon is on the celestial equator.

MOON RIDES HIGH/RUNS LOW: The Moon is highest above or farthest below the celestial equator.

MOONRISE/MOONSET: When the Moon rises above or sets below the horizon.

MOON'S PHASES: The changing appearance of the Moon, caused by the different angles at which it is illuminated by the Sun. **First Quarter:** Right half of the Moon is illuminated. **Full:** The Sun and the Moon are in opposition; the entire disk of the Moon is illuminated. **Last Quarter:** Left half of the Moon is illuminated. **New:** The Sun and the Moon are in conjunction; the Moon is darkened because it lines up between Earth and the Sun.

MOON'S PLACE, Astronomical: The position of the Moon within the constellations on the celestial sphere at midnight. **Astrological:** The position of the Moon within the tropical zodiac, whose twelve 30° segments (signs) along the ecliptic were named more than 2,000 years ago after constellations within each area. Because of precession and other factors, the zodiac signs no longer match actual constellation positions.

MORNING STAR: A planet that is above the eastern horizon at sunrise and less than 180° west of the Sun in right ascension.

NODE: Either of the two points where a celestial body's orbit intersects the ecliptic. **Ascending:** When the body is moving from south to north of the ecliptic. **Descending:** When the body is moving from north to south of the ecliptic.

OCCULTATION (OCCN.): When the Moon or a planet eclipses a star or planet.

OPPOSITION: The Moon or a planet appears on the opposite side of the sky from the Sun (elongation 180°).

PERIGEE (PERIG.): The point in the Moon's orbit that is closest to Earth.

PERIHELION (PERIH.): The point in a planet's orbit that is closest to the Sun.

PRECESSION: The slowly changing position of the stars and equinoxes in the sky caused by a slight wobble as Earth rotates around its axis.

RIGHT ASCENSION (R.A.): The celestial longitude of an object in the sky, measured eastward along the celestial equator in hours of time from the vernal equinox; comparable to longitude on Earth.

SOLSTICE, Summer: When the Sun reaches its greatest declination (23½°) north of the celestial equator, around June 21. **Winter:** When the Sun reaches its greatest declination (23½°) south of the celestial equator, around December 21.

STATIONARY (STAT.): The brief period of apparent halted movement of a planet against the background of the stars shortly before it appears to move backward/westward (retrograde motion) or forward/eastward (direct motion).

SUN FAST/SLOW: When a sundial is ahead of (fast) or behind (slow) clock time.

SUNRISE/SUNSET: The visible rising/setting of the upper edge of the Sun's disk across the unobstructed horizon of an observer whose eyes are 15 feet above ground level.

TWILIGHT: See **page 106.** ∎

Note: These definitions apply to the Northern Hemisphere; some do not hold true for locations in the Southern Hemisphere.

Stand Up Straight and Feel Better

Discover the Perfect Walker, the better way to walk safely and more naturally

NEW

Well, cheer up! There's finally a product designed to enable us all to walk properly and stay on the go. It's called the Perfect Walker, and it can truly change your life.

Traditional rollators and walkers simply aren't designed well. They require you to hunch over and shuffle your feet when you walk. This puts pressure on your back, your neck, your wrists and your hands. Over time, this makes walking

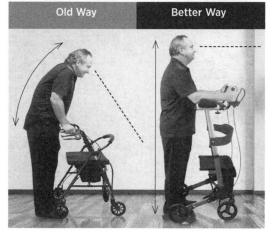

Old Way   Better Way

uncomfortable and can result in a variety of health issues. That's all changed with the Perfect Walker. Its upright design and padded elbow rests enable you to distribute your weight across your arms and shoulders, not your hands and wrists. Its unique frame gives you plenty of room to step, and the oversized wheels help

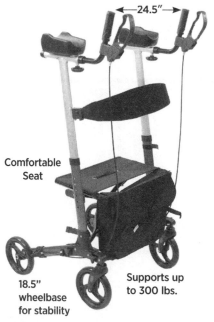

←—24.5"—→

Comfortable Seat

18.5" wheelbase for stability

Supports up to 300 lbs.

you glide across the floor. Once you've reached your destination you can use the hand brakes to gently slow down, and there's even a handy seat with a storage compartment. Its sleek, lightweight design makes it easy to use indoors and out and it folds up for portability and storage.

Why spend another day hunched over and shuffling along. Call now, and find out how you can try out a Perfect Walker for yourself... in your own home. You'll be glad you did.

Perfect Walker

Call now Toll-Free

1-888-348-0249

Please mention promotion code
112951 when ordering.

BBB
ACCREDITED BUSINESS
Rating of A+

© 2020 *first*STREET for Boomers and Beyond, Inc.

84514

2020

JANUARY
```
 S  M  T  W  T  F  S
          1  2  3  4
 5  6  7  8  9 10 11
12 13 14 15 16 17 18
19 20 21 22 23 24 25
26 27 28 29 30 31
```

FEBRUARY
```
 S  M  T  W  T  F  S
                   1
 2  3  4  5  6  7  8
 9 10 11 12 13 14 15
16 17 18 19 20 21 22
23 24 25 26 27 28 29
```

MARCH
```
 S  M  T  W  T  F  S
 1  2  3  4  5  6  7
 8  9 10 11 12 13 14
15 16 17 18 19 20 21
22 23 24 25 26 27 28
29 30 31
```

APRIL
```
 S  M  T  W  T  F  S
          1  2  3  4
 5  6  7  8  9 10 11
12 13 14 15 16 17 18
19 20 21 22 23 24 25
26 27 28 29 30
```

MAY
```
 S  M  T  W  T  F  S
                1  2
 3  4  5  6  7  8  9
10 11 12 13 14 15 16
17 18 19 20 21 22 23
24 25 26 27 28 29 30
31
```

JUNE
```
 S  M  T  W  T  F  S
    1  2  3  4  5  6
 7  8  9 10 11 12 13
14 15 16 17 18 19 20
21 22 23 24 25 26 27
28 29 30
```

JULY
```
 S  M  T  W  T  F  S
          1  2  3  4
 5  6  7  8  9 10 11
12 13 14 15 16 17 18
19 20 21 22 23 24 25
26 27 28 29 30 31
```

AUGUST
```
 S  M  T  W  T  F  S
                   1
 2  3  4  5  6  7  8
 9 10 11 12 13 14 15
16 17 18 19 20 21 22
23 24 25 26 27 28 29
30 31
```

SEPTEMBER
```
 S  M  T  W  T  F  S
       1  2  3  4  5
 6  7  8  9 10 11 12
13 14 15 16 17 18 19
20 21 22 23 24 25 26
27 28 29 30
```

OCTOBER
```
 S  M  T  W  T  F  S
             1  2  3
 4  5  6  7  8  9 10
11 12 13 14 15 16 17
18 19 20 21 22 23 24
25 26 27 28 29 30 31
```

NOVEMBER
```
 S  M  T  W  T  F  S
 1  2  3  4  5  6  7
 8  9 10 11 12 13 14
15 16 17 18 19 20 21
22 23 24 25 26 27 28
29 30
```

DECEMBER
```
 S  M  T  W  T  F  S
       1  2  3  4  5
 6  7  8  9 10 11 12
13 14 15 16 17 18 19
20 21 22 23 24 25 26
27 28 29 30 31
```

2021

JANUARY
```
 S  M  T  W  T  F  S
                1  2
 3  4  5  6  7  8  9
10 11 12 13 14 15 16
17 18 19 20 21 22 23
24 25 26 27 28 29 30
31
```

FEBRUARY
```
 S  M  T  W  T  F  S
    1  2  3  4  5  6
 7  8  9 10 11 12 13
14 15 16 17 18 19 20
21 22 23 24 25 26 27
28
```

MARCH
```
 S  M  T  W  T  F  S
    1  2  3  4  5  6
 7  8  9 10 11 12 13
14 15 16 17 18 19 20
21 22 23 24 25 26 27
28 29 30 31
```

APRIL
```
 S  M  T  W  T  F  S
                1  2  3
 4  5  6  7  8  9 10
11 12 13 14 15 16 17
18 19 20 21 22 23 24
25 26 27 28 29 30
```

MAY
```
 S  M  T  W  T  F  S
                   1
 2  3  4  5  6  7  8
 9 10 11 12 13 14 15
16 17 18 19 20 21 22
23 24 25 26 27 28 29
30 31
```

JUNE
```
 S  M  T  W  T  F  S
       1  2  3  4  5
 6  7  8  9 10 11 12
13 14 15 16 17 18 19
20 21 22 23 24 25 26
27 28 29 30
```

JULY
```
 S  M  T  W  T  F  S
             1  2  3
 4  5  6  7  8  9 10
11 12 13 14 15 16 17
18 19 20 21 22 23 24
25 26 27 28 29 30 31
```

AUGUST
```
 S  M  T  W  T  F  S
 1  2  3  4  5  6  7
 8  9 10 11 12 13 14
15 16 17 18 19 20 21
22 23 24 25 26 27 28
29 30 31
```

SEPTEMBER
```
 S  M  T  W  T  F  S
          1  2  3  4
 5  6  7  8  9 10 11
12 13 14 15 16 17 18
19 20 21 22 23 24 25
26 27 28 29 30
```

OCTOBER
```
 S  M  T  W  T  F  S
                1  2
 3  4  5  6  7  8  9
10 11 12 13 14 15 16
17 18 19 20 21 22 23
24 25 26 27 28 29 30
31
```

NOVEMBER
```
 S  M  T  W  T  F  S
    1  2  3  4  5  6
 7  8  9 10 11 12 13
14 15 16 17 18 19 20
21 22 23 24 25 26 27
28 29 30
```

DECEMBER
```
 S  M  T  W  T  F  S
          1  2  3  4
 5  6  7  8  9 10 11
12 13 14 15 16 17 18
19 20 21 22 23 24 25
26 27 28 29 30 31
```

2022

JANUARY
```
 S  M  T  W  T  F  S
                   1
 2  3  4  5  6  7  8
 9 10 11 12 13 14 15
16 17 18 19 20 21 22
23 24 25 26 27 28 29
30 31
```

FEBRUARY
```
 S  M  T  W  T  F  S
       1  2  3  4  5
 6  7  8  9 10 11 12
13 14 15 16 17 18 19
20 21 22 23 24 25 26
27 28
```

MARCH
```
 S  M  T  W  T  F  S
       1  2  3  4  5
 6  7  8  9 10 11 12
13 14 15 16 17 18 19
20 21 22 23 24 25 26
27 28 29 30 31
```

APRIL
```
 S  M  T  W  T  F  S
                1  2
 3  4  5  6  7  8  9
10 11 12 13 14 15 16
17 18 19 20 21 22 23
24 25 26 27 28 29 30
```

MAY
```
 S  M  T  W  T  F  S
 1  2  3  4  5  6  7
 8  9 10 11 12 13 14
15 16 17 18 19 20 21
22 23 24 25 26 27 28
29 30 31
```

JUNE
```
 S  M  T  W  T  F  S
          1  2  3  4
 5  6  7  8  9 10 11
12 13 14 15 16 17 18
19 20 21 22 23 24 25
26 27 28 29 30
```

JULY
```
 S  M  T  W  T  F  S
                1  2
 3  4  5  6  7  8  9
10 11 12 13 14 15 16
17 18 19 20 21 22 23
24 25 26 27 28 29 30
31
```

AUGUST
```
 S  M  T  W  T  F  S
    1  2  3  4  5  6
 7  8  9 10 11 12 13
14 15 16 17 18 19 20
21 22 23 24 25 26 27
28 29 30 31
```

SEPTEMBER
```
 S  M  T  W  T  F  S
             1  2  3
 4  5  6  7  8  9 10
11 12 13 14 15 16 17
18 19 20 21 22 23 24
25 26 27 28 29 30
```

OCTOBER
```
 S  M  T  W  T  F  S
                   1
 2  3  4  5  6  7  8
 9 10 11 12 13 14 15
16 17 18 19 20 21 22
23 24 25 26 27 28 29
30 31
```

NOVEMBER
```
 S  M  T  W  T  F  S
       1  2  3  4  5
 6  7  8  9 10 11 12
13 14 15 16 17 18 19
20 21 22 23 24 25 26
27 28 29 30
```

DECEMBER
```
 S  M  T  W  T  F  S
             1  2  3
 4  5  6  7  8  9 10
11 12 13 14 15 16 17
18 19 20 21 22 23 24
25 26 27 28 29 30 31
```

Love calendar lore? Find more at Almanac.com.

A CALENDAR OF THE HEAVENS FOR 2021

—Beth Krommes

CALENDAR

The Calendar Pages (120–147) are the heart of *The Old Farmer's Almanac.* They present sky sightings and astronomical data for the entire year and are what make this book a true almanac, a "calendar of the heavens." In essence, these pages are unchanged since 1792, when Robert B. Thomas published his first edition. The long columns of numbers and symbols reveal all of nature's precision, rhythm, and glory, providing an astronomical look at the year 2021.

HOW TO USE THE CALENDAR PAGES

The astronomical data on the **Calendar Pages (120–147)** are calculated for Boston (where Robert B. Thomas learned to calculate the data for his first Almanac). Guidance for calculating the times of these events for your locale appears on **pages 116–117.** Note that the results will be *approximate.* For the *exact* time of any astronomical event at your locale, go to **Almanac.com/ Astronomy** and enter your zip code. While you're there, print the month's "Sky Map," useful for viewing with "Sky Watch" in the Calendar Pages.

For a list of 2021 holidays and observances, see **pages 148–149.** Also check out the **Glossary of Almanac Oddities** on **pages 152–153,** which describes some of the more obscure entries traditionally found on the **Right-Hand Calendar Pages (121–147).**

ABOUT THE TIMES: All times are given in ET (Eastern Time), except where otherwise noted as AT (Atlantic Time, +1 hour), CT (Central Time, –1), MT (Mountain Time, –2), PT (Pacific Time, –3), AKT (Alaska Time, –4), or HAT (Hawaii-Aleutian Time, –5). Between 2:00 A.M., March 14, and 2:00 A.M., November 7, Daylight Saving Time is assumed in those locales where it is observed.

ABOUT THE TIDES: Tide times for Boston appear on **pages 120–146;** for Boston tide heights, see **pages 121–147.** Tide Corrections for East Coast locations appear on **pages 236–237.** Tide heights and times for locations across the United States and Canada are available at **Almanac.com/Tides.**

The Left-Hand Calendar Pages, 120 to 146

On these pages are the year's astronomical predictions for Boston (42°22' N, 71°3' W). Learn how to calculate the times of these events for your locale here or go to **Almanac.com/Rise** and enter your zip code.

A SAMPLE MONTH

SKY WATCH: The paragraph at the top of each Left-Hand Calendar Page describes the best times to view conjunctions, meteor showers, planets, and more. (Also see **How to Use the Right-Hand Calendar Pages, p. 118.**)

1 **2** **3** **4** **5** **6** **7** **8**

DAY OF YEAR	DAY OF MONTH	DAY OF WEEK	☀ RISES H. M.	RISE KEY	☀ SETS H. M.	SET KEY	LENGTH OF DAY H. M.	SUN FAST M.	SUN DECLINATION ° '	HIGH TIDE TIMES BOSTON	☾ RISES H. M.	RISE KEY	☾ SETS H. M.	SET KEY	☾ ASTRON. PLACE	☾ AGE
60	1	Fr.	6:20	D	5:34	C	11 14	4	7 s. 30	7¼ 8	3:30	E	12:58	B	SAG	25
61	2	Sa.	6:18	D	5:35	C	11 17	4	7 s. 07	8¼ 9	4:16	E	1:51	B	SAG	26
62	3	**F**	6:17	D	5:36	C	11 19	4	6 s. 44	9¼ 9¾	4:56	E	2:47	B	CAP	27
63	4	M.	6:15	D	5:37	C	11 22	4	6 s. 21	10 10½	5:31	E	3:45	C	CAP	28

1. To calculate the sunrise time in your locale: Choose a day. Note its Sun Rise Key Letter. Find your (nearest) city on **page 238**. Add or subtract the minutes that correspond to the Sun Rise Key Letter to/from the sunrise time for Boston.

EXAMPLE:

To calculate the sunrise time in Denver, Colorado, on day 1:

Sunrise, Boston,
with Key Letter D (above)   6:20 A.M. ET

Value of Key Letter D
for Denver (p. 238)   + 11 minutes

Sunrise, Denver   6:31 A.M. MT

To calculate your sunset time, repeat, using Boston's sunset time and its Sun Set Key Letter value.

2. To calculate the length of day: Choose a day. Note the Sun Rise and Sun Set Key Letters. Find your (nearest) city on **page 238**. Add or subtract the minutes that correspond to the Sun Set Key Letter to/from Boston's length of day. *Reverse* the sign (e.g., minus to plus) of the

Sun Rise Key Letter minutes. Add or subtract it to/from the first result.

EXAMPLE:

To calculate the length of day in Richmond, Virginia, on day 1:

Length of day, Boston (above)   11h.14m.
Sunset Key Letter C
for Richmond (p. 242)   + 25m.
    11h.39m.
Reverse sunrise Key Letter D
for Richmond (p. 242, +17 to -17)   - 17m.
Length of day, Richmond   11h.22m.

3. Use Sun Fast to change sundial time to clock time. A sundial reads natural (Sun) time, which is neither Standard nor Daylight time. To calculate clock time on a sundial in Boston, subtract the minutes given in this column; add the minutes when preceded by an asterisk [*].

–Beth Krommes

To convert the time to your (nearest) city, use Key Letter C on **page 238.**

EXAMPLE:

To change sundial to clock time in Boston or Salem, Oregon, on day 1:

Sundial reading (Boston or Salem)	12:00 noon
Subtract Sun Fast (p. 116)	- 4 minutes
Clock time, Boston	11:56 A.M. ET**
Use Key Letter C for Salem (p. 241)	+ 27 minutes
Clock time, Salem	12:23 P.M. PT**

**Note: Add 1 hour to the results in locations where Daylight Saving Time is currently observed.

4. This column gives the degrees and minutes of the Sun from the celestial equator at noon ET.

5. This column gives the approximate times of high tide in Boston. For example, the first high tide occurs at 7:15 A.M. and the second occurs at 8:00 P.M. the same day. (A dash indicates that high tide occurs on or after midnight and is recorded on the next day.) Figures for calculating approximate high tide times for localities other than Boston are given in the **Tide Corrections** table on page **236.**

6. To calculate the moonrise time in your locale: Choose a day. Note the Moon Rise Key Letter. Find your (nearest) city on **page 238.** Add or subtract the minutes that correspond to the Moon Rise Key Letter to/from the moonrise time given for Boston.

LONGITUDE OF CITY	CORRECTION MINUTES	LONGITUDE OF CITY	CORRECTION MINUTES
58°–76°	0	116°–127°	+4
77°–89°	+1	128°–141°	+5
90°–102°	+2	142°–155°	+6
103°–115°	+3		

(A dash indicates that the moonrise occurs on/after midnight and is recorded on the next day.) Find the longitude of your (nearest) city on **page 238.** Add a correction in minutes for your city's longitude (see table, bottom left). Use the same procedure with Boston's moonset time and the Moon Set Key Letter value to calculate the time of moonset in your locale.

EXAMPLE:

To calculate the time of moonset in Lansing, Michigan, on day 1:

Moonset, Boston, with Key Letter B (p. 116)	12:58 P.M. ET
Value of Key Letter B for Lansing (p. 240)	+ 53 minutes
Correction for Lansing longitude, 84°33'	+ 1 minute
Moonset, Lansing	1:52 P.M. ET

7. This column gives the Moon's *astronomical* position among the constellations (not zodiac) at midnight. For *astrological* data, see **pages 224–227.**

Constellations have irregular borders; on successive nights, the midnight Moon may enter one, cross into another, and then move to a new area of the previous. It visits the 12 zodiacal constellations, as well as Auriga **(AUR),** a northern constellation between Perseus and Gemini; Cetus **(CET),** which lies south of the zodiac, just south of Pisces and Aries; Ophiuchus **(OPH),** primarily north of the zodiac but with a small corner between Scorpius and Sagittarius; Orion **(ORI),** whose northern limit first reaches the zodiac between Taurus and Gemini; and Sextans **(SEX),** which lies south of the zodiac except for a corner that just touches it near Leo.

8. This column gives the Moon's age: the number of days since the previous new Moon. (The average length of the lunar month is 29.53 days.) *(continued)*

The Right-Hand Calendar Pages, 121 to 147

The Right-Hand Calendar Pages contain celestial events; religious observances; proverbs and poems; civil holidays; historical events; folklore; tide heights; weather prediction rhymes; Farmer's Calendar essays; and more.

A SAMPLE MONTH

	1	**2**	**3**	**4**	**5**	**6**		**7**	**8**	**9**	**10**
1	Fr.	ALL FOOLS' •		*If you want to make a fool of yourself,* *you'll find a lot of people ready to help you.*				*Flakes*			an inch long, who v
2	Sa.		Tap dancer Charles "Honi" Coles born, 1911 • Tides {9.5 9.0					*alive!*			in fresh water, pro pond across the
3	**B**	2nd ☉. of Easter •		Writer F. Scott Fitzgerald married Zelda Sayre, 1920				*Spring's*			emerged a month c
4	M.	Annunciation^T • ♂♆☾ •		*Ben Hur* won 11 Academy Awards, 1960				*arrived!*			to spend the next 3
5	Tu.	☾ AT ☍ •	Blizzard left 27.2" snow, St. John's, Nfld., 1999			• Tides {10.8 10.8		*Or is this*			on land before ret their wet world.
6	W.	☾ ON EQ. • ♂♀☾ •		Twin mongoose lemurs born, Busch Gardens, Tampa, Fla., 2012				*warmth*			You can't mis

1. The bold letter is the Dominical Letter (from A to G), a traditional ecclesiastical designation for Sunday determined by the date on which the year's first Sunday falls. For 2021, the Dominical Letter is **C**.

2. Civil holidays and astronomical events.

3. Religious feasts: A^T indicates a major feast that the church has this year temporarily transferred to a date other than its usual one.

4. Sundays and special holy days.

5. Symbols for notable celestial events. For example, ♂♆☾ on the 4th day means that a conjunction (♂) of Neptune (♆) and the Moon (☾) occurs.

6. Proverbs, poems, and adages.

7. Noteworthy historical events, folklore, and legends.

8. High tide heights, in feet, at Boston, Massachusetts.

9. Weather prediction rhyme.

10. Farmer's Calendar essay.

Celestial Symbols

☉ Sun	⊕ Earth	♅ Uranus	♂ Conjunction	☋ Descending node
○●☾ Moon	♂ Mars	♆ Neptune	(on the same	☌ Opposition
☿ Mercury	♃ Jupiter	♇ Pluto	celestial longitude)	(180 degrees
♀ Venus	♄ Saturn		☊ Ascending node	from Sun)

PREDICTING EARTHQUAKES

Note the dates in the Right-Hand Calendar Pages when the Moon rides high or runs low. The date of the high begins the most likely 5-day period of earthquakes in the Northern Hemisphere; the date of the low indicates a similar 5-day period in the Southern Hemisphere. Also noted are the 2 days each month when the Moon is on the celestial equator, indicating the most likely time for earthquakes in either hemisphere.

EARTH AT PERIHELION AND APHELION
Perihelion: January 2, 2021 (EST). Earth will be 91,399,454 miles from the Sun. **Aphelion:** July 5, 2021 (EDT). Earth will be 94,510,886 miles from the Sun.

CALENDAR

Why We Have Seasons

−Beth Krommes

The seasons occur because as Earth revolves around the Sun, its axis remains tilted at 23.5 degrees from the perpendicular. This tilt causes different latitudes on Earth to receive varying amounts of sunlight throughout the year.

In the Northern Hemisphere, the summer solstice marks the beginning of summer and occurs when the North Pole is tilted toward the Sun. The winter solstice marks the beginning of winter and occurs when the North Pole is tilted away from the Sun.

The equinoxes occur when the hemispheres equally face the Sun. At this time, the Sun rises due east and sets due west. The vernal equinox marks the beginning of spring; the autumnal equinox marks the beginning of autumn.

In the Southern Hemisphere, the seasons are the reverse of those in the Northern Hemisphere.

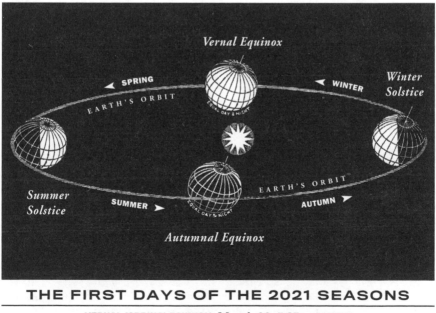

THE FIRST DAYS OF THE 2021 SEASONS

VERNAL (SPRING) EQUINOX:	March 20, 5:37 A.M. EDT
SUMMER SOLSTICE:	June 20, 11:32 P.M. EDT
AUTUMNAL (FALL) EQUINOX:	Sept. 22, 3:21 P.M. EDT
WINTER SOLSTICE:	Dec. 21, 10:59 A.M. EST

NOVEMBER

SKY WATCH: Except for Mercury in the predawn east, all of the planets fade a bit. Venus sinks lower each morning but is still conspicuous before dawn. Look for the thin crescent Moon between Mercury and Venus on the 13th and below them on the 14th. Venus hovering above Mercury is an easy observation from the 8th to the 18th, 40 minutes before sunrise, for those with an unobstructed eastern horizon. When evening dusk fades, Jupiter continues its steady march toward Saturn, with the pair now visible only in the first few hours of each night. The Moon floats near the two planets on the 18th and 19th.

◑ **LAST QUARTER** 8th day 8:46 A.M.   ◐ **FIRST QUARTER** 21st day 11:45 P.M.
● **NEW MOON** 15th day 12:07 A.M.   ○ **FULL MOON** 30th day 4:30 A.M.

After 2:00 A.M. on November 1, Eastern Standard Time is given.

GET THESE PAGES WITH TIMES SET TO YOUR ZIP CODE AT ALMANAC.COM/ACCESS.

DAY OF YEAR	DAY OF MONTH	DAY OF WEEK	☼ RISES H. M.	RISE KEY	☼ SETS H. M.	SET KEY	LENGTH OF DAY H. M.	SUN FAST M.	SUN DECLINATION ° '	HIGH TIDE TIMES BOSTON		☾ RISES H. M.	RISE KEY	☾ SETS H. M.	SET KEY	☾ ASTRON. PLACE	☾ AGE
306	1	**D**	6:18	D	**4:37**	B	10 19	32	14 s. 43	12¼	11½	**5:25**	B	7:05	E	ARI	16
307	2	M.	6:19	D	**4:36**	B	10 17	32	15 s. 02	12	12	**5:55**	B	8:06	E	TAU	17
308	3	Tu.	6:21	D	**4:34**	B	10 13	32	15 s. 21	12½	12½	**6:31**	B	9:08	E	TAU	18
309	4	W.	6:22	D	**4:33**	B	10 11	32	15 s. 39	1¼	1¼	**7:14**	B	10:07	E	TAU	19
310	5	Th.	6:23	E	**4:32**	B	10 09	32	15 s. 57	2	2	**8:04**	B	11:03	E	GEM	20
311	6	Fr.	6:24	E	**4:31**	B	10 07	32	16 s. 15	2¾	2¾	**9:03**	B	11:54	E	GEM	21
312	7	Sa.	6:26	E	**4:30**	B	10 04	32	16 s. 33	3½	3½	**10:08**	B	**12:38**	E	CAN	22
313	8	**D**	6:27	E	**4:29**	B	10 02	32	16 s. 50	4½	4½	**11:17**	C	**1:17**	E	CAN	23
314	9	M.	6:28	E	**4:28**	B	10 00	32	17 s. 07	5¼	5½	—	-	**1:50**	E	LEO	24
315	10	Tu.	6:29	E	**4:26**	B	9 57	32	17 s. 24	6¼	6½	12:29	C	**2:20**	D	LEO	25
316	11	W.	6:31	E	**4:25**	B	9 54	32	17 s. 40	7¼	7½	1:43	D	**2:48**	D	VIR	26
317	12	Th.	6:32	E	**4:25**	B	9 53	32	17 s. 56	8	8½	2:58	D	**3:16**	C	VIR	27
318	13	Fr.	6:33	E	**4:24**	B	9 51	31	18 s. 12	9	9½	4:16	E	**3:45**	C	VIR	28
319	14	Sa.	6:34	E	**4:23**	B	9 49	31	18 s. 27	9¾	10¼	5:35	E	**4:17**	B	LIB	29
320	15	**D**	6:36	E	**4:22**	B	9 46	31	18 s. 43	10¾	11¼	6:56	E	**4:55**	B	LIB	0
321	16	M.	6:37	E	**4:21**	B	9 44	31	18 s. 57	11½	—	8:15	E	**5:40**	B	OPH	1
322	17	Tu.	6:38	E	**4:20**	B	9 42	31	19 s. 12	12	12¼	9:28	E	**6:33**	B	OPH	2
323	18	W.	6:39	E	**4:19**	B	9 40	30	19 s. 26	1	1¼	10:32	E	**7:33**	B	SAG	3
324	19	Th.	6:40	E	**4:19**	B	9 39	30	19 s. 40	2	2	11:25	E	**8:39**	B	SAG	4
325	20	Fr.	6:42	E	**4:18**	B	9 36	30	19 s. 53	2¾	3	**12:08**	E	**9:45**	B	CAP	5
326	21	Sa.	6:43	E	**4:17**	B	9 34	30	20 s. 06	3¾	4	**12:42**	E	**10:51**	C	CAP	6
327	22	**D**	6:44	E	**4:17**	B	9 33	29	20 s. 19	4¾	5	**1:11**	E	**11:55**	C	AQU	7
328	23	M.	6:45	E	**4:16**	B	9 31	29	20 s. 32	5¾	6	**1:35**	D	—	-	AQU	8
329	24	Tu.	6:46	E	**4:15**	A	9 29	29	20 s. 43	6¾	7	**1:58**	D	12:56	D	AQU	9
330	25	W.	6:48	E	**4:15**	A	9 27	29	20 s. 55	7½	8	**2:19**	C	1:57	D	CET	10
331	26	Th.	6:49	E	**4:14**	A	9 25	28	21 s. 06	8¼	8¾	**2:40**	C	2:56	D	PSC	11
332	27	Fr.	6:50	E	**4:14**	A	9 24	28	21 s. 17	9	9½	**3:03**	C	3:56	E	PSC	12
333	28	Sa.	6:51	E	**4:13**	A	9 22	28	21 s. 27	9¾	10¼	**3:28**	B	4:56	E	ARI	13
334	29	**D**	6:52	E	**4:13**	A	9 21	27	21 s. 37	10¼	11	**3:57**	B	5:58	E	TAU	14
335	30	M.	6:53	E	**4:13**	A	9 20	27	21 s. 47	11	11½	**4:31**	B	7:00	E	TAU	15

NOVEMBER

The genuine food / Of every plant is earth:
hence their increase,
Their strength and substance.
–Robert Dodsley

DAY OF MONTH	DAY OF WEEK	DATES, FEASTS, FASTS, ASPECTS, TIDE HEIGHTS, AND WEATHER	
1	D	All Saints' • DAYLIGHT SAVING TIME ENDS, 2:00 A.M. • Tides {9.5 9.4	*Mild,*
2	M.	All Souls' • For 1st time since 1908, Chicago Cubs won World Series, 2016 • {10.1 —	*murky;*
3	Tu.	ELECTION DAY • ☾ AT ☊ • ☿ STAT. • Tides {9.2 10.0	*order*
4	W.	*A high wind prevents frost.* • *EPOXI* spacecraft flew by comet Hartley 2, 2010 • Tides {9.0 9.9	*the*
5	Th.	☾ RIDES HIGH • 2" snow, Salisbury, Mo., 1995 • Tides {8.7 9.7	*turkey!*
6	Fr.	Deadly tornado struck near Evansville, Ind., 2005 • {8.6 9.6	*White-*
7	Sa.	Sadie Hawkins Day • Last spike of transcontinental Can. Pacific Rwy. driven, Craigellachie, B.C., 1885	*out,*
8	D	23rd S. af. P. • 1st storm warning (for Great Lakes) by U.S. Signal Corps weather service, 1870	*then*
9	M.	Astronomer Carl Sagan born, 1934 • Tides {8.8 9.6	*bright*
10	Tu.	☿ GR. ELONG. (19° WEST) • 71°F, East Milford, N.H., 2009 • {9.3 9.9	*out.*
11	W.	St. Martin of Tours • VETERANS DAY • G. Bowering 1st Parliamentary Poet Laureate (Can.), 2002	*Great*
12	Th.	Indian Summer • ☾ ON EQ. • ☌♀☾ • Tides {10.6 10.6	*for*
13	Fr.	☌☿☾ • ☌♃♇ • Writer Robert Louis Stevenson born, 1850 • {11.3 10.9	*animal*
14	Sa.	☾ AT PERIG. • *Do good, if you expect to receive it.* • Tides {11.9 11.0	*tracks*
15	D	24th S. af. P. • NEW ● • ♂ STAT. • {12.2 11.0	*exposed:*
16	M.	☾ AT ☋ • Inaugural concert of Philadelphia Orchestra, 1900 • {12.3 —	*First*
17	Tu.	St. Hugh of Lincoln • Douglas C. Engelbart received patent for computer mouse, 1970 • {10.8 12.1	*it*
18	W.	St. Hilda of Whitby • ☾ RUNS LOW • Tides {10.5 11.7	*rains,*
19	Th.	☌♃☾ • ☌♄☾ • ☌♇☾ • Tides {10.0 11.1	*then it*
20	Fr.	U.S. attorney general Robert F. Kennedy born, 1925 • Tides {9.6 10.5	*snows.*
21	Sa.	*Mayflower* Compact signed (Nov. 11, Julian calendar), 1620 • Composer Henry Purcell died, 1695	*Rinse,*
22	D	25th S. af. P. • British clipper *Cutty Sark* launched, 1869 • {9.0 9.4	*repeat—*
23	M.	St. Clement • ☌♆☾ • Pathologist Walter Reed died, 1902 • {8.9 9.1	*Hey,*
24	Tu.	14.04-lb. saugeye caught, Antrim Lake, Ohio, 2004 • Tides {9.0 9.0	*let's*
25	W.	☾ ON EQ. • ☌♂☾ • Industrialist Andrew Carnegie born, 1835 • Tides {9.2 8.9	*eat!*
26	Th.	THANKSGIVING DAY • ☾ AT APO. • *Gratitude preserves old friendship and procures new.*	*Autumn*
27	Fr.	☌♅☾ • C.A.R.E. founded, 1945 • Tides {9.6 9.0	*lingers*
28	Sa.	Navigator Ferdinand Magellan reached Pacific, emerging from what is now Strait of Magellan, 1520	*with*
29	D	1st S. of Advent • ♆ STAT. • 1st helicopter hoist rescue, Penfield Reef, Conn., 1945	*cold,*
30	M.	St. Andrew • FULL BEAVER ○ • ECLIPSE ☾ • {10.1 9.0	*gray fingers.*

Farmer's Calendar

When the new woodstove arrived, it sat unevenly until the deliveryman supplied a quarter and a nickel and stacked them under the stove's short foot. His 30 cents endures, even as the steady stove's been dark and cold for months, serving as an overbuilt pedestal for vases displaying the summer's array, from aconite to zinnias. Once, on an excessively sultry day, I caught the cat draped across its soapstone top. Not anymore: Now orange flames flicker within and both the cat and the dog have succumbed to its heat, basking before it, on the floor. I'm keeping the fire alive by feeding it pages of old notebooks full of my expired ideas and crossed out scrawl. Later I'll shovel these ashes into a wide tin pail, the one I'll carry out to the snow-fleeced pasture. There, I'll scatter and dump these soots to sweeten the grasses' roots, which will bring on lavish clovers later, when the snow is over and the coin-size Sun again burns steady in the sky and finds me lugging buckets of water out to the grazing lambs. Then an idea might spark my mind and I'll dash back to the desk beside the chilly stove to scribble new lines on a white page.

Listen to the Farmer's Calendar at Almanac.com/Podcast.

DECEMBER

SKY WATCH: We welcome winter with the "Great Conjunction," which unfolds every two decades and has been celebrated since ancient times. The Moon is near the two giant worlds of Jupiter and Saturn on the 16th and 17th. Then Jupiter passes extremely close to Saturn from the 20th to the 22nd, coming closest on the 21st—the solstice. So close are the two planets that they merge almost into a single "star," near enough to fit together in the same telescope field of view and very much visible with the naked eye. Look for them 45 minutes after local sunset, low in fading evening twilight, roughly 14 degrees above the southwestern horizon. Often too close to the Sun to be observable (as in 2000), this conjunction is truly great and not to be missed!

◗ **LAST QUARTER** 7th day 7:37 P.M. ◖ **FIRST QUARTER** 21st day 6:41 P.M.
● **NEW MOON** 14th day 11:17 A.M. ○ **FULL MOON** 29th day 10:28 P.M.

All times are given in Eastern Standard Time.

GET THESE PAGES WITH TIMES SET TO YOUR ZIP CODE AT ALMANAC.COM/ACCESS.

DAY OF YEAR	DAY OF MONTH	DAY OF WEEK	☼ RISES H.M.	RISE KEY	☼ SETS H.M.	SET KEY	LENGTH OF DAY H.M.	SUN FAST M.	SUN DECLINATION ° '	HIGH TIDE TIMES BOSTON		☾ RISES H.M.	RISE KEY	☾ SETS H.M.	SET KEY	☾ ASTRON. PLACE	☾ AGE
336	1	Tu.	6:54	E	4:12	A	9 18	26	21 s. 56	11½	—	5:12	B	8:01	E	TAU	16
337	2	W.	6:55	E	4:12	A	9 17	26	22 s. 05	12¼	12¼	6:00	B	8:59	E	GEM	17
338	3	Th.	6:56	E	4:12	A	9 16	26	22 s. 13	12¾	12¾	6:56	B	9:52	E	GEM	18
339	4	Fr.	6:57	E	4:12	A	9 15	25	22 s. 21	1½	1½	7:59	B	10:38	E	GEM	19
340	5	Sa.	6:58	E	4:12	A	9 14	25	22 s. 28	2¼	2¼	9:06	B	11:18	E	CAN	20
341	6	**D**	6:59	E	4:12	A	9 13	24	22 s. 35	3	3¼	10:16	C	11:52	E	LEO	21
342	7	M.	7:00	E	4:11	A	9 11	24	22 s. 42	4	4¼	11:27	C	12:22	E	LEO	22
343	8	Tu.	7:01	E	4:11	A	9 10	24	22 s. 48	4¾	5¼	—	-	12:50	D	LEO	23
344	9	W.	7:02	E	4:11	A	9 09	23	22 s. 54	5¾	6¼	12:39	D	1:16	D	VIR	24
345	10	Th.	7:03	E	4:12	A	9 09	23	22 s. 59	6¾	7¼	1:53	E	1:43	C	VIR	25
346	11	Fr.	7:04	E	4:12	A	9 08	22	23 s. 04	7¾	8¼	3:08	E	2:12	C	VIR	26
347	12	Sa.	7:04	E	4:12	A	9 08	22	23 s. 08	8½	9¼	4:26	E	2:46	B	LIB	27
348	13	**D**	7:05	E	4:12	A	9 07	21	23 s. 12	9½	10	5:45	E	3:26	B	LIB	28
349	14	M.	7:06	E	4:12	A	9 06	21	23 s. 15	10¼	11	7:01	E	4:15	B	OPH	0
350	15	Tu.	7:07	E	4:12	A	9 05	20	23 s. 18	11¼	11¾	8:12	E	5:12	B	SAG	1
351	16	W.	7:07	E	4:13	A	9 06	20	23 s. 21	12	—	9:12	E	6:17	B	SAG	2
352	17	Th.	7:08	E	4:13	A	9 05	19	23 s. 22	12¾	12¾	10:01	E	7:26	B	CAP	3
353	18	Fr.	7:09	E	4:14	A	9 05	19	23 s. 24	1½	1¾	10:40	E	8:34	C	CAP	4
354	19	Sa.	7:09	E	4:14	A	9 05	18	23 s. 25	2½	2½	11:12	E	9:41	C	AQU	5
355	20	**D**	7:10	E	4:15	A	9 05	18	23 s. 26	3¼	3½	11:38	D	10:44	C	AQU	6
356	21	M.	7:10	E	4:15	A	9 05	17	23 s. 26	4¼	4½	12:02	D	11:46	D	AQU	7
357	22	Tu.	7:11	E	4:16	A	9 05	17	23 s. 25	5	5¼	12:23	D	—	-	PSC	8
358	23	W.	7:11	E	4:16	A	9 05	16	23 s. 24	6	6¼	12:45	C	12:46	D	CET	9
359	24	Th.	7:12	E	4:17	A	9 05	16	23 s. 23	6¾	7¼	1:07	C	1:46	E	PSC	10
360	25	Fr.	7:12	E	4:17	A	9 05	15	23 s. 21	7½	8¼	1:31	B	2:46	E	ARI	11
361	26	Sa.	7:12	E	4:18	A	9 06	15	23 s. 19	8½	9	1:58	B	3:47	E	ARI	12
362	27	**D**	7:13	E	4:19	A	9 06	14	23 s. 16	9	9¾	2:30	B	4:49	E	TAU	13
363	28	M.	7:13	E	4:19	A	9 06	14	23 s. 13	9¾	10½	3:08	B	5:51	E	TAU	14
364	29	Tu.	7:13	E	4:20	A	9 07	13	23 s. 10	10½	11¼	3:54	B	6:51	E	TAU	15
365	30	W.	7:13	E	4:21	A	9 08	13	23 s. 05	11¼	11¾	4:49	B	7:47	E	GEM	16
366	31	Th.	7:13	E	4:22	A	9 09	13	23 s. 01	11¾	—	5:51	B	8:36	E	GEM	17

DECEMBER

DECEMBER HATH 31 DAYS

Look! the massy trunks are cased in the pure crystal;
Each light spray nodding and tinkling in the breath of heaven.
–William Cullen Bryant, of trees glazed with ice

DAY OF MONTH	DAY OF WEEK	DATES, FEASTS, FASTS, ASPECTS, TIDE HEIGHTS, AND WEATHER	
1	Tu.	☾ AT ☊ • Astronaut Bob Thirsk returned to Earth after 6 mos. on ISS, 2009 • {10.2 / —	*Two-*
2	W.	St. Viviana • ☾ RIDES HIGH • Environmental Protection Agency (EPA) began operation, 1970	*faced—*
3	Th.	*If snowflakes increase in size, a thaw will follow.* • Tides {8.9 / 10.1	*snow's*
4	Fr.	Historian Thomas Carlyle born, 1795 • Tides {8.8 / 10.0	*erased*
5	Sa.	1st large hydroponicum established, Montebello, Calif., 1935 • Tides {8.8 / 9.9	*by*
6	**D**	**2nd S. of Advent** • **St. Nicholas** • {8.8 / 9.8	*rain*
7	M.	St. Ambrose • **National Pearl Harbor Remembrance Day** • {9.0 / 9.7	*and*
8	Tu.	Inventor Eli Whitney born, 1765 • Tides {9.3 / 9.7	*southern*
9	W.	☾ ON EQ. • 1st Heisman Trophy, awarded to Jay Berwanger, 1935 • {9.7 / 9.7	*breezes.*
10	Th.	St. Eulalia • Chanukah begins at sundown • Tides {10.3 / 9.9	*Flakefest,*
11	Fr.	2.1" rain, Vancouver, B.C., 1925 • Conservationist Benton MacKaye died, 1975	*then*
12	Sa.	**Our Lady of Guadalupe** • ☾ AT PERIG. • OCCN. ♀☾ • {11.4 / 10.2	*a*
13	**D**	**3rd S. of Advent** • **St. Lucia** • Tides {11.8 / 10.4	*rest*
14	M.	Halcyon Days begin. • **NEW** ● • **ECLIPSE** ☉ • ☾ AT ☋ • ☌☿☾	*(still,*
15	Tu.	☾ RUNS LOW • *He who prizes little things is worthy of great ones.* • Tides {12.0 / 10.3	*it*
16	W.	Ember Day • ☌♃☾ • ☌♇☾ • 2nd Cape Hatteras, N.C., lighthouse likely 1st lit, 1870	*freezes).*
17	Th.	☌♄☾ • Composer Ludwig van Beethoven baptized, 1770 • Tides {10.1 / 11.4	*Polar*
18	Fr.	Ember Day • Great Comet reached perihelion, 1680 • Tides {9.8 / 10.9	*pelting,*
19	Sa.	Ember Day • ☿ IN SUP. ☌ • Beware the Pogonip. • Tides {9.5 / 10.3	*followed*
20	**D**	**4th S. of Advent** • ☌♆☾ • Mo. imposed $1 tax on bachelors, 1820	*by*
21	M.	St. Thomas • **WINTER SOLSTICE** • ☌♃♄ • Tides {9.0 / 9.2	*melting,*
22	Tu.	☾ ON EQ. • Writer George Eliot died, 1880 • {8.9 / 8.7	*Santa*
23	W.	☌♂☾ • Reginald Fessenden 1st to transmit voice over wireless radio, 1900 • {8.9 / 8.5	*can't a-*
24	Th.	☾ AT APO. • ☌♅☾ • CONAD (later NORAD) began to track Santa Claus, 1955 • {9.0 / 8.4	*bide.*
25	Fr.	**Christmas** • Bytown (Ottawa) and Prescott Rwy. opened, Ont., 1854 • {9.1 / 8.4	*Such*
26	Sa.	St. Stephen • **Boxing Day (Canada)** • **First Day of Kwanzaa** • {9.4 / 8.5	*contrasting*
27	**D**	**1st S. af. Ch.** • *The more haste, the worse speed.* • Tides {9.6 / 8.6	*forecasting*
28	M.	Holy Innocents • ☾ AT ☊ • Writer Theodore Dreiser died, 1945 • {9.9 / 8.7	*means*
29	Tu.	St. John[T] • **FULL COLD** ○ • Texas statehood, 1845 • {10.1 / 8.8	*a*
30	W.	☾ RIDES HIGH • 1st photo of Earth's curvature exhibited, Cleveland, Ohio, 1930 • {10.3 / 9.0	*bumpy*
31	Th.	St. Sylvester • Gymnast Gabby Douglas born, 1995 • {10.4 / —	*ride!*

Farmer's Calendar

Clues #1 and #2: The room stank with a funky musk, and the cat hunched, its full attention given to the heating vent. When I snapped on the lamp, A-ha! Eye-shine glimmered from the open vent, and then a flash of white as something dashed under the dresser. After extracting the cat and shutting the door, I made an ignominious phone call to someone I'd heard was handy with these sort of predicaments. Hello, I greeted the person and got straight to the point: There's a weasel in my bedroom.

"Ermine" is the winter word for this creature whose brownish coat has turned pure white, a camouflage in snowy environs. Shouldn't I have been grateful for a lithe carnivore to feed on the unseen things constantly scrabbling in the walls—Mice? Squirrels? Chipmunks? Every night, I bang to quiet them. Futilely. But whose bedroom is big enough to host both cats and weasels? After the Good Samaritan arrived and set up his trap, I expected a prolonged scuffle—so I closed the door and wished him luck. But before 5 minutes had elapsed, my uninvited roommate was caged and leaving the premises, on his way to a spacious field that matched his hue.

JANUARY

SKY WATCH: Earth comes closest to the Sun on the 2nd for an unusually early perihelion. The year also begins with Jupiter and Saturn still close together after their historically tight conjunction 10 days earlier. While Jupiter is bright enough to be viewed easily in evening twilight, much dimmer and lower Saturn may be hard to spot. Bright Mercury joins them on the 10th, but this planet triangle is just 6 degrees high 40 minutes after sunset and challengingly low. In the predawn eastern sky, Venus is low but easy to see, especially on the 11th, when it's joined by the thin crescent Moon for a striking display. Bright Mars gets into the action on the 20th, when it hovers next to the first-quarter Moon.

| ☽ LAST QUARTER | 6th day | 4:37 A.M. | ☾ FIRST QUARTER | 20th day | 4:02 P.M. |
| ● NEW MOON | 13th day | 12:00 A.M. | ○ FULL MOON | 28th day | 2:16 P.M. |

All times are given in Eastern Standard Time.

GET THESE PAGES WITH TIMES SET TO YOUR ZIP CODE AT ALMANAC.COM/ACCESS.

DAY OF YEAR	DAY OF MONTH	DAY OF WEEK	☼ RISES H. M.	RISE KEY	☼ SETS H. M.	SET KEY	LENGTH OF DAY H. M.	SUN FAST M.	SUN DECLINATION ° '	HIGH TIDE TIMES BOSTON		☽ RISES H. M.	RISE KEY	☽ SETS H. M.	SET KEY	☽ ASTRON. PLACE	☽ AGE
1	1	Fr.	7:13	E	4:23	A	9 10	12	22 s. 56	12½	12½	6:58	B	9:19	E	CAN	18
2	2	Sa.	7:13	E	4:24	A	9 11	12	22 s. 50	1¼	1¼	8:08	C	9:55	E	LEO	19
3	3	**C**	7:13	E	4:24	A	9 11	11	22 s. 44	2	2	9:18	C	10:26	E	LEO	20
4	4	M.	7:13	E	4:25	A	9 12	11	22 s. 38	2¾	2¾	10:29	D	10:54	D	LEO	21
5	5	Tu.	7:13	E	4:26	A	9 13	10	22 s. 31	3½	3¾	11:41	D	11:20	D	VIR	22
6	6	W.	7:13	E	4:27	A	9 14	10	22 s. 24	4¼	4¾	—	-	11:46	C	VIR	23
7	7	Th.	7:13	E	4:28	A	9 15	9	22 s. 16	5¼	5¾	12:53	E	12:13	C	VIR	24
8	8	Fr.	7:13	E	4:29	A	9 16	9	22 s. 08	6¼	6¾	2:08	E	12:44	B	LIB	25
9	9	Sa.	7:13	E	4:30	A	9 17	9	21 s. 59	7¼	8	3:23	E	1:20	B	LIB	26
10	10	**C**	7:12	E	4:32	A	9 20	8	21 s. 50	8¼	9	4:39	E	2:03	B	OPH	27
11	11	M.	7:12	E	4:33	A	9 21	8	21 s. 41	9¼	10	5:50	E	2:55	B	OPH	28
12	12	Tu.	7:12	E	4:34	A	9 22	7	21 s. 31	10	10¾	6:55	E	3:56	B	SAG	29
13	13	W.	7:11	E	4:35	A	9 24	7	21 s. 21	11	11¾	7:49	E	5:03	B	SAG	0
14	14	Th.	7:11	E	4:36	A	9 25	7	21 s. 10	11¾	—	8:33	E	6:13	B	CAP	1
15	15	Fr.	7:11	E	4:37	A	9 26	6	20 s. 59	12½	12½	9:08	E	7:22	C	CAP	2
16	16	Sa.	7:10	E	4:38	A	9 28	6	20 s. 47	1¼	1¼	9:38	E	8:28	C	AQU	3
17	17	**C**	7:10	E	4:40	A	9 30	6	20 s. 35	2	2¼	10:03	D	9:32	D	AQU	4
18	18	M.	7:09	E	4:41	A	9 32	5	20 s. 23	2¾	3	10:26	D	10:33	D	PSC	5
19	19	Tu.	7:08	E	4:42	B	9 34	5	20 s. 10	3½	3¾	10:47	C	11:34	D	CET	6
20	20	W.	7:08	E	4:43	B	9 35	5	19 s. 57	4¼	4¾	11:09	C	—	-	PSC	7
21	21	Th.	7:07	E	4:45	B	9 38	4	19 s. 44	5	5½	11:32	B	12:34	E	CET	8
22	22	Fr.	7:06	E	4:46	B	9 40	4	19 s. 30	6	6½	11:58	B	1:34	E	ARI	9
23	23	Sa.	7:06	E	4:47	B	9 41	4	19 s. 16	6¾	7½	12:27	B	2:36	E	TAU	10
24	24	**C**	7:05	E	4:48	B	9 43	4	19 s. 01	7¾	8½	1:03	B	3:38	E	TAU	11
25	25	M.	7:04	E	4:50	B	9 46	3	18 s. 46	8½	9¼	1:46	B	4:38	E	TAU	12
26	26	Tu.	7:03	E	4:51	B	9 48	3	18 s. 31	9¼	10	2:37	B	5:36	E	GEM	13
27	27	W.	7:02	E	4:52	B	9 50	3	18 s. 16	10	10¾	3:37	B	6:29	E	GEM	14
28	28	Th.	7:01	E	4:53	B	9 52	3	18 s. 00	10¾	11½	4:44	B	7:15	E	CAN	15
29	29	F.	7:00	E	4:55	B	9 55	3	17 s. 44	11½	—	5:54	C	7:54	E	CAN	16
30	30	Sa.	6:59	E	4:56	B	9 57	3	17 s. 27	12	12¼	7:07	C	8:27	E	LEO	17
31	31	**C**	6:58	E	4:57	B	9 59	2	17 s. 10	12¾	1	8:20	D	8:57	D	LEO	18

To use this page, see p. 116; for Key Letters, see p. 238. LIGHT = A.M. BOLD = P.M. 2021

JANUARY

A good New Year to one and all, / And many may ye see;
And during all the years to come, / O happy may ye be.
–traditional Scottish poem

DAY OF MONTH	DAY OF WEEK	DATES, FEASTS, FASTS, ASPECTS, TIDE HEIGHTS, AND WEATHER	
1	Fr.	Holy Name • NEW YEAR'S DAY • Kathleen Casey-Kirschling, 1st baby boomer in U.S., born, 1946	*Baby*
2	Sa.	⊕ AT PERIHELION • Canadian Group of Seven artist Frederick Varley born, 1881 • { 9.1 / 10.5	*New*
3	C	2nd S. af. Ch. • 3-day storm left 8" ice, Idaho, 1961 • Tides { 9.3 / 10.4	*Year's*
4	M.	St. Elizabeth Ann Seton • ☌☿♇ • Utah became 45th U.S. state, 1896 • { 9.4 / 10.2	*a*
5	Tu.	Twelfth Night • ☾ ON EQ. • Quebec City mayor Jean-Paul L'Allier died, 2016 • { 9.6 / 9.9	*shivery*
6	W.	Epiphany • Indianapolis designated as capital of Ind., 1821 • Tides { 9.8 / 9.6	*delivery.*
7	Th.	Distaff Day • *Action is the proper fruit of knowledge.* • Tides { 10.1 / 9.4	*Rain*
8	Fr.	Entertainer Elvis Presley born, 1935 • Barge accidentally rammed Jacques Cousteau's *Calypso,* Singapore, 1996	*and*
9	Sa.	☾ AT PERIG. • ☌☿♄ • Yellow-bellied sea snake found on shore, Newport Beach, Calif., 2018	*snow*
10	C	1st S. af. Ep. • ☾ AT ☋ • Writer Sinclair Lewis died, 1951 • { 11.0 / 9.4	*together;*
11	M.	Plough Monday • ☌☿♃ • ☌♀☾ • Tides { 11.2 / 9.6	*sunny*
12	Tu.	☾ RUNS LOW • –35°F, Chester, Mass., 1981 • { 11.4 / 9.7	*weather.*
13	W.	St. Hilary • NEW ● • ☌♃☾ • ☌♄☾ • ☌♇☾	*It's*
14	Th.	☌☿☾ • ☌♇☉ • ♅ STAT. • American/British general Benedict Arnold born, 1741	*bitter—*
15	Fr.	*Stardust* capsule landed in Utah, after record re-entry speed of 28,860 mph, 2006 • { 9.7 / 11.0	*winter's*
16	Sa.	*A northern air, / Brings weather fair.* • Tides { 9.6 / 10.5	*no*
17	C	2nd S. af. Ep. • ☌♆☾ • U.S. statesman Benjamin Franklin born, 1706	*quitter!*
18	M.	MARTIN LUTHER KING JR.'S BIRTHDAY, OBSERVED • 95°F, Los Angeles and Palm Springs, Calif., 1971	*Rain*
19	Tu.	☾ ON EQ. • Last old-style, German-made Volkswagen Beetle left plant in Emden, Germany, 1978 • { 9.1 / 8.9	*falls,*
20	W.	INAUGURATION DAY • Solar activity disabled two Canadian satellites, 1994 • { 8.9 / 8.5	*flakes*
21	Th.	☾ AT APO. • ☌♂☾ • ☌♂♅ • ☌♅☾ • Tides { 8.8 / 8.1	*flitter,*
22	Fr.	St. Vincent • Philosopher Sir Francis Bacon born, 1561 • Tides { 8.8 / 7.9	*every*
23	Sa.	☌♄☉ • ☿ GR. ELONG. (19° EAST) • –80°F, Prospect Creek, Alaska, 1971 • { 8.9 / 7.9	*day's*
24	C	3rd S. af. Ep. • Change a Pet's Life Day • ☾ AT ☊ • { 9.1 / 8.0	*a snow*
25	M.	Conversion of Paul • January thaw traditionally begins about now. • { 9.4 / 8.2	*spitter.*
26	Tu.	Sts. Timothy & Titus • ☾ RIDES HIGH • Hockey player Wayne Gretzky born, 1961	*Request*
27	W.	*Neither praise nor dispraise thyself; thine actions serve the turn.* • Tides { 10.1 / 8.8	*a vest*
28	Th.	St. Thomas Aquinas • FULL WOLF ○ • ☌♀♇ • ☌♃☉ • { 10.5 / 9.2	*from*
29	Fr.	☿ STAT. • Kansas became 34th U.S. state, 1861 • Tides { 10.8 / —	*a*
30	Sa.	American seamstress Betsy Ross died, 1836 • Raccoons mate now. • Tides { 9.5 / 10.9	*friendly*
31	C	Septuagesima • Eunice Sanborn died at age 114, 2011 • { 9.8 / 10.9	*knitter!*

Farmer's Calendar

Promptly on the bitterest winter mornings there appears at my bird feeder one or more, often a pair, of purple finches. They are bright little birds, and their punctuality is reassuring. Yet they fill me with puzzlement: The purple finch has a flaw. Purple it is not.

The purple finch is the color of an overripe strawberry. Am I missing something? There are plenty of misnomers in the world of birds that are related to behavior. A whole family of birds of worldwide distribution, including the whippoorwills and nighthawks, has the odd name goatsucker (Caprimulgidae) because they were anciently believed to suckle at the teats of milking goats. Sufficiently nutty, but not hard to account for: Some Dark Age goatherd with too much mead under his belt discovered a whippoorwill flying around his milking stand, found the nannies dry, and drew a peasant's conclusion.

It's one thing for a bird to be mistakenly associated with an event or action, but what am I to make of a system of names that tells me a red bird is purple, a brown one black? It's the unapologetic falsity of the thing. If I were a purple finch, I would be made quite uncomfortable.

FEBRUARY

SKY WATCH: Jupiter and Saturn, after passing behind the Sun during January's last week, have deserted the evening sky, leaving low Mercury alone to finish up its own challenging apparition. Mars also appears in the evening sky, much higher, on the Aries/Taurus boundary; although fading, the Red Planet is still conspicuous at magnitude 0.76. Watch it hover dramatically just above the waxing gibbous Moon on the 18th. Low in the predawn eastern sky at month's end, the Jupiter–Saturn–Mercury threesome has been copied and pasted from their January evening-sky venue, but the grouping is just 7 degrees high in the brightening twilight, requiring an unobstructed, oceanlike horizon. The asteroid Vesta, in the tail of Leo, can be easily seen with binoculars at magnitude 6.3.

◑ **LAST QUARTER** 4th day 12:37 P.M.　　● **FIRST QUARTER** 19th day 1:47 P.M.

● **NEW MOON** 11th day 2:06 P.M.　　○ **FULL MOON** 27th day 3:17 A.M.

All times are given in Eastern Standard Time.

GET THESE PAGES WITH TIMES SET TO YOUR ZIP CODE AT ALMANAC.COM/ACCESS.

DAY OF YEAR	DAY OF MONTH	DAY OF WEEK	☼ RISES H. M.	RISE KEY	☼ SETS H. M.	SET KEY	LENGTH OF DAY H. M.	SUN FAST M.	SUN DECLINATION ° ′	HIGH TIDE TIMES BOSTON		☾ RISES H. M.	RISE KEY	☾ SETS H. M.	SET KEY	☾ ASTRON. PLACE	☾ AGE
32	1	M.	6:57	E	4:59	B	10 02	2	16 s. 53	1½	1¾	9:32	D	9:24	D	VIR	19
33	2	Tu.	6:56	E	5:00	B	10 04	2	16 s. 36	2¼	2½	10:45	E	9:50	C	VIR	20
34	3	W.	6:55	E	5:01	B	10 06	2	16 s. 18	3	3½	11:58	E	10:17	C	VIR	21
35	4	Th.	6:54	E	5:03	B	10 09	2	16 s. 00	4	4½	—	-	10:46	B	LIB	22
36	5	Fr.	6:53	D	5:04	B	10 11	2	15 s. 42	4¾	5½	1:12	E	11:19	B	LIB	23
37	6	Sa.	6:52	D	5:05	B	10 13	2	15 s. 23	5¾	6½	2:26	E	11:58	B	SCO	24
38	7	**C**	6:51	D	5:07	B	10 16	2	15 s. 04	7	7¾	3:38	E	12:46	B	OPH	25
39	8	M.	6:49	D	5:08	B	10 19	2	14 s. 45	8	8¾	4:43	E	1:42	B	SAG	26
40	9	Tu.	6:48	D	5:09	B	10 21	2	14 s. 26	9	9¾	5:40	E	2:46	B	SAG	27
41	10	W.	6:47	D	5:10	B	10 23	2	14 s. 07	10	10½	6:27	E	3:54	B	CAP	28
42	11	Th.	6:46	D	5:12	B	10 26	2	13 s. 47	10¾	11¼	7:05	E	5:03	C	CAP	0
43	12	Fr.	6:44	D	5:13	B	10 29	2	13 s. 27	11½	—	7:37	E	6:10	C	AQU	1
44	13	Sa.	6:43	D	5:14	B	10 31	2	13 s. 06	12	12¼	8:03	D	7:16	C	AQU	2
45	14	**C**	6:42	D	5:16	B	10 34	2	12 s. 46	12¾	1	8:27	D	8:19	D	AQU	3
46	15	M.	6:40	D	5:17	B	10 37	2	12 s. 25	1½	1¾	8:49	D	9:21	D	CET	4
47	16	Tu.	6:39	D	5:18	B	10 39	2	12 s. 04	2	2½	9:11	C	10:21	E	PSC	5
48	17	W.	6:37	D	5:19	B	10 42	2	11 s. 43	2¾	3¼	9:33	C	11:22	E	PSC	6
49	18	Th.	6:36	D	5:21	B	10 45	2	11 s. 22	3½	4	9:58	B	—	-	ARI	7
50	19	Fr.	6:35	D	5:22	B	10 47	2	11 s. 01	4¼	4¾	10:25	B	12:23	E	TAU	8
51	20	Sa.	6:33	D	5:23	B	10 50	2	10 s. 39	5	5¾	10:58	B	1:24	E	TAU	9
52	21	**C**	6:32	D	5:25	B	10 53	2	10 s. 17	6	6¾	11:37	B	2:25	E	TAU	10
53	22	M.	6:30	D	5:26	B	10 56	3	9 s. 56	7	7¾	12:24	B	3:24	E	GEM	11
54	23	Tu.	6:29	D	5:27	B	10 58	3	9 s. 34	8	8½	1:20	B	4:18	E	GEM	12
55	24	W.	6:27	D	5:28	B	11 01	3	9 s. 11	8¾	9½	2:23	B	5:06	E	GEM	13
56	25	Th.	6:25	D	5:30	B	11 05	3	8 s. 49	9½	10¼	3:33	B	5:48	E	CAN	14
57	26	Fr.	6:24	D	5:31	B	11 07	3	8 s. 27	10¼	11	4:46	C	6:25	E	LEO	15
58	27	Sa.	6:22	D	5:32	C	11 10	3	8 s. 04	11	11½	6:01	D	6:56	E	LEO	16
59	28	**C**	6:21	D	5:33	C	11 12	3	7 s. 41	11¾	—	7:16	D	7:24	D	VIR	17

THE SECOND MONTH • 2021 **FEBRUARY** FEBRUARY HATH 28 DAYS

Have you heard the snowdrops ringing / Their bells to themselves?
Smaller and whiter than the singing / Of any fairy elves.
–**Sydney Thompson Dobell**

DAY OF MONTH	DAY OF WEEK	DATES, FEASTS, FASTS, ASPECTS, TIDE HEIGHTS, AND WEATHER	
1	M.	St. Brigid • 1st Marine Division (U.S.) activated, 1941 • Tides 10.1 / 10.8	*Groundhogs*
2	Tu.	Candlemas • Groundhog Day • ☾ on Eq. • Tides 10.2 / 10.4	*shy*
3	W.	☾ at perig. • Elizabeth Blackwell, 1st woman to earn medical degree in U.S., born, 1821	*from*
4	Th.	Mormon exodus began, 1846 • 395 ice skaters lined up to set world record, Winnipeg, Man., 2018	*sunny*
5	Fr.	St. Agatha • Yankees bought 10 acres in Bronx for stadium, 1921 • Tides 10.3 / 9.1	*sky.*
6	Sa.	☾ at ☋ • ☌♀♄ • Alan Shepard became 1st person to hit golf ball on Moon, 1971	*Mild*
7	**C**	**Sexagesima** • Aviatrix Amelia Earhart wed George Putnam, 1931 • 10.3 / 8.8	*reprieve,*
8	M.	☾ runs low • ☿ in inf. ☌ • *Good counsel never comes too late.* • 10.5 / 9.0	*we*
9	Tu.	☌♇☾ • Naturalist/artist Hans Albert Hochbaum born, 1911 • 10.6 / 9.2	*do*
10	W.	☌☿☾ • ☌♀☾ • ☌♃☾ • ☌♄☾ • Tides 10.8 / 9.4	*believe.*
11	Th.	NEW ● • ☌♀♃ • Alban Michael, last fluent speaker of Nuchatlaht language, died, 2016	*Slushy;*
12	Fr.	**Chinese New Year (Ox)** • ☌☿♀ • U.S. president Abraham Lincoln born, 1809	*Valentine's*
13	Sa.	☌☿♃ • ☌♆☾ • 1st women RCAF pilots graduated, 1981 • 9.7 / 10.6	*Day's*
14	**C**	**Quinquagesima** • **Valentine's Day** • *To St. Valentine, the spring is a neighbor.*	*mushy!*
15	M.	**Presidents' Day** • ☾ on Eq. • Social reformer Susan B. Anthony born, 1820 • 9.6 / 9.9	*Bright*
16	Tu.	Shrove Tuesday • Winter's back breaks. • Tides 9.5 / 9.4	*beams*
17	W.	**Ash Wednesday** • ☌♅☾ • Myles Standish commander of Plymouth Col., Mass., 1621	*are*
18	Th.	☾ at apo. • ☌♂☾ • 72°F, Providence, R.I., 1981 • 9.1 / 8.4	*melting*
19	Fr.	1st official U.S. government weather predictions published, 1871 • Tides 8.9 / 8.0	*streams,*
20	Sa.	☾ at ☊ • ☿ stat. • *Every light is not the Sun.* • 8.7 / 7.7	*and*
21	**C**	**1st S. in Lent** • Actor Alan Rickman born, 1946 • 8.7 / 7.7	*steam's*
22	M.	☾ rides high • U.S. president George Washington born, 1732 • 8.9 / 7.8	*rising*
23	Tu.	Tootsie Roll introduced, 1896 • Tides 9.2 / 8.2	*from*
24	W.	St. Matthias • Ember Day • Discovery of 1st pulsar announced, 1968	*ski-race*
25	Th.	First state gasoline tax began (Oreg.), 1919 • Tides 10.2 / 9.2	*toilers*
26	Fr.	Ember Day • Buffalo Bill born, 1846 • 1st sextuplets to be born in Ohio (Akron), 2004	*and*
27	Sa.	Ember Day • **FULL SNOW** ○ • Tides 11.1 / 10.2	*maple*
28	**C**	**2nd S. in Lent** • Skunks mate now. • 11.3 / —	*boilers.*

Q: Why did the doughnut visit the dentist?
A: He needed a chocolate filling.

Farmer's Calendar

February 28. The end of the last fully winter month. I got in the car and headed northwest to Burlington, by the long way: say 150 miles. A journey to the edge.

My side of Vermont is a close country, narrow, wooded, but west of the mountains you get into a country of broad valleys, real farmland, with flat, wide fields and blue silos. I stopped to buy a doughnut in Whiting, a little village built up on top of a hill with plowed fields spreading down and away in all directions. Pretty weather—cold, though. The lakes and ponds still frozen hard.

From Whiting you can look west and see, for the first time, the Adirondacks, blue and gray in the distance; I ate my doughnut and admired them, not without misgivings. Somewhere between here and those peaks is a borderline. Over this is not New England. Beyond the Adirondacks there is an enormous country, a continent, a nation, and from this little hilltop it all seems at the same time very far off and very near, almost as though you could walk over to those mountains, climb up, and look out over the whole republic spread before you: the Great Lakes, the Plains, the Rockies, and the Golden Gate.

MARCH

SKY WATCH: This month's action happens mainly in the morning, when Jupiter, Saturn, and Mercury line up low in the east on the 1st. On the 5th, Mercury and Jupiter essentially merge into a single bright "star"—a "don't miss" event, except that at just 6 degrees high, it requires a flat eastern horizon for viewing. A much easier-to-see conjunction unfolds on the 10th, when the three planets form a small triangle that's 8 degrees up 40 minutes before sunrise. By month's end, Jupiter and Saturn are an even easier-to-view 10 to 15 degrees high in that same predawn eastern locale. On the evening of the 19th, the Moon closely meets Mars just above the orange Taurus star Aldebaran. The equinox brings spring to the Northern Hemisphere on the 20th at 5:37 A.M. EDT.

◗ **LAST QUARTER** 5th day 8:30 P.M. ◐ **FIRST QUARTER** 21st day 10:40 A.M.

● **NEW MOON** 13th day 5:21 A.M. ○ **FULL MOON** 28th day 2:48 P.M.

After 2:00 A.M. on March 14, Eastern Daylight Time is given.

GET THESE PAGES WITH TIMES SET TO YOUR ZIP CODE AT ALMANAC.COM/ACCESS.

DAY OF YEAR	DAY OF MONTH	DAY OF WEEK	☀ RISES H. M.	RISE KEY	☀ SETS H. M.	SET KEY	LENGTH OF DAY H. M.	SUN FAST M.	SUN DECLINATION ° '	HIGH TIDE TIMES BOSTON		☾ RISES H. M.	RISE KEY	☾ SETS H. M.	SET KEY	☾ ASTRON. PLACE	☾ AGE
60	1	M.	6:19	D	5:34	C	11 15	4	7 s. 18	12¼	12½	8:31	E	7:51	D	VIR	18
61	2	Tu.	6:17	D	5:36	C	11 19	4	6 s. 55	1	1½	9:47	E	8:18	C	VIR	19
62	3	W.	6:16	D	5:37	C	11 21	4	6 s. 32	1¾	2¼	11:03	E	8:47	C	VIR	20
63	4	Th.	6:14	D	5:38	C	11 24	4	6 s. 09	2¾	3¼	—	-	9:19	B	LIB	21
64	5	Fr.	6:13	D	5:39	C	11 26	5	5 s. 46	3½	4¼	12:18	E	9:57	B	SCO	22
65	6	Sa.	6:11	D	5:40	C	11 29	5	5 s. 23	4½	5¼	1:31	E	10:42	B	OPH	23
66	7	C	6:09	D	5:42	C	11 33	5	5 s. 00	5½	6½	2:38	E	11:35	B	SAG	24
67	8	M.	6:08	C	5:43	C	11 35	5	4 s. 36	6¾	7½	3:36	E	12:36	B	SAG	25
68	9	Tu.	6:06	C	5:44	C	11 38	6	4 s. 13	7¾	8½	4:25	E	1:42	B	CAP	26
69	10	W.	6:04	C	5:45	C	11 41	6	3 s. 49	8¾	9½	5:05	E	2:50	B	CAP	27
70	11	Th.	6:02	C	5:46	C	11 44	6	3 s. 26	9¾	10¼	5:38	E	3:57	C	CAP	28
71	12	Fr.	6:01	C	5:48	C	11 47	6	3 s. 02	10½	11	6:06	E	5:03	C	AQU	29
72	13	Sa.	5:59	C	5:49	C	11 50	7	2 s. 38	11¼	11¾	6:30	D	6:06	D	AQU	0
73	14	C	6:57	C	6:50	C	11 53	7	2 s. 15	1	—	7:52	D	8:09	D	PSC	1
74	15	M.	6:56	C	6:51	C	11 55	7	1 s. 51	1¼	1½	8:14	C	9:10	E	CET	2
75	16	Tu.	6:54	C	6:52	C	11 58	7	1 s. 27	1¾	2¼	8:36	C	10:11	E	PSC	3
76	17	W.	6:52	C	6:53	C	12 01	8	1 s. 03	2½	3	8:59	B	11:12	E	ARI	4
77	18	Th.	6:50	C	6:55	C	12 05	8	0 s. 40	3	3½	9:25	B	—	-	ARI	5
78	19	Fr.	6:49	C	6:56	C	12 07	8	0 s. 16	3¾	4¼	9:55	B	12:13	E	TAU	6
79	20	Sa.	6:47	C	6:57	C	12 10	9	0 N. 07	4½	5¼	10:30	A	1:14	E	TAU	7
80	21	C	6:45	C	6:58	C	12 13	9	0 N. 30	5½	6	11:13	B	2:13	E	TAU	8
81	22	M.	6:44	C	6:59	C	12 15	9	0 N. 54	6¼	7	12:04	B	3:08	E	GEM	9
82	23	Tu.	6:42	C	7:00	C	12 18	9	1 N. 18	7¼	8	1:04	B	3:58	E	GEM	10
83	24	W.	6:40	C	7:01	C	12 21	10	1 N. 41	8¼	9	2:10	B	4:42	E	CAN	11
84	25	Th.	6:38	C	7:03	C	12 25	10	2 N. 05	9¼	9¾	3:21	C	5:20	E	LEO	12
85	26	Fr.	6:37	C	7:04	C	12 27	10	2 N. 29	10	10½	4:35	C	5:53	E	LEO	13
86	27	Sa.	6:35	C	7:05	C	12 30	11	2 N. 52	10¾	11¼	5:50	D	6:22	D	LEO	14
87	28	C	6:33	C	7:06	C	12 33	11	3 N. 15	11¾	—	7:07	D	6:50	D	VIR	15
88	29	M.	6:31	C	7:07	D	12 36	11	3 N. 39	12	12½	8:25	E	7:17	C	VIR	16
89	30	Tu.	6:30	C	7:08	D	12 38	12	4 N. 02	12¾	1¼	9:44	E	7:46	C	VIR	17
90	31	W.	6:28	C	7:09	D	12 41	12	4 N. 25	1½	2¼	11:03	E	8:17	B	LIB	18

To use this page, see p. 116; for Key Letters, see p. 238. LIGHT = A.M. BOLD = P.M. **2021**

CALENDAR

RUSH!
Priority Order!

BUSINESS REPLY MAIL
FIRST-CLASS MAIL   PERMIT NO. 51   PALM COAST FL

POSTAGE WILL BE PAID BY ADDRESSEE

THE OLD FARMER'S ALMANAC
Subscriptions
PO BOX 420001
PALM COAST FL 32142-9900

RUSH!
Priority Order!

NO POSTAGE
NECESSARY
IF MAILED
IN THE
UNITED STATES

BUSINESS REPLY MAIL
FIRST-CLASS MAIL   PERMIT NO. 51   PALM COAST FL

POSTAGE WILL BE PAID BY ADDRESSEE

THE OLD FARMER'S ALMANAC
Subscriptions
PO BOX 420001
PALM COAST FL 32142-9900

MARCH

MARCH HATH 31 DAYS

Now feel the gentle zephyrs, / Warmth throughout they bring.
Carrying a familiar message, / Again the taste of spring.
–Donald Webber

DAY OF MONTH	DAY OF WEEK	DATES, FEASTS, FASTS, ASPECTS, TIDE HEIGHTS, AND WEATHER	
1	M.	St. David • ☾ ON EQ. • Peace Corps established, 1961 • Tides {10.7 11.3	*It's*
2	Tu.	St. Chad • ☾ AT PERIG. • Redesigned U.S. $10 bill circulated, 2006 • {11.0 11.0	*cold,*
3	W.	"Star-Spangled Banner" became official U.S. national anthem, 1931 • Tides {11.1 10.6	*we're*
4	Th.	Vermont statehood, 1791 • Comedienne/singer Minnie Pearl died, 1996	*told,*
5	Fr.	St. Piran • ☾ AT ☋ • ☌☿♃ • Tides {10.7 9.4	*with*
6	Sa.	☿ GR. ELONG. (27° WEST) • 1st machine patent issued in North America, 1646	*goose-down*
7	**C**	**3rd S. in Lent** • ☾ RUNS LOW • Hummingbirds migrate north now.	*snow,*
8	M.	☌♇☾ • *A peck of March dust is worth a king's ransom.* • Tides {10.0 8.7	*followed*
9	Tu.	☌♄☾ • Napoleon married Josephine, 1796 • Tides {10.0 8.9	*by a*
10	W.	☌☿☾ • ☌♃☾ • ☌♆☉ • Writer E. Pauline Johnson born, 1861	*three-*
11	Th.	Space probe *Pioneer 5* launched, Cape Canaveral, Fla., 1960 • {10.3 9.5	*day*
12	Fr.	☌♀☾ • ☌♆☾ • Historian Olive P. Dickason died, 2011 • {10.4 9.7	*blow!*
13	Sa.	NEW ● • ☌♀♆ • Uranus discovered, 1781 • {10.4 9.9	*Hip, hip,*
14	**C**	**4th S. in Lent** • **DAYLIGHT SAVING TIME BEGINS, 2:00 A.M.** • ☾ ON EQ.	*hurray*
15	M.	Clean Monday • Beware the ides of March. • Tides {9.9 10.0	*for*
16	Tu.	☌♅☾ • Botanist/photographer Anna Atkins born, 1799 • Tides {9.9 9.7	*St. Patty's*
17	W.	**ST. PATRICK'S DAY** • *Luck comes to those who look after it.* • {9.8 9.3	*Day!*
18	Th.	☾ AT APO. • 6.27" rain (plus 4.05" next day), Pinkham Notch, N.H., 1936 • {9.6 8.9	*Splish,*
19	Fr.	St. Joseph • ☾ AT ☊ • ☌♂☾ • Tides {9.3 8.4	*splash,*
20	Sa.	**VERNAL EQUINOX** • 1st U.S. figure skating championship in "international style," New Haven, Conn., 1914	*corned*
21	**C**	**5th S. in Lent** • Henry M. Stanley began search for David Livingstone, 1871	*beef*
22	M.	☾ RIDES HIGH • Artist Randolph Caldecott born, 1846 • {8.8 7.8	*hash*
23	Tu.	*Mir* space station deorbited as planned, falling into ocean, 2001 • Tides {8.9 8.0	*and*
24	W.	Politician Claire Kirkland-Casgrain died, 2016	*heaping*
25	Th.	**Annunciation** • Musician Jeffrey Healey born, 1966 • {9.8 9.1	*spuds.*
26	Fr.	♀ IN SUP. ☌ • 2-lb. 5-oz. yellow hybrid bass caught, Kiamichi River, Okla., 1991	*Leaping*
27	Sa.	Passover begins at sundown • ~800 students wished janitor H. Mabry a happy 80th birthday, Zebulon, Ga., 2019	*over*
28	**C**	**Palm Sunday** • FULL WORM ○ • ☾ ON EQ. • Tides {11.2 —	*a*
29	M.	☌☿♆ • *Cheerfulness and goodwill make labor light.* • Tides {11.1 11.4	*million*
30	Tu.	☾ AT PERIG. • Chipmunks emerge from hibernation now. • {11.5 11.3	*mud-*
31	W.	Philosopher René Descartes born, 1596 • Poet Andrew Marvell born, 1621 • {11.7 11.1	*puds!*

Farmer's Calendar

All around the bend in the river road, cars are pulled over to the side and on the bridge people have gathered. They come and go all day. They're gawking at the ice. The breaking up of the ice down the river is winter's last big show, a view of the underside of winter, the engine room, the groaning, grinding machinery.

The river is no more than 150 feet across where it makes a bend, following which the channel widens out some. There the ice, floating down from upriver, is apt to get stuck. A dam of ice begins to rise. More ice comes down the river, meets the dam, tries to push through it, fails, tries to climb over it, fails. The dam grows deeper, higher. The ice blocks are 4, 5 feet thick, gray or green, sometimes pale blue like the spring sky. The weight of the ice sheets is unimaginable, and yet they are flung up at all angles on the dam. They are shot out to the sides of the channel, where they scour the riverbanks and mow down good-size trees. As big as the ice blocks are, what is pushing them is bigger. They will go where they are pointed, and there is not too much that can stop them. The people watch silently, from a safe distance.

APRIL

SKY WATCH: The morning conjunctions of Jupiter and Saturn are now higher up and thus easier to see in the east, just before dawn's twilight becomes too bright. On the 6th, look for Saturn as the "star" above the crescent Moon, with much brighter Jupiter to the left. On the 7th, Jupiter floats above the Moon; look for Saturn to their upper right. On the 15th, in the western evening sky, the Moon stands to the right of the orange Taurus star Aldebaran. Look for Mars above the waxing crescent Moon on the 16th and below the Moon on the 17th. Don't bother seeking Venus; our nearest planet neighbor lurks behind the Sun during March and April, never more than 9 degrees from the blinding disk.

☽ **LAST QUARTER** 4th day 6:02 A.M.　　● **FIRST QUARTER** 20th day 2:59 A.M.
● **NEW MOON** 11th day 10:31 P.M.　　○ **FULL MOON** 26th day 11:32 P.M.

All times are given in Eastern Daylight Time.

GET THESE PAGES WITH TIMES SET TO YOUR ZIP CODE AT ALMANAC.COM/ACCESS.

DAY OF YEAR	DAY OF MONTH	DAY OF WEEK	☼ RISES H. M.	RISE KEY	☼ SETS H. M.	SET KEY	LENGTH OF DAY H. M.	SUN FAST M.	SUN DECLINATION ° ′	HIGH TIDE TIMES BOSTON		☾ RISES H. M.	RISE KEY	☾ SETS H. M.	SET KEY	☾ ASTRON. PLACE	☾ AGE
91	1	Th.	6:26	C	7:10	D	12 44	12	4 N. 48	2½	3	—	-	8:54	B	LIB	19
92	2	Fr.	6:24	C	7:12	D	12 48	12	5 N. 11	3¼	4	12:19	E	9:37	B	OPH	20
93	3	Sa.	6:23	C	7:13	D	12 50	13	5 N. 34	4¼	5	1:31	E	10:29	B	SAG	21
94	4	**C**	6:21	C	7:14	D	12 53	13	5 N. 57	5¼	6	2:33	E	11:29	B	SAG	22
95	5	M.	6:19	C	7:15	D	12 56	13	6 N. 20	6¼	7¼	3:26	E	**12:34**	B	SAG	23
96	6	Tu.	6:18	B	7:16	D	12 58	14	6 N. 43	7½	8¼	4:08	E	**1:41**	B	CAP	24
97	7	W.	6:16	B	7:17	D	13 01	14	7 N. 05	8½	9¼	4:42	E	**2:48**	C	CAP	25
98	8	Th.	6:14	B	7:18	D	13 04	14	7 N. 28	9½	10¼	5:10	E	**3:54**	C	AQU	26
99	9	Fr.	6:13	B	7:19	D	13 06	14	7 N. 50	10½	11	5:35	D	**4:57**	D	AQU	27
100	10	Sa.	6:11	B	7:21	D	13 10	15	8 N. 12	11¼	11½	5:57	D	**5:59**	D	PSC	28
101	11	**C**	6:09	B	7:22	D	13 13	15	8 N. 34	12	—	6:18	C	**7:01**	D	CET	0
102	12	M.	6:08	B	7:23	D	13 15	15	8 N. 56	12¼	12½	6:40	C	**8:02**	E	PSC	1
103	13	Tu.	6:06	B	7:24	D	13 18	15	9 N. 18	12¾	1¼	7:02	B	**9:03**	E	CET	2
104	14	W.	6:04	B	7:25	D	13 21	16	9 N. 39	1¼	1¾	7:27	B	**10:04**	E	ARI	3
105	15	Th.	6:03	B	7:26	D	13 23	16	10 N. 01	2	2½	7:55	B	**11:05**	E	TAU	4
106	16	Fr.	6:01	B	7:27	D	13 26	16	10 N. 22	2½	3	8:28	B	—	-	TAU	5
107	17	Sa.	6:00	B	7:28	D	13 28	16	10 N. 43	3¼	3¾	9:08	A	**12:05**	E	TAU	6
108	18	**C**	5:58	B	7:30	D	13 32	17	11 N. 04	4	4¾	9:55	A	**1:01**	E	GEM	7
109	19	M.	5:56	B	7:31	D	13 35	17	11 N. 25	4¾	5½	10:50	B	**1:53**	E	GEM	8
110	20	Tu.	5:55	B	7:32	D	13 37	17	11 N. 45	5¾	6½	11:52	B	**2:38**	E	CAN	9
111	21	W.	5:53	B	7:33	D	13 40	17	12 N. 06	6¾	7½	**12:59**	B	**3:17**	E	CAN	10
112	22	Th.	5:52	B	7:34	D	13 42	17	12 N. 26	7¾	8¼	**2:10**	C	**3:51**	E	LEO	11
113	23	Fr.	5:50	B	7:35	D	13 45	18	12 N. 46	8½	9¼	**3:23**	D	**4:21**	E	LEO	12
114	24	Sa.	5:49	B	7:36	D	13 47	18	13 N. 05	9½	10	**4:38**	D	**4:48**	D	VIR	13
115	25	**C**	5:47	B	7:37	D	13 50	18	13 N. 25	10½	10¾	**5:55**	E	**5:15**	C	VIR	14
116	26	M.	5:46	B	7:39	D	13 53	18	13 N. 44	11¼	11½	**7:14**	E	**5:42**	C	VIR	15
117	27	Tu.	5:45	B	7:40	D	13 55	18	14 N. 03	12	—	**8:35**	E	**6:12**	B	LIB	16
118	28	W.	5:43	B	7:41	D	13 58	18	14 N. 22	12½	1	**9:57**	E	**6:46**	B	LIB	17
119	29	Th.	5:42	B	7:42	E	14 00	18	14 N. 41	1¼	1¾	**11:14**	E	**7:28**	B	OPH	18
120	30	Fr.	5:40	B	7:43	E	14 03	19	14 N. 59	2	2¾	—	-	**8:18**	B	OPH	19

APRIL

Where the calm river glides along,
The patient angler takes his seat.
–Thomas Miller

Farmer's Calendar

Long before the garden begins to produce, it achieves perfection, a condition from which its subsequent career, however fruitful, can be only a decline. Where I live, that moment comes, say, two-thirds of the way through April, when you plant the peas and radishes and lay out the rows for the rest of the garden.

It's in the laying out of the rows that you can make your garden a success of a kind impossible in later months. I split new stakes and get a ball of twine to mark the rows. I get a 20-foot tape so I can keep the rows honest. Putting them in by eyeball would be good enough for the plants, but it wouldn't be good enough for the mind and it's the mind I'm gardening for. I make sure the twine is taut, the lines straight, and the corners square. I take these pains in the garden before it really is a garden because doing so is a kind of magic to make me a better gardener. I'm trying to fool myself. It doesn't work. In six weeks, the garden will be a mess; in ten, it will be a jungle. But for right now, it looks pretty sharp, doesn't it? Today the garden looks for all the world as though somebody around here knew what he was doing.

DAY OF MONTH	DAY OF WEEK	DATES, FEASTS, FASTS, ASPECTS, TIDE HEIGHTS, AND WEATHER	
1	Th.	Maundy Thursday • **ALL FOOLS'** • $\mathbb{C}$ AT $\otimes$ • $\{^{11.7}_{10.6}$	*Fooled*
2	Fr.	**Good Friday** • Rare 0.1" snowfall, Charlotte, N.C., 2019 • $\{^{11.4}_{10.0}$	*us,*
3	Sa.	$\mathbb{C}^{RUNS}_{LOW}$ • Tsawwassen First Nation Final Agreement (w/Canada and B.C.) went into effect, 2009	*cooled*
4	**C**	**Easter** • Lock inventor Linus Yale Jr. born, 1821 • $\{^{10.5}_{9.0}$	*us,*
5	M.	Easter Monday • $\sigma\mathbb{P}\mathbb{C}$ • *One joy scatters a hundred griefs.* • $\{^{10.0}_{8.8}$	*spring*
6	Tu.	$\sigma\hbar\mathbb{C}$ • 1st modern Olympic Games opened, Athens, Greece, 1896 • $\{^{9.8}_{8.9}$	*has*
7	W.	$\sigma\mathbb{24}\mathbb{C}$ • Everglades conservationist Marjory Stoneman Douglas born, 1890	*schooled*
8	Th.	Baseball pitcher James Augustus "Catfish" Hunter born, 1946 • Tides $\{^{9.8}_{9.4}$	*us:*
9	Fr.	$\sigma\Psi\mathbb{C}$ • *Nature* magazine published longest known scientific name (~207,000 letters), 1981	*Expect*
10	Sa.	$\mathbb{C}$ ON EQ. • 5-lb. white crappie caught, Bibb County pond, Ga., 1984 • $\{^{10.0}_{9.9}$	*the*
11	**C**	2nd $\mathfrak{S}$. of Easter • NEW ● • $\sigma\mathbb{Q}\mathbb{C}$ • $\{^{9.9}_{—}$	*unexpected.*
12	M.	Ramadan begins at sundown • $\sigma\mathbb{Q}\mathbb{C}$ • Terry Fox began "Marathon of Hope," 1980	*Hot*
13	Tu.	$\sigma\hat{o}\mathbb{C}$ • U.S. president Thomas Jefferson born, 1743 • $\{^{10.1}_{9.7}$	*as*
14	W.	$\mathbb{C}$ AT APO. • *Apr. 14–15:* 87" snow fell in 27.5 hours, Silver Lake, Colo., 1921 • $\{^{10.1}_{9.4}$	*blazes,*
15	Th.	Actress Emma Watson born, 1990 • Tides $\{^{10.0}_{9.1}$	*it*
16	Fr.	$\mathbb{C}$ AT $\otimes$ • Native Am. leader Mary "Molly" Brant died, 1796 • Tides $\{^{9.8}_{8.8}$	*won't*
17	Sa.	$\sigma\sigma\mathbb{C}$ • *The morning is wiser than the evening.* • Tides $\{^{9.6}_{8.5}$	*faze*
18	**C**	3rd $\mathfrak{S}$. of Easter • $\mathbb{C}^{RIDES}_{HIGH}$ • $\varnothing^{IN}_{SUP.}$ σ • $\{^{9.3}_{8.3}$	*us;*
19	M.	American statesman Roger Sherman born, 1721 • $\{^{9.2}_{8.1}$	*curtains*
20	Tu.	Christopher Robin Milne (son of Winnie the Pooh writer A. A. Milne) died, 1996 • $\{^{9.1}_{8.2}$	*of*
21	W.	Traditional date when Rome was founded by Romulus, 753 B.C. • Tides $\{^{9.2}_{8.5}$	*rain*
22	Th.	**EARTH DAY** • $\sigma\mathbb{Q}\hat{o}$ • R. Keech drove 207.552 mph in "White Triplex" car, 1928	*are*
23	Fr.	St. George • Playwright William Shakespeare likely born (1564) and died (1616)	*certain*
24	Sa.	$\sigma\mathbb{Q}\hat{o}$ • *The Old Farmer's Almanac* founder Robert B. Thomas born, 1766 • $\{^{10.3}_{10.5}$	*to*
25	**C**	4th $\mathfrak{S}$. of Easter • $\mathbb{C}^{ON}_{EQ.}$ • 362 twisters, eastern half of U.S., 2011	*wane.*
26	M.	St. Mark^T • **FULL PINK** ○ • $\sigma\mathbb{Q}\mathbb{Q}$ • 1st U.S. weather report broadcast, 1921	*April*
27	Tu.	$\mathbb{C}$ AT PERIG. • *A willing mind makes a light foot.* • Tides $\{^{11.2}_{—}$	*days*
28	W.	$\mathbb{P}$ STAT. • *Soyuz-TM 32* launched, carrying world's 1st space tourist, Dennis Tito, to ISS, 2001	*always*
29	Th.	$\mathbb{C}$ AT $\otimes$ • Mikah Meyer completed 3-yr. journey to visit all 419 U.S. National Park Service sites, 2019	*amaze*
30	Fr.	$\sigma\hat{o}\odot$ • Poplars leaf out about now. • Tides $\{^{12.0}_{10.5}$	*us.*

MAY

SKY WATCH: In the predawn east on the 3rd, Saturn is to the upper left of the crescent Moon before forming a triangle with Jupiter and the Moon on the 4th. Jupiter, which enters Aquarius this month, floats above the crescent Moon on the 5th. Extremely low in the western evening twilight, Venus returns and hovers above Mercury on the 1st. On the 12th, look for Venus to the right of the thin crescent Moon, with Mercury now far above them both. The 13th brings the best conjunction: Mercury hovers just to the right of the thin Moon, an easy 15 degrees high. A deep lunar eclipse is seen throughout North America in the predawn hours of the 26th, with the Moon dramatically setting while the eclipse is in progress.

◑ LAST QUARTER	3rd day 3:50 P.M.	◐ FIRST QUARTER	19th day 3:13 P.M.
● NEW MOON	11th day 3:00 P.M.	○ FULL MOON	26th day 7:14 A.M.

All times are given in Eastern Daylight Time.

GET THESE PAGES WITH TIMES SET TO YOUR ZIP CODE AT ALMANAC.COM/ACCESS.

Day of Year	Day of Month	Day of Week	☼ Rises H. M.	Rise Key	☼ Sets H. M.	Set Key	Length of Day H. M.	Sun Fast M.	Sun Declination °	Sun Declination '	High Tide Times Boston		☾ Rises H. M.	Rise Key	☾ Sets H. M.	Set Key	☾ Astron. Place	☾ Age
121	1	Sa.	5:39	B	**7:44**	E	14 05	19	15 N.	17	3	**3¾**	12:23	E	9:17	B	SAG	20
122	2	**C**	5:38	B	**7:45**	E	14 07	19	15 N.	35	4	**4¾**	1:22	E	10:22	B	SAG	21
123	3	M.	5:36	B	**7:46**	E	14 10	19	15 N.	52	5	**5¾**	2:08	E	11:31	B	CAP	22
124	4	Tu.	5:35	B	**7:47**	E	14 12	19	16 N.	10	6	**6¾**	2:45	E	**12:40**	B	CAP	23
125	5	W.	5:34	B	**7:49**	E	14 15	19	16 N.	27	7¼	**8**	3:16	E	**1:46**	C	AQU	24
126	6	Th.	5:33	B	**7:50**	E	14 17	19	16 N.	44	8¼	**8¾**	3:41	D	**2:50**	C	AQU	25
127	7	Fr.	5:31	B	**7:51**	E	14 20	19	17 N.	00	9¼	**9¾**	4:04	D	**3:53**	D	PSC	26
128	8	Sa.	5:30	B	**7:52**	E	14 22	19	17 N.	16	10	**10½**	4:25	C	**4:54**	D	CET	27
129	9	**C**	5:29	B	**7:53**	E	14 24	19	17 N.	32	10¾	**11**	4:46	C	**5:54**	E	PSC	28
130	10	M.	5:28	B	**7:54**	E	14 26	19	17 N.	48	11½	**11¾**	5:07	C	**6:55**	E	CET	29
131	11	Tu.	5:27	B	**7:55**	E	14 28	19	18 N.	03	**12¼**	—	5:31	B	**7:56**	E	ARI	0
132	12	W.	5:26	B	**7:56**	E	14 30	19	18 N.	18	12¼	**12¾**	5:57	B	**8:58**	E	TAU	1
133	13	Th.	5:24	A	**7:57**	E	14 33	19	18 N.	33	12¾	**1½**	6:29	B	**9:59**	E	TAU	2
134	14	Fr.	5:23	A	**7:58**	E	14 35	19	18 N.	47	1½	**2**	7:06	B	**10:56**	E	TAU	3
135	15	Sa.	5:22	A	**7:59**	E	14 37	19	19 N.	02	2	**2¾**	7:51	A	**11:50**	E	GEM	4
136	16	**C**	5:21	A	**8:00**	E	14 39	19	19 N.	15	2¾	**3½**	8:43	B	—	-	GEM	5
137	17	M.	5:20	A	**8:01**	E	14 41	19	19 N.	29	3½	**4¼**	9:42	B	12:36	E	GEM	6
138	18	Tu.	5:20	A	**8:02**	E	14 42	19	19 N.	42	4¼	**5**	10:46	B	1:17	E	CAN	7
139	19	W.	5:19	A	**8:03**	E	14 44	19	19 N.	55	5¼	**6**	11:54	C	1:51	E	LEO	8
140	20	Th.	5:18	A	**8:04**	E	14 46	19	20 N.	07	6	**6¾**	**1:04**	C	2:22	E	LEO	9
141	21	Fr.	5:17	A	**8:05**	E	14 48	19	20 N.	19	7	**7¾**	**2:15**	D	2:49	D	LEO	10
142	22	Sa.	5:16	A	**8:06**	E	14 50	19	20 N.	31	8	**8½**	**3:29**	D	3:14	D	VIR	11
143	23	**C**	5:15	A	**8:07**	E	14 52	19	20 N.	42	9	**9½**	**4:45**	E	3:40	C	VIR	12
144	24	M.	5:15	A	**8:08**	E	14 53	19	20 N.	53	10	**10¼**	**6:04**	E	4:08	C	VIR	13
145	25	Tu.	5:14	A	**8:09**	E	14 55	19	21 N.	04	10¾	**11¼**	**7:25**	E	4:39	B	LIB	14
146	26	W.	5:13	A	**8:10**	E	14 57	19	21 N.	14	11¾	—	**8:46**	E	5:17	B	LIB	15
147	27	Th.	5:13	A	**8:11**	E	14 58	18	21 N.	24	12	**12¾**	**10:02**	E	6:03	B	OPH	16
148	28	Fr.	5:12	A	**8:12**	E	15 00	18	21 N.	34	12¾	**1½**	**11:08**	E	6:58	B	SAG	17
149	29	Sa.	5:11	A	**8:12**	E	15 01	18	21 N.	43	1¾	**2½**	—	-	8:04	B	SAG	18
150	30	**C**	5:11	A	**8:13**	E	15 02	18	21 N.	52	2¾	**3½**	12:02	E	9:14	B	CAP	19
151	31	M.	5:10	A	**8:14**	E	15 04	18	22 N.	00	3½	**4½**	12:44	E	10:25	B	CAP	20

 To use this page, see p. 116; for Key Letters, see p. 238. LIGHT = A.M. **BOLD** = P.M.

MAY

Oh! fragrant is the breath of May
In tranquil garden closes.
–**William Hamilton Hayne**

DAY OF MONTH	DAY OF WEEK	DATES, FEASTS, FASTS, ASPECTS, TIDE HEIGHTS, AND WEATHER	
1	Sa.	Sts. Philip & James • May Day • ☾ runs low • {11.6 / 10.0	*Sunshine*
2	C	5th S. of Easter • Orthodox Easter • ☌♇☾ • {11.0 / 9.5	*spackling,*
3	M.	☌♄☾ • *Kindnesses, like grain, increase by sowing.* • Tides {10.5 / 9.2	*lightning*
4	Tu.	☌♃☾ • Rain caused deadly sinkhole/landslide, St.-Jean-Vianney, Que., 1971	*crackling,*
5	W.	Claude Stanley Choules, last known WWI combat veteran, died at the age of 110, 2011 • {9.6 / 9.1	*gardeners*
6	Th.	☌♆☾ • Successful flight of Samuel Langley's *Aerodrome No. 5* aircraft, 1896	*tackling*
7	Fr.	Haworth Parsonage recipient of 1st copies of Brontë sisters' *Poems,* 1846 • Tides {9.4 / 9.6	*the*
8	Sa.	St. Julian of Norwich • ☾ on Eq. • Coca-Cola 1st went on sale (in Atlanta, Ga.), 1886 • {9.4 / 9.8	*tilling,*
9	C	Rogation Sunday • Mother's Day • EF1 tornado, Washington, Vt., 2009	*God*
10	M.	☌♅☾ • Mathematician Gaspard Monge born, 1746 • {9.4 / 10.1	*willing,*
11	Tu.	New ● • ☾ at apo. • Astronomer John Herschel died, 1871 • Three	*while*
12	W.	☌♀☾ • Discovery of what is likely Library of Alexandria announced, 2004 • Chilly	*rain*
13	Th.	Ascension • ☾ at ☊ • ☌☿☾ • Cranberries in bud now. • Saints	*the*
14	Fr.	Racehorse *Winning Brew* ran ¼ mile in 20.57 secs., Penn Nat'l Race Course, Grantville, Pa., 2008	*gutters*
15	Sa.	☾ rides high • "Baily's Beads" solar eclipse phenomenon 1st described, 1836 • {9.9 / 8.8	*fills.*
16	C	1st S. af. Asc. • Shavuot begins at sundown • ☌♂☾ • {9.8 / 8.6	*Thunder*
17	M.	☿ Gr. Elong. (22° East) • Manufacturer John Deere died, 1886 • {9.6 / 8.5	*mutters*
18	Tu.	*Mist in May, heat in June, Make the harvest come right soon.* • Tides {9.5 / 8.6	*imprecations,*
19	W.	St. Dunstan • Robert B. Thomas, founder of *The Old Farmer's Almanac,* died, 1846	*children*
20	Th.	Singer Cher born, 1946 • 680-lb. goliath grouper (now protected) caught, Fernandina Beach, Fla., 1961	*dream*
21	Fr.	1st U.S. speed limit law for motor vehicles passed (12 mph city/15 country), Conn., 1901 • {9.7 / 9.7	*of*
22	Sa.	☾ on Eq. • 1st permanent IMAX theater opened, Toronto, Ont., 1971 • Tides {9.9 / 10.3	*school*
23	C	Whit S. • Pentecost • ♄ stat. • {10.2 / 11.0	*vacations,*
24	M.	Victoria Day (Canada) • *Patience is a flower that grows not in every garden.*	*temperatures*
25	Tu.	St. Bede • ☾ at perig. • Millions of people joined Hands Across America, 1986	*and*
26	W.	Ember Day • Vesak • Full Flower ○ • Eclipse ☾ • ☾ at ☋	
27	Th.	Ben Sawyer Bridge stuck open due to high temps, Sullivan's Island, S.C., 2019 • {10.7 / —	*expectations*
28	Fr.	Ember Day • ☾ runs low • Large hail hit areas of Pa., N.Y., N.J., 2019 • {12.3 / 10.5	*lift their*
29	Sa.	Ember Day • ☌☿♀ • ☌♇☾ • ☿ stat. • Tides {12.0 / 10.3	*heads*
30	C	Trinity • ☌♄☾ • *May 30–31:* 8 co-champions declared, Scripps Spelling Bee, 2019	*like*
31	M.	Visit. of Mary • Memorial Day, observed • Baltimore Basilica dedicated, Md., 1821	*daffodils.*

Farmer's Calendar

In the first days of May appears the red trillium *(Trillium erectum).* It's a vigorous plant a foot or more high, with three broad leaves atop its stalk. In their axis is the slightly drooping red-brown flower—a plain thing distinguished by its scent: that of dead mice. Yet its reek seems to win it friends. If a well-loved child has many names, then this trillium must be a favorite. Books on wild plants give it at least 16 common or local names. Two—stinking Benjamin and wet-dog trillium—come from the flower's outrageous smell. Others allude to the plant's supposed medicinal properties. It is thought to aid in childbirth, and Native Americans used it for snakebite—hence, birthroot, Indian balm, squawroot. Another name for this flower is wake-robin. Perhaps this flower's blooming coincides with, and thus signals, the spring arrival of the robin. But it doesn't around here. When our wake-robin comes out, the robins have been here for weeks. I think the robin who is fancifully being waked by *T. erectum* is not a bird but a boy, a man, in particular a simple country fellow, a ploughman, whose busy season on the land this flower's bloom announces.

JUNE

SKY WATCH: In evening twilight, 40 minutes after sunset, Venus now stands 8 degrees up—not high, but a marked improvement from last month. An annular solar eclipse will be visible from northern and northeastern North America on the 10th. On the 11th, Venus will float to the left of the thin crescent Moon, while the dark of the Moon glows brightly with earthshine. On the 13th, look for Mars, now fairly dim at magnitude 1.8, to be dangling below the Moon. The solstice brings summer to the Northern Hemisphere on the 20th at 11:32 P.M EDT. The Moon hovers to the right of Saturn on the 26th and just below brilliant Jupiter on the 28th and 29th; both giant planets will be rising just before midnight.

☽ **LAST QUARTER**	2nd day	3:24 A.M.	● **FIRST QUARTER**	17th day 11:54 P.M.
● **NEW MOON**	10th day	6:53 A.M.	○ **FULL MOON**	24th day 2:40 P.M.

All times are given in Eastern Daylight Time.

GET THESE PAGES WITH TIMES SET TO YOUR ZIP CODE AT ALMANAC.COM/ACCESS.

DAY OF YEAR	DAY OF MONTH	DAY OF WEEK	☼ RISES H. M.	RISE KEY	☼ SETS H. M.	SET KEY	LENGTH OF DAY H. M.	SUN FAST M.	SUN DECLINATION ° '	HIGH TIDE TIMES BOSTON		☽ RISES H. M.	RISE KEY	☽ SETS H. M.	SET KEY	☽ ASTRON. PLACE	☽ AGE
152	1	Tu.	5:10	A	8:15	E	15 05	18	22 N. 08	4½	5½	1:18	E	11:35	C	AQU	21
153	2	W.	5:09	A	8:16	E	15 07	18	22 N. 16	5½	6¼	1:45	D	12:41	C	AQU	22
154	3	Th.	5:09	A	8:16	E	15 07	17	22 N. 23	6¾	7¼	2:09	D	1:45	D	AQU	23
155	4	Fr.	5:09	A	8:17	E	15 08	17	22 N. 30	7¾	8¼	2:31	D	2:46	D	CET	24
156	5	Sa.	5:08	A	8:18	E	15 10	17	22 N. 37	8½	9	2:52	C	3:47	E	PSC	25
157	6	**C**	5:08	A	8:18	E	15 10	17	22 N. 43	9½	9¾	3:13	C	4:48	E	PSC	26
158	7	M.	5:08	A	8:19	E	15 11	17	22 N. 49	10¼	10½	3:35	B	5:49	E	ARI	27
159	8	Tu.	5:07	A	8:20	E	15 13	17	22 N. 54	11	11	4:01	B	6:50	E	TAU	28
160	9	W.	5:07	A	8:20	E	15 13	16	22 N. 59	11¾	11¾	4:31	B	7:52	E	TAU	29
161	10	Th.	5:07	A	8:21	E	15 14	16	23 N. 03	12¼	—	5:06	B	8:51	E	TAU	0
162	11	Fr.	5:07	A	8:21	E	15 14	16	23 N. 07	12¼	1	5:48	A	9:46	E	TAU	1
163	12	Sa.	5:07	A	8:22	E	15 15	16	23 N. 11	1	1¾	6:38	B	10:35	E	GEM	2
164	13	**C**	5:07	A	8:22	E	15 15	15	23 N. 14	1¾	2¼	7:35	B	11:18	E	GEM	3
165	14	M.	5:07	A	8:23	E	15 16	15	23 N. 17	2¼	3	8:38	B	11:54	E	CAN	4
166	15	Tu.	5:07	A	8:23	E	15 16	15	23 N. 20	3	3¾	9:45	B	—	-	LEO	5
167	16	W.	5:07	A	8:23	E	15 16	15	23 N. 22	4	4½	10:53	C	12:25	E	LEO	6
168	17	Th.	5:07	A	8:24	E	15 17	15	23 N. 23	4¾	5½	12:02	C	12:52	D	LEO	7
169	18	Fr.	5:07	A	8:24	E	15 17	14	23 N. 25	5¾	6¼	1:12	D	1:17	D	VIR	8
170	19	Sa.	5:07	A	8:24	E	15 17	14	23 N. 25	6½	7¼	2:24	E	1:42	C	VIR	9
171	20	**C**	5:07	A	8:25	E	15 18	14	23 N. 26	7½	8	3:39	E	2:07	C	VIR	10
172	21	M.	5:07	A	8:25	E	15 18	14	23 N. 26	8½	9	4:57	E	2:36	B	LIB	11
173	22	Tu.	5:08	A	8:25	E	15 17	14	23 N. 25	9½	9¾	6:17	E	3:09	B	LIB	12
174	23	W.	5:08	A	8:25	E	15 17	13	23 N. 24	10½	10¾	7:36	E	3:49	B	OPH	13
175	24	Th.	5:08	A	8:25	E	15 17	13	23 N. 23	11½	11¾	8:47	E	4:40	B	OPH	14
176	25	Fr.	5:09	A	8:25	E	15 16	13	23 N. 21	12½	—	9:48	E	5:41	B	SAG	15
177	26	Sa.	5:09	A	8:25	E	15 16	13	23 N. 19	12½	1¼	10:37	E	6:50	B	SAG	16
178	27	**C**	5:09	A	8:25	E	15 16	13	23 N. 17	1½	2¼	11:15	E	8:04	B	CAP	17
179	28	M.	5:10	A	8:25	E	15 15	12	23 N. 14	2¼	3	11:46	E	9:16	C	CAP	18
180	29	Tu.	5:10	A	8:25	E	15 15	12	23 N. 11	3¼	4	—	-	10:26	C	AQU	19
181	30	W.	5:11	A	8:25	E	15 14	12	23 N. 07	4¼	4¾	12:12	D	11:33	C	AQU	20

THE SIXTH MONTH • 2021 **JUNE** JUNE HATH 30 DAYS

Hark, the honeybee's low hum
Tells us that the summer's come!
–Frank Dempster Sherman

DAY OF MONTH	DAY OF WEEK	DATES, FEASTS, FASTS, ASPECTS, TIDE HEIGHTS, AND WEATHER	
1	Tu.	☌♃☾ • Tenn. became 16th U.S. state, 1796 • Tides {10.4 9.4	*Dreamy,*
2	W.	☌♆☾ • U.S. first lady Martha Washington born, 1731 • *Surveyor 1* landed on Moon, 1966	*steamy*
3	Th.	Flood caused major devastation, Pueblo, Colo., 1921 • Tides {9.4 9.3	*days, can't*
4	Fr.	☾ ON EQ. • Snapchat cofounder Evan Spiegel born, 1990 • Tides {9.1 9.4	*beat 'em,*
5	Sa.	St. Boniface • *Deliver your words not by number but by weight.* • {9.0 9.6	*showers*
6	**C**	**Corpus Christi** • D-Day, 1944 • Harbo and Samuelson began 55-day row across Atlantic, 1896	*cool 'em,*
7	M.	☾ AT APO. • ☌⛢☾ • Tennis player Anna Kournikova born, 1981 • {8.9 9.9	*sun*
8	Tu.	Ives McGaffey granted patent for 1st U.S. hand-pumped vacuum cleaner, 1869 • {8.9 10.0	*reheats 'em.*
9	W.	☾ AT ☊ • Alma struck Fla., earliest hurricane landfall on U.S. continent since 1825, 1966	*Swarming*
10	Th.	**Orthodox Ascension** • **NEW** ● • **ECLIPSE** ☉ • ☌☿☾ • ☿ IN INF. ☌	
11	Fr.	St. Barnabas • Football player Joe Montana born, 1956 • Tides {10.1 8.9	*storms:*
12	Sa.	☾ RIDES HIGH • ☌♀☾ • Dallas Mavericks won NBA championship for 1st time, 2011	*Sleepers'*
13	**C**	**3rd S. af. P.** • ☌♂☾ • Actresses Mary-Kate and Ashley Olsen born, 1986	*rest*
14	M.	St. Basil • **FLAG DAY** • Quotations publisher John Bartlett born, 1820 • {10.0 8.9	*is*
15	Tu.	Ark. became 25th U.S. state, 1836 • Jazz singer Ella Fitzgerald died, 1996 • {10.0 8.9	*often*
16	W.	*A dripping June / Brings all things in tune.* • {9.9 9.1	*shattered*
17	Th.	1st U.S. mobile telephone commercial service inaugurated, St. Louis, Mo., 1946 • {9.8 9.4	*and*
18	Fr.	☾ ON EQ. • 103-yr.-old Julia Hawkins won 100-meter dash, Nat'l Senior Games, 2019	*graduates'*
19	Sa.	1st baseball game with set rules played between 2 clubs, Hoboken, N.J., 1846 • {9.7 10.3	*tasseled*
20	**C**	**4th S. af. P.** • Orthodox Pentecost • **FATHER'S DAY** • **SUMMER SOLSTICE**	*caps*
21	M.	♃ STAT. • Momsen Lung inventor VADM Charles B. Momsen born, 1896 • {9.9 11.2	*are*
22	Tu.	St. Alban • ☿ STAT. • Explorer Henry Hudson, son, and 7 crew set adrift by mutineers, 1611	*scattered.*
23	W.	☾ AT ☋ • ☾ AT PERIG. • TV producer Aaron Spelling died, 2006 • {10.1 12.0	*It's*
24	Th.	Nativ. John the Baptist • **MIDSUMMER DAY** • **FULL STRAWBERRY** ○	*cool;*
25	Fr.	☾ RUNS LOW • *Do nothing hastily but the catching of fleas.* • Tides {10.3 —	*no*
26	Sa.	☌♇☾ • ♆ STAT. • Sculptress Norma Lyon ("Butter Cow Lady") died, 2011	*more*
27	**C**	**5th S. af. P.** • Orthodox All Saints' • ☌♄☾ • {11.8 10.1	*school;*
28	M.	St. Irenaeus • ☌♃☾ • Tornado tossed tractor 1.5 miles, Camp Crook, S.Dak., 2018	*prom*
29	Tu.	Sts. Peter & Paul • The Rooms cultural facility opened, N.L., 2005 • {10.8 9.8	*queens*
30	W.	☌♆☾ • 1st photo of confirmed baby planet (PDS 70b) announced, 2018 • {10.2 9.6	*rule!*

Farmer's Calendar

Most years, it's sometime in June that the mosquitoes arrive to finish up whatever blood has been left us by the blackflies, whose high season comes a few weeks earlier. Whereas the fly is little more than a black speck that somehow bites, the mosquito is a creature whose menace is evident in its form: a syringe with wings.

Still, the mosquitoes hereabouts are neither particularly large nor particularly aggressive. In these parts, mosquitoes come and go. Some years there will be few or none. Fortunately, we needn't be without them, even in an off year. Benjamin Franklin, in *Poor Richard's Almanack* for 1748, gives a recipe for mosquitoes. "In a scarce summer," Ben writes, "any citizen may provide Musketoes sufficient for his own family, by leaving tubs of rain water uncover'd in his yard; for in such water they lay their eggs, which when hatch'd. . . . put forth legs and wings, leave the water, and fly into your windows." Make of that what you like. Ben worked in Philadelphia, but he was a Boston man by birth and schooling, and he has the anarchic, deadpan Yankee wit that looks you blandly in the face and dares you to doubt.

JULY

SKY WATCH: Earth arrives at its annual far point from the Sun—aphelion—on the 5th. When overhead, the Sun appears 7 percent dimmer than it looked in January. In the western sky after sunset, Venus and Mars meet in conjunction on the 11th, with both just to the left of the crescent Moon. These three nearest bodies to Earth stand about 10 degrees high during mid-twilight. The Moon moves on, but the two planets come very close together on the 12th and 13th; Mars's dimness at magnitude 1.84 means that binoculars should be used for the very best view. On the 24th, the Moon forms a nice triangle with Saturn on the right and Jupiter on the left. Jupiter is below the Moon on the 25th.

◑ LAST QUARTER	1st day	5:11 P.M.	○ FULL MOON	23rd day 10:37 P.M.
● NEW MOON	9th day	9:17 P.M.	◐ LAST QUARTER	31st day 9:16 A.M.
◐ FIRST QUARTER	17th day	6:11 A.M.		

All times are given in Eastern Daylight Time.

GET THESE PAGES WITH TIMES SET TO YOUR ZIP CODE AT ALMANAC.COM/ACCESS.

DAY OF YEAR	DAY OF MONTH	DAY OF WEEK	☼ RISES H. M.	RISE KEY	☼ SETS H. M.	SET KEY	LENGTH OF DAY H. M.	SUN FAST M.	SUN DECLINATION ° '	HIGH TIDE TIMES BOSTON		☽ RISES H. M.	RISE KEY	☽ SETS H. M.	SET KEY	☽ ASTRON. PLACE	☽ AGE
182	1	Th.	5:11	A	8:25	E	15 14	12	23 N. 03	5	5¾	12:35	D	12:36	D	PSC	21
183	2	Fr.	5:12	A	8:25	E	15 13	12	22 N. 58	6	6½	12:56	C	1:38	D	CET	22
184	3	Sa.	5:12	A	8:24	E	15 12	11	22 N. 53	7	7½	1:17	C	2:39	E	PSC	23
185	4	**C**	5:13	A	8:24	E	15 11	11	22 N. 48	8	8¼	1:39	C	3:40	E	ARI	24
186	5	M.	5:14	A	8:24	E	15 10	11	22 N. 42	8¾	9	2:04	B	4:41	E	ARI	25
187	6	Tu.	5:14	A	8:24	E	15 10	11	22 N. 36	9¾	9¾	2:32	B	5:43	E	TAU	26
188	7	W.	5:15	A	8:23	E	15 08	11	22 N. 30	10½	10½	3:05	B	6:43	E	TAU	27
189	8	Th.	5:16	A	8:23	E	15 07	11	22 N. 23	11¼	11¼	3:45	B	7:40	E	TAU	28
190	9	Fr.	5:16	A	8:22	E	15 06	10	22 N. 16	12	—	4:33	A	8:32	E	GEM	0
191	10	Sa.	5:17	A	8:22	E	15 05	10	22 N. 08	12	12½	5:29	B	9:17	E	GEM	1
192	11	**C**	5:18	A	8:21	E	15 03	10	22 N. 00	12¾	1¼	6:31	B	9:55	E	CAN	2
193	12	M.	5:18	A	8:21	E	15 03	10	21 N. 51	1¼	2	7:37	B	10:28	E	CAN	3
194	13	Tu.	5:19	A	8:20	E	15 01	10	21 N. 43	2	2¾	8:45	C	10:56	E	LEO	4
195	14	W.	5:20	A	8:20	E	15 00	10	21 N. 33	2¾	3¼	9:54	C	11:22	D	LEO	5
196	15	Th.	5:21	A	8:19	E	14 58	10	21 N. 24	3½	4	11:03	D	11:46	D	VIR	6
197	16	Fr.	5:22	A	8:18	E	14 56	10	21 N. 14	4¼	5	12:13	E	—	-	VIR	7
198	17	Sa.	5:23	A	8:18	E	14 55	10	21 N. 04	5¼	5¾	1:25	E	12:10	C	VIR	8
199	18	**C**	5:23	A	8:17	E	14 54	9	20 N. 53	6¼	6¾	2:40	E	12:37	C	VIR	9
200	19	M.	5:24	A	8:16	E	14 52	9	20 N. 42	7¼	7½	3:56	E	1:07	B	LIB	10
201	20	Tu.	5:25	A	8:15	E	14 50	9	20 N. 31	8¼	8½	5:13	E	1:43	B	SCO	11
202	21	W.	5:26	A	8:15	E	14 49	9	20 N. 19	9¼	9½	6:27	E	2:27	B	OPH	12
203	22	Th.	5:27	A	8:14	E	14 47	9	20 N. 07	10¼	10½	7:32	E	3:22	B	SAG	13
204	23	Fr.	5:28	A	8:13	E	14 45	9	19 N. 55	11¼	11½	8:26	E	4:28	B	SAG	14
205	24	Sa.	5:29	A	8:12	E	14 43	9	19 N. 42	12¼	—	9:09	E	5:39	B	CAP	15
206	25	**C**	5:30	A	8:11	E	14 41	9	19 N. 29	12¼	1	9:44	E	6:54	B	CAP	16
207	26	M.	5:31	B	8:10	E	14 39	9	19 N. 16	1¼	1¾	10:12	E	8:06	C	AQU	17
208	27	Tu.	5:32	B	8:09	E	14 37	9	19 N. 02	2	2¾	10:36	D	9:15	C	AQU	18
209	28	W.	5:33	B	8:08	E	14 35	9	18 N. 48	2¾	3½	10:59	C	10:21	D	PSC	19
210	29	Th.	5:34	B	8:07	E	14 33	9	18 N. 34	3¾	4¼	11:20	C	11:25	D	CET	20
211	30	Fr.	5:35	B	8:06	E	14 31	9	18 N. 19	4½	5	11:42	C	12:27	E	PSC	21
212	31	Sa.	5:36	B	8:05	E	14 29	9	18 N. 05	5½	5¾	—	-	1:29	E	CET	22

CALENDAR

Day of glory! Welcome day!
Freedom's banners greet thy ray.
–**John Pierpont**

DAY OF MONTH	DAY OF WEEK	DATES, FEASTS, FASTS, ASPECTS, TIDE HEIGHTS, AND WEATHER	
1	Th.	CANADA DAY • ☾ ON EQ. • Librarian William Howard Brett born, 1846 • {9.7/9.4	*Nature's*
2	Fr.	Alligator fell from sky during storm, Charleston, S.C., 1843 • Tides {9.2/9.4	*fireworks*
3	Sa.	Dog Days begin. • *Dog Days bright and clear, Indicate a happy year.* • Tides {8.8/9.3	*outglow*
4	C	6th S. af. P. • INDEPENDENCE DAY • ☌♅☾ • ☿ GR. ELONG. (22° WEST)	
5	M.	☾ AT APO. • ⊕ AT APHELION • *July 5–17:* Fruit baked on trees (>111°F) in Man./Ont., 1936	*the*
6	Tu.	☾ AT ☊ • Musician Louis Armstrong died, 1971 • Tides {8.4/9.7	*patriotic*
7	W.	2" snow fell, Utqiagvik (Barrow), Alaska, 2018 • Armadillos mate now. • Tides {8.5/9.8	*show;*
8	Th.	☌☿☾ • Ballerina Cynthia Gregory born, 1946 • NASA's last space shuttle launched, 2011	*every*
9	Fr.	NEW ● • ☾ RIDES HIGH • Wildlife statistician Douglas George Chapman died, 1996	*night's a*
10	Sa.	His Master's Voice trademark (dog Nipper and gramophone) registered in U.S., 1900 • {8.8/—	*cannonade!*
11	C	7th S. af. P. • Wilfrid Laurier became prime minister of Canada, 1896	*Perfect*
12	M.	☌♀☾ • ☌♂☾ • Cornscateous air is everywhere. • Tides {10.3/9.1	*days for*
13	Tu.	☌♀♂ • *A good neighbor, a good morrow.* • {10.4/9.3	*lemonade,*
14	W.	Bastille Day • Human chain rescued swimmer in rip current, Panama City Beach, Fla., 2019	*nights*
15	Th.	St. Swithin • Artist Rembrandt born, 1606 • Tides {10.2/9.8	*of*
16	Fr.	☾ ON EQ. • Giuseppe Piazzi, 1st to discover an asteroid, born, 1746 • {10.0/10.0	*flashes*
17	Sa.	♇ AT ☍ • Spain formally ceded Fla. to U.S., 1821 • Tides {9.8/10.3	*and*
18	C	8th S. af. P. • Astronaut John Glenn Jr. born, 1921 • {9.6/10.6	*thunder*
19	M.	Plant breeder Elwyn Meader died, 1996 • {9.5/10.9	*crashes!*
20	Tu.	☾ AT ☋ • B.C. joined Canadian Confederation, 1871 • Tides {9.4/11.1	*Coolish:*
21	W.	☾ AT PERIG. • Poet Robert Burns died, 1796 • {9.5/11.4	*Even*
22	Th.	St. Mary Magdalene • ☾ RUNS LOW • Black-eyed Susans in bloom now. • {9.7/11.6	*Yankees*
23	Fr.	FULL BUCK ○ • ☌♇☾ • *Mirth and motion prolong life.*	*pull*
24	Sa.	☌♄☾ • Archaeologist Hiram Bingham "discovered" Machu Picchu Incan ruins, Peru, 1911	*up*
25	C	9th S. af. P. • ☌♃☾ • Seth Wheeler's "Improvement in Wrapping-Papers" patented, 1871	
26	M.	St. James[T] • Adult gypsy moths emerge. • {11.4/10.1	*blankies.*
27	Tu.	☌♆☾ • Donovan Bailey won men's 100m dash in 9.84 secs., Summer Olympics, 1996	*Keep*
28	W.	Writer Beatrix Potter born, 1866 • Tides {10.6/9.8	*the*
29	Th.	St. Martha • ☾ ON EQ. • Lightning caused deadly fire, Cochrane and Matheson, Ont., 1916	*sunblock*
30	Fr.	*Apollo 15* landed on Moon, 1971 • Tides {9.4/9.5	*in*
31	Sa.	St. Ignatius of Loyola • ☌♅☾ • *Viking I*'s "Face on Mars" photo released, 1976 • {8.9/9.3	*stock!*

Farmer's Calendar

The humblest rodent can tell of catastrophes. Late one night, investigating a faint sound that came from the kitchen closet, I found a mouse trapped in a glass bottle up on a high shelf. It was a deer mouse, an outdoor creature, usually, and a great gatherer of seeds and nuts. The bottle was a clean, empty quart. The mouse had evidently discovered our supply of birdseed and had hit on the plan of dropping sunflower seeds into the bottle for safekeeping. With the bottle a quarter full of seeds, the mouse must have decided to visit his assets. Once in there, he couldn't get out.

I took the bottle down from the shelf. As I held him in his bottle, he looked up at me. I laid the bottle on its side in the closet and left it, so the mouse could walk out. Half an hour later he was still there. He couldn't or wouldn't leave. I could think of only one solution—a crash. I took the bottle outside, tilted it so seeds and mouse slid toward the neck, and gave its base a smart rap with a hammer. Nothing. Again. An explosion of glass, seeds, and escaping mouse. Sweeping up, I wondered what in the world he would tell his friends. Where would he begin?

AUGUST

SKY WATCH: Saturn (on the 2nd) and Jupiter (the 19th) both come to opposition this month, when they are optimally bright, big, and out all night. Venus brightens in the evening twilight, but Mars now drops too low into solar glare, bringing its fine 2-year apparition to an end. On the 11th, look for brilliant Venus below the crescent Moon, which sets early enough to bring full darkness and let the Perseid meteors perform at full glory on the 11th and 12th. The post-midnight hours are best for viewing these very fast shooting stars. Jupiter retrogrades back into Capricornus on the 18th and hovers just above the Moon on the 21st. Telescope users can find the glorious planet Saturn by pointing at the "star" just above the Moon on the 20th.

● **NEW MOON** 8th day 9:50 A.M. ○ **FULL MOON** 22nd day 8:02 A.M.
◐ **FIRST QUARTER** 15th day 11:20 A.M. ◑ **LAST QUARTER** 30th day 3:13 A.M.

All times are given in Eastern Daylight Time.

GET THESE PAGES WITH TIMES SET TO YOUR ZIP CODE AT ALMANAC.COM/ACCESS.

DAY OF YEAR	DAY OF MONTH	DAY OF WEEK	☼ RISES H. M.	RISE KEY	☼ SETS H. M.	SET KEY	LENGTH OF DAY H. M.	SUN FAST M.	SUN DECLINATION ° ′	HIGH TIDE TIMES BOSTON		☽ RISES H. M.	RISE KEY	☽ SETS H. M.	SET KEY	☽ ASTRON. PLACE	☽ AGE
213	1	**C**	5:37	B	**8:03**	E	14 26	9	17 N. 49	6¼	6¾	12:05	B	**2:31**	E	ARI	23
214	2	M.	5:38	B	**8:02**	E	14 24	10	17 N. 34	7¼	7½	12:32	B	**3:32**	E	TAU	24
215	3	Tu.	5:39	B	**8:01**	E	14 22	10	17 N. 18	8¼	8¼	1:03	B	**4:33**	E	TAU	25
216	4	W.	5:40	B	**8:00**	E	14 20	10	17 N. 02	9	9¼	1:41	A	**5:32**	E	TAU	26
217	5	Th.	5:41	B	**7:59**	E	14 18	10	16 N. 46	10	10	2:26	A	**6:25**	E	GEM	27
218	6	Fr.	5:42	B	**7:57**	E	14 15	10	16 N. 29	10¾	10¾	3:19	B	**7:13**	E	GEM	28
219	7	Sa.	5:43	B	**7:56**	E	14 13	10	16 N. 12	11½	11½	4:19	B	**7:54**	E	CAN	29
220	8	**C**	5:44	B	**7:55**	E	14 11	10	15 N. 55	12¼	—	5:25	B	**8:29**	E	CAN	0
221	9	M.	5:45	B	**7:53**	E	14 08	10	15 N. 38	12¼	12¾	6:34	C	**8:59**	E	LEO	1
222	10	Tu.	5:46	B	**7:52**	E	14 06	11	15 N. 20	1	1½	7:44	C	**9:26**	D	LEO	2
223	11	W.	5:47	B	**7:51**	E	14 04	11	15 N. 03	1¾	2¼	8:54	D	**9:50**	D	VIR	3
224	12	Th.	5:48	B	**7:49**	E	14 01	11	14 N. 44	2½	2¾	10:05	D	**10:15**	C	VIR	4
225	13	Fr.	5:49	B	**7:48**	D	13 59	11	14 N. 26	3¼	3½	11:17	E	**10:40**	C	VIR	5
226	14	Sa.	5:51	B	**7:46**	D	13 55	11	14 N. 08	4	4½	12:30	E	**11:08**	B	VIR	6
227	15	**C**	5:52	B	**7:45**	D	13 53	11	13 N. 49	5	5¼	1:45	E	**11:42**	B	LIB	7
228	16	M.	5:53	B	**7:43**	D	13 50	12	13 N. 30	6	6¼	3:01	E	—	-	LIB	8
229	17	Tu.	5:54	B	**7:42**	D	13 48	12	13 N. 11	7	7¼	4:14	E	12:22	B	OPH	9
230	18	W.	5:55	B	**7:40**	D	13 45	12	12 N. 51	8	8¼	5:20	E	1:12	A	SAG	10
231	19	Th.	5:56	B	**7:39**	D	13 43	12	12 N. 32	9¼	9½	6:17	E	2:12	B	SAG	11
232	20	Fr.	5:57	B	**7:37**	D	13 40	13	12 N. 12	10¼	10¼	7:03	E	3:20	B	SAG	12
233	21	Sa.	5:58	B	**7:36**	D	13 38	13	11 N. 52	11	11¼	7:41	E	4:32	B	CAP	13
234	22	**C**	5:59	B	**7:34**	D	13 35	13	11 N. 32	12	—	8:11	E	5:45	C	AQU	14
235	23	M.	6:00	B	**7:33**	D	13 33	13	11 N. 11	12	12¾	8:37	D	6:56	C	AQU	15
236	24	Tu.	6:01	B	**7:31**	D	13 30	14	10 N. 51	1	1½	9:00	D	8:04	D	AQU	16
237	25	W.	6:02	B	**7:29**	D	13 27	14	10 N. 30	1¾	2	9:22	C	9:10	D	CET	17
238	26	Th.	6:03	B	**7:28**	D	13 25	14	10 N. 09	2½	2¾	9:44	C	10:13	E	PSC	18
239	27	Fr.	6:04	B	**7:26**	D	13 22	14	9 N. 48	3¼	3½	10:06	B	11:16	E	PSC	19
240	28	Sa.	6:05	B	**7:24**	D	13 19	15	9 N. 27	4	4¼	10:32	B	12:18	E	ARI	20
241	29	**C**	6:06	B	**7:23**	D	13 17	15	9 N. 06	4¾	5	11:01	B	1:21	E	TAU	21
242	30	M.	6:07	B	**7:21**	D	13 14	15	8 N. 44	5½	5¾	11:36	A	2:22	E	TAU	22
243	31	Tu.	6:09	B	**7:19**	D	13 10	16	8 N. 22	6½	6¾	—	-	3:21	E	TAU	23

To use this page, see p. 116; for Key Letters, see p. 238. LIGHT = A.M. BOLD = P.M. **2021**

THE EIGHTH MONTH • 2021 **AUGUST** AUGUST HATH 31 DAYS

It is so deep in summer now / The pasture bars are almost hid
In daisies, where I call my cow / And listen to the katydid.
–**Anna Boynton Averill**

DAY OF MONTH	DAY OF WEEK	DATES, FEASTS, FASTS, ASPECTS, TIDE HEIGHTS, AND WEATHER	
1	**C**	**10th S. af. P.** • Lammas Day • ☿ in sup. ☌ • Colo. became 38th U.S. state, 1876	*The*
2	M.	**Civic Holiday (Canada)** • ☾ at ☊ • ☾ at apo. • ♄ at ☍	*coastline's*
3	Tu.	*August sunshine and bright nights ripen the grapes.* • Tides {8.1 9.3	*roasted,*
4	W.	108°F, Spokane, Wash., 1961 • Tides {8.1 9.4	*don't*
5	Th.	☾ rides high • 1st U.S. federal income tax imposed, 1861 • {8.3 9.7	*get toasted!*
6	Fr.	Transfiguration • Penicillin-discoverer Sir Alexander Fleming born, 1881 • {8.5 10.0	*A*
7	Sa.	Katie Ledecky swam 400m freestyle in 3:56.46, setting world record, Summer Olympics, 2016	*hurricane*
8	**C**	**11th S. af. P.** • First of Muharram begins at sundown • New ● • ☌☿☾	
9	M.	☌♂☾ • Ragweed in bloom. • Tides {10.5 9.4	*could*
10	Tu.	St. Lawrence • Mo. became 24th U.S. state, 1821 • Smithsonian Institution established, 1846	*be*
11	W.	St. Clare • Dog Days end. • ☌♀☾ • Tides {10.7 10.0	*nearing—*
12	Th.	☾ on Eq. • 1.8" rain, San Diego, Calif., 1873 • Gray squirrels have second litters now.	*skies*
13	Fr.	Writer H. G. Wells died, 1946 • Tides {10.5 10.5	*clearing.*
14	Sa.	*Honor and ease are seldom bedfellows.* • Tides {10.1 10.6	*Put*
15	**C**	**Assumption** • Writer Sir Walter Scott born, 1771 • {9.8 10.6	*your*
16	M.	☾ at ☋ • Gold discovered in Rabbit Creek, Y.T., starting Klondike Gold Rush, 1896	*feet*
17	Tu.	Cat Nights commence. • ☾ at perig. • Tides {9.2 10.7	*up.*
18	W.	☾ runs low • "Starman" Tesla completed 1st orbit around Sun, 2019 • {9.1 10.8	*Pennant*
19	Th.	☌☿♂ • ☌♇☾ • ⛢ stat. • ♃ at ☍ • Aviator Orville Wright born, 1871	*races*
20	Fr.	☌♄☾ • Strowger firm applied for patent for 1st telephone rotary dial, 1896 • {9.4 11.1	*heat*
21	Sa.	Painter Asher Brown Durand born, 1796 • Tides {9.7 11.2	*up!*
22	**C**	**13th S. af. P.** • Full Sturgeon ○ • ☌♃☾	*Lightning*
23	M.	☌♆☾ • *Nothing is impossible to a willing mind.* • Tides {11.1 10.1	*chases*
24	Tu.	St. Bartholomew • Hummingbirds migrate south. • Tides {11.0 10.1	*golfers*
25	W.	☾ on Eq. • Largest (60 million cu. ft.) successfully launched NASA balloon set world record, 2002	*from*
26	Th.	Bill 101 passed, making French official language of Quebec, 1977 • Tides {10.2 9.9	*their*
27	Fr.	Photographer Margaret Bourke-White died, 1971 • {9.7 9.7	*sport*
28	Sa.	St. Augustine of Hippo • ☌⛢☾ • Scientist John Herbert Chapman born, 1921 • {9.2 9.5	*and*
29	**C**	**14th S. af. P.** • ☾ at apo. • 1st *Peppersass* demo, Mt. Wash. cog rwy., N.H., 1866	*sailors*
30	M.	☾ at ☊ • Vicki Keith became 1st person to swim across all five Great Lakes, 1988 • {8.3 9.0	*into*
31	Tu.	Deadly 7.3 (est.) moment magnitude earthquake, Charleston, S.C., 1886 • Tides {8.0 9.0	*port.*

Farmer's Calendar

Every year I remember to do so, I plant a row of sunflowers in my vegetable patch; and every year I forget, I miss them. The sunflower is one of the flowers that every garden should by no means be without. I understand there are 70 species of sunflower (genus *Helianthus*), perennials and annuals, wild and cultivated, some grown for crops, most for fun. Some of the perennials are demure and well-mannered flowers. They do not interest me. I like the big, loud annuals that produce flowers the size of dinner plates, having raggedy, butter-yellow petals and fat, bulging centers. These flowers are essential because of their high spirits and because the sunflower is all flowers, the epitome.

There is something touching about the sunflower as well, something to do with its famous turning after the Sun. You can see its heavy flowerhead bend on its stalk to follow the Sun through its daily arc. That faithful, mechanical movement has a sadness: Its faint sorrow marks the passing summer. Especially at this time of year, the Sun it watches is going away unmistakably farther each day, and where it's going, the rooted sunflower can't follow.

SEPTEMBER

SKY WATCH: A nice series of conjunctions happens in the west in evening twilight. On the 1st, dazzling Venus is to the upper left of Mercury, with that innermost planet very low but bright at exactly magnitude 0.0. Look for Mercury below the thin crescent Moon on the 8th. The Moon will stand to the right of Venus on the 9th before forming a lineup on the 10th; from lowest right to highest left, this alignment will feature Mercury, Virgo's blue star Spica, Venus, and the crescent Moon. The Moon floats below Saturn on the 16th and below Jupiter on the 17th. Autumn begins at the moment of the equinox—3:21 P.M. EDT—on the 22nd.

● **NEW MOON** 6th day 8:52 P.M. ○ **FULL MOON** 20th day 7:55 P.M.
◐ **FIRST QUARTER** 13th day 4:39 P.M. ◑ **LAST QUARTER** 28th day 9:57 P.M.

All times are given in Eastern Daylight Time.

GET THESE PAGES WITH TIMES SET TO YOUR ZIP CODE AT ALMANAC.COM/ACCESS.

DAY OF YEAR	DAY OF MONTH	DAY OF WEEK	☼ RISES H.M.	RISE KEY	☼ SETS H.M.	SET KEY	LENGTH OF DAY H.M.	SUN FAST M.	SUN DECLINATION ° '	HIGH TIDE TIMES BOSTON		☾ RISES H.M.	RISE KEY	☾ SETS H.M.	SET KEY	☾ ASTRON. PLACE	☾ AGE
244	1	W.	6:10	B	7:18	D	13 08	16	8 N. 01	7½	7¾	12:17	A	4:17	E	GEM	24
245	2	Th.	6:11	B	7:16	D	13 05	16	7 N. 39	8½	8½	1:07	A	5:07	E	GEM	25
246	3	Fr.	6:12	B	7:14	D	13 02	17	7 N. 17	9¼	9½	2:04	B	5:50	E	GEM	26
247	4	Sa.	6:13	B	7:13	D	13 00	17	6 N. 54	10¼	10¼	3:08	B	6:27	E	CAN	27
248	5	**C**	6:14	C	7:11	D	12 57	17	6 N. 32	10¾	11	4:17	B	6:59	E	LEO	28
249	6	M.	6:15	C	7:09	D	12 54	18	6 N. 10	11½	11¾	5:28	C	7:27	D	LEO	0
250	7	Tu.	6:16	C	7:07	D	12 51	18	5 N. 47	12¼	—	6:39	D	7:53	D	LEO	1
251	8	W.	6:17	C	7:06	D	12 49	18	5 N. 25	12½	1	7:52	D	8:18	C	VIR	2
252	9	Th.	6:18	C	7:04	D	12 46	19	5 N. 02	1¼	1¾	9:05	E	8:43	C	VIR	3
253	10	Fr.	6:19	C	7:02	D	12 43	19	4 N. 39	2	2½	10:20	E	9:11	B	VIR	4
254	11	Sa.	6:20	C	7:00	D	12 40	19	4 N. 17	2¾	3¼	11:36	E	9:42	B	LIB	5
255	12	**C**	6:21	C	6:59	C	12 38	20	3 N. 54	3¾	4	12:52	E	10:20	B	LIB	6
256	13	M.	6:22	C	6:57	C	12 35	20	3 N. 31	4¾	5	2:06	E	11:07	A	OPH	7
257	14	Tu.	6:23	C	6:55	C	12 32	20	3 N. 08	5¾	6	3:14	E	—	-	SAG	8
258	15	W.	6:24	C	6:53	C	12 29	21	2 N. 45	6¾	7	4:13	E	12:03	B	SAG	9
259	16	Th.	6:25	C	6:52	C	12 27	21	2 N. 21	8	8¼	5:01	E	1:08	B	SAG	10
260	17	Fr.	6:26	C	6:50	C	12 24	21	1 N. 58	9	9¼	5:40	E	2:18	B	CAP	11
261	18	Sa.	6:28	C	6:48	C	12 20	22	1 N. 35	10	10¼	6:12	E	3:30	B	CAP	12
262	19	**C**	6:29	C	6:46	C	12 17	22	1 N. 12	10¾	11	6:39	D	4:40	C	AQU	13
263	20	M.	6:30	C	6:45	C	12 15	23	0 N. 48	11½	11¾	7:02	D	5:49	C	AQU	14
264	21	Tu.	6:31	C	6:43	C	12 12	23	0 N. 25	12¼	—	7:24	C	6:55	D	PSC	15
265	22	W.	6:32	C	6:41	C	12 09	23	0 N. 02	12½	1	7:46	C	7:59	D	CET	16
266	23	Th.	6:33	C	6:39	C	12 06	24	0 s. 21	1¼	1½	8:08	C	9:03	E	PSC	17
267	24	Fr.	6:34	C	6:37	C	12 03	24	0 s. 44	2	2¼	8:32	B	10:06	E	ARI	18
268	25	Sa.	6:35	C	6:36	C	12 01	24	1 s. 07	2¾	2¾	9:00	B	11:08	E	ARI	19
269	26	**C**	6:36	C	6:34	C	11 58	25	1 s. 31	3¼	3½	9:32	B	12:11	E	TAU	20
270	27	M.	6:37	C	6:32	C	11 55	25	1 s. 54	4¼	4¼	10:10	A	1:11	E	TAU	21
271	28	Tu.	6:38	C	6:30	C	11 52	25	2 s. 17	5	5¼	10:56	A	2:08	E	TAU	22
272	29	W.	6:39	C	6:29	C	11 50	26	2 s. 41	6	6	11:49	A	3:00	E	GEM	23
273	30	Th.	6:40	C	6:27	C	11 47	26	3 s. 04	6¾	7	—	-	3:45	E	GEM	24

SEPTEMBER

The rain is o'er—How dense and bright
Yon pearly clouds reposing lie!
–**Andrews Norton**

DAY OF MONTH	DAY OF WEEK	DATES, FEASTS, FASTS, ASPECTS, TIDE HEIGHTS, AND WEATHER	
1	W.	☾ RIDES HIGH • Activist Nellie McClung died, 1951 • 23" Atl. grayling caught, Wolf Lake, Man., 1991	*Bright*
2	Th.	*Fields have eyes and woods have ears.* • Tides {8.0 9.3	*but*
3	Fr.	Hurricane caused 13' storm surge in N.Y.C., 1821 • Tides {8.3 9.6	*breezy,*
4	Sa.	Dust devil flipped small plane and scattered papers in NWS office, Flagstaff Pulliam Airport, Ariz., 1986	*ragweed*
5	C	**15th S. af. P.** • Lake water DNA analysis showed no Loch Ness Monster (but perhaps a giant eel), 2019	
6	M.	Rosh Hashanah begins at sundown • **LABOR DAY** • **NEW** ● • Tides {9.6 10.7	*makes us*
7	Tu.	☌♂☾ • Damaging hailstorm, Calgary, Alta., 1991 • Tides {10.1 —	*sneezy.*
8	W.	☾ ON EQ. • ☌☿☾ • Naturalist Euell Gibbons born, 1911 • {10.9 10.5	*Wetter:*
9	Th.	☌♀☾ • Bluegrass musician Bill Monroe died, 1996 • Tides {11.0 10.9	*Apple*
10	Fr.	Hurricane Irma made U.S. landfall at Cudjoe Key, Fla., 2017 • Tides {10.9 11.1	*pickers*
11	Sa.	**PATRIOT DAY** • ☾ AT PERIG. • Cranberry bog harvest begins, Cape Cod, Mass. • {10.6 11.1	*have*
12	C	**16th S. af. P.** • ☾ AT ☋ • Poets Elizabeth Barrett and Robert Browning eloped, 1846	*to*
13	M.	*Little and often fills the purse.* • Tides {9.7 10.8	*don*
14	Tu.	Holy Cross • ☾ RUNS LOW • ♆ AT ☍ • ☿ GR. ELONG. (27° EAST) • {9.3 10.5	*slickers*
15	W.	Ember Day • Yom Kippur begins at sundown • Greenpeace founded, 1971 • {9.0 10.4	*(and*
16	Th.	☌♄☾ • ☌♇☾ • Metropolitan Opera House opened, N.Y.C., 1966 • {9.0 10.4	*maybe*
17	Fr.	Ember Day • NASA unveiled 1st space shuttle, *Enterprise,* to public, 1976 • {9.2 10.5	*a*
18	Sa.	Ember Day • ☌♃☾ • Cornerstone for U.S. Capitol laid, D.C., 1793 • {9.5 10.6	*sweater).*
19	C	**17th S. af. P.** • Betty and Barney Hill claimed to have been abducted by UFO, N.H., 1961	*Now*
20	M.	Sukkoth begins at sundown • **FULL HARVEST** ○ • ☌♆☾ • Tides {10.1 10.6	*it's*
21	Tu.	St. Matthew • ☾ ON EQ. • Jingle writer Richard D. Trentlage died, 2016 • {10.2 —	*turning*
22	W.	Harvest Home • **AUTUMNAL EQUINOX** • 3.3 magnitude earthquake, Rathdrum, Idaho, 2003	*better—*
23	Th.	Neptune discovered, 1846 • Actor "Chief" Dan George died, 1981 • {10.2 10.2	*foliage*
24	Fr.	☌♅☾ • Writer F. Scott Fitzgerald born, 1896 • Football player Joe Greene born, 1946	*unfettered.*
25	Sa.	Woodchucks hibernate now. • Tides {9.4 9.8	*Balmy*
26	C	**18th S. af. P.** • ☾ AT ☊ • ☾ AT APO. • {9.0 9.5	*and*
27	M.	St. Vincent de Paul • ☿ STAT. • Composer Engelbert Humperdinck died, 1921 • {8.6 9.2	*blue*
28	Tu.	8 players indicted in Black Sox scandal, 1920 • {8.2 9.0	*for*
29	W.	St. Michael • ☾ RIDES HIGH • *The farther the sight, the nearer the rain.* • {8.0 8.9	*autumn's*
30	Th.	St. Gregory the Illuminator • Gymnast Dominique Moceanu born, 1981 • Tides {8.0 9.0	*debut!*

Farmer's Calendar

This house was once part of a hill farm that started around 1790 and was worked until about 1925. On the place today are five wells that served the old farm. One is a spring a couple of feet deep that's been scooped out and lined with stones. The others are more ambitious structures: 12 to 15 feet deep and lined with large stones laid skillfully in the manner of a house foundation. I try to imagine how you'd go about building such a well. You'd have to dig out the hole, plumb 6 or 7 feet wide and as deep as needed. Two or three workers could dig, but once the hole was dug and the work of laying up the stones begun, only one worker could carry on at a time; there is no room for more in the stone-sided cylinder. Putting up the stones, you'd be alone down there. And the stones would be above. Somebody would have to lower them to you on ropes. You'd want a good man up top. As the stones rose around you, you'd need staging to stand on and work from. You'd dismantle it when you were done. How long would it take to lay up a well? For an experienced stoneworker with good help, a day or two. Would you toss a penny down the finished well for good luck? I would.

CALENDAR

Listen to the Farmer's Calendar at Almanac.com/Podcast.

OCTOBER

SKY WATCH: On the 9th, in evening twilight, the crescent Moon hovers closely above now-brilliant Venus, nestled in the claws of Scorpius. A few nights after that dramatic conjunction, on the 13th, the just-past-first-quarter Moon stands to the right of Jupiter and Saturn; on the 14th, the three form a triangle, with the Moon in the upper middle, brilliant Jupiter to the lower left, and Saturn on the lower right. These three, now conveniently grouped together and optimally illuminated, offer the finest targets for small backyard telescopes. Venus meets Scorpius's famous orange star Antares from the 15th to the 17th, before crossing into the oft-called "13th zodiacal constellation" of Ophiuchus, the Serpent Bearer, on the 21st, where it will spend the next 10 evenings.

● **NEW MOON** 6th day 7:05 A.M.   ○ **FULL MOON** 20th day 10:57 A.M.
◐ **FIRST QUARTER** 12th day 11:25 P.M.   ◑ **LAST QUARTER** 28th day 4:05 P.M.

All times are given in Eastern Daylight Time.

GET THESE PAGES WITH TIMES SET TO YOUR ZIP CODE AT ALMANAC.COM/ACCESS.

DAY OF YEAR	DAY OF MONTH	DAY OF WEEK	☀ RISES H.M.	RISE KEY	☀ SETS H.M.	SET KEY	LENGTH OF DAY H.M.	SUN FAST M.	SUN DECLINATION ° '	HIGH TIDE TIMES BOSTON		☾ RISES H.M.	RISE KEY	☾ SETS H.M.	SET KEY	☾ ASTRON. PLACE	☾ AGE
274	1	Fr.	6:41	C	6:25	C	11 44	26	3 s. 27	7¾	8	12:50	B	4:24	E	CAN	25
275	2	Sa.	6:43	C	6:23	C	11 40	27	3 s. 50	8¾	8¾	1:56	B	4:58	E	CAN	26
276	3	C	6:44	C	6:22	C	11 38	27	4 s. 14	9½	9¾	3:06	C	5:27	E	LEO	27
277	4	M.	6:45	C	6:20	C	11 35	27	4 s. 37	10¼	10½	4:17	C	5:53	D	LEO	28
278	5	Tu.	6:46	D	6:18	C	11 32	28	5 s. 00	11	11¼	5:30	D	6:18	D	VIR	29
279	6	W.	6:47	D	6:17	C	11 30	28	5 s. 23	11¾	—	6:44	E	6:43	C	VIR	0
280	7	Th.	6:48	D	6:15	C	11 27	28	5 s. 46	12	12½	8:00	E	7:10	C	VIR	1
281	8	Fr.	6:49	D	6:13	C	11 24	28	6 s. 09	12¾	1¼	9:18	E	7:41	B	LIB	2
282	9	Sa.	6:50	D	6:12	C	11 22	29	6 s. 31	1¾	2	10:38	E	8:18	B	LIB	3
283	10	C	6:52	D	6:10	C	11 18	29	6 s. 54	2½	2¾	11:55	E	9:02	B	OPH	4
284	11	M.	6:53	D	6:08	C	11 15	29	7 s. 17	3½	3¾	1:08	E	9:56	B	OPH	5
285	12	Tu.	6:54	D	6:07	B	11 13	29	7 s. 39	4½	4¾	2:10	E	10:59	B	SAG	6
286	13	W.	6:55	D	6:05	B	11 10	30	8 s. 02	5½	5¾	3:02	E	—	-	SAG	7
287	14	Th.	6:56	D	6:03	B	11 07	30	8 s. 24	6¾	7	3:43	E	12:08	B	CAP	8
288	15	Fr.	6:57	D	6:02	B	11 05	30	8 s. 46	7¾	8	4:16	E	1:19	B	CAP	9
289	16	Sa.	6:58	D	6:00	B	11 02	30	9 s. 08	8¾	9	4:43	E	2:30	C	AQU	10
290	17	C	7:00	D	5:59	B	10 59	31	9 s. 30	9¾	10	5:07	D	3:38	C	AQU	11
291	18	M.	7:01	D	5:57	B	10 56	31	9 s. 52	10½	10¾	5:29	D	4:44	D	PSC	12
292	19	Tu.	7:02	D	5:56	B	10 54	31	10 s. 13	11¼	11½	5:50	C	5:48	D	CET	13
293	20	W.	7:03	D	5:54	B	10 51	31	10 s. 35	11¾	—	6:11	C	6:51	E	PSC	14
294	21	Th.	7:04	D	5:52	B	10 48	31	10 s. 56	12¼	12½	6:35	B	7:54	E	ARI	15
295	22	Fr.	7:06	D	5:51	B	10 45	31	11 s. 17	12¾	1	7:00	B	8:57	E	ARI	16
296	23	Sa.	7:07	D	5:50	B	10 43	32	11 s. 38	1½	1½	7:30	B	10:00	E	TAU	17
297	24	C	7:08	D	5:48	B	10 40	32	11 s. 59	2¼	2¼	8:06	A	11:01	E	TAU	18
298	25	M.	7:09	D	5:47	B	10 38	32	12 s. 20	3	3	8:49	A	12:00	E	TAU	19
299	26	Tu.	7:10	D	5:45	B	10 35	32	12 s. 40	3¾	3¾	9:39	A	12:53	E	GEM	20
300	27	W.	7:12	D	5:44	B	10 32	32	13 s. 01	4½	4½	10:36	B	1:41	E	GEM	21
301	28	Th.	7:13	D	5:42	B	10 29	32	13 s. 21	5¼	5½	11:38	B	2:21	E	CAN	22
302	29	Fr.	7:14	D	5:41	B	10 27	32	13 s. 40	6¼	6¼	—	-	2:56	E	CAN	23
303	30	Sa.	7:15	D	5:40	B	10 25	32	14 s. 00	7¼	7¼	12:45	B	3:26	E	LEO	24
304	31	C	7:17	D	5:38	B	10 21	32	14 s. 19	8	8¼	1:54	C	3:53	D	LEO	25

To use this page, see p. 116; for Key Letters, see p. 238. LIGHT = A.M. BOLD = P.M.   2021

OCTOBER

One star is trembling into sight,
And soft as sleep the darkness falls.
–**W. M.,** ***Chambers's Journal***

DAY OF MONTH	DAY OF WEEK	DATES, FEASTS, FASTS, ASPECTS, TIDE HEIGHTS, AND WEATHER	
1	Fr.	Walt Disney World opened, Orlando, Fla., 1971 • {8.1 9.2	*Rain's*
2	Sa.	Watch for banded woolly bear caterpillars now. • {8.5 9.6	*refrain*
3	C	**19th S. af. P.** • *Opportunity is the cream of time.* • {9.1 10.0	*brings*
4	M.	St. Francis of Assisi • NFL Patriots' Tom Brady threw 500th career regular-season touchdown pass, 2018	*sudden*
5	Tu.	World Series 1st broadcast on radio, 1921 • {10.3 10.8	*chills,*
6	W.	NEW ● • ☾ ON EQ. • ☌☿☾ • ☌♂☾ • ♇ STAT. • {10.9 —	*flurries*
7	Th.	12-yr.-old caught 618-lb. bluefin tuna, Northumberland Strait, Can., 2014 • Tides {11.0 11.4	*spread*
8	Fr.	☾ AT PERIG. • ☌♂☉ • Great Chicago Fire started, 1871 • Tides {11.1 11.6	*lace*
9	Sa.	☾ AT ☋ • ☌☿♂ • ☌♀☾ • ☿ IN INF. ☌ • Tides {10.9 11.7	*upon*
10	C	**20th S. af. P.** • ♄ STAT. • Sir Robert Borden became 8th prime minister of Canada, 1911	*the*
11	M.	**Columbus Day, observed** • **Indigenous Peoples' Day** • **Thanksgiving Day (Canada)**	*hills.*
12	Tu.	☾ RUNS LOW • *If animals crowd together, rain will follow.* • {9.6 10.8	*Leaves*
13	W.	☌♇☾ • Expo 86 ended, Vancouver, B.C., 1986 • Tides {9.2 10.4	*are*
14	Th.	☌♄☾ • Poland presented 5.5M goodwill signatures to U.S. for 150th anniv., 1926	*many-hued,*
15	Fr.	☌♃☾ • *American Angler,* 1st U.S. fishing magazine, debuted, 1881 • {9.1 10.0	*but*
16	Sa.	1st successful demonstration of ether, Mass. Gen. Hospital, Boston, Mass., 1846 • {9.4 10.1	*foliage*
17	C	**21st S. af. P.** • ☌♆☾ • ☿ STAT. • Tides {9.7 10.1	*tours*
18	M.	St. Luke • ♃ STAT. • St. Luke's little summer. • {10.0 10.1	*get a*
19	Tu.	☾ ON EQ. • Cornwallis surrendered to Washington, effectively ending Am. Rev. War, Yorktown, Va., 1781	*rude*
20	W.	FULL HUNTER'S ○ • Baseball player Mickey Mantle born, 1931	*awakening:*
21	Th.	☌⛢☾ • Little brown bats hibernate now. • {9.9 10.3	*Cold*
22	Fr.	Princeton University founded, 1746 • Tides {9.7 10.2	*showers*
23	Sa.	St. James of Jerusalem • ☾ AT ☊ • Major flooding, Chickasha, Okla., 2000 • {9.4 10.1	*and*
24	C	**22nd S. af. P.** • ☾ AT APO. • Singing telegram creator George P. Oslin died, 1996	*even*
25	M.	☿ GR. ELONG. (18° WEST) • Artist Pablo Picasso born, 1881 • Tides {8.8 9.6	*some*
26	Tu.	☾ RIDES HIGH • Game show host Pat Sajak born, 1946 • Tides {8.5 9.3	*flakening!*
27	W.	Timber rattlesnakes move to winter dens. • Tides {8.2 9.1	*More*
28	Th.	Sts. Simon & Jude • Statue of Liberty unveiled, N.Y. Harbor, 1886 • Tides {8.1 9.0	*tricky*
29	Fr.	♀ GR. ELONG. (47° EAST) • *2019:* Escape artist cat Quilty repeatedly freed friends from shelter's cat room, Houston, Tex.	
30	Sa.	*In a night's time springs up a mushroom.* • {8.4 9.2	*than treaty,*
31	C	**23rd S. af. P.** • All Hallows' Eve • Reformation Day • {8.9 9.5	*sweetie!*

Farmer's Calendar

The summer birds are gone. The last robin, bluebird, swallow have surreptitiously decamped. In the spring, they arrive in big, noisy flights full of greeting, but when they turn south, they go by ones and twos. According to the migration maps, the robin favors Florida in winter, the tree swallow Cuba and the Caribbean. It took a long time to figure that out. The annual disappearance of the common birds of passage remained a mystery longer than seems necessary. For most of history, the best scientists of their times believed that birds hibernated. Not until the 19th century was it known that the same species returned to the same winter ranges year after year.

I have always thought it strange that the solution to the mystery of migration, in its main outlines, should have taken centuries to find. After all, the robins, the warblers, and the rest aren't hiding out down there. They're easy to spot. And, since the Renaissance, navigators and other travelers have frequented the tropics of both hemispheres where migratory birds winter. Those old, bold navigators weren't paying attention, I guess.

NOVEMBER

SKY WATCH: Venus, at a dazzling magnitude –4.33, crosses into Sagittarius and floats directly in front of our galaxy's center, which is off in the far distance. On the 7th, the crescent Moon joins Venus there. The Moon forms a triangle with Jupiter and Saturn on the 10th and then dangles beneath Jupiter on the 11th. Venus reaches its most southerly zodiac position at midmonth. Its declination of –27 degrees makes it set as far left as possible, in the southwest instead of the west. The night of the 18th–19th brings another nearly total lunar eclipse in the hours before dawn. This 98 percent–eclipsed Moon will be a strange, coppery sight—well worth a look by early risers and insomniacs who have unobstructed views of the low western sky.

● NEW MOON	4th day	5:15 P.M.	○ FULL MOON	19th day	3:57 A.M.
◑ FIRST QUARTER	11th day	7:46 A.M.	◐ LAST QUARTER	27th day	7:28 A.M.

After 2:00 A.M. on November 7, Eastern Standard Time is given.

GET THESE PAGES WITH TIMES SET TO YOUR ZIP CODE AT ALMANAC.COM/ACCESS.

DAY OF YEAR	DAY OF MONTH	DAY OF WEEK	☼ RISES H. M.	RISE KEY	☼ SETS H. M.	SET KEY	LENGTH OF DAY H. M.	SUN FAST M.	SUN DECLINATION ° '	HIGH TIDE TIMES BOSTON	☽ RISES H. M.	RISE KEY	☽ SETS H. M.	SET KEY	☽ ASTRON. PLACE	☽ AGE
305	1	M.	7:18	D	5:37	B	10 19	32	14 s. 39	8¾ 9¼	3:05	D	4:18	D	LEO	26
306	2	Tu.	7:19	D	5:36	B	10 17	32	14 s. 58	9½ 10	4:17	D	4:42	C	VIR	27
307	3	W.	7:20	D	5:35	B	10 15	32	15 s. 16	10½ 10¾	5:32	E	5:08	C	VIR	28
308	4	Th.	7:22	D	5:33	B	10 11	32	15 s. 35	11¼ 11¾	6:51	E	5:37	B	VIR	0
309	5	Fr.	7:23	D	5:32	B	10 09	32	15 s. 53	12 —	8:11	E	6:11	B	LIB	1
310	6	Sa.	7:24	E	5:31	B	10 07	32	16 s. 11	12½ 12¾	9:33	E	6:53	B	SCO	2
311	7	**C**	6:25	E	4:30	B	10 05	32	16 s. 28	1¼ 12½	9:51	E	6:45	A	OPH	3
312	8	M.	6:27	E	4:29	B	10 02	32	16 s. 46	1¼ 1½	11:01	E	7:47	B	SAG	4
313	9	Tu.	6:28	E	4:28	B	10 00	32	17 s. 03	2¼ 2½	11:59	E	8:57	B	SAG	5
314	10	W.	6:29	E	4:27	B	9 58	32	17 s. 20	3¼ 3½	12:44	E	10:09	B	CAP	6
315	11	Th.	6:30	E	4:26	B	9 56	32	17 s. 36	4¼ 4½	1:20	E	11:21	C	CAP	7
316	12	Fr.	6:32	E	4:25	B	9 53	32	17 s. 52	5¼ 5½	1:49	E	—	-	AQU	8
317	13	Sa.	6:33	E	4:24	B	9 51	31	18 s. 08	6½ 6¾	2:13	D	12:30	C	AQU	9
318	14	**C**	6:34	E	4:23	B	9 49	31	18 s. 24	7½ 7¾	2:35	D	1:36	D	AQU	10
319	15	M.	6:35	E	4:22	B	9 47	31	18 s. 39	8¼ 8¾	2:56	C	2:40	D	CET	11
320	16	Tu.	6:37	E	4:21	B	9 44	31	18 s. 54	9 9½	3:17	C	3:43	E	PSC	12
321	17	W.	6:38	E	4:20	B	9 42	31	19 s. 09	9¾ 10¼	3:39	B	4:45	E	PSC	13
322	18	Th.	6:39	E	4:19	B	9 40	31	19 s. 23	10¼ 10¾	4:03	B	5:48	E	ARI	14
323	19	Fr.	6:40	E	4:19	B	9 39	30	19 s. 37	11 11½	4:32	B	6:51	E	TAU	15
324	20	Sa.	6:41	E	4:18	B	9 37	30	19 s. 50	11½ —	5:05	B	7:53	E	TAU	16
325	21	**C**	6:43	E	4:17	B	9 34	30	20 s. 03	12¼ 12¼	5:45	A	8:53	E	TAU	17
326	22	M.	6:44	E	4:17	A	9 33	30	20 s. 16	12¾ 12¾	6:33	B	9:48	E	GEM	18
327	23	Tu.	6:45	E	4:16	A	9 31	29	20 s. 29	1½ 1½	7:27	B	10:38	E	GEM	19
328	24	W.	6:46	E	4:15	A	9 29	29	20 s. 41	2¼ 2¼	8:27	B	11:20	E	GEM	20
329	25	Th.	6:47	E	4:15	A	9 28	29	20 s. 52	3 3	9:31	B	11:56	E	CAN	21
330	26	Fr.	6:48	E	4:14	A	9 26	28	21 s. 03	3¾ 3¾	10:37	C	12:27	E	LEO	22
331	27	Sa.	6:50	E	4:14	A	9 24	28	21 s. 14	4½ 4¾	11:45	C	12:54	E	LEO	23
332	28	**C**	6:51	E	4:14	A	9 23	28	21 s. 25	5½ 5¾	—	-	1:19	D	LEO	24
333	29	M.	6:52	E	4:13	A	9 21	27	21 s. 35	6¼ 6¾	12:54	D	1:42	D	VIR	25
334	30	Tu.	6:53	E	4:13	A	9 20	27	21 s. 45	7¼ 7½	2:06	D	2:06	C	VIR	26

To use this page, see p. 116; for Key Letters, see p. 238. LIGHT = A.M. **BOLD = P.M.**   **2021**

NOVEMBER

The farmer sat there milking Bess, / A-whistling all the while;
He was a sunburnt, stalwart man, / And had a kindly smile.
–Mary E. Wilkins

DAY OF MONTH	DAY OF WEEK	DATES, FEASTS, FASTS, ASPECTS, TIDE HEIGHTS, AND WEATHER	
1	M.	All Saints' • Writer Stephen Crane born, 1871 • {9.5 / 9.9}	*Bundle*
2	Tu.	All Souls' • **Election Day** • ☾ on Eq. • Tides {10.2 / 10.4}	*up*
3	W.	☌☿☾ • John Adams elected 2nd U.S. president, 1796 • Tides {10.9 / 10.7}	*to*
4	Th.	**NEW ●** • ☌♂☾ • ⛢ at ☍ • Tides {11.5 / 10.9}	*your*
5	Fr.	☾ at perig. • ☾ at ☋ • *Better untaught than ill taught.* • Tides {12.0 / —}	*necks*
6	Sa.	Sadie Hawkins Day • Basketball-game inventor James Naismith born, 1861 • {10.9 / 12.2}	*for*
7	C	**24th S. af. P.** • **Daylight Saving Time ends, 2:00 A.M.** • {10.7 / 12.1}	*the*
8	M.	☾ runs low • ☌♀☾ • Astronomer Edmond Halley born, 1656	*polar*
9	Tu.	☌☿♂ • ☌♇☾ • Maj. Robert White flew X-15 rocket plane at Mach 6.04, 1961	*vortex!*
10	W.	☌♄☾ • 70+ tornadoes developed, eastern half of U.S., 2002 • Tides {9.6 / 10.7}	*Cold's*
11	Th.	St. Martin of Tours • **Veterans Day** • ☌♃☾ • Tides {9.3 / 10.2}	*injurious,*
12	Fr.	Indian Summer • *The wind in the west suits everyone best.* • Tides {9.2 / 9.8}	*flurries*
13	Sa.	☌♆☾ • *Mariner 9* became 1st spacecraft to orbit another planet (Mars), 1971 • {9.3 / 9.6}	*furious.*
14	C	**25th S. af. P.** • U.S. first lady Mamie Eisenhower born, 1896 • {9.5 / 9.5}	*Hunters*
15	M.	☾ on Eq. • *Love Me Tender,* Elvis Presley's 1st movie, debuted, 1956 • {9.7 / 9.5}	*find*
16	Tu.	45°F plus 8.4" snow, Anchorage, Alaska, 2019 • Tides {9.9 / 9.4}	*plenty*
17	W.	St. Hugh of Lincoln • ☌⛢☾ • Social worker Grace Abbott born, 1878 • {10.1 / 9.4}	*of*
18	Th.	St. Hilda of Whitby • Standard Railway Time went into effect for most N.Am. railroads, 1883	*snow*
19	Fr.	**Full Beaver** ○ • **Eclipse** ☾ • ☾ at ☊ • Tides {10.2 / 9.2}	*for*
20	Sa.	☾ at apo. • Ballerina Maya Plisetskaya born, 1925 • {10.2 / —}	*tracking;*
21	C	**26th S. af. P.** • H. Truman became 2nd U.S. pres. to dive in sub (T. Roosevelt 1st), 1946	*turkey*
22	M.	☾ rides high • Agronomist William Evans born, 1786 • Comedian Rodney Dangerfield born, 1921	*roasters,*
23	Tu.	St. Clement • Horseshoe manufacturing machine patented, 1835 • Tides {8.6 / 9.7}	*let's*
24	W.	Baseball player Warren Spahn died, 2003 • Tides {8.5 / 9.5}	*get*
25	Th.	**Thanksgiving Day** • *A good tale is none the worse for being twice told.* • {8.3 / 9.3}	*cracking!*
26	Fr.	Buoy recorded 75-foot wave off Cape Mendocino, Calif., 2019 • Tides {8.3 / 9.2}	*Woodstove*
27	Sa.	Microsoft's *Internet Explorer 2.0* released, starting 1st "browser war" (with Netscape's *Navigator*), 1995	*owners*
28	C	**1st S. of Advent** • Chanukah begins at sundown • ☿ in sup. ☌	*better*
29	M.	☾ on Eq. • Ensemble of 1,013 cellists played in Kobe, Japan, setting world record, 1998	*start*
30	Tu.	St. Andrew • Deadly tornado, Simsboro, La., 1996 • Tides {9.9 / 9.7}	*stacking!*

Farmer's Calendar

"Every man looks at his woodpile with a kind of affection," wrote American essayist Henry David Thoreau (1817–62). He's right, too, isn't he? An ample woodpile has a familiar, reassuring presence. It's a satisfactory object in a way that's a little hard to account for. We respond to the sight of a good woodpile with a level of contentment.

What is it that contents us? Not use, or not use alone.

It's not as fuel that a woodpile makes its particular appeal. It's as a symbol. We are cheered and comforted by our woodpile today because a woodpile is one of the stations of the year and expresses the essential ambiguity of all seasonal work. It represents a job that we know we can do well enough but that we also know will never finally be done: Woodpiles are built up that they may be torn down. Massive as they are, they're ephemeral. You'll have to build another next year, which you will then once more throw down. The woodpile reminds us of the fix we're in just by being alive on Earth. It connects us with the years, and so it connects us with one another. We may as well look at our woodpile with affection, then, for it makes us be philosophers.

DECEMBER

SKY WATCH: On the 1st, Venus, now at its most brilliant, stands a comfortable 16 degrees high as the constellations emerge in the late evening twilight. On the 6th, it hovers just above the crescent Moon—a lovely sight. Also on the 6th, look for a planet bunch-up in the west after sunset: From lower right to upper left stand Venus, the Moon, Saturn, and Jupiter. The grouping remains on the 8th, with the crescent Moon now second from the top, below Jupiter, which moves back into Aquarius at midmonth. By the holidays, Mercury, at a bright magnitude –0.5, will be visible, too, dangling below Venus from the 24th to the 31st. It will stand left of Venus from the 29th to the 31st. The solstice brings winter to the Northern Hemisphere on the 21st at 10:59 A.M. EST.

● **NEW MOON** 4th day 2:43 A.M.   ○ **FULL MOON** 18th day 11:35 P.M.
◑ **FIRST QUARTER** 10th day 8:36 P.M.   ◐ **LAST QUARTER** 26th day 9:24 P.M.

All times are given in Eastern Standard Time.

GET THESE PAGES WITH TIMES SET TO YOUR ZIP CODE AT ALMANAC.COM/ACCESS.

DAY OF YEAR	DAY OF MONTH	DAY OF WEEK	☼ RISES H.M.	RISE KEY	☼ SETS H.M.	SET KEY	LENGTH OF DAY H.M.	SUN FAST M.	SUN DECLINATION ° '	HIGH TIDE TIMES BOSTON		☾ RISES H.M.	RISE KEY	☾ SETS H.M.	SET KEY	☾ ASTRON. PLACE	☾ AGE
335	1	W.	6:54	E	4:12	A	9 18	27	21 s. 54	8	8½	3:20	E	2:33	B	VIR	27
336	2	Th.	6:55	E	4:12	A	9 17	26	22 s. 03	8¾	9½	4:38	E	3:03	B	LIB	28
337	3	Fr.	6:56	E	4:12	A	9 16	26	22 s. 11	9¾	10¼	6:00	E	3:41	B	LIB	29
338	4	Sa.	6:57	E	4:12	A	9 15	25	22 s. 19	10½	11¼	7:22	E	4:28	B	OPH	0
339	5	**C**	6:58	E	4:12	A	9 14	25	22 s. 27	11½	—	8:39	E	5:27	A	SAG	1
340	6	M.	6:59	E	4:12	A	9 13	25	22 s. 34	12	12¼	9:45	E	6:36	B	SAG	2
341	7	Tu.	7:00	E	4:11	A	9 11	24	22 s. 40	1	1¼	10:38	E	7:51	B	SAG	3
342	8	W.	7:01	E	4:11	A	9 10	24	22 s. 47	2	2	11:19	E	9:06	B	CAP	4
343	9	Th.	7:02	E	4:11	A	9 09	23	22 s. 52	3	3	11:51	E	10:18	C	CAP	5
344	10	Fr.	7:03	E	4:12	A	9 09	23	22 s. 58	4	4	12:18	D	11:27	C	AQU	6
345	11	Sa.	7:03	E	4:12	A	9 09	23	23 s. 03	5	5¼	12:41	D	—	-	AQU	7
346	12	**C**	7:04	E	4:12	A	9 08	22	23 s. 07	6	6¼	1:02	C	12:32	D	PSC	8
347	13	M.	7:05	E	4:12	A	9 07	21	23 s. 11	6¾	7¼	1:23	C	1:35	E	PSC	9
348	14	Tu.	7:06	E	4:12	A	9 06	21	23 s. 14	7¾	8¼	1:44	C	2:38	E	PSC	10
349	15	W.	7:06	E	4:12	A	9 06	20	23 s. 17	8½	9	2:08	B	3:40	E	ARI	11
350	16	Th.	7:07	E	4:13	A	9 06	20	23 s. 20	9¼	9¾	2:34	B	4:42	E	ARI	12
351	17	Fr.	7:08	E	4:13	A	9 05	19	23 s. 22	9¾	10½	3:06	B	5:45	E	TAU	13
352	18	Sa.	7:08	E	4:13	A	9 05	19	23 s. 24	10½	11¼	3:44	A	6:45	E	TAU	14
353	19	**C**	7:09	E	4:14	A	9 05	18	23 s. 25	11¼	11¾	4:29	A	7:43	E	TAU	15
354	20	M.	7:10	E	4:14	A	9 04	18	23 s. 26	11¾	—	5:21	A	8:35	E	GEM	16
355	21	Tu.	7:10	E	4:14	A	9 04	17	23 s. 26	12½	12½	6:20	B	9:20	E	GEM	17
356	22	W.	7:11	E	4:15	A	9 04	17	23 s. 25	1	1	7:23	B	9:58	E	CAN	18
357	23	Th.	7:11	E	4:16	A	9 05	17	23 s. 25	1¾	1¾	8:28	C	10:30	E	CAN	19
358	24	Fr.	7:11	E	4:16	A	9 05	16	23 s. 24	2½	2½	9:34	C	10:57	E	LEO	20
359	25	Sa.	7:12	E	4:17	A	9 05	16	23 s. 22	3¼	3¼	10:41	D	11:22	D	LEO	21
360	26	**C**	7:12	E	4:18	A	9 06	15	23 s. 20	4	4¼	11:49	D	11:45	D	VIR	22
361	27	M.	7:12	E	4:18	A	9 06	15	23 s. 17	4¾	5¼	—	-	12:08	C	VIR	23
362	28	Tu.	7:13	E	4:19	A	9 06	14	23 s. 14	5¾	6	12:59	E	12:32	C	VIR	24
363	29	W.	7:13	E	4:20	A	9 07	14	23 s. 11	6½	7	2:13	E	12:59	B	VIR	25
364	30	Th.	7:13	E	4:21	A	9 08	13	23 s. 07	7½	8	3:30	E	1:32	B	LIB	26
365	31	Fr.	7:13	E	4:22	A	9 09	13	23 s. 02	8½	9	4:50	E	2:12	B	SCO	27

DECEMBER

Let Joy light up in every breast, / And brighten every eye,
Distressing Care be lull'd to rest, / And hush'd be every sigh.
–Peter Sherston

DAY OF MONTH	DAY OF WEEK	DATES, FEASTS, FASTS, ASPECTS, TIDE HEIGHTS, AND WEATHER	
1	W.	♆ STAT. • Holography pioneer Stephen Benton born, 1941 • {10.6 / 10.0	*More*
2	Th.	St. Viviana • ☌♂☾ • 1st unmanned landing on Mars, by USSR *Mars 3*, 1971 • {11.3 / 10.3	*snow*
3	Fr.	☾ AT ☋ • 68°F, Portland, Maine, 2009 • Tides {11.8 / 10.5	*than*
4	Sa.	NEW ● • ECLIPSE ⊙ • ☾ AT PERIG. • ☌☿☾ • ♀ GR. ILLUM. EXT.	*we*
5	C	2nd S. of Advent • ☾ RUNS LOW • Entrepreneur Walt Disney born, 1901	*reckoned*
6	M.	St. Nicholas • ☌♀☾ • ☌♇☾ • Tides {10.5 / 12.2	*for*
7	Tu.	St. Ambrose • NATIONAL PEARL HARBOR REMEMBRANCE DAY • ☌♄☾	*piles*
8	W.	John McCrae's *In Flanders Fields* poem published, 1915 • Tides {10.0 / 11.3	*up*
9	Th.	☌♃☾ • Robert Cushman preached 1st known Christian sermon in America, Plymouth (Mass.), 1621	*to*
10	Fr.	St. Eulalia • ☌♆☾ • Chemist Alfred Nobel died, 1896 • {9.5 / 10.0	*the*
11	Sa.	☌♀♇ • Statute of Westminster passed, 1931 • Tides {9.4 / 9.5	*second*
12	C	3rd S. of Advent • ☾ ON EQ. • Astronomer Henrietta Swan Leavitt died, 1921	*floor!*
13	M.	St. Lucia • Artist Grandma Moses died, 1961 • {9.4 / 8.9	*Brief*
14	Tu.	Halcyon Days begin. • 5.6-lb. avocado set world record for heaviest, Kahului, Hawaii, 2018	*relief,*
15	W.	Ember Day • ☌⛢☾ • U.S. Bill of Rights ratified, 1791 • Tides {9.6 / 8.7	*then*
16	Th.	☾ AT ☊ • *In courtesy, rather pay a penny too much than too little.* • {9.8 / 8.8	*good*
17	Fr.	Ember Day • ☾ AT APO. • 1st heart, lung, and liver transplant, 1986 • Tides {9.9 / 8.8	*grief!*
18	Sa.	Ember Day • FULL COLD ○ • ♀ STAT. • Film director Steven Spielberg born, 1946	*It's*
19	C	4th S. of Advent • ☾ RIDES HIGH • Mark Twain rec'd patent for suspenders, 1871	*true:*
20	M.	Beware the Pogonip. • Astrophysicist Carl Sagan died, 1996 • Tides {10.0 / —	*Even*
21	Tu.	St. Thomas • WINTER SOLSTICE • *After a rainy winter follows a fruitful spring.* • {8.7 / 10.0	*Santa's*
22	W.	Grote Reber, builder of 1st radio telescope, born, 1911 • Tides {8.7 / 9.9	*checking*
23	Th.	☌♀♇ • *Voyager* aircraft completed 1st nonstop flight around world w/o refueling (9 days 4 min.), 1986	*real*
24	Fr.	Eggnog Riot began, U.S. Military Academy at West Point, N.Y., 1826 • {8.7 / 9.6	*estate*
25	Sa.	Christmas • Poet William Collins born, 1721 • Am. Red Cross founder Clara Barton born, 1821	*in*
26	C	1st S. af. Ch. • BOXING DAY (CANADA) • FIRST DAY OF KWANZAA	*Malibu!*
27	M.	St. Stephen[T] • ☾ ON EQ. • Astronomer Johannes Kepler born, 1571 • {9.3 / 9.2	*Lips*
28	Tu.	St. John[T] • ☌☿♀ • Iowa became 29th U.S. state, 1846 • 31.5" snow in 24 hrs., Victoria, B.C., 1996	*will*
29	W.	Holy Innocents[T] • William Lyon Mackenzie King became 1st prime minister of Canada, 1921	*be*
30	Th.	☾ AT ☋ • ☌☿♇ • *A new broom sweeps clean.* • {10.7 / 9.5	*blue*
31	Fr.	St. Sylvester • ☌♂☾ • Baltimore, Md., incorporated, 1796 • {11.2 / 9.6	*in '22!*

Farmer's Calendar

Now, as the season of storms approaches, a bewildering multiplicity of snow shovels has been on display in practically every store in town. And what snow shovels they are! There are snow shovels with straight handles, snow shovels with bent handles, with fat blades, with thin blades, with D grips, with T grips. Some snow shovels are plastic and cost a couple of bucks; others are so expensive that it seems wrong to expose them to a substance, like snow, that comes for free.

What to do?

It took me a number of winters to discover that very often the best snow shovel is a simple broom, one with long, stiff straw. A broom will take care of better than half the snow you'll get in a winter, and it won't break your back, burst your heart, or dig up your grass by mistake. For cleaning snow off the car, the broom is far superior to the shovel because it can't scratch your paint job. And if you are equipped with a broom and you should, at last, get a fall of snow too deep to overcome, you can fly south until you get to a latitude where snow is unknown and the home centers sell only those shovels that come with pails for use at the beach.

Listen to the Farmer's Calendar at Almanac.com/Podcast.

HOLIDAYS AND OBSERVANCES

2021 HOLIDAYS
FEDERAL HOLIDAYS ARE LISTED IN BOLD.

JAN. 1: New Year's Day

JAN. 18: Martin Luther King Jr.'s Birthday, observed

JAN. 20: Inauguration Day

FEB. 2: Groundhog Day

FEB. 12: Abraham Lincoln's Birthday

FEB. 14: Valentine's Day

FEB. 15: Presidents' Day
Susan B. Anthony's Birthday *(Fla.)*

FEB. 16: Mardi Gras *(Baldwin & Mobile counties, Ala.; La.)*

FEB. 22: George Washington's Birthday

MAR. 2: Texas Independence Day
Town Meeting Day *(Vt.)*

MAR. 8: International Women's Day

MAR. 14: Daylight Saving Time begins at 2:00 A.M.

MAR. 17: St. Patrick's Day
Evacuation Day *(Suffolk Co., Mass.)*

MAR. 29: Seward's Day *(Alaska)*

MAR. 31: César Chávez Day

APR. 2: Pascua Florida Day

APR. 19: Patriots Day *(Maine, Mass.)*

APR. 21: San Jacinto Day *(Tex.)*

APR. 22: Earth Day

APR. 30: National Arbor Day

MAY 5: Cinco de Mayo

MAY 8: Truman Day *(Mo.)*

MAY 9: Mother's Day

MAY 15: Armed Forces Day

MAY 22: National Maritime Day

MAY 24: Victoria Day *(Canada)*

MAY 31: Memorial Day, observed

JUNE 5: World Environment Day

JUNE 11: King Kamehameha I Day *(Hawaii)*

JUNE 14: Flag Day

JUNE 17: Bunker Hill Day *(Suffolk Co., Mass.)*

JUNE 19: Emancipation Day *(Tex.)*

JUNE 20: Father's Day
West Virginia Day

JULY 1: Canada Day

JULY 4: Independence Day

JULY 24: National Day of the Cowboy
Pioneer Day *(Utah)*

AUG. 1: Colorado Day

AUG. 2: Civic Holiday *(parts of Canada)*

AUG. 16: Bennington Battle Day *(Vt.)*

AUG. 19: National Aviation Day

AUG. 26: Women's Equality Day

SEPT. 6: Labor Day

SEPT. 9: Admission Day *(Calif.)*

SEPT. 11: Patriot Day

SEPT. 12: Grandparents Day

SEPT. 17: Constitution Day

SEPT. 21: International Day of Peace

OCT. 4: Child Health Day

OCT. 9: Leif Eriksson Day

OCT. 11: Columbus Day, observed
Indigenous Peoples' Day *(parts of U.S.)*
Thanksgiving Day *(Canada)*

OCT. 18: Alaska Day

OCT. 24: United Nations Day

OCT. 29: Nevada Day

OCT. 31: Halloween

NOV. 2: Election Day

NOV. 4: Will Rogers Day *(Okla.)*

NOV. 7: Daylight Saving Time ends at 2:00 A.M.

NOV. 10: U.S. Marine Corps Birthday

NOV. 11: Veterans Day
Remembrance Day *(Canada)*

NOV. 19: Discovery of Puerto Rico Day

NOV. 25: Thanksgiving Day

NOV. 26: Acadian Day *(La.)*

DEC. 7: National Pearl Harbor Remembrance Day

DEC. 15: Bill of Rights Day

DEC. 17: Wright Brothers Day

DEC. 25: Christmas Day

DEC. 26: Boxing Day *(Canada)* First day of Kwanzaa

Movable Religious Observances

JAN. 31: Septuagesima Sunday

FEB. 16: Shrove Tuesday

FEB. 17: Ash Wednesday

MAR. 27: Passover begins at sundown

MAR. 28: Palm Sunday

APR. 2: Good Friday

APR. 4: Easter

APR. 12: Ramadan begins at sundown

MAY 2: Orthodox Easter

MAY 9: Rogation Sunday

MAY 13: Ascension Day

MAY 23: Whitsunday–Pentecost

MAY 30: Trinity Sunday

JUNE 6: Corpus Christi

SEPT. 6: Rosh Hashanah begins at sundown

SEPT. 15: Yom Kippur begins at sundown

NOV. 28: First Sunday of Advent Chanukah begins at sundown

CHRONOLOGICAL CYCLES

–Beth Krommes

Dominical Letter **C**

Epact **16**

Golden Number (Lunar Cycle) **8**

Roman Indiction **14**

Solar Cycle **14**

Year of Julian Period **6734**

ERAS

ERA	YEAR	BEGINS
Byzantine	7530	September 14
Jewish (A.M.)*	5782	September 6
Chinese (Lunar) [Year of the Ox]	4719	February 12
Roman (A.U.C.)	2774	January 14
Nabonassar	2770	April 18
Japanese	2681	January 1
Grecian (Seleucidae)	2333	September 14 (or October 14)
Indian (Saka)	1943	March 22
Diocletian	1738	September 11
Islamic (Hegira)* [FCNA date]	1443	August 8
Bahá'í*	178	March 19

*Year begins at sundown.

Natural device stops a cold before it starts

New research shows you can stop a cold in its tracks if you take one simple step with a new device when you feel a cold about to start.

Colds start after cold viruses get in your nose. Viruses multiply fast. If you don't stop them early, they spread and cause misery.

But scientists have found a quick way to kill a virus. Touch it with copper. Researchers at labs and universities agree, copper is "antimicrobial." It kills microbes, such as viruses and bacteria, just by touch.

New research: Copper stops colds if used early.

That's why ancient Greeks and Egyptians used copper to purify water and heal wounds. They didn't know about viruses and bacteria, but now we do.

Scientists say the high conductance of copper disrupts the electrical balance in a microbe cell and destroys the cell in seconds.

Tests by the EPA (Environmental Protection Agency) show germs die fast on copper. So some hospitals tried copper for touch surfaces like faucets and doorknobs. This cut the spread of MRSA and other illnesses by over half, and saved lives.

The strong scientific evidence gave inventor Doug Cornell an idea. When he felt a cold about to start he fashioned a smooth copper probe and rubbed it gently in his nose for 60 seconds.

"It worked!" he exclaimed. "The cold never got going." It worked again every time. He has not had a single cold for 7 years since.

He asked relatives and friends to try it. They said it worked for them, too, so he patented CopperZap™ and put it on the market.

Soon hundreds of people had tried it. Nearly 100% said the copper stops their colds if used within 3 hours after the first sign. Even up to 2 days, if they still get the cold it is milder and they feel better.

Users wrote things like, "It stopped my cold right away," and "Is it supposed to work that fast?"

"What a wonderful thing," wrote Physician's Assistant Julie. "Now I have this little magic wand, no more colds for me!"

Pat McAllister, age 70, received one for Christmas and called it "one of the best presents ever. This little jewel really works." Now thousands have simply stopped getting colds.

Copper can also stop flu that starts in the nose if used right away and for several days. In a lab test, scientists placed 25 million live flu viruses on a CopperZap. No viruses were found still alive soon after.

People often use CopperZap preventively. Frequent flier Karen Gauci used to get colds after crowded flights. Though skeptical, she tried it several times a day on travel days for 2 months. "Sixteen flights and not a sniffle!" she exclaimed.

Businesswoman Rosaleen says when people are sick around her she uses CopperZap morning and night. "It saved me last holidays," she said. "The kids had colds going round and round, but not me."

Some users say it also helps with sinuses. Attorney Donna Blight had a 2-day sinus headache. She tried CopperZap. "I am shocked!" she said. "My head cleared, no more headache, no more congestion."

One man suffered seasonal sinus problems for years. It ruined family vacations and even dinners out with friends. His wife Judy bought CopperZaps for both of them. He was so skeptical he said, "Oh Judy, you are such a whack job!" But he finally tried it and the copper cleared up his sinuses right away. Judy and their daughter both said, "It has changed our lives."

Some users say copper stops nighttime stuffiness, too, if they use it just before bed. One man said, "Best sleep I've had in years."

People have used it on cold sores and say it can completely prevent outbreaks. You can also use it on cuts, or lesions to combat infections.

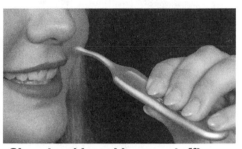

Sinus trouble, cold sores, stuffiness.

Copper even kills deadly germs that have become resistant to antibiotics. If you are near sick people, a moment of handling it may keep serious infection away. It may even save a life.

The EPA says copper still works even when tarnished. It kills hundreds of different disease germs so it can prevent serious illness.

CopperZap is made in the U.S. of pure copper. It has a 90-day full money back guarantee when used as directed to stop a cold. It is $69.95. Get $10 off each CopperZap with code **OFMA** at www.CopperZap.com or call toll-free 1-888-411-6114.

Buy once, use forever.

GLOSSARY OF ALMANAC ODDITIES

Many readers have expressed puzzlement over the rather obscure entries that appear on our **Right-Hand Calendar Pages, 121–147.** These "oddities" have long been fixtures in the Almanac, and are pleased to provide some definitions. Once explained, they may not seem so odd after all!

EMBER DAYS: These are the Wednesdays, Fridays, and Saturdays that occur in succession following (1) the First Sunday in Lent; (2) Whitsunday–Pentecost; (3) the Feast of the Holy Cross, September 14; and (4) the Feast of St. Lucia, December 13. The word *ember* is perhaps a corruption of the Latin *quatuor tempora,* "four times." The four periods are observed by some Christian denominations for prayer, fasting, and the ordination of clergy.

Folklore has it that the weather on each of the 3 days foretells the weather for the next 3 months; that is, in September, the first Ember Day, Wednesday, forecasts the weather for October; Friday predicts November; and Saturday foretells December.

DISTAFF DAY (JANUARY 7): This was the day after Epiphany, when women were expected to return to their spinning following the Christmas holiday. A distaff is the staff that women used for holding the flax or wool in spinning. (Hence the term "distaff" refers to women's work or the maternal side of the family.)

PLOUGH MONDAY (JANUARY): Traditionally, the first Monday after Epiphany was called Plough Monday because it was the day when men returned to their plough, or daily work, following the Christmas holiday. (Every few years, Plough Monday and Distaff Day fall on the same day.) It was customary at this time for farm laborers to draw a plough through the village, soliciting money for a "plough light,"

–Beth Krommes

which was kept burning in the parish church all year. This traditional verse captures the spirit of it:

Yule is come and Yule is gone,
and we have feasted well;
so Jack must to his flail again
and Jenny to her wheel.

THREE CHILLY SAINTS (MAY): Mamertus, Pancras, and Gervais were three early Christian saints whose feast days, on May 11, 12, and 13, respectively, are traditionally cold; thus they have come to be known as the Three Chilly Saints. An old French saying translates to "St. Mamertus, St. Pancras, and St. Gervais do not pass without a frost."

MIDSUMMER DAY (JUNE 24): To the farmer, this day is the midpoint of the growing season, halfway between planting and harvest. The Anglican Church considered it a "Quarter Day," one of the four major divisions of the liturgical year. It also marks the feast day of St. John the Baptist. (Midsummer Eve is an occasion for festivity and celebrates fertility.)

CORNSCATEOUS AIR (JULY): First used by early almanac makers, this term signifies warm, damp air. Although it signals ideal climatic conditions for growing corn, warm, damp air poses a danger to those affected by asthma and other respiratory problems.

DOG DAYS (JULY 3–AUGUST 11): These 40 days are traditionally the year's hottest and unhealthiest. They once coincided with the year's heliacal (at sunrise) rising of the Dog Star, Sirius. Ancient folks thought that the "combined heat" of Sirius and the Sun caused summer's swelter.

LAMMAS DAY (AUGUST 1): Derived from the Old English *hlaf maesse,* meaning "loaf mass," Lammas Day marked the beginning of the harvest. Traditionally, loaves of bread were baked from the first-ripened grain and brought to the churches to be consecrated. In Scotland, Lammastide fairs became famous as the time when trial marriages could be made. These marriages could end after a year with no strings attached.

CAT NIGHTS COMMENCE (AUGUST 17): This term harks back to the days when people believed in witches. An Irish legend says that a witch could turn into a cat and regain herself eight times, but on the ninth time (August 17), she couldn't change back and thus began her final life permanently as a cat. Hence the saying "A cat has nine lives."

HARVEST HOME (SEPTEMBER): In Britain and other parts of Europe, this marked the conclusion of the harvest and a period of festivals for feasting and thanksgiving. It was also a time to hold elections, pay workers, and collect rents. These festivals usually took place around the autumnal equinox. Certain groups in the United States, e.g., the Pennsylvania Dutch, have kept the tradition alive.

ST. LUKE'S LITTLE SUMMER (OCTOBER): This is a period of warm weather that occurs on or near St. Luke's feast day (usually October 18) and is sometimes called Indian summer.

INDIAN SUMMER (NOVEMBER): A period of warm weather following a cold spell or a hard frost, Indian summer can occur between St. Martin's Day (November 11) and November 20. Although there are differing dates for its occurrence, for more than 225 years the Almanac has adhered to the saying "If All Saints' [November 1] brings out winter, St. Martin's brings out Indian summer." The term may have come from early Native Americans, some of whom believed that the condition was caused by a warm wind sent from the court of their southwestern god, Cautantowwit.

HALCYON DAYS (DECEMBER): This period of about 2 weeks of calm weather often follows the blustery winds at autumn's end. Ancient Greeks and Romans experienced this weather at around the time of the winter solstice, when the halcyon, or kingfisher, was thought to brood in a nest floating on the sea. The bird was said to have charmed the wind and waves so that waters were especially calm at this time.

BEWARE THE POGONIP (DECEMBER): The word *pogonip* refers to frozen fog and was coined by Native Americans to describe the frozen fogs of fine ice needles that occur in the mountain valleys of the western United States and Canada. According to tradition, breathing the fog is injurious to the lungs. ■

–Beth Krommes

TEST YOUR SKY-Q

As a calendar of the heavens, this Almanac,
with Almanac.com/Astronomy, provides context
and helps you to scan the skies. Take this
quiz to gauge your knowledge of the universe.

Compiled by Bethany E. Cobb

FOR BEGINNER OBSERVERS

1. Which planets (not including Earth) can you easily see with the naked eye when they are up in the night sky?
a. Mercury, Venus, Mars
b. Mercury, Venus, Mars, Jupiter, Saturn
c. Venus, Mars, Jupiter, Saturn
d. Jupiter, Saturn, Uranus, Neptune

2. Why do astronomers use visible-light space–based telescopes like the Hubble Space Telescope (HST)?
a. These telescopes have a better view because they are nearer to the stars.
b. Because these telescopes are above the atmosphere, they can obtain clearer images than ground–based telescopes.
c. These telescopes are much larger than ground–based telescopes, so they can collect more light.
d. Digital imaging cameras work more efficiently in the coldness of space.

3. What causes the seasons?
a. The entire Earth is closer to the Sun in summer and farther from the Sun in winter.
b. The 23.5-degree tilt of Earth's axis results in one hemisphere of Earth being significantly closer to

the Sun in summer and significantly farther from the Sun in winter.
c. The 23.5-degree tilt of Earth's axis results in more direct sunlight and longer days in summer and less direct sunlight and shorter days in winter.
d. The Sun changes in brightness slightly over a year, being slightly brighter in summer and slightly dimmer in winter.

True or False?
4. Astronomers have detected hundreds of planets orbiting stars other than the Sun.

5. Astronomers have strong evidence that liquid water once flowed on Mars.

6. Astronomers have discovered conclusive proof that life once existed on Mars.

FOR INTERMEDIATE OBSERVERS
1. What was Galileo's major contribution to astronomy?
a. He invented the telescope.
b. He was the first to suggest that the Sun, not Earth, was the center of the solar system.
c. He used telescopes to

observe the phases of Venus and the moons of Jupiter, which helped to support the Sun-centered model of the solar system.
d. He developed the mathematics of gravity, which can be used to predict and explain the motions of the planets and stars in the universe.

2. Assume that you live on the Moon near the center of the side that faces Earth. When you see a "new" Earth in your sky, what phase of the Moon do people on Earth see?
a. New Moon
b. Crescent Moon
c. Full Moon
d. Third-quarter Moon

3. In which one of the following situations would total solar eclipses still occur?
a. The Moon orbits Earth at half its current distance.
b. The Moon is half its current diameter.
c. The Sun is twice its current diameter.
d. The Moon orbits Earth at twice its current distance.

True or False?
4. Astronomers have obtained direct images of extra-solar planets.

5. In about 5 billion years, the Sun will run out of hydrogen fuel and "die" in a supernova explosion.
(continued)

6. Astronomers have identified more than a dozen black holes in the Milky Way galaxy.

FOR ADVANCED OBSERVERS

1. What best describes the current rate of the expansion of the universe?
a. The expansion of the universe is slowing down (decelerating).
b. The expansion of the universe is speeding up (accelerating).
c. The expansion of the universe is constant (neither decelerating or accelerating).
d. The universe is not currently expanding.

2. Approximately what percent of the universe is composed of normal matter, the kind found in atoms, stars, planets, asteroids, humans, and this Almanac?
a. 100 percent
b. 75 percent
c. 50 percent
d. 5 percent

3. You are an alien observer who has installed spy telescopes on the Sun's equator to watch Earth. During your surveillance, what do you notice about

Earth's Moon?
a. The Moon is always in the full phase and never disappears behind Earth.
b. The Moon goes through a full set of phases and disappears behind Earth about twice a year.
c. The Moon is always in the full phase and disappears behind Earth about twice a year.
d. The Moon goes through a full set of phases and disappears behind Earth about once a month.

True or False?
4. If astronauts ever land on Mars, it will be possible to have a real-time conversation with them,

with a transmission delay of only a few seconds.

5. The solar system orbits the center of the Milky Way galaxy.

6. In about 4 billion years, the Milky Way galaxy and the Andromeda Galaxy will collide and combine to form a new galaxy.

ANSWERS TO "TEST YOUR SKY-Q"
Beginner
1. b. Planets are visible because they reflect sunlight. Uranus and Neptune are very far away—and thus very dim. You will always need a telescope to see Neptune, but if you know exactly where to

Illustration: den-belitsky

look on an extremely dark night (and have excellent eyesight), you might spot Uranus.

2. b. As light passes through inhomogeneities in the atmosphere, it gets bounced around, blurring images viewed through ground–based telescopes. HST, a 2.4–meter telescope, collects less light than larger (up to 10-meter), ground-based telescopes. However, because HST orbits above the atmosphere, it obtains much clearer images.

3. c. Seasons are caused by the tilt of Earth's axis. Summer is warmer because the Sun is above the horizon for a longer time and the sunlight is more direct, since the Sun is higher in the sky. Winter is cooler because days are shorter and the Sun is lower in the sky. If Earth had no axial tilt, we would not experience any seasonal variations!

4. True. More than 4,000 extrasolar planets have been confirmed, primarily by observing the gravitational influence that they exert on their parent stars and by the transit method. NASA's Kepler Space Telescope alone confirmed the existence of more than 2,000 via the transit method: It watched for the slight drops in stellar brightness that occur when planets cross between Earth and their parent stars.

5. True. It is believed that nearly 4 billion years ago, Mars was warmer and had a thicker atmosphere, allowing for liquid water to exist on its surface. Today, the surface shows now-dry valleys

Intermediate

1. c. Galileo was the first to use the telescope to systematically observe the night sky. His observations of moons orbiting Jupiter and the phases of Venus lent crucial support to the Copernican Revolution. (Copernicus first developed and published a "heliocentric" model of the solar system, which put the Sun, not Earth, at its center.) Galileo spent the last decade of his life under house arrest as a suspected heretic for supporting the heliocentric model.

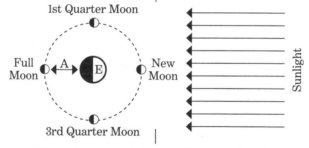

Figure 1. Answer to Intermediate question #2.

and channels that appear to have been carved by flowing water.

6. False. While Mars might have once been hospitable to life, no conclusive evidence exists to prove that life existed on Mars at any time.

2. c. To see a "new" Earth from the Moon, Earth must be directly between the Moon and the Sun. In that case, people on Earth would see a full Moon. See "A" view in *Figure 1*.

(continued)

3. a. For a total solar eclipse to occur, the apparent size of the Moon must be equal to or larger than that of the Sun. The Sun is physically larger than the Moon, but because it is farther away, it appears to be about the same size in the sky. If the Moon were closer, it would appear bigger and easily eclipse the Sun. Answers B, C, and D would all result in the Moon appearing smaller than the Sun, so only "annular" eclipses (in which a ring of full sunlight is visible around the Moon) could occur.

4. True. Stars greatly outshine planets, so taking a direct image of an exoplanet is extremely difficult—although it has indeed been accomplished in a number of cases.

5. False. While the Sun will run out of hydrogen fuel in its core in about 5 billion years, it isn't massive enough to undergo a spectacular supernova explosion.

6. True. While black holes can not be seen directly, their presence can be inferred by the gravitational influence that they have on a companion star. The Milky Way galaxy is also known to have at its center a supermassive black hole, one with a mass of more than 4 million Suns!

Advanced

1. b. Astronomers initially expected that the gravitational pull of the matter in the universe would be slowing down its expansion. In 1998, however, they measured that the universe's rate of expansion was increasing! While astronomers do not understand what is causing this accelerated expansion, they have labeled it "Dark Energy."

2. d. About 5 percent of the universe is made up of normal particles. Fully 23 percent of the universe is composed of "Dark Matter," which acts gravitationally like normal matter but does not emit light. The remaining 72 percent or so of the universe is the even more mysterious "Dark Energy."

3. c. Because the Sun illuminates the Moon, from your point of view, the Moon will always appear full. When Earth experiences a total lunar eclipse, the Moon will disappear behind Earth. This alignment occurs only about twice a year because the Moon's orbit is tilted.

4. False. When Mars and Earth are closest together, it will take a message about 3 minutes to travel one way. At greatest separation, it would take about 22 minutes!

5. True. The solar system orbits the supermassive black hole at the center of the Milky Way, completing one orbit every 200 million years!

6. True. Galaxies commonly undergo collisions. During this merger, the solar system will remain basically unaffected, but the night sky will change: The new galaxy will have more stars and a different shape. ■

Bethany E. Cobb is an associate professor of honors and physics at George Washington University.

Now available in the U.S. without a prescription!

Pill Used in Germany For 53 Years Relieves Joint Pain In 7 Days Without Side Effects

Approved by top doctors nationwide. Active ingredient numbs nerves that trigger pain. Relieves joint stiffness. Increases joint mobility and freedom.

By J.K. Roberts
Interactive News Media

INM — A pill that relieves joint pain and stiffness in 7 days without side effects has been used safely in Germany for 53 years. It is now available in the United States.

This pill contains an active ingredient that not only relieves pain quickly, but also works to rebuild damaged cartilage between bones for greater range of motion.

It can cut your pain relief costs up to 82% less than using pain relief drugs and pain relief cream and heat products.

An improved version of this pill is now being offered in the United States under the brand name FlexJointPlus.

FlexJointPlus relieves joint pain, back pain, neck pain, carpal tunnel, sprains, strains, sports injuries, and more. With daily use, users can expect to feel 24-hour relief.

"Relief in pain and stiffness is felt in as quickly as 7 days," said Roger Lewis, Chief Researcher for FlexJointPlus.

"And with regular use, you can expect even more reduction in the following 30-60 days," added Lewis.

WHAT SCIENTISTS DISCOVERED

FlexJointPlus contains an amazing compound with a known ability to rebuild damaged cartilage and ligaments associated with joint pain.

This compound is not a drug. It is the active ingredient in FlexJointPlus.

Studies show it naturally reduces inflammation while repairing bone and cartilage in the joint.

Many joint pain sufferers see an increase in flexibility and mobility. Others are able to get back to doing the things they love.

With so much positive feedback, it's easy to see why sales for this newly approved joint pain pill continue to climb every day.

IMPRESSIVE BENEFITS FOR JOINT PAIN SUFFERERS

The 8 week clinical study was carried out by scientists across six different clinic sites in Germany. The results were published in the Journal of Arthritis in July 2014.

The study involved patients with a variety of joint pain conditions associated with osteoarthritis. They were not instructed to change their daily routines. They were only told to take FlexJointPlus' active ingredient every day.

The results were incredible.

Taking FlexJointPlus' active ingredient just once daily significantly reduced both joint pain and stiffness compared to placebo at 7, 30, and 60 days.

In fact, many patients experienced greater than 50% reduction in pain and stiffness at 60 days.

They also enjoyed an improvement in stiffness when first getting out of the bed in the morning, and an improvement in pain when doing light household chores.

The findings are impressive, no doubt, but results will vary.

But with results like these it's easy to see why thousands of callers are jamming the phone lines trying to get their hands on FlexJointPlus.

HOW IT REBUILDS DAMAGED JOINTS

Scientists have discovered that after the age of 40 the body is no longer able to efficiently repair bone and cartilage in the joint. This results in deterioration and inflammation in the joint, leading to pain.

The natural compound found in FlexJointPlus contains the necessary ingredients needed for the body to rebuild damaged bone and cartilage.

This compound is known as 'NEM'®.

"Essentially, it contains the same elements found in your joints, which are needed to repair and rebuild cartilage and ligaments," explains chief researcher, Roger Lewis.

There also have been no adverse side effects reported with the use of NEM®.

This seems to be another reason why

Approved by U.S. Doctors: U.S. medical doctors are now recommending the powerful new pill FlexJointPlus. Participants in clinical studies reported noticeable results in just days.

FlexJointPlus' release has triggered such a frenzy of sales.

RECOMMENDED BY U.S. MEDICAL DOCTORS

"Based on my 20 years of experience treating people with osteoarthritis, FlexJointPlus receives my highest recommendation to any person suffering from joint pain and stiffness," said Dr. David Vallance, Rheumatologist from Ann Arbor, MI.

"I use FlexJointPlus every day for my stiff and aching joints. I also have my wife and daughter taking it regularly as well," said Dr. Oozer, G.P. from LaSalle, CA.

OLD FARMER'S ALMANAC READERS GET SPECIAL DISCOUNT SUPPLY

This is the official release of FlexJointPlus and so for a limited time, the company is offering a special discount supply to our readers. An Order Hotline has been set up for our readers to call, but don't wait. The special offer will not last forever. All you have to do is call TOLL FREE 1-800-540-7740. The company will do the rest.

IMPORTANT: Due to FlexJoint's recent media exposure, phone lines are often busy. If you call, and do not immediately get through, please be patient and call back. Current supplies of FlexJoint are limited, so consumers that don't get through to the order hotline will have to wait until more inventory is available. Call 1-800-540-7740 today!

WHEN
PREDATORS
COME
CALLING

WHAT TO EXPECT AND WHAT TO DO IN THE BACKYARD OR BARNYARD

BY JAN DOHNER

Many folks have engaged in a battle of wits with a raccoon or discovered bear damage to a cabin or beehive. Livestock and poultry owners are certainly very familiar with coyotes and other predators. The presence of animal predators large and small is growing as their populations and ranges extend right into our property. As a result, we are having more interactions with these animals. Gathering knowledge and using prevention strategies makes good sense. Let's take a look at a few of the most common animal predators. *(continued)*

Black Bears

Three species of bears live in North America: black, brown or grizzly, and polar. When European colonists arrived, black bears were found nearly everywhere, except in the deserts and arctic north. Experts believe that today's population of about 800,000 is nearly double their original number, despite the fact that they have been forced into smaller forested habitats.

Bears are the strongest large animals in North America—they can lift or drag objects much heavier than themselves. They often stand up to get a better look at things. Bears forage from dusk through night to avoid human contact. In late summer and early fall, they feed 20 hours per day in preparation for hibernation. Bear hibernation is actually a winter dormancy; they remain alert enough to be roused. Hunger makes them most unpredictable before and after hibernation.

Most interactions occur when humans move into bear habitat for recreation or housing. Bears will damage structures, crops, beehives, and orchards and occasionally kill livestock. Because reliance on human-provided food is dangerous to their long-term health, bears that become habituated to such sources are usually removed permanently.

SIGNS OF A VISIT
- Crushed vegetation and fur left in the area.
- Scat and hind foot tracks that resemble those of a human.
- Deep teeth and claw marks with extensive damage. Prey's carcass often skinned out.
- Remains not scattered after feeding; usually taken away and hidden nearby.

TO DETER
- Use electric fencing around beehives, buildings, pastures, and campsites.
- Use bearproof containers for food, scented items, and garbage.
- Clean outdoor cooking areas or fish-cleaning stations.
- Use round doorknobs, not levers, which bears can open.
- Cover compost piles.

Photo: Jillian Cooper/Getty Images

Coyotes

European colonists were familiar with the wolf and fox, but the coyote remained unknown until Meriwether Lewis (of Lewis & Clark fame) described him on the Great Plains in 1805. With deforestation and the loss of large predator competition, coyotes greatly expanded their range to fill the continent from coast to coast, even into urban areas. Experts can not even estimate the size of the current huge population.

Mating pairs often form lifelong bonds and may live in small family groups or packs. They have a large vocal repertoire and use howls to create social bonds and warn others off their territory. There are regional size differences between the smaller southwestern coyotes and their larger Eastern counterparts. Eastern coyotes possess small and varying amounts of wolf and dog DNA.

Most active at night and early morning, coyotes can habituate to human presence and food sources, although 90 percent of their diet is small animals, insects, fruit, and carrion. Coyotes are the most common farm and ranch predator, responsible for half of all young livestock deaths due to preda-tion. They also pose a threat to poultry, rabbits, and small pets. Coyotes consume garden crops, pet food, and garbage. Normally shy and reclusive, coyotes are most commonly encountered near open recreation land. *(continued)*

SIGNS OF A VISIT

- Feces are similar to dog scat but may include hair, feathers, bones, fruit, or seeds.
- Paw print is tighter and more oval than that of a dog.
- Prey are attacked with a bite to the top of head, throat, or back.
- Small animals go missing.
- Only one or two animals in a group killed.

TO DETER

- Persistently "haze," or frighten away.
- Walk dogs on a short leash to prevent an attack on the dog.
- Protect small animals and pets left alone in yards.
- Use livestock guardian dogs for stock protection.
- Cut down tall grass areas.

Raccoons

This animal family, including kinkajous and coatis, is found only in the Western Hemisphere. The northern raccoon, once found only in the wooded riverlands of the United States, has greatly expanded its range throughout most of United States and southern Canada, adapting to both urban and agricultural areas.

Raccoons can weigh from 4 to 40 pounds or more. Their hind legs are much longer than their front legs, giving them a hunched appearance. Raccoons are omnivores who usually forage at night. They do not deliberately wash their food but do so only because rubbing or dipping it in water helps them to gather more sensory information about what they are eating. Raccoons are clever and can open many latches and locks, solve complex tasks, and remember their solutions over time. Raccoons attack poultry or waterfowl, raid garbage or pet food, and eat garden or fruit crops. They are the most common complaint to pest removal agencies.

Warning: Raccoons are a major carrier of rabies and can transmit other serious diseases such as distemper. Handle raccoons and feces with gloves, wash and disinfect contaminated areas, and carefully dispose of feces, which may carry a potentially fatal parasite. Be especially cautious of raccoons spotted during the day. It is illegal to transport trapped raccoons in many areas due to the threat of disease.

SIGNS OF A VISIT
- Distinctive tracks on ground and structures.
- Scat size the same as that of a domestic cat but often contains fruit seeds.
- Several birds may be killed; heads may be bitten off.
- Eggs smashed and eaten in the nest or completely missing.

TO DETER
- Secure pet doors at night.
- Use raccoon-proof latches.
- Use hardware cloth, not chicken wire; cover all pens; and coop poultry or small animals at night.

Weasels

Members of the weasel family range in size from the least weasel, which can be 5 inches long and weigh 1 to 2 ounces, to the wolverine, which can weigh up to 40 pounds. Even though the animals that we commonly think of as weasels—such as the ermine—are relatively small, the family also includes minks, martens, fishers, and badgers. Agile, fast, and high-energy, weasels all have short legs; long, slender bodies; and nonretractable claws. Largely carnivorous and active both day and night, they are good climbers and have excellent senses of hearing, smell, and vision.

With a powerful bite, weasels can prey on animals larger than themselves, biting the back of the head and wrapping their body around their prey. Although other predators have this trait, the surplus killing of many animals at the same time is closely associated with weasels. This behavior is a response to abundant prey, especially in fall and winter, but can also be triggered in close quarters when animals panic and attempt to flee. *(continued)*

SIGNS OF A VISIT
- Tracks and scat are small, at 1½ inch or less.
- May leave tail drag marks.
- Eggs are eaten through a ½- to ¾-inch hole in the shell.
- May leave a pile of bodies, with only the head eaten.

TO DETER
- Use hardware cloth to cover openings in coops and pens, since weasels can slip through a 1-inch opening.

Raptors

The raptor family includes eagles, hawks, and vultures. As opposed to owls that hunt at night, raptors hunt by sight during the day or dusk. All raptors also scavenge carcasses. Long-lived and monogamous, raptors are highly adapted for soaring and equipped with sharp and strong hooked beaks and muscular legs. Female raptors are usually larger than the males—an example of reverse sexual dimorphism.

The only eagles found in North America are the bald and golden, but they are not closely related. Eagle eyesight is four to eight times better than humans' at distance, and they are able to spot a rabbit at 2 miles. With wind assistance, eagles are able to carry prey weighing up to 15 pounds. Larger prey may be eaten at the site or dismembered and carried away.

Hawks are 16 to 22 inches long and weigh 1 to 3 pounds. In other areas of the world, hawks are called buzzards, a name applied to vultures in North America. Among the most common hawks are the Cooper's, northern goshawk, red-tailed, and red-shouldered.

Vultures are primarily scavengers, but black vultures are an exception, actively preying on stock, poultry, and pets. Black vultures feed in groups, surrounding their prey. They are often attracted to carcasses first located by the turkey vulture, which has a greater sense of smell. Black vultures gather together in roosts as large as 1,000 birds, and their population and range are growing. ■

Jan Dohner lives on her family farm in Michigan. She is the author of *The Encyclopedia of Animal Predators* (Storey Publishing, 2017). Learn more at jandohner.com.

SIGNS OF A VISIT
- Entire bird or small animal may be missing, although some feathers may be left behind.
- Carcass may show talon punctures, which are deeper and less crushing than tooth punctures.

TO DETER
- Cover coops and runs.
- Cover larger areas with wire or reflective Mylar tape.
- Remove perching sites from the area and provide shelters for poultry.
- Use electric netting to cover areas for pastured poultry.
- Protect vulnerable newborn animals and their mothers.

Cooper's hawk

THE SAFE SIDE

To deter predators:
- Do not feed or encourage them.
- Secure all garbage and animal, bird, and pet feed—especially at night.
- Keep yards clean of refuse and clear brush near fences and buildings.
- Clean up fallen fruit or decaying vegetables and cover compost piles.
- Control rodent populations.
- Block access to potential hiding spaces.
- Use exclusion fencing around stock, poultry, gardens, and yards.
- Cover small animal runs, coop poultry at night, and use protected areas for stock at night.
- Use livestock guardians when appropriate.
- Warning: Lights and frightening devices work only temporarily.

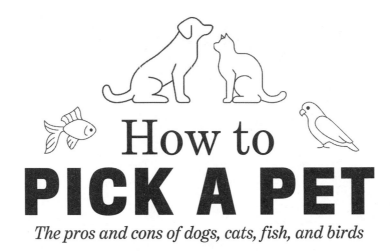

How to
PICK A PET

The pros and cons of dogs, cats, fish, and birds

BY JACK SAVAGE

L et it be said here that a life is not complete without the companionship of a beloved pet. Nearly 60 percent of households in the United States and Canada have pets of one kind or another. Most popular, of course, are dogs and cats. Almost 40 percent of U.S. households (41 percent in Canada) have at least one dog, with the average being 1.6 dogs. Apparently even half a dog is better than none. A quarter of all U.S. households have an average of 1.8 cats, or perhaps two cats who go missing 10 percent of the time, while in Canada, 38 percent of households have at least one cat.

Choosing a pet successfully requires knowing yourself and your lifestyle. Are you a dog person or a cat person? Or perhaps neither, and a fish or bird is more your style.

Pets take time and dedication. Will you really take the dog out for walks? Are you willing to clean your fish's tank?

Perhaps the best advice is to ask a trusted friend what kind of pet they think would be good for you. If they say "a bottle of wine on a leash," listen to them.

A good match between pet and pet owner/caretaker/provider may come as a result of natural symbiosis, an ideal complement of personalities and lifestyles. You get out of the relationship what you put into it. Your pet will live a better life thanks to your care, and they in turn will allow you to be a better person.

DOGS

DOGS are the best. Just ask the people who live with one (or 1.6). Not all dogs are the same, of course. If a dog's life is for you, read up on breeds and find a good match. There are apps (Barkbuddy or GetPet) where you can swipe right, and dogs never ghost you. If you already own a horse, you may feel inexplicably compelled to have a dog—80 percent of horse owners also own a dog.

WANT TO MEET SOMEONE NEW? DOGS ARE WAY BETTER THAN ONLINE DATING.

PROS

DOGS are known for their unconditional love and affection. Dogs make you happier. Resist intellectualizing dog love. Just revel in it.

DOGS get you outside, which is good for your well-being. (Pouring rain during the walk? *Woo-hoo!*) Remember, you're not taking the dog for a walk—he or she is taking you. Be grateful.

FOR dogs, the water bowl is always half-full. Kibble for breakfast? It's *the best!* Again for dinner? *Awesome!*

CONS

OK, there's the slobbering thing. And the eat-first-ask-questions-later thing, which leads to the puking thing. Then there's the not-quite-house-trained thing. Oh, and the watch-everything-you-do thing. Every. Thing. You. Do.

YOU have to run home after work to let a dog out. And then get up in the middle of the night to let it out. *(continued)*

DOGS SHED. THEY CHEW YOUR NEW SHOES. AND YOUR OLD SHOES.

CATS

CAT ancestors were solitary hunters. (Dogs evolved from pack-hunting wolves.) Even today, domestic cats are seen as more "independent" than dogs. This is among the reasons that many people find cats appealing as pets.

A CAT'S purr is created by the muscles that control the opening and closing of the vocal cords. As kittens, the purring reminds mama cat to keep nursing them; later in life, domestic cats purr to encourage you to pet them. Not only does a purring cat in your lap reduce stress, but also it is believed (by cat scientists) to have therapeutic healing effects on human muscle and bone tissue. House cats also "meow" in order to get attention.

PROS

CATS MAKE AWESOME YOUTUBE VIDEOS—THEY RULE THE INTERNET.

CATS are arguably less work than dogs; they can stay inside and be happy.

CATS chase a flashlight or laser on the wall. This is entertaining for you and the cat.

IF a cat does purr or meow or rub against you, you know that it is expressing affection.

CONS

YOU never really liked those floor-length curtains anyway, did you?

CATS don't fetch. They may leave a dead mouse at your feet, but that's about them, not you.

KITTY can be passive-aggressive; that broken lamp was no accident. And if cats could text, they wouldn't.

LITTER BOXES. ENOUGH SAID?

IF purring isn't for you, then consider the equally calming white noise of the bubbling fish tank. The well-curated aquarium makes an aesthetically pleasing statement in any home: pretty, colorful, exotic. Tropical fish are not very expensive, an aquarium doesn't take up a lot of space, and, at the bottom of the tank, you can stage scenes from your favorite pirate movie.

FISH

PROS

IF the cable goes out, you can always watch the aquarium.

KIDS love to gaze at fish in fish tanks and can be entertained for minutes at a time.

FISH TANKS HAVE TO BE CLEANED, AND THE WATER HAS TO BE MONITORED CAREFULLY— PH LEVEL, TEMPERATURE, AND SO ON. THIS TAKES WORK AND CAN BE MESSY.

YOU CAN WATCH THEM TO PRACTICE FOR "FISH FACE" SELFIES.

CONS

FISH do have to be fed daily and are hard-pressed to remind you.

YOU can't really pet a fish, and they can't sit in your lap. *(continued)*

BIRDS

BIRDS are fascinating to watch, and they often think the same about you. They're intelligent and have personality. They have evolved to flock, so they are naturally social: You can flock together even if your feathers don't match theirs.

PROS
THEY—OR RATHER, THEIR CAGES—DON'T TAKE UP MUCH ROOM.

THE cost to house and feed a bird is modest compared to room and board for other pets.

SOME birds say funny things or say things that are funny in a certain context. Like little brothers. Or like city folk when they visit a farm.

BIRDS like macaws can live up to 100 years, which means that you can leave them to your favorite (or least favorite) nephew or niece.

CONS

BIRDS can be messy and never clean up after themselves.

THEIR feed attracts mice.

THEY fly away.

BIRDS may well be gateway pets toward owning a snake, as 25 percent of snake owners also own a bird.

IF birds get sick, there are avian veterinarians, but it's not every vet practice that has a bird specialist on hand. In fact, find one on hand and they are worth two in the bush. ■

Jack Savage lives with his wife on Skydog Farm in New Hampshire, where they have been blessed with a menagerie of pets, farm animals, and surrounding wildlife.

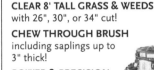

173

MAKE ROOM FOR MAPLE!

*Pure maple syrup (not to be confused with pancake syrup)
is a versatile ingredient. Here are some recipes for
making breakfast, lunch, and dinner just a little sweeter.*

BY SARAH PERREAULT, ALMANAC FOOD EDITOR

MAPLE GRANOLA

*This healthful granola is great with yogurt or
eaten straight out of the container!*

3½ cups old-fashioned rolled oats
⅔ cup maple syrup
½ cup shredded unsweetened coconut
½ cup chopped almonds (optional)
¼ cup vegetable oil
¼ cup pumpkin or sunflower seeds
1 cup raisins, dried cranberries, and/or dried cherries

Preheat oven to 225°F. Line a rimmed baking sheet with parchment paper.

In a bowl, combine oats, maple syrup, coconut, almonds (if using), oil, and pumpkin seeds. Spread on prepared baking sheet.

Bake until granola is golden brown, up to about 1½ hours. Remove from oven every 15 minutes to stir.

Transfer to a bowl and stir in raisins. When cooled, store in a container with a lid.

Makes about 6 cups.

THE HISTORY OF MAPLE SYRUP

We have Native Americans to thank for discovering maple syrup, although the exact telling of the tale varies. According to one legend, a chief stuck his tomahawk into a maple tree one spring night. In the morning, he pulled it out and went off hunting. His wife had placed a container under the tree, and the clear, watery sap dripped into it. Later, she needed water to cook some meat. She thought the liquid in the bucket was water, so she used it. As it cooked, the water evaporated until syrup was left. The sweet meat was the best that they had ever tasted, and soon the entire tribe was cooking with maple sap.

MAPLE-ORANGE GLAZED VEGETABLES

This easy glaze can be added to a variety of vegetables and is particularly good with baked squash—just brush it on during the last few minutes of cooking.

4 to 6 large carrots or parsnips,
  or a combination of both,
  peeled and cut into thick slices
1 tablespoon butter
¼ cup maple syrup
2 tablespoons frozen orange juice
  concentrate
pinch of salt
pinch of nutmeg
fresh thyme, for garnish

In a pot of salted, boiling water, cook carrots until tender but still firm. Drain and set aside.

In a skillet, melt butter. Add maple syrup, orange juice, salt, and nutmeg. Add carrots and stir until glazed, about 2 minutes.

Garnish with fresh thyme.

Makes 4 to 6 servings.

MAPLE MUSTARD

This spicy, sweet mustard is excellent for dipping veggies or pretzels. Add a little to mayonnaise for potato or pasta salads.

½ cup ground mustard
¼ cup brown sugar
2 teaspoons all-purpose flour
pinch of salt
½ cup maple syrup
¼ cup white vinegar

In a saucepan, combine mustard, brown sugar, flour, and salt. Stir in maple syrup and vinegar. Cook over medium heat, stirring with a whisk, until mixture boils and thickens slightly. Reduce heat and simmer for 2 minutes, stirring constantly. Cool and pour into small jars. Cover and store in the refrigerator.

Makes about ¾ cup.

Photos, from top: AnastasiaNurullina/Getty Images; La_vanda/Getty Images

MAPLE TERIYAKI CHICKEN

A hint of maple mellows the sweet-sour flavor of teriyaki.
For party food, prepare recipe using chicken wings.

¼ cup hoisin sauce
¼ cup soy sauce
¼ cup rice vinegar
¼ cup maple syrup
2 cloves garlic, minced
2 teaspoons minced
   fresh ginger
2 pounds chicken pieces
sesame seeds and sliced
   green onions, for
   garnish

In a bowl, combine hoisin sauce, soy sauce, vinegar, maple syrup, garlic, and ginger. Add chicken pieces and stir well to coat. Place in refrigerator for 2 to 6 hours.

Preheat oven to 375°F. Grease a baking sheet.

Arrange chicken on prepared baking sheet. Bake for 45 to 60 minutes or until well browned.

Garnish with sesame seeds and green onions.

Makes about 4 servings. ∎

HOW TO MAKE

Land that is left wholly to nature,
that has no improvement of
pasturage, tillage, or planting, is called,
as indeed it is, "waste."
–John Locke, English philosopher (1632–1704)

A FIELD

If you have unappreciated and/or overgrown land, here's how to regenerate it.

by Cynthia Van Hazinga

GOT A FIELD OF DREAMS?
Share your pics of it on 𝑷 @almanac
and 🅞 @theoldfarmersalmanac

BEFORE TACKLING ANY LAND RENOVATION, CONSIDER THE POSSIBILITIES. Walk around your property. Is the land rough, rocky, or sandy? Are there trees, shrubs, or saplings greater than 2 inches in diameter? Are there stumps left from logging? Wet spots? Think, dream, and scheme: How do you want to use the land? Perhaps you'd like to look out over an open green space or cultivate vegetables or flowers. Maybe you want to provide a habitat for birds or other wildlife. Do you want to sell hay? Pasture a horse or cow?

LEARN ALL YOU CAN

Begin regeneration by learning all you can about your land. Talk to neighbors or check town records to learn its prior use. Has it ever been used for a woodlot or to grow hay or vegetable crops? What use has been successful in the past?

Ken Van Hazinga, an organic grain farmer in western Vermont for more than 30 years (and my cousin), says that knowing the history of your land can be extremely helpful: "If you have a field next to a barn, for instance, it's likely to be rich, as it would likely have been spread heavily with manure. A field that grew corn is not as fertile as one that grew hay. These will be small changes in soil composition and

fertility, but over the years, they add up."

"Old-time farmers really knew their soil. Instead of watching TV, they watched the soil," says Van Hazinga. He recommends consulting the Farm Service Agency (FSA, part of the U.S. Department of Agriculture),

which often has crop records that have usually been saved at the county level. Soil maps, rigorously maintained by the FSA, add more relevant information. "These maps differentiate types of soil to even 10 feet, and they are constantly rechecking and re-calibrating them," Van Hazinga adds.

Soil testing is critical to understanding the earth's character and fertility. Rick Kersbergen, a University of Maine Extension educator, recommends taking at least 10 soil samples in neglected pastures. Your county's Cooperative Extension agent or Web site can help you with a test and suggest how to meet your soil's needs. Follow recommendations closely.

DIG IN

Assess your resources as well as your plans. Consider your time, money, and equipment.

If your land is forested, you'll have to cut trees (or hire a forester to do it) and then deal with stumps. It's a multistep process. A Bobcat or a bulldozer with a rock rake is usually required to remove large rocks and stumps, but more tillage operations may be in order. Plan to chip-cut branches and twigs for mulch or gather them into a burn pile.

Doing the work yourself can save money but take longer than if you enlist help and serious machinery. In moderately overgrown fields, you may get good results (e.g., success in clearing) with a mower attached to the back of a tractor, aka a brush hog. Likely you'll need to mow more than once.

Land that is free of small trees, stumps, or shrubs—merely abandoned and depleted—may require other machinery. Van Hazinga much prefers using a disk harrow to employing a moldboard plow; the plow turns up about 7 inches of soil, completely inverting it. "A disk harrow mixes growth—hay stems, weeds, and roots—in the top couple of inches" he says, "allowing for aerobic decomposition and the growth of bacteria and microflora, which actually feed the plants in a constant exchange. Photosynthesis powers the whole system, creating oxygen as it grows and decays."

You'll need patience, perseverance, and a very sharp spade and hatchet, plus safety gear, to clear overgrown land by hand. Small rocks may call for handpicking. Woody stumps need special attention: Cut stumps close to the ground, then burn them or fill drilled holes with salt to kill them. Or use a mechanical stumper with a mulching head to grind stumps into sawdust.

(continued)

CULTIVATE COVER CROPS

Once unwelcome plants, stones, and stumps have been removed, plant a restorative cover crop to outmaneuver the weeds that are ready to reclaim space. Be aware that eliminating established perennial weeds takes time because you

PHACELIA

must watch for eager new seedlings—and these tend to be numerous. First come perennial weeds and grasses like dandelions, milkweed, or burdock, followed by woody species: tree seedlings, exotic invaders such as Russian olives and Japanese barberries, and invasive brambles such as wild raspberries or thorny multiflora roses.

"It takes 2 or 3 years to clear overgrown space of unwanted plants and restore its ability to grow good vegetables," explains writer and home gardener Barbara

Pleasant, who renovated several of her previously logged acres in Floyd, Virginia. "You'll be humbled by the number of weeds and thug plants that quickly come back to life."

Cover-cropping is especially important if your goal is field regeneration to establish an

orchard or vineyard, grow vegetables or berries, or create habitats for wildlife. Animals from turtles to rabbits to bobolinks need edge-of-field native-plant habitats as well as open fields and thrive where there are wildflowers, hedges, nesting boxes, and small ponds.

Many plants work as soil-enriching cover crops. In spring or early fall, you might sow vigorous but controllable phacelia (aka leafy tansy) to form a dense carpet. It produces nectar-rich flowers when days are longer than 13 hours, and it's so beloved by bees that it's sometimes called

Bee's Friend. Buckwheat is a good summer cover crop. Fast-growing mustard, best as a fall crop, likes a cool climate, as does winter rye. When these cover crops flower but before they go to seed, till them into the soil. They will provide a layer of mulch to feed the soil food web as they decompose.

To revive and revitalize hay fields, Van Hazinga plants cover crops of clover and timothy. "It's not a good idea to cut all of the hay in a field," he says. "Let the grasses build up a root reserve. Three or four cuttings a year, not giving the plants a chance to renew themselves, is what has exhausted old hayfields." It's much better, he says, to let the hay grow and allow the soil to develop bacteria, fungi, and microflora.

For his wheat fields, Van Hazinga's favorite cover crop is more wheat. "If you have tree stumps, rye is probably better, but it can cause roots to clump, and wheat is higher in nutrition. For growing vegetables, I'd definitely choose wheat.

"As far as cover crops go, everything depends on your circumstances, and they change so radically. You have to figure out what's best each time. You really can't reduce it to a science. This is why farming is an art."

GENERATIONAL REGENERATION

We all benefit from regenerating land with an eye to a sustainable future. North Dakota farmer Gabe Brown subscribes to a holistic philosophy of farming in nature's image. Author of *Dirt to Soil* (Chelsea Green Publishing, 2018), Brown practices regenerative agriculture through a strategy of diverse cover and companion crops on his family's 5,000-acre ranch just east of Bismarck. Brown has seen the health of his soil and mineral and water cycles improve, providing a higher quality of life both for his family and for their cattle and sheep, while increasing production and profit. "We are moving toward sustainability not only for our future, but for future generations," Brown says. "It's the only way to go."

BECKON THE BARNYARD

Consider getting four-legged or feathered foragers to help you regenerate your land and keep it free of weeds. "Animals are still the best way for clearing land," says Van Hazinga, who hosts a neighbor's flock of sheep. "They work all the time. You need good fences, you can't let them stray, they need some care, and in some cases you have to feed them, but they root and fertilize without stopping."

Benefits of barnyard helpers:
• Sheep eat close to the ground, keep grass down, and help to eliminate weeds.
• Goats browse and eat thickets, underbrush, and other unwanted growth.
• Pigs till and fertilize the ground. Consider moving their pens frequently.
• Poultry break up soil and consume a wide variety of plant matter, as well as feast on insects.
• Cows are fussy eaters and require rich pastures to keep their production stable.

Rebecca Holland of Holland Homestead in New Hampshire, who has kept goats to clear rough land, adds: "Make sure that there are no poisonous plants on the land. Rhododendrons and azaleas are deadly to goats." ∎

Cynthia Van Hazinga, from a farming family, has always been interested in fields as well as flour and flowers. The author of 14 books, she can often be found in Greenwich Village (NYC) or New Hampshire.

TIME-TESTED TIPS
FOR FIGHTING COLDS AND FLU

Almost everyone gets colds and/or the flu (or "a" flu; there are many types) at some point in life. We've identified ways to lessen the chances of getting one or both of these, plus ways to endure them with as few ill effects as possible.

WHAT'S THE DIFFERENCE BETWEEN A COLD AND THE FLU?

Both illnesses are caused by viruses. Viruses are tiny microbes (1/900 the width of a human hair) that can infect plants and animals. The symptoms of each are different (e.g., the effects of a cold are usually far less severe than those of a flu). There is no "cure" for either one, but there are ways to ameliorate the conditions.

COLD VS. FLU

SIGNS AND SYMPTOMS	COLD	FLU
Symptom onset	Gradual	Abrupt
Fever	Rare	Usual
Aches	Slight	Usual
Chills	Uncommon	Fairly Common
Fatigue, weakness	Sometimes	Usual
Sneezing	Common	Sometimes
Chest discomfort, cough	Mild to moderate	Common
Stuffy nose	Common	Sometimes
Sore throat	Common	Sometimes
Headache	Rare	Common

–U.S. Centers for Disease Control and Prevention (CDC)

HOW TO AVOID THE FLU

1. Wash your hands frequently—the right way. (See "How—and When—to Wash Your Hands.")

2. Keep current on all inoculations (including a flu shot) and medications.

3. Eat a healthy diet.

4. Don't share food or drinks.

5. Drink plenty of liquids, especially water.

6. Get plenty of sleep.

7. Spend some time outdoors.

8. If you feel fine, exercise.

9. If someone sneezes or coughs without covering, avoid the air that they have just contaminated.

10. In public spaces such as restrooms, use paper towels or tissues to touch the faucet and door handles. Use your shoulder to open non-handled doors.

11. Avoid direct contact with handrails, handles, buttons, and the like in public spaces.

12. Avoid handshakes and hugs, and no kissing, even on cheeks!

13. Do not share washcloths or towels.

14. Avoid touching your fingers to your eyes, nose, mouth, or face.

15. Don't bite your nails. *(continued)*

Illustrations: Getty Images

HOW–AND WHEN– TO WASH YOUR HANDS

• Use lots of soap and lots of water. (The water temperature is not important.)

• Allow for 2 minutes (or, at least, 20 seconds) of vigorous scrub time after lathering.

• Scrub not only palms and fingers, but also the backs of hands, the skin between the fingers, and wrists. Use a nailbrush to scrub beneath fingernails.

When to wash your hands . . .

• Before and after they are near your face

• Before eating and cooking, and after handling any meat or garbage

• After using the bathroom, blowing your nose, and sneezing into a hand

• After changing diapers

• After touching animals or cleaning up after them

To avoid fall fevers, eat moderately, drink sparingly [not advised today],
lie not down on the damp earth, nor overheat yourself; but keep your
temper, and change your clothes as the weather changes.
–The Old Farmer's Almanac, *1852*

IF YOU GET THE FLU . . .

1. Contact your health provider to find out the best way to receive treatment.

2. Follow your health provider's instructions for easing your symptoms.

3. If you can, rest as soon as symptoms develop.

4. Wash your hands often to avoid contaminating those close to you.

5. Stay well hydrated.

6. Eat a healthy diet, especially fruit that's high in vitamin C, and veggies and grains (these help to cleanse your system).

7. Avoid sugars and alcoholic drinks.

8. Use a humidifier if the air is dry.

9. Sit in a steamy bathroom to ease congestion.

10. Stay at home if you are sick.

11. Cover your mouth and nose with a tissue when you sneeze or cough and discard the tissue. Don't have a tissue? Cough into your upper sleeve or elbow.

12. Clean and disinfect any surfaces that you may have touched.

13. Avoid contact with the elderly and those with weakened immune systems.

14. Avoid stress. Focus on doing things that will lead to wellness.

15. Be optimistic. A positive attitude always works wonders!

WHEN A COLD COMES ON . . .

1. Cook with and eat onions; they may have antibacterial qualities.

2. Got chills? Take fresh gingerroot.

3. Drink rose hip tea; it contains vitamin C and can help to relieve cold symptoms.

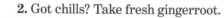

4. Consume prunes; they are rich in fiber, vitamins A and B, iron, calcium, and phosphorus.

5. Consume lemons, oranges, and apple cider.

6. Eat hot and spicy foods like chili to clear the sinuses.

7. Use horseradish; it generates lots of "heat" to help offset colds.

8. Add chopped garlic cloves to foods or consume small chunks of raw garlic as you would pills. This may reduce the frequency of colds.

SPICE UP YOUR LIFE—AND FEEL BETTER

TURMERIC *(CURCUMA LONGA)*
The active healing ingredient in golden-yellow hued turmeric is called curcumin, which studies show is an anti-oxidant and anti-inflammatory.

Add a teaspoon of turmeric to scrambled eggs or rice or sprinkle into soups, stews, or smoothies.

GINGER *(ZINGIBER OFFICINALE)*
Ginger is a pungent spice rich in phytonutrients known as gingerol. These are responsible for its pungency and its anti-oxidant, anti-inflammatory, and anti-viral properties. It also has anti-nausea properties.

Take ginger as tea: Allow a few slices of peeled fresh ginger root to steep in a cup of hot water. Ginger also can be added to baked goods, soups, stews, or smoothies.

THYME *(THYMUS VULGARIS)*
The antiseptic and antimicrobial properties found in thyme come from its thymol, a volatile oil that is a common ingredient in mouthwashes. The properties of thymol lend themselves to killing germs and fighting infection.

Using more thyme in cooking is easy: Just add to taste. Also, it is prominent in French *herbes de provence* and *bouquets garnis,* many Cajun blends, and the Middle Eastern spice blend called *za'atar.* ■

–Melissa Spencer

Illustrations: Getty Images

THE MOST
PRACTICED SPORT
IN THE WORLD
(for which no fancy gear is needed)

BY MARTIE MAJOROS

Who hasn't stood at the edge of a lake and hunted around for the perfect stone to skip over the water? Once one person does it, everyone wants to try. Soon, it's a friendly competition to see who can get the most skips from a single stone.

This age-old pastime was cited by the ancient Roman philosopher Minucius Felix in his *Octavius*. He described a group of young boys at the seashore vying with one another to see who could throw stones into the sea the farthest and with the most skips. It's reported that ancient Greeks used oyster shells instead of stones. Today, Arctic peoples skip stones on ice, while Bedouins skim stones on sand.

In Scotland, the hobby is known as "ducks and drakes," with a duck being a first skip and drakes, the subsequent ones. In Russia, the sport is known as baking pancakes; in Japan, cutting water; and in Sweden, throwing a sandwich.

MEET THE COMPETITION

The popularity of stone skipping or skimming has led to international competitions, with events in Japan, Scotland, Switzerland, the Netherlands, and Wales. The criteria vary for each contest; some count the number of skips, while others measure the distance that a stone travels as it skims across the water. The current distance records were set in 2018 at Abernant Lake, Wales: for women, 172 feet by Switzerland's Nina Luginbuhl; for men, 400 feet by Scotland's Dougie Isaacs.

The North American Stone Skipping Association (NASSA), founded in 1989 by Jerdone Coleman McGhee, sponsors annual U.S. championship tournaments on Mackinac Island, Michigan, and in Franklin, Pennsylvania. Both contests rely on the greatest number of skips to determine a winner. McGhee's enthusiasm was inspired while walking on a beach in Spain one evening. As he

DID YOU KNOW?

Maritime lore claims that throwing stones into the sea from a boat will cause storms and large ocean swells.

stopped to cast stones into the water, a crowd gathered and cheered as one of the rocks appeared to skip endlessly into the sunset. A short time later, he founded NASSA.

Decades before that, in 1969, residents of Mackinac Island, Michigan, were already celebrating the lure of stone skipping with their first annual Stone Skipping and Gerplunking Tournament, an event created by Michigan Upper Peninsula (U.P.) resident Bill Rabe. Every July 4, the event draws enthusiasts from throughout the United States who compete in professional, amateur, and children's contests. In the pro category, participants throw six stones. Six judges observe and count the number of skips for each throw. The scores are averaged to give a single final score. Victory is sweet for the winner, whose prize is a year's supply of fudge—about 4 pounds per month.

Children 12 and younger compete in the gerplunking division. Each child throws just one stone, and the stone with the best "gerplunking" sound is declared the winner.

In recent years, the event has been covered by ESPN, with Michigan native Eric Steiner providing commentary. Steiner's son, Max "Top Gun" Steiner, claimed the 2019 title with 20 skips, besting Guinness World Record holder Kurt "Mountain Man" Steiner (no relation), who scored a mere 18 skips. The 2019 scores were a bit lower than usual, as competitors had to deal with the unusually choppy waters of Lake Huron and the appearance of a family of ducks swimming in the area.

ROCK STARS

The sport—at least on Mackinac Island—is indebted to two legendary ambassadors: Bill Rabe and U.S. Navy Commander Tom Tellefson. In 2011, both men were inducted into the Is-

---

ROCK-ET SCIENTISTS

1. NASA physicists use stone-skipping principles to model a spacecraft's reentry into the atmosphere. For a safe reentry, a spacecraft needs to enter Earth's dense atmosphere at a precise angle and speed. If it hits the atmosphere at too steep an angle or with too much speed, it could burn up. If it enters the atmosphere at too

Sir Barnes Wallis

shallow an angle, it could bounce back into space.

2. Sir Barnes Wallis, a World War II British engineer, relied on the physics of stone skipping to invent circular bombs that spun while they were in the air and could bounce across water before sinking right before they hit their target. In 1943, the bombs were used successfully to attack Germany's Mohne and Eder dams and power stations.

THE PERFECT PITCH

The two most important factors for any aspiring stone skipper to keep in mind are spin and speed. When a thrown stone has spin, the rotational force helps to stabilize its plane in relation to the water. The speed of the stone keeps it from sinking. With enough spin and speed, the stone bounces off the surface to skip again. However, with each subsequent skip, the stone loses speed because of the friction created by contact with the air and water. As the friction increases, the speed decreases, and the stone eventually sinks.

Research has shown that in addition to carrying adequate spin and speed, stones that

enter the water at a 10- to 20-degree angle have the best chance of producing multiskip throws. (Yes, professional and amateur scientists have studied stone skipping.)

To up your skips, try some of these tips from the pros:
• Choose a uniformly thick, oval stone that's neither too heavy nor too light. Rectangular stones tend to go off at an angle; triangular stones do best on choppy water.
• Hold it between your thumb and index finger. It should fit easily in the palm of your hand.
• Throw the stone quickly, flicking your wrist as you release it to add spin.
• Aim to keep the stone parallel with and as close to the surface as possible when it hits the water.
• The stone should enter the water no more than 15 feet from shore, at an angle of between 10 and 20 degrees.
• Hold a few stones in your nonthrowing hand for a counterweight.
• For best results, try skipping in the morning or evening, when waters are usually calmer.

land's Stone Skipping Hall of Fame.

Rabe founded the Mackinac Island Stone Skipping and Gerplunking Club. As tournament director and publisher of the stone-skipping journal *The Boulder,* he promoted the sport throughout the U.P.

Tellefson, regarded as the "grand old man of stone skipping," began his skipping career with an impressive 17 skips in 1932. For many years until his death in 2008, he opened the Island tournament with his traditional call that continues to this day: "Let he who is without Frisbee cast the first stone!"

"Mountain Man" Steiner set a record for the *Guinness Book of World Records* with 88 skips in 2013 in Kane, Pennsylvania, with a stone estimated to have traveled at 43 miles per hour. ■

Martie Majoros is a graduate of the University of New Hampshire who lives in Burlington, Vermont.

How to Clean Your Chimney

The down-and-dirty details of how one couple got stuck between a rock and a hard place.

BY TIM CLARK

ILLUSTRATION BY TIM ROBINSON

Cleaning a chimney is a dirty job. Ordinarily, I would not dream of taking on such a task by myself. But when my wife and I moved into a charmingly ramshackle cottage in New Hampshire several years ago, we discovered that our chimney (to which a woodstove, our sole source of heat, was to be connected) had not been cleaned. Ever. My wife insisted that we do it ourselves. Being half thrifty Yankee and half practical Midwesterner, she had no sympathy for my horizontalist tendencies.

But how to do it? I vaguely remembered reading about the methods of chimney sweeps and promptly set about constructing a wire brush that could be dragged with a rope up and down the flue, thus scouring it clean. Within a few minutes, I had assembled, with chicken wire and bricks (for weight), a device that resembled a piece of modern sculpture.

My wife eyed the monstrosity dubiously but said nothing. This was early in our married life, and she had not yet learned to recognize the fatal point at which my knowledge of the facts runs out and unrestrained whimsy begins.

I explained that the next step was to drop a weighted rope down the chimney. The wire brush would be attached to the rope at the bottom end (where there was a door for cleaning out ashes and such), and then we would simply haul the brush up and down, cleaning the chimney without dirtying our hands. The whimsy was in full control by now.

While she waited in the basement, I mounted the roof, equipped with a rope and a rock about the size of a grapefruit. I wrapped one end of the rope around the rock, tied a knot, and then dropped it into the chimney.

The rock fell about 4 feet and then stopped, stuck in the constricted opening. It was clearly too large. So I pulled up the rope to try again with a smaller rock.

All I got was rope. My knot had apparently slipped off.

The rock was too far down the chimney to reach with my arms. I spied on the roof a long 2x4 that the previous owners had used to hammer open a passageway for the smoke. With the madness of those whom the gods would destroy, I picked it up and began thumping the rock, hoping, I suppose, to force it down the flue with mighty strokes, like a colonial soldier loading his musket. Of course, I succeeded in wedging the rock irretrievably into the maw of the chimney.

When my wife finally came out from under the house to find out what was happening, I was sitting on the rooftop in an attitude of despair. I could think of no way

The creosote spilled out of the flue like a bituminous shower. I pushed and pulled, singing coal mining songs between coughing fits.

of getting the rock out, short of dismantling the chimney brick by brick. It seemed to be a choice of that, selling the house, or installing a whole new heating system. Jumping off the roof also crossed my mind.

Fortunately, my wife is made of sterner stuff. She quickly sized up the problem and came up with an ingenious solution.

Following her instructions, I returned to the ground (by the ladder) and cut down a sapling tree, about 20 feet in height and no more than 2 inches thick at the base. I dragged it into the living room, where the hole in the chimney for the woodstove was, and pushed the supple tree up into the flue. By forcing it up and then pulling it back down rapidly, I could use the sapling like a giant pipe cleaner. The room began to fill with creosote dust. All the while, my wife was sitting atop the chimney, diligently chipping at the creosote around the rock with a knife lashed to a broomstick.

The creosote spilled out of the flue like a bituminous shower. I pushed and pulled, singing coal mining songs between coughing fits.

After an hour or so of toil, there was a minor avalanche, and my wife cried out that the rock had disappeared. It had, in fact, fallen past the hole in the chimney where I was working, and lodged itself a few feet farther down. I pulled my sapling out of the flue, took it to the basement cleaning door, and set back to work.

Clunk. There in the heaped-up creosote shavings was a black grapefruit. I seized it with a triumphant cry, coughed again, and marched out into the sunlight with my by-now-defoliated sapling.

From the roof, my wife shouted that I should go back in and look up the chimney. When I did, I discovered that I could see her grinning down from the top. The chimney was clean as a whistle. In our desperation to get the rock out, we had entirely forgotten our original intent. But now we had a spotless flue—far cleaner, I suspect, than it might have been without the rock crisis. We had had incentive, you see.

So, if you want a chimney that you can be proud of and you are skeptical of your staying power at the job, do as I did. Drop a rock in it. Leave yourself no alternative.

Or call a chimney sweep. ∎

Tim Clark still relies on wood to help heat his home in Dublin, New Hampshire.

SECRET Symbols
of CEMETERIES

By Courtney Henderson

A walk through a cemetery when researching ancestors can be a haunting yet beautiful and reflective experience. Aside from the names, birthdates, and death dates, what other secrets might their tombstones reveal?

Those majestic, weather-worn stone carvings that you see (popularized by those cipher-loving Victorians from 1839 to 1920) are more than pure decoration. They mean something: a virtue the person ex-

emplified, a value they held dear, or a nod to how they earned their living.

The table opposite gives the meanings behind 21 popular gravestone symbols. (There are many more.) A revelation about your ancestor's life may just be right in front of you, hidden in plain sight!

Courtney Henderson is the digital editor of our sister publication *Family Tree* magazine. For much more information about all things genealogical, go to Familytreemagazine.com.

MEANINGS OF GRAVESTONE SYMBOLS

SYMBOL	MEANING
ACORN	Prosperity; power; triumph
ANCHOR; SEXTANT	Mariner
ANVIL AND HAMMER	Blacksmith
BASKET	Fertility; maternal bond
BIRD	Flight of the soul
CANDLE	Life
COLUMN/PILLAR (BROKEN)	Life cut short; sudden death
EVERGREEN	Faithfulness; remembrance
FERN	Sincerity; humility; solitude
FRUIT	Eternal plenty
IHS MONOGRAM	Christian; name of Jesus
KEY	Knowledge; entrance into heaven
LAMP	Knowledge; spiritual immortality
LILY	Innocence, purity, and the resurrection (Easter); marriage and fidelity (calla); innocence and humility (lily-of-the-valley)
OAK LEAF	Strength; stability; endurance
OLIVE TREE	Peace; reconciliation between God and man
PALM	Life conquering death
PLOW; HOE; RACK; STALK OF CORN; SHOCK OF WHEAT	Farmer
ROSE	Love; beauty; virtue; strong bond (intertwined); youthful death (rosebud)
SPHINX	Courage; honor; power
TREE-SHAPED	Possible member of the Modern Woodmen of America or Woodmen of the World fraternal organization member ∎

CONVINCING SIGNS

By Celeste Longacre

ARIES
(MARCH 21–APRIL 20)

Individuals born under this sign jump into things. When seeking help from an Aries friend, be ready to begin immediately; they will want to get started right away. If the details are not final, they can help with the planning; be sure that you have something for them to do now. Otherwise, wait to involve this individual until everything is set to move forward.

Be ready to begin immediately; Aries will want to get started right away.

TAURUS
(APRIL 21–MAY 20)

Taurean individuals look for value. They want to know that something is worth doing and how they will benefit. Approach them with details in a written proposal. Identify the steps that need to be taken, approximate the time necessary to accomplish the goal, and estimate the reward. These people will want to think it over before committing, so give them time.

Approach Taureans with details in a written proposal.

GEMINI
(MAY 21–JUNE 20)

Geminis will want to participate in a project that is captivating and fun. These individuals become bored easily, so present the project through several avenues of expression and in different pieces. They love a process that involves humor. If you can convince them that it will be light and lively, you will have a solid partner. Don't expect them to sign on for a dull trudge or a tedious plan.

If you can convince a Gemini that it will be light and lively, you will have a solid partner.

**WANT TO ENLIST OR ENGAGE SOMEONE IN A PROJECT?
PLAY TO THEIR STRENGTHS AND
EXPECTATIONS, BASED ON THEIR ZODIAC SIGN.**

CANCER
(JUNE 21-JULY 22)

Cancers are dedicated to their homes and families. If you can convince these sensitive individuals that your idea will be of benefit to those around them, they will take it into consideration. To spark their interest, offer specific benefits (e.g., financial gain, ability to work from home). Gentle persuasion works best; forcefulness turns them off.

Cancers want ideas that will benefit those around them.

LEO
(JULY 23-AUGUST 22)

Leos enjoy the spotlight. These individuals are naturally talented, so let them know that their help would be invaluable. They like to have a hand in the details; if you can defer to them in any way, even better. As the project moves forward, compliment their progress. They want their efforts to be noticed and appreciated. With regular pats on the back, these people will continue to give until complete success is achieved.

Leos like to have a hand in the details.

VIRGO
**(AUGUST 23-
SEPTEMBER 22)**

Virgos like order and precision. These individuals want to see the progression, step by step, as well as the final outcome. Writing a proper prospectus could ensure success. If you can present your idea as a perfect fit into one of their own plans and show how the project benefits them, even better. Iron out all of the details ahead of time; these people will spot a flaw instantly.

Virgos like order and precision.

(continued)

LIBRA
(SEPTEMBER 23– OCTOBER 22)

Libras thrive on relationships. These individuals want to live, work, and play in partnerships. They have a strong sense of art and design. To make your plan most attractive, present it as a group endeavor with the highest aesthetic qualities. Emphasize that you can use their tactfulness and diplomacy and offer sincere compliments; they will be appreciated.

Libras want to live, work, and play in partnerships.

SCORPIO
(OCTOBER 23– NOVEMBER 22)

Scorpios are passionate and driven to succeed. These individuals will want to know that you have a plan and a backup plan and that all of the details have been addressed. Results are important: Delineate the benefits and advantages in ___concrete, precise language, and you will catch their attention. These people enjoy a challenge if it is reasonable and doable. Show strength.

Scorpios will want to know that you have a plan and a backup plan.

SAGITTARIUS
(NOVEMBER 23– DECEMBER 21)

Sagittarians are freedom-loving and dedicated to truth. These individuals have a philosophy of life and a big-picture view. They will be captivated by grand plans that have far-reaching consequences. They will be drawn to projects that uplift and educate. Appeal to their sense of humanity—and be prepared for an honest evaluation, as these people can not lie.

Sagittarians will be captivated by grand plans that have far-reaching consequences.

CAPRICORN
(DECEMBER 22–JANUARY 19)

Capricorns are the workers of the world. These individuals are goal-oriented and can anticipate all of the steps along the way. They want to be part of organized, detailed plans and will respond well to a written proposal. Truly knowing what you want to do will give them the confidence that they need to join you, but expect to be grilled on the details. Express the benefits for them, but also ask for their expertise.

Capricorns will respond well to a written proposal.

AQUARIUS
(JANUARY 20–FEBRUARY 19)

Aquarians are the world's futurists. They see things as they should be or could be, rather than as they are. Humanitarian to the core, these individuals can be motivated by ideas that are good for us all. They will want the freedom to be able to pursue a project in their own way. Intuition is their guide; they often perform best when operating outside of the box. A willingness to try new and different avenues of expression will be met with positivity. Be creative.

Aquarians can be motivated by ideas that are good for us all.

PISCES
(FEBRUARY 20–MARCH 20)

Pisces are the world's dreamers. Blessed with a tremendous amount of creativity, these individuals have the ability to understand those around them. Environmental harmony is important; a project that can be met with universal acceptance and works for everybody is appealing. Feelings are strong, so a plea that can promote positive emotions will be engaging. Give them time to weigh the details before making a decision. ■

Pisces are the world's dreamers.

Celeste Longacre, an Aries, says that her ability to jump into things gives her projects great momentum. However, if her partner fails to provide details in a timely fashion, her momentum fades.

HOW WE PREDICT THE WEATHER

We derive our weather forecasts from a secret formula that was devised by the founder of this Almanac, Robert B. Thomas, in 1792. Thomas believed that weather on Earth was influenced by sunspots, which are magnetic storms on the surface of the Sun.

Over the years, we have refined and enhanced this formula with state-of-the-art technology and modern scientific calculations. We employ three scientific disciplines to make our long-range predictions: solar science, the study of sunspots and other solar activity; climatology, the study of prevailing weather patterns; and meteorology, the study of the atmosphere. We predict weather trends and events by comparing solar patterns and historical weather conditions with current solar activity.

Our forecasts emphasize temperature and precipitation deviations from averages, or normals. These are based on 30-year statistical averages prepared by government meteorological agencies and updated every 10 years. The most-recent tabulations span the period 1981 through 2010.

The borders of the 16 weather regions of the contiguous states (page 205) are based primarily on climatology and the movement of weather systems. For example, while the average weather in Richmond, Virginia, and Boston, Massachusetts, is very different (although both are in Region 2), both areas tend to be affected by the same storms and high-pressure centers and have weather deviations from normal that are similar.

We believe that nothing in the universe happens haphazardly, that there is a cause-and-effect pattern to all phenomena. However, although neither we nor any other forecasters have as yet gained sufficient insight into the mysteries of the universe to predict the weather with total accuracy, our results are almost always very close to our traditional claim of 80%.

WEATHER

Drug Companies Fear Release of the New AloeCure®

Big Pharma execs stand to lose billions as doctors' recommend drug-free "health cocktail" that adjusts and corrects your body's health conditions.

By David Waxman
Seattle Washington:

Drug company execs are nervous. That's because the greatest health advance in decades has hit the streets. And analysts expect it to put a huge crimp in "Big Pharma" profits.

So what's all the fuss about? It's about a new ingredient that's changing the lives of people who use it. Some call it "the greatest discovery since penicillin"! And others call it "a miracle!"

The name of the product is the AloeCure. It's not a drug. It's something completely different. And the product is available to anyone who wants it, at a reasonable price.

Top Doc Warns: Digestion Drugs Can Cripple You!

Company spokesperson, Dr. Liza Leal; a leading integrative health specialist out of Texas recommends Aloecure before she decides to prescribe any digestion drug. Especially after the FDA's stern warning about long-term use of drugs classified as proton pump inhibitors like **Prilosec®, Nexium®, and Prevacid®.** In a nutshell, the FDA statement warned people should avoid taking these digestion drugs for longer than three 14-day treatment periods because there is an increased risk of bone fractures. Many people take them daily and for decades.

Dr. Leal should know. Many patients come to her with bone and joint complaints and she does everything she can to help them. One way for digestion sufferers to help avoid possible risk of tragic joint and bone problems caused by overuse of digestion drugs is to take the AloeCure.

The secret to AloeCure's "health adjusting" formula is scientifically tested Acemannan, a polysaccharide extracted from Aloe Vera. But not the same aloe vera that mom used to apply to your cuts, scrapes and burns. This is a perfect strain of aloe that is organically grown in special Asian soil; under very strict conditions. AloeCure is so powerful it begins to benefit your health the instant you take it. It soothes intestinal discomfort and you can avoid the possibility of bone and health damage caused by overuse of digestion drugs.

Helps the Immune System to Calm Inflammation

According to a leading aloe research, when correctly processed for digesting, the Aloe plant has a powerful component for regulating your immune system called Acemannan. So whether it's damage that is physical, bacterial, chemical or autoimmune; the natural plant helps the body stay healthy.

Rapid Acid and Heartburn Neutralizer

Aloe has proved to have an astonishing effect on users who suffer with digestion problems like bouts of acid reflux, heartburn, cramping, gas and constipation because it acts as a natural acid buffer and soothes the digestive system. But new studies prove it does a whole lot more.

Side-Step Heart Concerns

So you've been taking proton pump inhibitors (PPI's) for years and you feel just fine. In June of 2015 a major study shows that chronic PPI use increases the risk of heart attack in general population.

Debilitating brain disorders are on the rise. New studies show PPI's are linked to an increased risk of dementia. Studies show that your brain needs the healthy bacteria from your gut in order to function at its best. Both low and high dosages of digestion drugs are proven to destroy that healthy bacteria and get in the way of brain function. So you're left with a sluggish, slow-to-react brain without a lot of room to store information. The acemannan used in AloeCure actually makes your gut healthier, so healthy bacteria flows freely to your brain so you think better, faster and with a larger capacity for memory.

Sleep Like A Baby

A night without sleep really damages your body. And continued lost sleep can lead to all sorts of health problems. But what you may not realize is the reason why you're not sleeping. I sometimes call it "Ghost Reflux". A low-intensity form of acid discomfort that quietly keeps you awake in the background. AloeCure helps digestion so you may find yourself sleeping through the night.

Save Your Kidney

National and local news outlets are reporting Kidney Failure linked to PPI's. Your Kidney extracts waste from blood, balance body fluids, form urine, and aid in other important functions of the body. Without it your body would be overrun by deadly toxins. Aloe helps your kidney function properly.

Guaranteed Results Or Double Your Money Back

Due to the incredible results people are reporting, AloeCure is being sold with an equally incredible guarantee.

Take the pill exactly as directed. You must see and feel remarkable improvements in your digestive health, your mental health, in your physical appearance, the amount inflammation you have throughout your body – even in your ability to fall asleep at night!

Otherwise, simply return the empty bottles with a short note about how you took the pills and followed the simple instructions and the company will send you...Double your money back!

How To Get AloeCure

This is the official nationwide release of the new AloeCure pill in the United States. And so, the company is offering our readers up to 3 FREE bottles with their order.

All you have to do is call **TOLL-FREE 1-800-561-6637**.

HOW ACCURATE WAS OUR FORECAST LAST WINTER?

Our overall accuracy rates in forecasting the direction of the change in temperature compared with the actual previous winter season across the 18 regions of the United States was 72.2%, while our accuracy rate in forecasting the change in precipitation was 88.9%. So, our overall accuracy rate was 80.5%, which is slightly above our traditional average rate of 80%. The only regions in which our temperature forecasts were incorrect were the Atlantic Corridor, Florida, Intermountain, Pacific Southwest, and Hawaii. In precipitation, we were correct in all regions with the exception of the Ohio Valley and Upper Midwest.

Most of the places in our "A Parade of Snowstorms" area (the northern tier of states) had above-normal snowfall. We also forecast "Snowy" in Alaska, and many parts of the state did have above-normal snowfall. Nearly every place else that normally has winter snowfall was below normal. We did forecast below-normal snowfall in most of these areas, but we forecast too much snow in most spots from the Appalachians westward to the Intermountain region.

The table below shows how the actual average temperature differed from our forecast for November through March for one city in each region. On average, these actual winter temperatures differed from our forecasts by 1.08 degrees F.

REGION/ CITY	Nov.-Mar. Temp Variations From Normal (degrees) PREDICTED	ACTUAL	REGION/ CITY	Nov.-Mar. Temp Variations From Normal (degrees) PREDICTED	ACTUAL
1. Caribou, ME	1.3	1.8	10. St. Louis, MO	0.6	1.8
2. Philadelphia, PA	2.0	2.6	11. Oklahoma City, OK	0.7	0.5
3. Roanoke, VA	1.6	3.2	12. Denver, CO	−0.2	0.6
4. Raleigh, NC	1.0	3.2	13. Grand Junction, CO	−0.6	0.7
5. Miami, FL	1.2	2.9	14. Phoenix, AZ	−1.8	0.4
6. Rochester, NY	1.8	2.0	15. Seattle, WA	2.0	1.3
7. Pittsburgh, PA	1.2	2.6	16. San Francisco, CA	−0.6	1.6
8. Little Rock, AR	1.4	1.2	17. Juneau, AK	2.3	2.2
9. Minneapolis, MN	2.2	2.1	18. Honolulu, HI	−0.4	1.9

WEATHER

WEATHER REGIONS

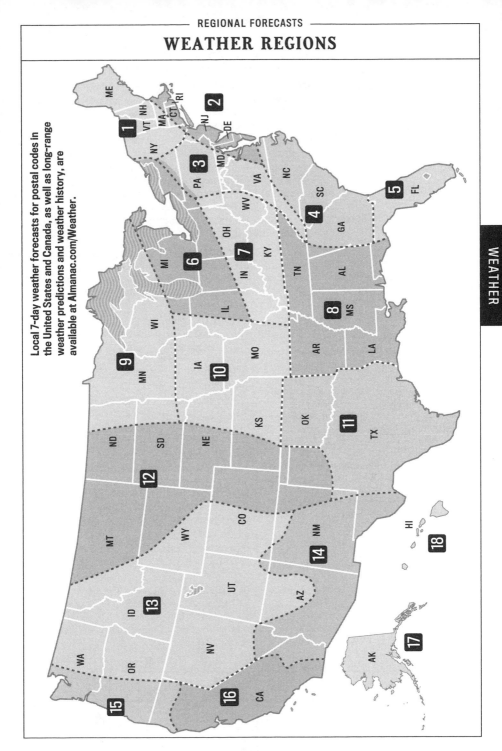

Local 7-day weather forecasts for postal codes in the United States and Canada, as well as long-range weather predictions and weather history, are available at Almanac.com/Weather.

NORTHEAST

SUMMARY: Winter will be colder than normal in the north and warmer in the south, with above-normal precipitation and snowfall. The coldest periods will be in mid-December and mid-January, with the snowiest periods in mid-December, early January, and early to mid-March. **April** and **May** will be warmer and slightly rainier than normal, with an early hot spell in early to mid-April. **Summer** temperatures will be slightly cooler than normal, on average, with above-normal rainfall. The hottest periods will be in late June, early to mid-July, and early August. Watch for a hurricane in early to mid-August. **September** and **October** will be cooler and rainier than normal.

NOV. 2020: Temp. 42° (1° below avg. north, 5° above south); precip. 4" (0.5" above avg.). 1–4 Rainy, mild. 5–8 Rain to snow. 9–13 Sunny, mild. 14–21 Rain and snow showers, turning cold. 22–30 Snow showers, cold.

DEC. 2020: Temp. 24° (4° below avg.); precip. 3.5" (0.5" above avg.). 1–4 Rainy periods, mild. 5–10 Flurries, cold. 11–18 Snowstorm, then flurries, very cold. 19–23 Snowstorm, then flurries, cold. 24–28 Snowy periods, mild. 29–31 Sunny, cold.

JAN. 2021: Temp. 18° (5° below avg.); precip. 4.5" (1.5" above avg.). 1–6 Snowy periods, cold. 7–12 Rain and snow, then sunny, cold. 13–18 Snow showers, very cold. 19–22 Snow north, rain south; mild. 23–31 Snow showers, turning cold.

FEB. 2021: Temp. 28° (2° above avg. north, 8° above south); precip. 3" (0.5" above avg.). 1–3 Sunny, mild. 4–8 Rain and snow showers, mild. 9–16 Periods of rain and snow, mild. 17–21 Sunny, mild. 22–28 Rain and snow showers; cold, then mild.

MAR. 2021: Temp. 36° (2° above avg.); precip. 3.5" (0.5" above avg.). 1–8 Snow showers, cold. 9–12 Snowstorm, then flurries, cold. 13–17 Showers, then sunny, mild. 18–27 Rainy periods, turning warm. 28–31 Sunny, mild.

APR. 2021: Temp. 49° (3° above avg.); precip. 2.5" (0.5" below avg.). 1–6 Sunny, turning cold. 7–13 Showers, then sunny, hot. 14–21 Showers, turning cool. 22–30 Rainy periods, cool.

MAY 2021: Temp. 55° (avg.); precip. 4.5" (1" above avg.). 1–3 Sunny, cool. 4–7 T-storms, cool. 8–15 Rainy periods, warm, then cool. 16–24 Isolated t-storms, turning warm. 25–31 Sunny, warm.

JUNE 2021: Temp. 69° (4° above avg.); precip. 4.5" (1" above avg.). 1–4 Sunny, hot. 5–10 Showers, cool, then warm. 11–17 Scattered t-storms, hot. 18–25 T-storms, turning cool. 26–30 Sunny, hot.

JULY 2021: Temp. 66° (4° below avg.); precip. 5" (2" above avg. north, avg. south). 1–10 Scattered t-storms, cool. 11–13 Sunny, hot. 14–17 T-storms, warm. 18–25 A few t-storms, cool. 26–31 Sunny, then t-storms, cool.

AUG. 2021: Temp. 65° (1° below avg.); precip. 4.5" (0.5" above avg.). 1–7 Scattered t-storms, turning hot. 8–10 Hurricane threat. 11–18 Sunny, cool, then warm. 19–25 A few t-storms, turning cool. 26–31 Sunny, cool.

SEPT. 2021: Temp. 59° (avg.); precip. 3.5" (0.5" below avg.). 1–2 Sunny, cool. 3–9 Rain, then sunny, warm. 10–14 Showers, warm. 15–21 Rainy periods, cool. 22–30 Sunny, turning warm.

OCT. 2021: Temp. 44° (4° below avg.); precip. 5.5" (2" above avg.). 1–9 Rainy periods, cool. 10–12 Snow showers, cold. 13–19 Rainy periods, chilly. 20–23 Sunny, cool. 24–31 Periods of rain and snow, cold.

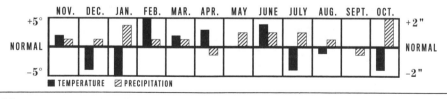

Get your local forecast at Almanac.com/Weather.

ATLANTIC CORRIDOR

SUMMARY: Winter temperatures will be above normal, on average, with the coldest periods in mid-December and early and mid-January. Precipitation will be near normal, with mostly below-normal snowfall. The snowiest periods will occur in mid-December and early March. **April** and **May** will be warmer and drier than normal, with an early hot spell in early to mid-April. **Summer** will be hotter than normal, with the hottest periods in early and mid-June, early to mid-July, and early to mid-August. Rainfall will be near normal, especially in the south. Watch for a hurricane in early August. **September** and **October** will be cooler and mostly rainier than normal. Watch for a tropical storm threat in early to mid-September.

Boston
Providence
Hartford
New York
Philadelphia
Atlantic City
Baltimore
Washington, D.C.
Richmond

NOV. 2020: Temp. 50° (3° above avg.); precip. 4" (1" above avg.). 1–6 Rainy, mild. 7–13 Sunny; cool, then mild. 14–19 Rain, then sunny, cool. 20–24 Rainy periods; cool, then mild. 25–28 Sunny, cool. 29–30 Rain.

DEC. 2020: Temp. 38° (1° below avg.); precip. 4" (0.5" below avg.). 1–5 Rain, then sunny, cold. 6–10 Showers, mild. 11–17 Snowstorm north, flurries south; then sunny, very cold. 18–27 Rainy periods, milder. 28–31 Sunny, cold.

JAN. 2021: Temp. 32° (3° below avg.); precip. 4.25" (1.5" above avg. north, avg. south). 1–6 Snow showers, cold. 7–12 Rain, then sunny, very cold. 13–16 Rain and snow north, sunny south; cold. 17–21 Rainy, mild. 22–24 Sunny, cold. 25–31 Periods of rain and snow, cold.

FEB. 2021: Temp. 42° (8° above avg.); precip. 1.5" (1.5" below avg.). 1–5 Sunny, mild. 6–15 Rainy periods, mild. 16–23 Sunny; cold, then mild. 24–26 Snow north, showers south. 27–28 Sunny, mild.

MAR. 2021: Temp. 45° (1° above avg.); precip. 3.5" (0.5" below avg.). 1–6 Snowy periods north, rain south; cold. 7–11 Snow showers, cold. 12–14 Showers, warm. 15–19 Sunny; cold, then warm. 20–26 Rainy periods, mild. 27–31 Sunny, warm.

APR. 2021: Temp. 57° (5° above avg.); precip. 2.5" (1" below avg.). 1–7 A few showers, turning warm. 8–13 Sunny, hot. 14–17 Showers, warm. 18–24 Rainy periods, cool. 25–30 Showers, warm.

MAY 2021: Temp. 61° (1° below avg.); precip. 2" (1" below avg.). 1–6 Showers, cool. 7–14 Rainy periods; warm, then cool. 15–19 Sunny, cool. 20–26 Rainy periods, cool. 27–31 Sunny, cool.

JUNE 2021: Temp. 75° (4° above avg.); precip. 2" (1.5" below avg.). 1–6 Sunny; hot, then cool. 7–13 Scattered showers, warm. 14–19 Isolated t-storms, hot. 20–30 Scattered t-storms, turning cool.

JULY 2021: Temp. 75° (1° below avg.); precip. 3.5" (0.5" below avg.). 1–9 Scattered t-storms, cool. 10–13 Sunny, hot. 14–19 Scattered t-storms, cool. 20–25 A few t-storms, turning cool. 26–31 Sunny, cool.

AUG. 2021: Temp. 73° (1° below avg.); precip. 4" (1.5" above avg. north, 2" below south). 1–4 Hurricane risk. 5–8 A few t-storms, turning hot. 9–18 Sunny; cool, then hot. 19–25 T-storms, then sunny, cool. 26–31 Scattered t-storms, cool.

SEPT. 2021: Temp. 68° (1° above avg.); precip. 4" (1" below avg. north, 2" above south). 1–5 T-storms, then sunny, cool. 6–9 Scattered t-storms, warm. 10–13 Tropical storm risk. 14–18 Sunny, cool. 19–26 Rainy periods, cool. 27–30 Sunny, warm.

OCT. 2021: Temp. 53° (3° below avg.); precip. 4.5" (avg. north, 2" above avg. south). 1–8 T-storms, then sunny, cool. 9–12 Showers, cool. 13–19 Rainy periods, cool. 20–22 Sunny, cold. 23–31 Rain, then sunny, cool.

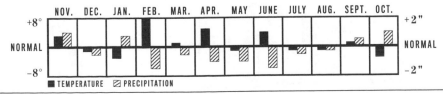

APPALACHIANS

Elmira
Scranton •
Harrisburg •
Frederick •
Roanoke •
Asheville •

WEATHER

SUMMARY: Winter will be warmer than normal, with precipitation above normal in the north and below normal in the south. The coldest periods will be in mid- and late December and throughout January. Snowfall will be below normal, with the snowiest period in early March. **April** and **May** will be warmer and drier than normal, with an early hot spell in early to mid-April. **Summer** will be drier than normal, with temperatures near normal in the north and below normal in the south. The hottest periods will be in early June and mid-August. **September** and **October** will be cooler and rainier than normal.

NOV. 2020: Temp. 47° (3° above avg.); precip. 3.5" (avg.). 1–5 Rainy periods, warm. 6–8 Rain to snow. 9–13 Sunny, warm. 14–19 Rainy periods, cool. 20–24 Showers, mild. 25–30 Sunny; cold, then mild.

DEC. 2020: Temp. 35° (1° below avg.); precip. 2.5" (0.5" below avg.). 1–7 Showers, then sunny, mild. 8–17 Showers, then flurries, cold. 18–25 Periods of rain and snow, mild. 26–31 Snow showers, very cold.

JAN. 2021: Temp. 28° (2° below avg.); precip. 2.5" (1" above avg., north, 1" below south). 1–9 Snow showers; cold, then mild. 10–12 Sunny, frigid. 13–17 Snow, then flurries, cold. 18–22 Rain to snow. 23–27 Rain and snow. 28–31 Snow showers, cold.

FEB. 2021: Temp. 39° (9° above avg.); precip. 1.5" (1" above avg.). 1–5 Sunny, turning mild. 6–15 Rainy periods, mild. 16–23 Sunny; cold, then quite mild. 24–28 Rainy periods, quite mild.

MAR. 2021: Temp. 41° (1° above avg.); precip. 4" (1" above avg.). 1–2 Rain to snow. 3–8 Rain and snow showers. 9–12 Snow showers, cold. 13–16 Rainy, mild, then sunny, cold. 17–25 Rainy periods, mild. 26–31 Showers, cool.

APR. 2021: Temp. 53° (3° above avg.); precip. 1" (1.5" below avg.). 1–3 Sunny, cool. 4–15 Showers, then sunny, turning hot. 16–22 Rainy periods, cool. 23–27 Showers, cool. 28–30 Sunny, warm.

MAY 2021: Temp. 58° (2° below avg.); precip. 5.5" (1" above avg.). 1–3 Sunny, cool. 4–14 Rainy periods, turning warm. 15–18 Sunny, cool. 19–27 Rainy periods, cool. 28–31 Sunny, cool.

JUNE 2021: Temp. 68° (3° above avg. north, 1° below south); precip. 4.5" (0.5" above avg.). 1–6 Sunny, warm. 7–18 T-storms, warm. 19–25 Showers north, sunny south; cool. 26–30 Showers, cool.

JULY 2021: Temp. 71° (2° below avg.); precip. 2.5" (1" below avg.). 1–9 A few t-storms; mild north, hot south. 10–13 Sunny, warm. 14–20 T-storms, then sunny, cool. 21–28 T-storms, then sunny, cool. 29–31 T-storms.

AUG. 2021: Temp. 72° (1° below avg.); precip. 2" (1.5" below avg.). 1–8 Showers, cool. 9–18 Sunny, turning hot. 19–25 T-storms, then sunny, cool. 26–31 T-storms, then sunny, cool.

SEPT. 2021: Temp. 64° (avg.); precip. 5" (1.5" above avg.). 1–2 Sunny, warm. 3–13 Showers; cool, then warm. 14–18 Sunny, cool. 19–26 Rainy periods. 27–30 Sunny, warm.

OCT. 2021: Temp. 47° (6° below avg.); precip. 6" (3" above avg.). 1–5 Rain, then sunny, cool. 6–12 Showers, then sunny, cold. 13–19 Rainy periods, chilly. 20–23 Sunny, cold. 24–28 Rain, then sunny, cold. 29–31 Snow north, showers south.

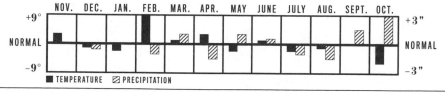

	NOV.	DEC.	JAN.	FEB.	MAR.	APR.	MAY	JUNE	JULY	AUG.	SEPT.	OCT.	
+9°													+3"
NORMAL													NORMAL
-9°													-3"

■ TEMPERATURE ▨ PRECIPITATION

SOUTHEAST

SUMMARY: Winter temperatures will be above normal, on average, with the coldest periods in mid- and late December and throughout January. Precipitation will be above normal in the north and below normal in the south. Snowfall generally will be below normal, with the best chance for snow in early January. **April** and **May** will be a bit cooler than normal, with above-normal rainfall. **Summer** will be cooler and drier than normal, with the hottest period in mid-July. Watch for a hurricane threat in early August and a tropical storm threat in mid-August. **September** and **October** will be cooler than normal, with near-normal precipitation. Expect a tropical storm threat in early to mid-September.

NOV. 2020: Temp. 56° (1° above avg.); precip. 3" (2" above avg. north, 2" below south). 1–5 Rainy periods, warm. 6–13 Sunny; cold, then mild. 14–24 Rainy periods; cold, then mild. 25–30 Sunny, turning warm.

DEC. 2020: Temp. 44° (3° below avg.); precip. 3" (1" above avg. north, 2" below south). 1–8 Rainy, cool, then sunny, warm. 9–17 Rain, then sunny, cold. 18–22 Rain, then sunny, cool. 23–31 Rainy periods; mild, then cold.

JAN. 2021: Temp. 41° (3° below avg.); precip. 4" (0.5" below avg.). 1–4 Snow north, rain south, then sunny, cold. 5–9 Showers, cool. 10–18 Sunny; cold, then mild. 19–24 Rain, then sunny, cold. 25–31 Rain, then sunny, turning mild.

FEB. 2021: Temp. 55° (9° above avg.); precip. 2" (2" below avg.). 1–6 Sunny, mild. 7–14 Scattered showers, warm. 15–26 Sunny, warm. 27–28 Rainy, mild.

MAR. 2021: Temp. 56° (1° above avg.); precip. 6.5" (2" above avg.). 1–9 Rainy periods; mild, then chilly. 10–17 Sunny, mild. 18–24 Rainy periods, mild. 25–31 Sunny, cool.

APR. 2021: Temp. 64° (1° above avg.); precip. 2" (1" below avg.). 1–12 Sunny, turning warm. 13–18 Scattered showers, warm. 19–22 Sunny, cool. 23–28 T-storms, then sunny, cool. 29–30 Rainy.

MAY 2021: Temp. 69° (2° below avg.); precip. 6.5" (3" above avg.). 1–3 Showers, cool. 4–10 Rainy periods; cool north, warm south. 11–15 Sunny, cool. 16–28 Scattered t-storms, cool. 29–31 Sunny, cool.

JUNE 2021: Temp. 76° (2° below avg.); precip. 5.5" (1" below avg. north, 3" above south). 1–9 Sunny, warm. 10–18 T-storms, then sunny, cool. 19–24 Scattered t-storms, warm. 25–30 Rainy periods, cool.

JULY 2021: Temp. 81° (1° below avg.); precip. 1.5" (3" below avg.). 1–8 Sunny, warm. 9–14 T-storms, then sunny, cool. 15–19 Sunny, hot. 20–26 Scattered t-storms; comfortable north, hot south. 27–31 Showers, cool.

AUG. 2021: Temp. 79° (1° below avg.); precip. 3" (2" below avg.). 1–4 Hurricane threat. 5–12 Sunny north, t-storms south; cool. 13–15 Tropical storm threat. 16–22 A few t-storms, warm. 23–31 Scattered t-storms, cool.

SEPT. 2021: Temp. 72° (2° below avg.); precip. 4.5" (avg.). 1–6 Scattered t-storms, cool. 7–11 Tropical storm threat. 12–18 Sunny, cool. 19–27 T-storms, then sunny, cool. 28–30 T-storms, warm.

OCT. 2021: Temp. 59° (5° below avg.); precip. 4" (avg.). 1–9 Rain, then sunny, cool. 10–18 Rainy periods, chilly. 19–22 Sunny, cold. 23–31 Showers, then sunny, cold.

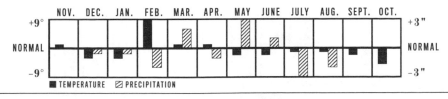

FLORIDA

Jacksonville
Orlando
Tampa
Miami

SUMMARY: Winter will be milder and drier than normal, with the coldest temperatures in mid-December, early January, and early February. **April** and **May** will have near-normal temperatures, with above-normal rain. Watch for a tropical storm threat in mid-May. **Summer** will be slightly cooler than normal, with near-normal rainfall. The hottest periods will be in early and mid- to late July. Watch for a tropical storm threat in early to mid-August. **September** and **October** will be cooler and drier than normal, despite a hot spell in mid-September. Expect a tropical storm threat in early to mid-September.

NOV. 2020: Temp. 68° (1° below avg.); precip. 1.5" (1" below avg.). 1–5 A few showers, warm. 6–10 Sunny, cold. 11–14 T-storms, warm. 15–19 Showers, chilly. 20–24 Sunny, warm. 25–30 Showers, mild.

DEC. 2020: Temp. 62° (1° below avg.); precip. 2" (1" below avg.). 1–5 Showers, then sunny, cool. 6–10 Scattered showers, warm. 11–17 Sunny, cold. 18–24 T-storms, turning warm. 25–31 Sunny, then showers; cool.

JAN. 2021: Temp. 58° (2° below avg.); precip. 2.5" (avg.). 1–3 Showers, then sunny, cold. 4–9 Scattered t-storms, warm. 10–17 Sunny, cool. 18–20 T-storms, warm. 21–27 Scattered t-storms, cool. 28–31 T-storms, warm.

FEB. 2021: Temp. 65° (4° above avg.); precip. 1.5" (2" below avg. north, avg. south). 1–11 Sunny; cold, then warm. 12–22 Scattered t-storms, mild. 23–28 Sunny, warm.

MAR. 2021: Temp. 69° (2° above avg.); precip. 2.5" (0.5" below avg.). 1–8 T-storms, then sunny, warm. 9–12 A few showers, cool. 13–21 Sunny, mild. 22–25 T-storms, warm. 26–31 Sunny, cool.

APR. 2021: Temp. 72° (1° above avg.); precip. 3.5" (1" above avg.). 1–8 Scattered t-storms, cool. 9–18 A few t-storms, warm. 19–23 Sunny, warm. 24–30 Scattered t-storms, warm.

MAY 2021: Temp. 76° (1° below avg.); precip. 7" (3" above avg.). 1–9 A few t-storms, warm. 10–15 Sunny, cool. 16–21 Tropical storm threat. 22–31 Scattered t-storms, cool.

JUNE 2021: Temp. 81° (1° below avg.); precip. 7" (0.5" above avg.). 1–7 Sunny north, t-storms south; cool. 8–16 Sunny, warm. 17–25 Sunny, cool. 26–30 A few t-storms, warm.

JULY 2021: Temp. 84° (1° above avg.); precip. 3.5" (3" below avg.). 1–6 A few t-storms, turning hot. 7–17 Sunny, warm. 18–25 Scattered t-storms, hot. 26–31 T-storms, cool.

AUG. 2021: Temp. 81° (1° below avg.); precip. 10" (2.5" above avg.). 1–9 A few t-storms, warm. 10–14 Tropical storm threat. 15–22 Scattered t-storms, cool. 23–31 A few t-storms, warm.

SEPT. 2021: Temp. 79° (1° below avg.); precip. 3" (4" below avg. north, 1" below south). 1–7 Daily t-storms, cool. 8–12 Tropical storm threat. 13–22 Scattered t-storms, hot. 23–30 Sunny, cool.

OCT. 2021: Temp. 72° (4° below avg. north, 2° below south); precip. 3" (1" below avg.). 1–7 Rain, then sunny, cool. 8–13 Rainy periods, warm. 14–17 Sunny, chilly. 18–27 A few showers, cool. 28–31 Sunny, cold.

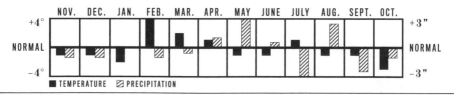

LOWER LAKES

SUMMARY: Winter temperatures will be much above normal, on average, despite cold periods in early and mid-December, from late December into early January, in early to mid-January, and in late January. Precipitation will be near normal. Snowfall will be below normal in most areas, with the snowiest periods in early and mid-December, mid- to late February, and early to mid-March. **April** and **May** will have near-normal temperatures, on average, with precipitation a bit above normal in the east and below normal in the west. **Summer** will be warmer and rainier than normal in the east but cooler and drier in the west. The hottest periods will be in early June, from late June to early July, and in mid-August. **September** and **October** will be cooler than normal, with precipitation a bit above normal in the east and below normal in the west.

WEATHER

NOV. 2020: Temp. 44° (3° above avg.); precip. 1.5" (1" below avg.). 1–5 Rainy periods, mild. 6–8 Rain to snow. 9–14 Rainy periods, mild. 15–16 Sunny, cold. 17–21 Periods of rain and snow, cold. 22–23 Rainy, mild. 24–27 Snow showers, cold. 28–30 Rainy, mild.

DEC. 2020: Temp. 31.5° (2° below avg. east, 1° above west); precip. 4" (1" above avg.). 1–3 Snowy, cold. 4–8 Rainy periods, mild. 9–18 Lake snows, cold. 19–25 Snow, then flurries, mild. 26–31 Snowy periods, cold.

JAN. 2021: Temp. 23° (4° below avg.); precip. 2.5" (avg.). 1–4 Lake snows, very cold. 5–9 Periods of snow, mild. 10–14 Snow showers; bitter cold, then milder. 15–17 Lake snows, frigid. 18–22 Snow showers, mild. 23–31 Snowy periods, cold.

FEB. 2021: Temp. 37° (10° above avg.); precip. 4" (2" above avg.). 1–7 Sunny, mild. 8–14 Rainy periods, quite mild. 15–21 Sunny, quite mild. 22–25 Rain to snow, colder. 26–28 Rainy, mild.

MAR. 2021: Temp. 41° (3° above avg.); precip. 2.5" (0.5" below avg.). 1–6 Rain and snow showers, mild. 7–11 Snowstorm, then sunny, cold. 12–20 Rainy periods, warm. 21–24 Sunny, then rainy, cooler. 25–31 Sunny, cold.

APR. 2021: Temp. 50° (2° above avg.); precip. 4.5" (1" above avg.). 1–6 Showers, cool. 7–14 Showers, then sunny, hot. 15–22 Rainy periods, turning cold. 23–30 Showers, mild.

MAY 2021: Temp. 56° (2° below avg.); precip. 2.5" (avg. east, 2" below west). 1–3 Sunny, warm. 4–12 T-storms; warm east, turning chilly west. 13–21 Sunny, turning warm. 22–28 Rain, then sunny, cool. 29–31 Sunny east, t-storms west; warm.

JUNE 2021: Temp. 67.5° (4° above avg. east, 1° below west); precip. 3.5" (avg.). 1–3 Sunny, hot. 4–8 Scattered t-storms, hot. 9–22 A few t-storms, warm. 23–27 T-storms, cool. 28–30 Sunny, hot.

JULY 2021: Temp. 69.5° (1° below avg.); precip. 4" (2" above avg. east, 1" below west). 1–4 A few t-storms, hot. 5–11 Scattered t-storms, cool. 12–24 A few t-storms, warm. 25–28 Sunny, cool. 29–31 T-storms, cool.

AUG. 2021: Temp. 68° (1° below avg.); precip. 3" (1" below avg.). 1–5 Sunny, turning warm. 6–12 T-storms, then sunny, cool. 13–19 Sunny, hot. 20–31 T-storms, then sunny, cooler.

SEPT. 2021: Temp. 62° (avg.); precip. 4.5" (avg.). 1–2 Sunny, hot. 3–8 T-storms, then sunny, hot. 9–20 Rainy periods, turning cool. 21–27 Sunny, turning warm. 28–30 Showers, cool.

OCT. 2021: Temp. 47° (5° below avg.); precip. 2.5" (1" above avg. east, 1" below west). 1–2 Rain east, sunny west; cool. 3–5 Sunny. 6–11 Rain, then sunny, cold. 12–19 Rainy periods, chilly. 20–21 Wet snow. 22–31 Rain and snow showers, cold.

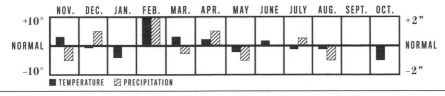

OHIO VALLEY

SUMMARY: Winter temperatures will be much above normal, on average, despite cold periods in early and mid-December, from late December into early January, in early to mid-January, and in late January. Precipitation and snowfall will be below normal in most areas, with the snowiest periods in early and mid-December and from early to mid-March. **April** and **May** will have near-normal temperatures, on average, with below-normal precipitation. **Summer** will be cooler than normal, with rainfall below normal in the east and above normal in the west. The hottest periods will be in early June and mid-August. **September** and **October** will be cooler than normal, despite a hot spell in early September, with above-normal precipitation.

NOV. 2020: Temp. 47° (1° above avg.); precip. 3" (0.5" below avg.). 1–5 Rainy periods, warm. 6–8 Rain to snow, then sunny, cold. 9–13 Sunny, mild. 14–17 Rain, then sunny, cold. 18–21 Snow showers, cold. 22–26 Rain, then flurries, cold. 27–30 Rainy, mild.

DEC. 2020: Temp. 37.5° (0.5° above avg.); precip. 4" (1" above avg.). 1–8 Snow to rain, then showers, mild. 9–12 Flurries, cold. 13–17 Snow showers, cold. 18–27 Periods of rain and snow, mild. 28–31 Snow, then flurries, cold.

JAN. 2021: Temp. 30° (3° below avg.); precip. 2.5" (0.5" below avg.). 1–3 Snowy, cold. 4–8 Rainy periods, mild. 9–16 Snow showers, cold. 17–24 Periods of rain and wet snow, mild. 25–31 Snow showers, cold.

FEB. 2021: Temp. 44° (10° above avg.); precip. 2.5" (avg. east, 1.5" below west). 1–3 Snow showers, cold. 4–15 Rainy periods, mild. 16–24 Sunny, warm. 25–28 Rainy, turning cold.

MAR. 2021: Temp. 47° (2° above avg.); precip. 3.5" (0.5" below avg.). 1–7 Periods of rain and snow, cold. 8–11 Snow showers, cold. 12–14 Rainy, mild. 15–23 Showers, warm. 24–31 Snow showers, then sunny, cool.

APR. 2021: Temp. 57° (2° above avg.); precip. 2" (1.5" below avg.). 1–6 Showers, cool. 7–13 Sunny, turning hot. 14–18 Rainy periods, warm. 19–23 Sunny, cool. 24–25 Rainy, mild.

26–30 A few showers, cool.

MAY 2021: Temp. 61° (2° below avg.); precip. 2" (1.5" below avg.). 1–4 Showers, cool. 5–11 Rainy periods; warm, then cool. 12–17 Sunny, cool. 18–26 Rainy periods, mild. 27–31 Sunny, cool.

JUNE 2021: Temp. 71° (1° below avg.); precip. 4.5" (1" below avg. east, 2" above west). 1–7 Sunny, hot. 8–18 Rainy periods, turning cool. 19–30 Scattered t-storms, cool.

JULY 2021: Temp. 73° (2° below avg.); precip. 4" (1" above avg. east, 1" below west). 1–9 A few t-storms, cool. 10–16 Sunny, warm. 17–24 Scattered t-storms, warm. 25–31 Sunny, cool.

AUG. 2021: Temp. 70° (3° below avg.); precip. 3.5" (2" below avg. east, 1" above west). 1–4 Sunny, cool. 5–8 T-storms, warm. 9–18 Sunny, turning hot. 19–25 Scattered t-storms, turning cool. 26–31 Sunny, cool.

SEPT. 2021: Temp. 65° (2° below avg.); precip. 4" (1" above avg.). 1–7 T-storms, then sunny, warm. 8–14 Rainy periods, cool. 15–18 Sunny, cool. 19–24 Rainy periods, cool. 25–30 Sunny, mild, then rain.

OCT. 2021: Temp. 50° (7° below avg.); precip. 3" (0.5" above avg.). 1–2 Rainy, cool. 3–7 Sunny, cool. 8–18 Rainy periods, chilly. 19–22 Sunny, cold. 23–31 Rain, then sunny, cold.

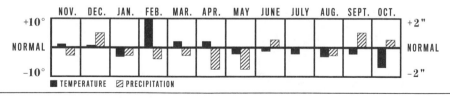

DEEP SOUTH

SUMMARY: Winter will be warmer than normal, on average, especially across the north. The coldest periods will be in early and mid-December and in early to mid- and late January. Rainfall will be below normal, with the best threats for snow in the north in late December and late January. **April** and **May** will be cooler than normal, with near-normal rainfall. **Summer** will be cooler and rainier than normal, with the hottest period in mid-July. **September** and **October** will be cooler than normal. Rainfall will be above normal in the north and below normal in the south.

WEATHER

NOV. 2020: Temp. 54° (avg. north, 2° below south); precip. 3" (2" below avg.). 1–8 Rain, then sunny, cold. 9–12 Sunny, warm. 13–18 Rain, then sunny, cold. 19–30 Rain, then sunny, turning mild.

DEC. 2020: Temp. 47° (1° above avg. north, 3° below south); precip. 5" (avg.). 1–3 Showers, cold. 4–7 Sunny, warm. 8–17 Rain, then sunny, cold. 18–26 Rainy periods, turning mild. 27–31 Rainy periods, wet snow north; chilly.

JAN. 2021: Temp. 45° (avg.); precip. 5" (1" below avg. north, 0.5" above south). 1–6 Showers, turning mild. 7–11 Sunny, turning cold. 12–19 Rainy periods, turning mild. 20–23 Sunny, mild. 24–27 Snow north, sunny south. 28–31 Rainy periods, cold.

FEB. 2021: Temp. 54.5° (10° above avg. north, 5° above south); precip. 3.5" (1.5" below avg.). 1–3 Sunny, turning warm. 4–14 Rainy periods, quite mild. 15–25 Sunny; cool, then warm. 26–28 Rain, then cooler.

MAR. 2021: Temp. 57.5° (3° above avg. north, 0.5° above south); precip. 5" (1" below avg.). 1–6 Rainy periods, mild. 7–11 Sunny, cool. 12–24 Rainy periods, mild. 25–31 Sunny, mild.

APR. 2021: Temp. 63° (avg.); precip. 2.5" (2" below avg.). 1–6 Scattered showers, mild. 7–11 Sunny, warm. 12–17 Scattered t-storms, warm. 18–22 Sunny, cool. 23–30 Rain, then sunny, cool.

MAY 2021: Temp. 68° (3° below avg.); precip. 7" (2" above avg.). 1–2 Sunny, cool. 3–10 Rain and heavy t-storms, warm. 11–14 Sunny, cool. 15–21 Rainy periods, cool. 22–31 A few t-storms, mild.

JUNE 2021: Temp. 76° (2° below avg.); precip. 6" (1" above avg.). 1–7 Sunny, warm. 8–16 A few t-storms, cool. 17–22 T-storms, mainly north; warm. 23–30 A few t-storms, cool.

JULY 2021: Temp. 80° (1° below avg.); precip. 4.5" (1.5" below avg. north, 1.5" above south). 1–9 Scattered t-storms, warm. 10–17 Sunny north, a few t-storms south; turning hot. 18–25 Scattered t-storms, warm. 26–31 Isolated t-storms, cool.

AUG. 2021: Temp. 78° (2° below avg.); precip. 5" (3" above avg. north, 2" below south). 1–6 Sunny, cool. 7–9 T-storms. 10–15 Sunny, cool. 16–22 A few t-storms, warm. 23–31 Scattered t-storms, cool.

SEPT. 2021: Temp. 74° (2° below avg.); precip. 4" (1" above avg. north, 2" below south). 1–9 Rain, then sunny, cool. 10–22 A few showers, cool. 23–27 Sunny, turning warm. 28–30 Rainy, cool.

OCT. 2021: Temp. 60° (5° below avg.); precip. 3.5" (0.5" above avg.). 1–8 Rain, then sunny, cool. 9–18 Rainy periods, chilly. 19–21 Sunny, cold. 22–31 Rain, then sunny, cold.

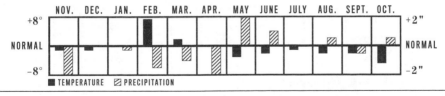

SUMMARY: Winter temperatures and precipitation will be above normal, while snowfall will be above normal in the east and below normal in the west. The coldest periods will be in early to mid- and late December, late January, and late February. The snowiest periods will be in late December, early and late January, late February, and early March. **April** and **May** will be warmer and drier than normal. **Summer** will be hotter and drier than normal, with the hottest periods in early June, early July, and mid- and late August. **September** and **October** will have below-normal temperatures and precipitation.

NOV. 2020: Temp. 29° (avg.); precip. 3" (2" above avg. east, avg. west). 1–7 Rain to snow, then sunny, cold. 8–11 Sunny, mild. 12–16 Rain to snow, then flurries, cold. 17–26 Snow showers, cold. 27–30 Flurries, mild.

DEC. 2020: Temp. 17.5° (1.5° above avg.); precip. 1.5" (0.5" above avg.). 1–5 Flurries, mild. 6–11 Snow showers, very cold. 12–24 Flurries, turning mild. 25–31 Snowy periods, turning cold.

JAN. 2021: Temp. 13° (2° below avg. east, 2° above west); precip. 0.8" (0.2" below avg.). 1–2 Sunny, cold. 3–6 Snowy, mild. 7–16 Snow showers; cold east, mild west. 17–24 Flurries, mild. 25–31 Snow, then flurries, cold.

FEB. 2021: Temp. 18° (6° above avg.); precip. 2" (2" above avg. east, avg. west). 1–13 Snow showers, mild. 14–16 Flurries, cold. 17–20 Sunny, mild. 21–25 Snowy periods, cold. 26–28 Snowstorm, then frigid.

MAR. 2021: Temp. 31° (3° above avg.); precip. 1.5" (avg.). 1–5 Snowy periods, cold. 6–13 Flurries; cold, then mild. 14–18 Snow, then sunny, mild. 19–23 Rainy periods, mild. 24–31 Sunny, mild.

APR. 2021: Temp. 44° (2° above avg.); precip. 1.5" (0.5" below avg.). 1–5 Showers, cool. 6–9 Sunny, warm. 10–16 Rainy periods, turning cool. 17–22 Sunny, cool. 23–30 Rain and wet snow, then sunny, cold.

MAY 2021: Temp. 57.5° (1° above avg. east, 4° above west); precip. 2" (1" below avg.). 1–3 Sunny, warm. 4–9 Rainy periods, cool. 10–18 Sunny; cool east, turning warm west. 19–31 T-storms, then sunny, hot.

JUNE 2021: Temp. 65° (2° above avg.); precip. 3.5" (avg. east, 1" below west). 1–11 A few t-storms; hot, then cool. 12–16 Sunny, warm. 17–25 Scattered t-storms, cool. 26–30 Sunny, warm.

JULY 2021: Temp. 69° (1° above avg.); precip. 2.5" (1" below avg.). 1–7 A few t-storms, turning hot. 8–12 Sunny, warm. 13–23 Scattered t-storms, warm. 24–31 Isolated t-storms, warm.

AUG. 2021: Temp. 70° (4° above avg.); precip. 1.5" (2" below avg.). 1–6 A few t-storms, warm. 7–18 Sunny, hot. 19–23 T-storms, then sunny, cool. 24–31 Scattered t-storms, turning hot.

SEPT. 2021: Temp. 57° (1° below avg.); precip. 1" (2" below avg.). 1–6 Isolated t-storms, warm. 7–11 Sunny, warm. 12–20 Showers, cool. 21–26 Sunny, turning warm. 27–30 Showers, chilly.

OCT. 2021: Temp. 43° (4° below avg.); precip. 0.5" (2" below avg.). 1–4 Sunny, mild. 5–7 Rainy periods, mild. 8–20 Snow showers, cold. 21–26 Sunny, turning mild. 27–31 Rain to snow east, sunny west; chilly.

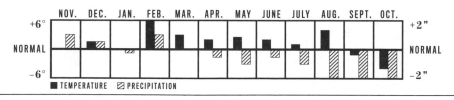

WEATHER

HEARTLAND

SUMMARY: Winter temperatures will be well above normal, on average, with the coldest periods in mid-December, from late December into early January, and in late February. Precipitation will be below normal, with snowfall below normal in most places. The snowiest periods will be in mid-November, early to mid-December, and mid-February. **April** and **May** temperatures will be above normal in the north and below normal in the south, with below-normal rain. **Summer** will be cooler and drier than normal, with the hottest periods in early July and mid-August. **September** and **October** will bring below-normal temperatures and rainfall.

Des Moines
Omaha
Kansas City
Topeka
St. Louis

NOV. 2020: Temp. 45° (4° above avg. north, avg. south); precip. 2.5" (avg.). 1–4 Rainy periods, mild. 5–8 Snow showers, cold. 9–12 Sunny, warm. 13–18 Snowy periods, cold. 19–21 Snowstorm, then sunny, cold. 22–30 Rainy periods, turning mild.

DEC. 2020: Temp. 33.5° (3° above avg. north, avg. south); precip. 0.5" (1" below avg.). 1–7 Rainy periods, mild. 8–16 Snow, then sunny, cold. 17–26 Rain and snow showers, mild. 27–31 Flurries, cold.

JAN. 2021: Temp. 31° (2° above avg.); precip. 0.5" (0.5" below avg.). 1–9 Sunny; cold, then mild. 10–18 Scattered showers, mild. 19–20 Rain and wet snow. 21–31 Snow showers, cold.

FEB. 2021: Temp. 41° (10° above avg.); precip. 1.5" (avg.). 1–8 Sunny, quite mild. 9–14 Rainy periods, mild. 15–23 Snow, then sunny, mild. 24–25 Flurries, very cold. 26–28 Snow north, rain south.

MAR. 2021: Temp. 48° (4° above avg.); precip. 1.5" (1" below avg.). 1–5 Rain arriving, turning mild. 6–13 Snow, then sunny, warm. 14–23 Showers, mild. 24–31 Rain, then sunny, warm.

APR. 2021: Temp. 55° (3° above avg. north, 1° below south); precip. 3.5" (avg.). 1–7 Sunny; warm north, cool south. 8–11 T-storms, warm. 12–24 Rainy periods, cool. 25–30 Scattered t-storms, cool.

MAY 2021: Temp. 63° (1° above avg. north, 3° below south); precip. 3" (1.5" below avg.). 1–5 Sunny; warm north, cool south. 6–10 Rainy periods, cool. 11–15 Sunny, turning warm. 16–28 Scattered t-storms, cool. 29–31 Sunny, warm.

JUNE 2021: Temp. 71° (1° below avg.); precip. 4.5" (avg.). 1–3 Sunny, warm. 4–11 A few t-storms, turning cool. 12–17 Sunny north, t-storms south; cool. 18–22 Scattered t-storms, warm. 23–30 Isolated t-storms, warm.

JULY 2021: Temp. 76° (1° below avg.); precip. 2" (2" below avg.). 1–7 Sunny, hot. 8–12 T-storms, then sunny, cool. 13–22 A few t-storms, hot. 23–31 Scattered t-storms, turning cool.

AUG. 2021: Temp. 74° (1° below avg.); precip. 1.5" (2" below avg.). 1–4 Sunny, turning warm. 5–11 T-storms, then sunny, cool. 12–19 Sunny, hot. 20–31 T-storms, then sunny, warm.

SEPT. 2021: Temp. 66° (1° below avg.); precip. 2" (1.5" below avg.). 1–4 T-storms, cool. 5–12 Sunny, warm. 13–21 Rainy periods, cool. 22–26 Sunny, warm. 27–30 Rainy, turning chilly.

OCT. 2021: Temp. 51° (5° below avg.); precip. 1.5" (1.5" below avg.). 1–6 Sunny, turning warm. 7–11 Sunny, turning cold. 12–18 Rainy periods, chilly. 19–21 Sunny, cold. 22–31 Rain, then sunny, cold.

WEATHER

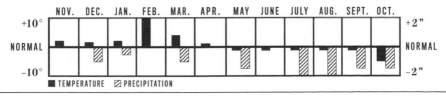

| | NOV. | DEC. | JAN. | FEB. | MAR. | APR. | MAY | JUNE | JULY | AUG. | SEPT. | OCT. |

+10°
NORMAL
−10°
+2"
NORMAL
−2"

■ TEMPERATURE ▨ PRECIPITATION

TEXAS-OKLAHOMA

Oklahoma City•

Dallas •

San   Houston
Antonio •

SUMMARY: Winter will be milder and drier than normal, with below-normal snowfall in places that normally receive snow. The coldest periods will be in mid-November, early to mid-December, and late January. The best chance for snow will be in late January. **April** and **May** will be cooler and rainier than normal. **Summer** will be cooler than normal, with the hottest periods in mid-June, mid- to late July, and mid-August. Rainfall will be below normal in the north and above normal in the south. **September** and **October** will be cooler than normal, with rainfall below normal in the north and above normal in the south.

NOV. 2020: Temp. 58° (1° above avg.); precip. 2" (1" below avg.). 1–6 Sunny, turning cold. 7–11 Sunny, warm. 12–18 Rain, then sunny, cold. 19–22 Snow north, rain south, then sunny, cold. 23–30 Showers, turning mild.

DEC. 2020: Temp. 52° (1° below avg.); precip. 1.5" (1" below avg.). 1–5 Sunny, warm. 6–12 Showers, turning cold. 13–22 Rainy periods, turning milder. 23–28 Sunny, cold. 29–31 Showers.

JAN. 2021: Temp. 52.5° (4° above avg. north, 1° above south); precip. 1" (1" below avg.). 1–6 Sunny, turning mild. 7–11 Showers, then sunny, mild. 12–16 Showers, then sunny, mild. 17–23 Showers, then sunny; mild north, cold south. 24–28 Sunny, turning mild. 29–31 Snow north, rain south; cold.

FEB. 2021: Temp. 57.5° (10° above avg. north, 5° above south); precip. 1" (1" below avg.). 1–9 Sunny, turning warm. 10–14 Rainy periods, mild. 15–23 Sunny, mild. 24–28 Rain, then sunny, cold.

MAR. 2021: Temp. 60° (1° above avg.); precip. 1.5" (1" below avg.). 1–8 Rainy periods; turning cold north, warm south. 9–13 Sunny, warm. 14–22 A few t-storms, turning cooler. 23–26 Sunny, cool. 27–31 T-storms, warm.

APR. 2021: Temp. 66° (avg.); precip. 5" (2" above avg.). 1–4 Sunny, warm. 5–13 A few t-storms, warm. 14–23 Rainy periods, turning cool. 24–28 Sunny, cool. 29–30 T-storms.

MAY 2021: Temp. 70° (3° below avg.); precip. 5.5" (2" above avg. east, 1" below west). 1–6 T-storms, mild. 7–12 Sunny, cool. 13–23 A few t-storms; warm, then cool. 24–31 Isolated t-storms, warm.

JUNE 2021: Temp. 78° (1° below avg.); precip. 4.5" (2" below avg. north, 3" above south). 1–6 Sunny, warm. 7–18 Scattered t-storms, warm. 19–23 T-storms, hot. 24–30 A few t-storms, turning cool.

JULY 2021: Temp. 79° (2° below avg.); precip. 4" (1" below avg. north, 3" above south). 1–9 A few t-storms, cool. 10–15 Sunny, warm. 16–26 Isolated t-storms, turning hot. 27–31 Scattered t-storms, warm.

AUG. 2021: Temp. 81° (avg.); precip. 2.5" (avg.). 1–4 Sunny north, t-storms south; warm. 5–14 Scattered t-storms, warm. 15–19 Sunny north, t-storms south; hot. 20–25 Scattered t-storms, cool. 26–31 Sunny, warm.

SEPT. 2021: Temp. 74° (2° below avg.); precip. 4.5" (1" above avg.). 1–6 A few t-storms; cool north, hot south. 7–18 Scattered t-storms, hot. 19–23 T-storms, cool. 24–30 A few t-storms, turning chilly.

OCT. 2021: Temp. 61° (6° below avg.); precip. 5" (2" below avg. north, 4" above south). 1–7 Sunny, cool. 8–23 Rainy periods, cool. 24–31 Sunny, cool.

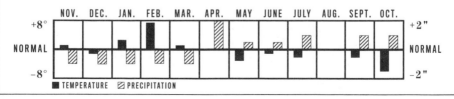

WEATHER

HIGH PLAINS

SUMMARY: Winter will be milder than normal, with the coldest periods in mid-November, early to mid- and late December, late January, and late February. Precipitation will be above normal in the north and slightly below normal in the south. Snowfall will be above normal in most places, with the snowiest periods in mid-November, early and late December, mid- and late January, mid- to late February, and early March. **April** and **May** will see temperatures above normal in the north and below normal in the south, and overall the months will be slightly rainier than normal. **Summer** will be warmer than normal, with the hottest periods in early and late June, early and mid-July, and early to mid-August. Rainfall will be near to below normal. **September** and **October** will have below-normal temperatures, with precipitation below normal in the north and above normal in the south.

Billings • Bismarck •
Rapid • City
• Cheyenne
Denver •
Amarillo •

WEATHER

NOV. 2020: Temp. 35° (1° below avg.); precip. 1.5" (0.5" above avg.). 1–8 Snow showers, then sunny, mild. 9–15 Snow showers, then sunny, cold. 16–23 Snow, then flurries, very cold. 24–30 Sunny, mild.

DEC. 2020: Temp. 29° (1° below avg.); precip. 1" (1.5" above avg. north, 0.5" below south). 1–2 Sunny, mild. 3–9 Snowy periods, very cold. 10–17 Sunny, mild. 18–23 Rain and snow showers, mild. 24–31 Snowy periods, cold.

JAN. 2021: Temp. 32.5° (5° above avg.); precip. 0.5" (avg.). 1–5 Sunny, mild. 6–12 Snow showers, mild. 13–16 Sunny, warm. 17–25 Snow, then sunny, warm. 26–31 Snowy periods, cold.

FEB. 2021: Temp. 33° (5° above avg.); precip. 0.5" (avg.). 1–11 Rain and snow showers, mild. 12–19 Snow, then sunny, turning mild. 20–28 Snowy periods, turning very cold.

MAR. 2021: Temp. 42° (3° above avg.); precip. 0.5" (0.5" below avg.). 1–8 Snowy periods, cold. 9–12 Sunny, warm. 13–18 Showers, mild. 19–23 Snow, then sunny, cold. 24–31 Snow north, showers south; then sunny, mild.

APR. 2021: Temp. 47° (1° below avg.); precip. 3" (1" above avg.). 1–5 Sunny, warm. 6–21 Rainy periods, cool. 22–26 Sunny, mild. 27–30 Rainy periods, cool.

MAY 2021: Temp. 58.5° (3° above avg. north, 2° below south); precip. 2" (0.5" below avg.).

1–6 Showers, turning warm. 7–12 Scattered t-storms; warm north, cool south. 13–19 Scattered t-storms, cool. 20–31 Isolated t-storms; hot north, cool south.

JUNE 2021: Temp. 66° (1° below avg.); precip. 2.5" (avg.). 1–3 Sunny, hot. 4–12 Rainy periods north, sunny south; cool. 13–19 A few t-storms, cool. 20–30 Sunny, turning hot.

JULY 2021: Temp. 72.5° (0.5° above avg.); precip. 2" (avg.). 1–4 Sunny, hot. 5–9 A few t-storms, turning cool. 10–17 Scattered t-storms, turning hot. 18–26 A few t-storms, turning cool. 27–31 Sunny, warm.

AUG. 2021: Temp. 73° (2° above avg.); precip. 1" (avg. north, 2" below south). 1–8 Scattered t-storms, warm. 9–19 A few t-storms, hot. 20–31 Scattered t-storms, warm.

SEPT. 2021: Temp. 60.5° (1° above avg. north, 2° below south); precip. 2.5" (avg. north, 2" above south). 1–3 Sunny, cool. 4–11 A few t-storms, turning hot. 12–16 Sunny; warm north, cool south. 17–24 T-storms, then sunny; cool, then warm. 25–30 Rainy periods, turning cool.

OCT. 2021: Temp. 47° (2° below avg.); precip. 0.5" (0.5" below avg.). 1–7 Sunny, cool. 8–20 Periods of rain and snow, cold. 21–31 Sunny, mild.

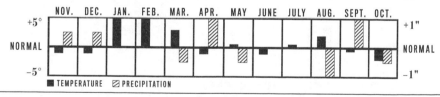

INTERMOUNTAIN

Spokane
• Pendleton
Boise •
Reno •   Salt • Lake City
Grand Junction •
Flagstaff •

SUMMARY: Winter temperatures and precipitation will be slightly below normal, on average. The coldest periods will be in early to mid-December, late January, and late February. Snowfall will be near normal, with the snowiest periods in early and late December, late January, and late February. **April** and **May** temperatures will be below normal in the north and above normal in the south, with near-normal precipitation. **Summer** temperatures will be cooler than normal in the north and above normal in the south, and it will be slightly rainier than normal. The hottest periods will be in late June, mid-July, and mid- to late August. **September** and **October** will be warmer than normal, with near-normal precipitation.

NOV. 2020: Temp. 38° (2° below avg.); precip. 1.5" (avg.). 1–6 Snow showers, then sunny, cool. 7–8 Showers, mild. 9–23 Snow showers, cold. 24–30 Rainy periods north, sunny south; mild.

DEC. 2020: Temp. 33° (2° above avg. north, 2° below south); precip. 1.5" (avg.). 1–4 Sunny, mild. 5–14 Snowstorm, then sunny, cold. 15–23 Rain and snow showers, mild. 24–31 Snowy periods, turning mild.

JAN. 2021: Temp. 34° (2° above avg.); precip. 1" (0.5" below avg.). 1–6 Rain and snow showers, mild. 7–15 Sunny, turning cold. 16–26 Snow showers, then sunny, mild. 27–31 Snowy periods, cold.

FEB. 2021: Temp. 33.5° (3° below avg. north, 2° above south); precip. 2" (0.5" above avg.). 1–7 Rainy periods, mild. 8–13 Snow showers, turning cold. 14–17 Sunny, mild. 18–28 Snowy periods, then sunny, cold.

MAR. 2021: Temp. 42° (1° below avg.); precip. 1" (0.5" below avg.). 1–8 Snow showers, then sunny, cold. 9–17 Rain and snow showers north; sunny, mild south. 18–26 Snow showers, cold. 27–31 Showers, mild.

APR. 2021: Temp. 49° (avg.); precip. 1" (avg.). 1–4 Sunny, mild. 5–11 Rainy periods north, snowstorm south; cool. 12–17 Showers, cool north; sunny, mild south. 18–24 Sunny, mild. 25–30 Rainy periods, mild.

MAY 2021: Temp. 58° (1° below avg. north, 3° above south); precip. 1" (avg.). 1–10 Rain, then sunny, turning warm. 11–17 Rainy periods, cool. 18–20 Sunny, warm. 21–25 Rainy periods, cool north; sunny, warm south. 26–31 Sunny, warm.

JUNE 2021: Temp. 65° (1° below avg.); precip. 0.3" (0.2" below avg.). 1–9 Rainy periods, cool. 10–14 Sunny, warm. 15–20 Showers, then sunny, cool. 21–30 Isolated t-storms, turning hot.

JULY 2021: Temp. 73° (avg.); precip. 1.5" (1" above avg.). 1–7 A few t-storms, turning cool. 8–19 Scattered t-storms, hot. 20–31 T-storms, then sunny, cool.

AUG. 2021: Temp. 71.5° (3° below avg. north, 2° above south); precip. 1" (0.5" above avg. north, 0.5" below south). 1–11 T-storms, then sunny, cool. 12–18 T-storms, warm. 19–28 Sunny, hot. 29–31 Showers, cool.

SEPT. 2021: Temp. 64° (2° above avg.); precip. 1.5" (0.5" above avg.). 1–9 Sunny, warm north; rainy periods south. 10–19 Sunny, warm north; showers, cool south. 20–25 Sunny, warm. 26–30 Showers, then sunny, cool.

OCT. 2021: Temp. 52° (1° above avg.); precip. 0.5" (0.5" below avg.). 1–13 Sunny; warm, then cool. 14–18 Rainy periods, cool. 19–31 Scattered showers, turning warm.

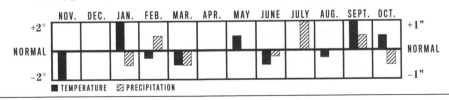

| | NOV. | DEC. | JAN. | FEB. | MAR. | APR. | MAY | JUNE | JULY | AUG. | SEPT. | OCT. | |

+2°   +1"

NORMAL   NORMAL

−2°   −1"

■ TEMPERATURE ▨ PRECIPITATION

WEATHER

DESERT SOUTHWEST

SUMMARY: Winter will be colder and drier than normal, with the coldest periods in mid- and late December and mid- and late February. Snowfall will be below normal in most areas that normally receive snow, with the snowiest periods in late December and late February. **April** and **May** will be cooler than normal in the east and warmer in the west, with above-normal rainfall.

Summer will be cooler than normal, with near-normal rainfall. The hottest periods will occur in mid-June and late August. **September** and **October** will be cooler than normal, with near- to slightly above-normal precipitation.

NOV. 2020: Temp. 54° (2° below avg.); precip. 0.7" (0.3" below avg.). 1–10 Sunny; cool, then warm. 11–19 Showers, then sunny, cool. 20–22 Showers, cold. 23–30 Sunny, turning warmer.

DEC. 2020: Temp. 46° (2° below avg.); precip. 0.4" (0.1" below avg.). 1–4 Sunny, warm. 5–11 Showers, then sunny, cold. 12–17 Rainy periods, wet snow east. 18–23 Sunny; cold east, mild west. 24–31 Snow showers east, then sunny, cold.

JAN. 2021: Temp. 49° (1° below avg. east, 3° above west); precip. 0.5" (avg.). 1–11 Sunny, turning warm. 12–17 Showers east; sunny, mild west. 18–27 Sunny; cool east, mild west. 28–31 Rainy periods, mild.

FEB. 2021: Temp. 52° (3° above avg. east, 1° below west); precip. 0.5" (avg.). 1–7 Rainy periods, mild. 8–16 Sunny, cold. 17–23 Sunny, warm. 24–28 Rain and snow showers, cold.

MAR. 2021: Temp. 56° (2° below avg.); precip. 0.3" (avg. east, 0.4" below west). 1–2 Sunny, cool. 3–9 Snow showers, then sunny, cool. 10–18 Sunny, turning warm. 19–23 Snow showers east, sunny west; cold. 24–31 Sunny, cool.

APR. 2021: Temp. 55° (2° below avg.); precip. 1.5" (1" above avg.). 1–4 Sunny, warm. 5–12 Rain, then sunny, cool. 13–20 Sunny; warm east, turning cool west. 21–24 Sunny; cool east, warm west. 25–30 Rainy periods, cool.

MAY 2021: Temp. 74.5° (2° below avg. east, 3°

above west); precip. 0.5" (avg.). 1–9 Sunny, turning hot. 10–15 A few showers, cooler. 16–20 Sunny, warm. 21–31 Isolated t-storms, turning cooler.

JUNE 2021: Temp. 81° (2° below avg.); precip. 0.5" (avg.). 1–8 Sunny, cool. 9–14 Sunny, hot. 15–22 Isolated t-storms, hot. 23–30 Scattered t-storms, warm.

JULY 2021: Temp. 84° (3° below avg.); precip. 2" (0.5" above avg.). 1–10 A few t-storms, turning cooler. 11–16 T-storms east, sunny west; warm. 17–24 A few t-storms, warm. 25–31 Isolated t-storms, warm.

AUG. 2021: Temp. 84° (1° below avg.); precip. 1" (1" below avg. east, avg. west). 1–6 A few t-storms east, sunny west; warm. 7–13 Isolated t-storms east, sunny west; cool. 14–23 Isolated t-storms, cool east; sunny, hot west. 24–31 Scattered t-storms; hot, then cooler.

SEPT. 2021: Temp. 76° (3° below avg.); precip. 1.5" (avg. east, 1" above west). 1–6 Rain, then sunny, cooler. 7–13 Showers, then sunny, cool. 14–20 Rainy periods, cool. 21–30 Scattered t-storms, cool.

OCT. 2021: Temp. 67.5° (3° below avg. east, 2° above west); precip. 1" (avg.). 1–4 Sunny, cool. 5–12 Scattered showers; warm, then cool. 13–22 Rainy periods east, sunny west; turning chilly. 23–31 Sunny, turning warm.

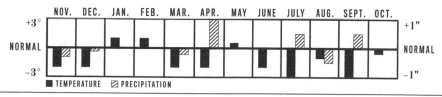

PACIFIC NORTHWEST

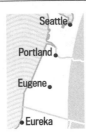

Seattle
Portland
Eugene
Eureka

SUMMARY: Winter temperatures and precipitation will be close to normal, on average, with below-normal snowfall. The coldest periods will occur in mid-January and early and late February. The snowiest periods will occur in early December and from mid- to late February. **April** and **May** will be slightly cooler and drier than normal. **Summer** will have slightly above-normal temperatures, on average, with above-normal precipitation. The hottest periods will be in mid-June, mid-July, and mid-August. **September** and **October** will be warmer and drier than normal.

NOV. 2020: Temp. 48° (1° above avg.); precip. 7.5" (1" above avg.). 1–8 Rainy periods; cold, then mild. 9–14 Occasional rain, cool. 15–20 Rainy; mild, then cool. 21–23 Snow north, rain south. 24–30 Rain, some heavy; mild.

DEC. 2020: Temp. 45° (2° above avg.); precip. 7.5" (avg. north, 2" above south). 1–3 Rainy periods. 4–8 Rain and snow. 9–13 Sunny, cold. 14–22 Rainy periods, mild. 23–26 Sunny, cold. 27–31 Rainy periods, cool.

JAN. 2021: Temp. 44° (1° above avg.); precip. 3.5" (1" below avg. north, 4" below south). 1–8 Rainy periods, turning mild. 9–18 A few showers, turning cold. 19–24 Rain, then sunny, cool. 25–31 Sprinkles and flurries, cold.

FEB. 2021: Temp. 43° (1° below avg.); precip. 6" (1" above avg.). 1–3 Sunny, cold. 4–13 Rainy periods; mild, then cold. 14–15 Sunny, cool. 16–20 Rainy periods; cold north, mild south. 21–28 Snow, then sunny, cold.

MAR. 2021: Temp. 45° (2° below avg.); precip. 4" (avg.). 1–8 Rainy periods, cool. 9–12 Showers, mild. 13–20 Rainy periods, cool. 21–25 Rain and wet snow, cold. 26–31 Sunny, then rain; mild.

APR. 2021: Temp. 50° (avg.); precip. 3" (avg.). 1–5 Showers, mild. 6–17 Rainy periods, cool.

18–23 Sunny, turning warm. 24–30 Rainy periods, mild.

MAY 2021: Temp. 54° (1° below avg.); precip. 1.5" (0.5" below avg.). 1–9 Showers, then sunny, warm. 10–15 Sunny, cool. 16–24 Rainy periods, cool. 25–31 Sunny, cool.

JUNE 2021: Temp. 60° (avg.); precip. 1.5" (avg.). 1–9 Showers, cool. 10–15 Sunny, warm. 16–21 Showers, then sunny, hot. 22–30 Scattered t-storms; cool, then warm.

JULY 2021: Temp. 66° (1° above avg.); precip. 1" (0.5" above avg.). 1–4 Showers, cool. 5–11 Sunny, warm. 12–18 Showers, turning hot. 19–25 Sunny, cool. 26–31 T-storms, cool.

AUG. 2021: Temp. 65.5 (0.5° below avg.); precip. 2" (1" above avg.). 1–5 Sunny, cool. 6–19 Rainy periods, cool. 20–27 Sunny, hot. 28–31 T-storms, cool.

SEPT. 2021: Temp. 64° (3° above avg.); precip. 0.5" (1" below avg.). 1–9 A few showers, cool. 10–14 Sunny, warm. 15–22 Showers, then sunny, warm. 23–30 Scattered showers, warm.

OCT. 2021: Temp. 56° (2° above avg.); precip. 1" (2" below avg.). 1–4 Showers, warm. 5–15 Sunny, turning cool. 16–25 Rainy periods, mild. 26–31 Sunny, warm.

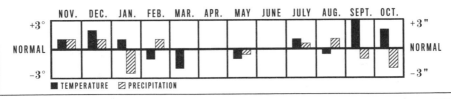

	NOV.	DEC.	JAN.	FEB.	MAR.	APR.	MAY	JUNE	JULY	AUG.	SEPT.	OCT.	
+3°													+3"
NORMAL													NORMAL
–3°													–3"

■ TEMPERATURE ▨ PRECIPITATION

WEATHER

PACIFIC SOUTHWEST

SUMMARY: Winter will be cooler and drier than normal, with below-normal mountain snows. The coldest temperatures will occur in late December, late January, and mid- to late February. The stormiest periods will be from late January into early February, mid- to late February, and late March into early April. **April** and **May** will be cooler than normal, with rainfall below normal in the north and above normal in the south. **Summer** temperatures will be cooler than normal inland and warmer near the coast, with slightly above-normal rainfall. The hottest periods will be in mid-June and mid- to late August. **September** and **October** will be warmer and rainier than normal.

San Francisco

Fresno

Los Angeles

San Diego

WEATHER

NOV. 2020: Temp. 56° (2° below avg.); precip. 0.5" (1" below avg.). 1–8 Rain, then sunny, cool north; sunny, turning warm south. 9–15 Scattered showers, cool. 16–19 Sunny, warm. 20–30 Rain, then sunny, cool.

DEC. 2020: Temp. 52° (2° below avg.); precip. 0.5" (1.5" below avg.). 1–6 Rainy periods, cool. 7–12 Sunny, cool. 13–16 Showers, cool. 17–22 Sunny, warm. 23–31 Sunny, cold.

JAN. 2021: Temp. 55.5° (avg. north, 3° above south); precip. 2" (1" below avg.). 1–6 Rain, then sunny, cool. 7–15 Sunny, turning warm. 16–20 Sunny, cool. 21–26 Sunny, warm. 27–31 Rainy, cold.

FEB. 2021: Temp. 53° (2° below avg.); precip. 2.5" (1" below avg. north, 2" above south). 1–12 Rainy periods, cool. 13–21 Sunny, cool. 22–25 Rain, some heavy; cold. 26–28 Sunny, cool.

MAR. 2021: Temp. 57.5° (1° below avg. north, 2° above south); precip. 0.5" (2" below avg.). 1–9 Showers, then sunny, turning warm. 10–20 Showers, then sunny; cool north, warm south. 21–26 A few showers north; sunny, mild south. 27–31 Rainy periods, cool.

APR. 2021: Temp. 59° (1° below avg.); precip. 1.3" (0.5" below avg. north, 1" above south). 1–8 Rainy periods, cool. 9–15 Scattered showers, cool. 16–24 Sunny, turning warm. 25–30 Scattered showers, cooler.

MAY 2021: Temp. 63.5° (avg.); precip. 0.3" (0.2" below avg.). 1–4 Sunny, warm inland; A.M. sprinkles, P.M. sunny coast. 5–9 Sunny;

hot north, warm south. 10–18 Sunny, cool. 19–24 Sunny inland; A.M. sprinkles, P.M. sunny coast; cool. 25–31 Sunny, cool.

JUNE 2021: Temp. 68.5° (2° below avg. east, 3° above west); precip. 0.2" (0.1" above avg.). 1–5 Showers, then sunny, cool. 6–9 Sunny; hot north, cool south. 10–15 Sunny, cool. 16–21 Sunny, hot. 22–30 A.M. sprinkles, P.M. sunny, cool north; sunny, hot south.

JULY 2021: Temp. 70.5° (2° below avg. east, 1° above west); precip. 0.01" (0.01" above avg.). 1–6 Sunny, cool inland; A.M. sprinkles, P.M. sunny, warm coast. 7–19 Isolated showers, cool. 20–23 Sunny, warm. 24–31 Sunny, cool inland; A.M. sprinkles, P.M. sunny coast.

AUG. 2021: Temp. 70° (1° below avg.); precip. 0.35" (0.5" above avg. north, avg. south). 1–3 Sunny, cool. 4–12 A few showers; cold inland, warm coast. 13–20 Isolated showers; cool inland, warm coast. 21–26 Sunny, warm. 27–31 Scattered showers; cool north, warm south.

SEPT. 2021: Temp. 70° (avg.); precip. 1.2" (1" above avg.). 1–4 Showers, turning cooler. 5–16 Sunny, cool. 17–25 Rainy periods, cool north; sunny, warm south. 26–30 Sunny, warm.

OCT. 2021: Temp. 68° (1° above avg. north, 5° above south); precip. 0.5" (avg.). 1–12 Sunny; hot, then cooler. 13–18 Showers, then sunny, cool. 19–24 Sunny; cool north, warm south. 25–31 Sunny; warm north, hot south.

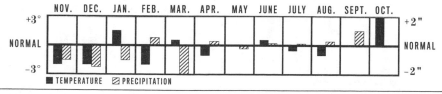

| | NOV. | DEC. | JAN. | FEB. | MAR. | APR. | MAY | JUNE | JULY | AUG. | SEPT. | OCT. | |

■ TEMPERATURE ☒ PRECIPITATION

SUMMARY: Winter season temperatures will be milder than normal, with the coldest periods in late November, early January, and early and mid-February. Precipitation will be slightly above normal. Snowfall will be above normal in the north and below normal in the south, with the snowiest periods in late March N, mid-November C, and early December and early to mid-March S. **April** and **May** will be warmer than normal, with slightly below-normal precipitation. **Summer** will be warmer and drier than normal, with the hottest periods in early June and throughout July. **September** and **October** will be milder than normal, with precipitation below normal N and above S.

KEY: north (N), central (C), south (S), elsewhere (EW).

NOV. 2020: Temp. –3° N, 31° S (5° below avg.); precip. 0.3" N, 4" S (0.1" below avg. N, 1" below S). 1–10 Snow showers, cold. 11–16 Sunny, mild. 17–21 Snowy periods, mild. 22–30 Sunny, frigid.

DEC. 2020: Temp. –5° N, 33° S (2° above avg.); precip. 0.1" N, 4.9" S (0.1" below avg.). 1–8 Snow showers N+C, snowy periods S; cold. 9–18 Flurries, cold N; snow, then clear, mild EW. 19–24 Flurries, cold N; snow showers, mild EW. 25–31 Flurries; mild N, cold EW.

JAN. 2021: Temp. –10° N, 37° S (2° above avg. N, 8° above S); precip. 0.1" N, 8" S (0.1" below avg. N, 3" above S). 1–10 Flurries; cold, then mild. 11–21 Flurries, cold N; snowy periods, mild S. 22–28 Snowy periods, mild. 29–31 Flurries; cold N, mild EW.

FEB. 2021: Temp. –17° N, 28° S (3° below avg.); precip. 0.1" N, 2.5" S (0.1" below avg. N, 1.5" below S). 1–4 Clear N, snow showers EW; cold. 5–15 Clear, cold. 16–24 Clear, turning mild N; snow showers, cold S. 25–28 Flurries, quite mild.

MAR. 2021: Temp. –8° N, 39° S (5° above avg.); precip. 1" N, 5.5" S (0.5" above avg.). 1–5 Snow showers; cold N, mild S. 6–13 Clear, mild N; snowy periods, cold EW. 14–21 Snow showers, mild. 22–31 Snow showers; cold N, mild S.

APR. 2021: Temp. 5° N, 44° S (3° above avg.); precip. 0.2" N, 2.5" S (0.5" below avg.). 1–6 Snowy periods, mild. 7–11 Sunny; cold N, mild S. 12–16 Snow showers N, sunny S; mild. 17–19 Snow showers, cold. 20–30 Flurries,

mild N; scattered showers, warm S.

MAY 2021: Temp. 20° N, 46° EW (1° below avg.); precip. 0.6" N, 3" S (avg.). 1–12 Flurries N, scattered showers S; mild. 13–22 Flurries N, showers S; cool. 23–31 A few showers, mild.

JUNE 2021: Temp. 34° N, 54° EW (1° below avg.); precip. 1" N, 2" S (0.3" above avg. N, 1" below S). 1–8 Showers, then sunny, warm. 9–18 A few showers, mild. 19–27 Scattered showers, cool. 28–30 Showers; cool N, warm S.

JULY 2021: Temp. 44° N, 59° EW (2° above avg.); precip. 0.7" N, 3.5" S (0.5" below avg.). 1–8 Sunny, warm. 9–16 A few showers; warm N+S, hot C. 17–24 Scattered showers, warm. 25–31 Showers, mild.

AUG. 2021: Temp. 42° N, 58° EW (2° above avg.); precip. 0.7" N, 4.5" S (0.5" below avg.). 1–9 Showers, cool. 10–16 A few showers; cool N, warm EW. 17–24 Isolated showers, cool. 25–31 Rainy periods N+C, sunny S; cool.

SEPT. 2021: Temp. 37° N, 59° EW (5° above avg.); precip. 0.6" N, 8" S (0.5" below avg. N, 1" above S). 1–14 Rainy periods, mild. 15–21 Showers, mild. 22–30 Snow showers N, a few showers EW; mild.

OCT. 2021: Temp. 16° N, 47° S (1° below avg. N, 5° above S); precip. 0.5" N, 7" S (avg.). 1–7 Snow showers, turning cold N+C; sunny, cool S. 8–15 Flurries N, showers EW; mild. 16–24 Snow showers N+C; snow, then sunny S; turning cold. 25–31 Snow showers; cold N, mild S.

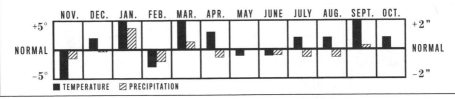

Get your local forecast at Almanac.com/Weather.

HAWAII

SUMMARY: Winter season temperatures will be below average in the east and above average in the west, with the coolest periods in early and mid-December, mid-January, early February, and early March. Rainfall will be above normal in the east and below normal in the west, with the stormiest periods in mid-November, from late January into early February, and in early to mid-March. **April** and **May** will be cooler than normal in the east and warmer than normal in the west. The months will be slightly drier than normal overall. **Summer** will be slightly cooler than normal, with the warmest period in late July. Rainfall will be below normal in the east and above normal in the west. **September** and **October** will be cooler than normal, with the hottest period in mid-September. Rainfall will be below normal in the east and near normal in the west.

KEY: east (E), central (C), west (W). Note: Temperature and precipitation are substantially based upon topography. The detailed forecast focuses on the Honolulu–Waikiki area and provides general trends elsewhere.

NOV. 2020: Temp. 77.8° (0.5° below avg. E, 1° above W); precip. 2.5" (1" above avg. E, 5" above C, 3" below W). 1–8 A few showers, cool. 9–16 Scattered showers, warm; heavy rain E. 17–20 Heavy rain. 21–30 A few showers, warm; heavy rain E.

DEC. 2020: Temp. 75° (avg.); precip. 2.3" (1" above avg. E, 4" below W). 1–7 Showers, cool. 8–19 Sunny, cool. 20–31 Rainy periods E+W, isolated showers C; warm.

JAN. 2021: Temp. 72.5° (0.5° below avg.); precip. 2.5" (2" below avg. E, 3" above C, 1" below W). 1–7 Rainy periods E+W, sunny C; warm. 8–21 A few showers, cool. 22–28 Rain, then sunny, cool. 29–31 Heavy rain, cool.

FEB. 2021: Temp. 73.5° (avg. E, 1° above W); precip. 3.5" (6" above avg. E, 3" below W). 1–4 Rainy periods, cool. 5–16 Heavy rain E; a few showers, cool C+W. 17–22 Heavy rain E; sunny, cool C+W. 23–28 Rainy periods, seasonable.

MAR. 2021: Temp. 73.5° (0.5° below avg.); precip. 4" (2" above avg.). 1–8 Heavy rain E; scattered showers, cool C+W. 9–17 Showers and t-storms, warm. 18–31 Showers, turning cooler.

APR. 2021: Temp. 76° (0.5° below avg. E, 1.5° above W); precip. 0.2" (0.5" below avg.). 1–8 Scattered showers, seasonable. 9–21 Showers, cool. 22–30 Rainy E, a few showers C+W; seasonable.

MAY 2021: Temp. 77.5° (1° below avg. E, 2° above W); precip. 0.2" (0.5" below avg.). 1–3 Sunny, warm. 4–14 Showers, seasonable. 15–21 Scattered showers, seasonable. 22–31 A few showers, cool.

JUNE 2021: Temp. 79.5° (avg.); precip. 0.2" (0.2" below avg.). 1–12 Scattered showers, cool. 13–20 Rainy periods E+W, isolated showers C; seasonable. 21–30 Daily showers E and W, isolated showers C; warm.

JULY 2021: Temp. 81° (avg.); precip. 0.5" (2" below avg. E, 2" above W). 1–15 Daily showers, warm. 16–23 Showers E and W, isolated showers C; cool. 24–31 A few showers, warm.

AUG. 2021: Temp. 81° (0.5° below avg.); precip. 0.6" (2" below avg. E, 2" above W). 1–10 A few showers, cool. 11–17 Showers E and W, sunny C; seasonable. 18–31 Rainy periods, warm E; a few showers, cool C+W.

SEPT. 2021: Temp. 80° (1.5° below avg.); precip. 0.8" (2" below avg. E, 2" above W). 1–13 A few showers, cool. 14–21 Showers, warm. 22–30 Scattered showers, cool.

OCT. 2021: Temp. 80° (1° above avg. E, 1° below W); precip. 1.5" (1" above avg. E, 2" below W). 1–11 Showers, warm E; isolated showers, cool C+W. 12–21 Rainy periods, some heavy E; scattered showers C+W; warm. 22–31 Showers, warm.

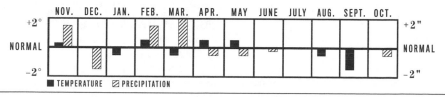

SECRETS OF THE ZODIAC

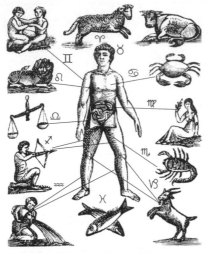

The Man of the Signs

Ancient astrologers believed that each astrological sign influenced a specific part of the body. The first sign of the zodiac—Aries—was attributed to the head, with the rest of the signs moving down the body, ending with Pisces at the feet.

♈ Aries, head	ARI	*Mar. 21–Apr. 20*
♉ Taurus, neck	TAU	*Apr. 21–May 20*
♊ Gemini, arms	GEM	*May 21–June 20*
♋ Cancer, breast	CAN	*June 21–July 22*
♌ Leo, heart	LEO	*July 23–Aug. 22*
♍ Virgo, belly	VIR	*Aug. 23–Sept. 22*
♎ Libra, reins	LIB	*Sept. 23–Oct. 22*
♏ Scorpio, secrets	SCO	*Oct. 23–Nov. 22*
♐ Sagittarius, thighs	SAG	*Nov. 23–Dec. 21*
♑ Capricorn, knees	CAP	*Dec. 22–Jan. 19*
♒ Aquarius, legs	AQU	*Jan. 20–Feb. 19*
♓ Pisces, feet	PSC	*Feb. 20–Mar. 20*

ASTROLOGY VS. ASTRONOMY

Astrology is a tool we use to plan events according to the placements of the Sun, the Moon, and the planets in the 12 signs of the zodiac. In astrology, the planetary movements do not cause events; rather, they explain the path, or "flow," that events tend to follow. *The Moon's astrological place is given on the next page.* **Astronomy** is the study of the actual placement of the known planets and constellations. The Moon's astronomical place is given in the **Left-Hand Calendar Pages, 120–146.** *(The placement of the planets in the signs of the zodiac is not the same astrologically and astronomically.)*

The dates in the **Best Days** table, **pages 226–227,** are based on the astrological passage of the Moon.

WHEN MERCURY IS RETROGRADE

Sometimes the other planets appear to be traveling backward through the zodiac; this is an illusion. We call this illusion *retrograde motion.*

Mercury's retrograde periods can cause our plans to go awry. However, intuition is high during these periods and coincidences can be extraordinary.

When Mercury is retrograde, stay flexible, allow more time for travel, and don't sign contracts. Review projects and plans but wait until Mercury is direct again to make final decisions.

In 2021, Mercury will be retrograde during **January 30–February 21, May 29–June 22,** and **September 27–October 23**.

–Celeste Longacre

GARDENING BY THE MOON'S SIGN

USE CHART ON NEXT PAGE TO FIND THE BEST DATES FOR THE FOLLOWING GARDEN TASKS . . .

PLANT, TRANSPLANT, AND GRAFT: Cancer, Scorpio, Pisces, or Taurus
HARVEST: Aries, Leo, Sagittarius, Gemini, or Aquarius
BUILD/FIX FENCES OR GARDEN BEDS: Capricorn

CONTROL INSECT PESTS, PLOW, AND WEED: Aries, Gemini, Leo, Sagittarius, or Aquarius
PRUNE: Aries, Leo, or Sagittarius. During a waxing Moon, pruning encourages growth; during a waning Moon, it discourages it.

Get your zodiac profile at Almanac.com/BestDays/Zodiac.

SETTING EGGS BY THE MOON'S SIGN

Chicks take about 21 days to hatch. Those born under a waxing Moon in Cancer, Scorpio, or Pisces are healthier and mature faster. To ensure that chicks are born during these times, "set eggs" (place eggs in an incubator or under a hen) 21 days before the desired hatching dates.

EXAMPLE:
The Moon is new on May 11 and full on May 26 (EDT). Between these dates, the Moon is in the sign of Cancer on May 15 and 16. To have chicks born on May 15, count back 21 days; set eggs on April 24.

Below are the best days to set eggs in 2021, using only the fruitful dates between the new and full Moons, and counting back 21 days:

JAN.: 5, 6, 22, 23
FEB.: 1, 2, 20, 28
MAR.: 1, 2, 28, 29

APR.: 5, 24, 25
MAY: 3, 4, 21–23, 30, 31
JUNE: 18, 19, 27, 28

JULY: 24, 25
AUG.: 1, 20, 21, 29, 30
SEPT.: 16, 17, 25, 26

OCT.: 14, 15, 22, 23
NOV.: 18–20
DEC.: 16, 17, 25–27

The Moon's Astrological Place, 2020–21

	NOV.	DEC.	JAN.	FEB.	MAR.	APR.	MAY	JUNE	JULY	AUG.	SEPT.	OCT.	NOV.	DEC.
1	TAU	GEM	LEO	LIB	LIB	SAG	CAP	PSC	ARI	TAU	CAN	LEO	VIR	SCO
2	GEM	CAN	LEO	LIB	LIB	SAG	CAP	PSC	ARI	GEM	CAN	LEO	LIB	SCO
3	GEM	CAN	VIR	SCO	SCO	CAP	AQU	PSC	TAU	GEM	LEO	VIR	LIB	SAG
4	GEM	LEO	VIR	SCO	SCO	CAP	AQU	ARI	TAU	GEM	LEO	VIR	SCO	SAG
5	CAN	LEO	LIB	SCO	SAG	AQU	PSC	ARI	TAU	CAN	LEO	LIB	SCO	CAP
6	CAN	LEO	LIB	SAG	SAG	AQU	PSC	TAU	GEM	CAN	VIR	LIB	SAG	CAP
7	LEO	VIR	SCO	SAG	CAP	AQU	ARI	TAU	GEM	LEO	VIR	SCO	SAG	AQU
8	LEO	VIR	SCO	CAP	CAP	PSC	ARI	TAU	CAN	LEO	LIB	SCO	CAP	AQU
9	VIR	LIB	SAG	CAP	AQU	PSC	ARI	GEM	CAN	VIR	LIB	SAG	CAP	PSC
10	VIR	LIB	SAG	AQU	AQU	ARI	TAU	GEM	CAN	VIR	SCO	SAG	AQU	PSC
11	LIB	SCO	CAP	AQU	PSC	ARI	TAU	CAN	LEO	VIR	SCO	SAG	AQU	PSC
12	LIB	SCO	CAP	PSC	PSC	TAU	GEM	CAN	LEO	LIB	SAG	CAP	PSC	ARI
13	SCO	SAG	AQU	PSC	PSC	TAU	GEM	CAN	VIR	LIB	SAG	CAP	PSC	ARI
14	SCO	SAG	AQU	ARI	ARI	TAU	GEM	LEO	VIR	SCO	CAP	AQU	ARI	TAU
15	SAG	CAP	AQU	ARI	ARI	GEM	CAN	LEO	LIB	SCO	CAP	AQU	ARI	TAU
16	SAG	CAP	PSC	ARI	TAU	GEM	CAN	VIR	LIB	SAG	AQU	PSC	ARI	TAU
17	CAP	AQU	PSC	TAU	TAU	GEM	LEO	VIR	LIB	SAG	AQU	PSC	TAU	GEM
18	CAP	AQU	ARI	TAU	TAU	CAN	LEO	LIB	SCO	CAP	AQU	ARI	TAU	GEM
19	CAP	PSC	ARI	GEM	GEM	CAN	LEO	LIB	SCO	CAP	PSC	ARI	GEM	CAN
20	AQU	PSC	ARI	GEM	GEM	LEO	VIR	SCO	SAG	AQU	PSC	ARI	GEM	CAN
21	AQU	PSC	TAU	GEM	CAN	LEO	VIR	SCO	SAG	AQU	ARI	TAU	GEM	CAN
22	PSC	ARI	TAU	CAN	CAN	VIR	LIB	SAG	CAP	PSC	ARI	TAU	CAN	LEO
23	PSC	ARI	GEM	CAN	CAN	VIR	LIB	SAG	CAP	PSC	TAU	GEM	CAN	LEO
24	ARI	TAU	GEM	LEO	LEO	LIB	SCO	CAP	AQU	PSC	TAU	GEM	LEO	VIR
25	ARI	TAU	GEM	LEO	LEO	LIB	SCO	CAP	AQU	ARI	TAU	GEM	LEO	VIR
26	ARI	TAU	CAN	LEO	VIR	SCO	SAG	AQU	PSC	ARI	GEM	CAN	LEO	LIB
27	TAU	GEM	CAN	VIR	VIR	SCO	SAG	AQU	PSC	TAU	GEM	CAN	VIR	LIB
28	TAU	GEM	LEO	VIR	LIB	SAG	CAP	AQU	ARI	TAU	CAN	LEO	VIR	LIB
29	GEM	CAN	LEO	—	LIB	SAG	CAP	PSC	ARI	GEM	CAN	LEO	LIB	SCO
30	GEM	CAN	VIR	—	SCO	CAP	AQU	PSC	ARI	GEM	CAN	LEO	LIB	SCO
31	—	CAN	VIR	—	SCO	—	AQU	—	TAU	GEM	—	VIR	—	SAG

BEST DAYS FOR 2021

This chart is based on the Moon's sign and shows the best days each month for certain activities. –*Celeste Longacre*

	JAN.	FEB.	MAR.	APR.	MAY	JUNE	JULY	AUG.	SEPT.	OCT.	NOV.	DEC.
Quit smoking	4, 8, 31	5, 28	4, 30, 31	9, 27	6, 28	3, 8, 30	5, 27, 31	6, 24, 28	25, 30	3, 22, 31	1, 28	2, 19, 25
Bake	26, 27	22, 23	21–23	18, 19	15, 16	11–13	8–10	5, 6	1, 2, 28–30	26, 27	22, 23	19–21
Brew	7, 8	3–5	3, 4, 30, 31	26, 27	24, 25	20, 21	18, 19	14, 15	10, 11	7, 8	4, 5	1, 2, 29, 30
Dry fruit, vegetables, or meat	1, 2, 29	6, 7	5, 6	1, 2	7–9	4, 5	1, 2, 28–30	7, 25, 26	3–5	1, 2, 28–30	24–26	3, 22, 23
Make jams or jellies	16, 17	12, 13	11–13	8, 9	5, 6	1–3, 29, 30	26, 27	22–24	19, 20	16, 17	12, 13	9–11
Can, pickle, or make sauerkraut	7, 8	3–5	3, 4, 30, 31	8, 9	5, 6	1–3, 29, 30	8, 9, 26, 27	23, 24	1, 2, 28–30	26, 27	22, 23	20, 21
Begin diet to lose weight	4, 8, 31	5, 28	4, 30, 31	9, 27	6, 28	3, 8, 30	5, 27, 31	6, 24, 28	25, 30	3, 22, 31	1, 28	2, 19, 25
Begin diet to gain weight	17, 22	13, 18	18, 27	14, 23	15, 24	17, 21	14, 19	11, 15	7, 11	8, 17	5, 13, 18	9, 19
Cut hair to encourage growth	16, 17, 21, 22	17, 18	17, 18	12–14	22, 23	18, 19	15–17	12, 13	8, 9	16, 17	12, 13	14–16
Cut hair to discourage growth	5, 6, 29	1, 2	1, 2, 29	9, 10	5, 6, 10	6–8	3–5	1, 27, 28	23–25	5, 21, 22	2, 3, 29, 30	26–28
Perm hair	13–15	10, 11	9, 10	5–7	3, 4, 30, 31	26–28	24, 25	20, 21	16–18	14, 15	10, 11	7, 8
Color hair	21, 22	17, 18	16–18	12–14	10, 11	6–8	3–5, 31	1, 27, 28	23–25	21, 22	17, 18	14–16
Straighten hair	9, 10	6, 7	5, 6	1, 2, 28, 29	26, 27	22, 23	20, 21	16, 17	12, 13	9–11	6, 7	3, 4, 31
Have dental care	3, 4, 30, 31	27, 28	26, 27	22, 23	20, 21	16, 17	13, 14	9–11	6, 7	3, 4, 31	1, 27, 28	24, 25
Start projects	14	12	14	12	12	11	10	9	7	7	5	5
End projects	12	10	12	10	10	9	8	7	5	5	3	3
Demolish	7, 8	3–5	3, 4, 30, 31	26, 27	24, 25	20, 21	18, 19	14, 15	10, 11	7, 8	4, 5	1, 2, 29, 30
Lay shingles	1, 2, 28, 29	24–26	24, 25	20, 21	17–19	14, 15	11, 12	7, 8	3–5	1, 2, 28–30	24–26	22, 23
Paint	5, 6	1, 2	1, 2, 28, 29	24, 25	22, 23	18, 19	15–17	12, 13	8, 9	5, 6	2, 3, 29, 30	26–28
Wash windows	18–20	14–16	14, 15	10, 11	7–9	4, 5	1, 2, 28–30	25, 26	21, 22	18–20	14–16	12, 13
Wash floors	16, 17	12, 13	11–13	8, 9	5, 6	1–3, 29, 30	26, 27	22–24	19, 20	16, 17	12, 13	9–11
Go camping	9, 10	6, 7	5, 6	1, 2, 28, 29	26, 27	22, 23	20, 21	16, 17	12, 13	9–11	6, 7	3, 4, 31

	JAN.	FEB.	MAR.	APR.	MAY	JUNE	JULY	AUG.	SEPT.	OCT.	NOV.	DEC.
Entertain	1, 2, 28, 29	24–26	24, 25	20, 21	17–19	14, 15	11, 12	7, 8	3–5	1, 2, 28–30	24–26	22, 23
Travel for pleasure	1, 2, 28, 29	24–26	24, 25	20, 21	17–19	14, 15	11, 12	7, 8	3–5	1, 2, 28–30	24–26	22, 23
Get married	5, 6	1, 2	1, 2, 28, 29	24, 25	22, 23	18, 19	15–17	12, 13	8, 9	5, 6	2, 3, 29, 30	26–28
Ask for a loan	7, 8	3–5	3, 4, 30, 31	8, 9	5, 6, 10	6–8	3–5	7, 25, 26	23–25	21, 22	24–26	1, 2, 29, 30
Buy a home	21, 22	17, 18	16, 17	12–14	24, 25	20, 21	18, 19	14, 15	10, 11	7, 8	5, 17, 18	14–16
Move (house/household)	23–25	19–21	19, 20	15–17	12–14	9, 10	6, 7	2–4	26, 27	23–25	19–21	17, 18
Advertise to sell	21, 22	17, 18	16–18	12–14	24, 25	20, 21	18, 19	14, 15	10, 11	7, 8	17, 18	14–16
Mow to promote growth	18–20	14–16	14, 15	12–14	24, 25	20, 21	18, 19	14, 15	10, 11	18, 19	14–16	12, 13
Mow to slow growth	7, 8	3–5	3, 4, 30, 31	10, 27	7–9	4, 5	1, 2, 28–30	7, 25, 26	3–5, 21, 22	1, 2, 28–30	24–26	29, 30
Plant aboveground crops	16, 17, 26, 27	12, 13, 22, 23	21–23	18, 19	15, 16, 24, 25	11–13	18, 19	14, 15	10, 11, 19	7, 8, 16	12, 13	9–11
Plant belowground crops	7, 8	3–5	3, 4, 30, 31	8, 9	5, 6	1–3, 29, 30	8, 26, 27	5, 6, 23, 24	1, 2, 28–30	26, 27	22, 23	1, 2, 29, 30
Destroy pests and weeds	18–20	14–16	14, 15	10, 11	7–9	4, 5	1, 2, 28–30	25, 26	21, 22	18–20	14–16	12, 13
Graft or pollinate	26, 27	22, 23	21–23	18, 19	15, 16	11–13	8–10	5, 6	1, 2, 28–30	26, 27	22, 23	19–21
Prune to encourage growth	18–20	14–16	14, 15	20, 21	17–19	14, 15	11, 12	16, 17	12, 13	18, 19	14–16	12, 13
Prune to discourage growth	1, 2, 29	6, 7	5, 6	1, 2, 10	7–9	4, 5	1, 2, 28–30	7, 25, 26	3–5	1, 2, 28–30	24–26	3, 31
Pick fruit	3, 4, 30, 31	27, 28	26, 27	22, 23	20, 21	16, 17	13, 14	9–11	6, 7	3, 4, 31	1, 27, 28	24, 25
Harvest above-ground crops	21, 22	17, 18	16–18	12–14	20, 21	16, 17	13, 14	9–11	14, 15	12, 13	17, 18	14–16
Harvest below-ground crops	3, 4, 30, 31	8, 9, 28	7, 8	3, 4, 30	1, 2, 28, 29	6–8	3–5, 31	1, 27, 28	23–25	3, 4, 31	27, 28	24, 25
Cut hay	18–20	14–16	14, 15	10, 11	7–9	4, 5	1, 2, 28–30	25, 26	21, 22	18–20	14–16	12, 13
Begin logging, set posts, pour concrete	11, 12	8, 9	7, 8	3, 4, 30	1, 2, 28, 29	24, 25	22, 23	18, 19	14, 15	12, 13	8, 9	5, 6
Purchase animals	26, 27	22, 23	21–23	18, 19	15, 16	11–13	8–10	5, 6	1, 2, 28–30	26, 27	22, 23	19–21
Breed animals	7, 8	3–5	3, 4, 30, 31	26, 27	24, 25	20, 21	18, 19	14, 15	10, 11	7, 8	4, 5	1, 2, 29, 30
Wean children or animals	4, 8, 31	5, 28	4, 30, 31	9, 27	6, 28	3, 8, 30	5, 27, 31	6, 24, 28	25, 30	3, 22, 31	1, 28	2, 19, 25
Castrate animals	13–15	10, 11	9, 10	5–7	3, 4, 30, 31	26–28	24, 25	20, 21	16–18	14, 15	10, 11	7, 8
Slaughter livestock	7, 8	3–5	3, 4, 30, 31	26, 27	24, 25	20, 21	18, 19	14, 15	10, 11	7, 8	4, 5	1, 2, 29, 30

BEST FISHING DAYS AND TIMES

The best times to fish are when the fish are naturally most active. The Sun, Moon, tides, and weather all influence fish activity. For example, fish tend to feed more at sunrise and sunset, and also during a full Moon (when tides are higher than average). However, most of us go fishing simply when we can get the time off. But there are best times, according to fishing lore:

■ One hour before and one hour after high tides, and one hour before and one hour after low tides. The times of high tides for Boston are given on **pages 120–146; also see pages 236–237.** (Inland, the times for high tides correspond with the times when the Moon is due south. Low tides are halfway between high tides.)

GET TIDE TIMES AND HEIGHTS NEAREST TO YOUR LOCATION AT ALMANAC.COM/TIDES.

■ During the "morning rise" (after sunup for a spell) and the "evening rise" (just before sundown and the hour or so after).

■ During the rise and set of the Moon.

■ When the barometer is steady or on the rise. (But even during stormy periods, the fish aren't going to give up feeding. The clever angler will find just the right bait.)

■ When there is a hatch of flies—caddis flies or mayflies, commonly.

■ When the breeze is from a westerly quarter, rather than from the north or east.

■ When the water is still or slightly rippled, rather than during a wind.

THE BEST FISHING DAYS FOR 2021, WHEN THE MOON IS BETWEEN NEW AND FULL

January 13–28
February 11–27
March 13–28
April 11–26
May 11–26
June 10–24
July 9–23
August 8–22
September 6–20
October 6–20
November 4–19
December 4–18

Dates based on Eastern Time.

HOW TO ESTIMATE THE WEIGHT OF A FISH

Measure the fish from the tip of its nose to the tip of its tail. Then measure its girth at the thickest portion of its midsection.

The weight of a fat-bodied fish (bass, salmon) =
(length x girth x girth)/800

SALMON

The weight of a slender fish (trout, northern pike) =
(length x girth x girth)/900

TROUT

EXAMPLE: If a trout is 20 inches long and has a 12-inch girth, its estimated weight is
(20 x 12 x 12)/900 =
2,880/900 = 3.2 pounds

CATFISH

GESTATION AND MATING TABLES

		PROPER AGE OR WEIGHT FOR FIRST MATING	PERIOD OF FERTILITY (YRS.)	NUMBER OF FEMALES FOR ONE MALE	PERIOD OF GESTATION (DAYS) AVERAGE	RANGE
CATTLE:	Cow	15–18 mos.[1]	10–14		283	279–290[2] 262–300[3]
	Bull	1 yr., well matured	10–12	50[4] / thousands[5]		
GOAT:	Doe	10 mos. or 85–90 lbs.	6		150	145–155
	Buck	well matured	5	30		
HORSE:	Mare	3 yrs.	10–12		336	310–370
	Stallion	3 yrs.	12–15	40–45[4] / record 252[5]		
PIG:	Sow	5–6 mos. or 250 lbs.	6		115	110–120
	Boar	250–300 lbs.	6	50[6] / 35–40[7]		
RABBIT:	Doe	6 mos.	5–6		31	30–32
	Buck	6 mos.	5–6	30		
SHEEP:	Ewe	1 yr. or 90 lbs.	6		147 / 151[8]	142–154
	Ram	12–14 mos., well matured	7	50–75[6] / 35–40[7]		
CAT:	Queen	12 mos.	6		63	60–68
	Tom	12 mos.	6	6–8		
DOG:	Bitch	16–18 mos.	8		63	58–67
	Male	12–16 mos.	8	8–10		

[1]Holstein and beef: 750 lbs.; Jersey: 500 lbs. [2]Beef; 8–10 days shorter for Angus. [3]Dairy. [4]Natural. [5]Artificial. [6]Hand-mated. [7]Pasture. [8]For fine wool breeds.

INCUBATION PERIOD OF POULTRY (DAYS)

Chicken	21
Duck	26–32
Goose	30–34
Guinea	26–28
Turkey	28

AVERAGE LIFE SPAN OF ANIMALS IN CAPTIVITY (YEARS)

Cat (domestic)	14	Goose (domestic)	20
Chicken (domestic)	8	Horse	22
Dog (domestic)	13	Pig	12
Duck (domestic)	10	Rabbit	6
Goat (domestic)	14	Turkey (domestic)	10

	ESTRAL/ESTROUS CYCLE (INCLUDING HEAT PERIOD) AVERAGE	RANGE	LENGTH OF ESTRUS (HEAT) AVERAGE	RANGE	USUAL TIME OF OVULATION	WHEN CYCLE RECURS IF NOT BRED
Cow	21 days	18–24 days	18 hours	10–24 hours	10–12 hours after end of estrus	21 days
Doe goat	21 days	18–24 days	2–3 days	1–4 days	Near end of estrus	21 days
Mare	21 days	10–37 days	5–6 days	2–11 days	24–48 hours before end of estrus	21 days
Sow	21 days	18–24 days	2–3 days	1–5 days	30–36 hours after start of estrus	21 days
Ewe	16½ days	14–19 days	30 hours	24–32 hours	12–24 hours before end of estrus	16½ days
Queen cat		15–21 days	3–4 days, if mated	9–10 days, in absence of male	24–56 hours after coitus	Pseudo-pregnancy
Bitch	24 days	16–30 days	7 days	5–9 days	1–3 days after first acceptance	Pseudo-pregnancy

PLANTING BY THE MOON'S PHASE

ACCORDING TO THIS AGE-OLD PRACTICE, CYCLES OF THE MOON AFFECT PLANT GROWTH.

Plant annual flowers and vegetables that bear crops above ground during the light, or waxing, of the Moon: from the day the Moon is new to the day it is full.

Plant flowering bulbs, biennial and perennial flowers, and vegetables that bear crops below ground during the dark, or waning, of the Moon: from the day after it is full to the day before it is new again.

The Planting Dates columns give the safe periods for planting in areas that receive frost. (See **page 232** for frost dates in your area.) The Moon Favorable columns give the best planting days within the Planting Dates based on the Moon's phases for 2021. (See **pages 120–146** for the exact days of the new and full Moons.)

The dates listed in this table are meant as general guidelines only. For seed-sowing dates based on frost dates in your local area, go to **Almanac.com/PlantingTable.**

Aboveground crops are marked *.
(E) means early; (L) means late.

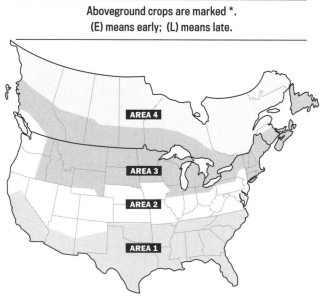

* Barley	
* Beans	(E)
	(L)
Beets	(E)
	(L)
* Broccoli plants	(E)
	(L)
* Brussels sprouts	
* Cabbage plants	
Carrots	(E)
	(L)
* Cauliflower plants	(E)
	(L)
* Celery plants	(E)
	(L)
* Collards	(E)
	(L)
* Corn, sweet	(E)
	(L)
* Cucumbers	
* Eggplant plants	
* Endive	(E)
	(L)
* Kale	(E)
	(L)
Leek plants	
* Lettuce	
* Muskmelons	
* Okra	
Onion sets	
* Parsley	
Parsnips	
* Peas	(E)
	(L)
* Pepper plants	
Potatoes	
* Pumpkins	
Radishes	(E)
	(L)
* Spinach	(E)
	(L)
* Squashes	
Sweet potatoes	
* Swiss chard	
* Tomato plants	
Turnips	(E)
	(L)
* Watermelons	
* Wheat, spring	
* Wheat, winter	

AREA 1		AREA 2		AREA 3		AREA 4	
PLANTING DATES	MOON FAVORABLE	PLANTING DATES	MOON FAVORABLE	PLANTING DATES	MOON FAVORABLE	PLANTING DATES	MOON FAVORABLE
2/15-3/7	2/15-27	3/15-4/7	3/15-28	5/15-6/21	5/15-26, 6/10-21	6/1-30	6/10-24
3/15-4/7	3/15-28	4/15-30	4/15-26	5/7-6/21	5/11-26, 6/10-21	5/30-6/15	6/10-15
8/7-31	8/8-22	7/1-21	7/9-21	6/15-7/15	6/15-24, 7/9-15	—	—
2/7-28	2/7-10, 2/28	3/15-4/3	3/29-4/3	5/1-15	5/1-10	5/25-6/10	5/27-6/9
9/1-30	9/1-5, 9/21-30	8/15-31	8/23-31	7/15-8/15	7/24-8/7	6/15-7/8	6/25-7/8
2/15-3/15	2/15-27, 3/13-15	3/7-31	3/13-28	5/15-31	5/15-26	6/1-25	6/10-24
9/7-30	9/7-20	8/1-20	8/8-20	6/15-7/7	6/15-24	—	—
2/11-3/20	2/11-27, 3/13-20	3/7-4/15	3/13-28, 4/11-15	5/15-31	5/15-26	6/1-25	6/10-24
2/11-3/20	2/11-27, 3/13-20	3/7-4/15	3/13-28, 4/11-15	5/15-31	5/15-26	6/1-25	6/10-24
2/15-3/7	2/28-3/7	3/7-31	3/7-12, 3/29-31	5/15-31	5/27-31	5/25-6/10	5/27-6/9
8/1-9/7	8/1-7, 8/23-9/5	7/7-31	7/7-8, 7/24-31	6/15-7/21	6/25-7/8	6/15-7/8	6/25-7/8
2/15-3/7	2/15-27	3/15-4/7	3/15-28	5/15-31	5/15-26	6/1-25	6/10-24
8/7-31	8/8-22	7/1-8/7	7/9-23	6/15-7/21	6/15-24, 7/9-21	—	—
2/15-28	2/15-27	3/7-31	3/13-28	5/15-6/30	5/15-26, 6/10-24	6/1-30	6/10-24
9/15-30	9/15-20	8/15-9/7	8/15-22, 9/6-7	7/15-8/15	7/15-23, 8/8-15	—	—
2/11-3/20	2/11-27, 3/13-20	3/7-4/7	3/13-28	5/15-31	5/15-26	6/1-25	6/10-24
9/7-30	9/7-20	8/15-31	8/15-22	7/1-8/7	7/9-23	—	—
3/15-31	3/15-28	4/1-17	4/11-17	5/10-6/15	5/11-26, 6/10-15	5/30-6/20	6/10-20
8/7-31	8/8-22	7/7-21	7/9-21	6/15-30	6/15-24	—	—
3/7-4/15	3/13-28, 4/11-15	4/7-5/15	4/11-26, 5/11-15	5/7-6/20	5/11-26, 6/10-20	5/30-6/15	6/10-15
3/7-4/15	3/13-28, 4/11-15	4/7-5/15	4/11-26, 5/11-15	6/1-30	6/10-24	6/15-30	6/15-24
2/15-3/20	2/15-27, 3/13-20	4/7-5/15	4/11-26, 5/11-15	5/15-31	5/15-26	6/1-25	6/10-24
8/15-9/7	8/15-22, 9/6-7	7/15-8/15	7/15-23, 8/8-15	6/7-30	6/10-24	—	—
2/11-3/20	2/11-27, 3/13-20	3/7-4/7	3/13-28	5/15-31	5/15-26	6/1-15	6/10-15
9/7-30	9/7-20	8/15-31	8/15-22	7/1-8/7	7/9-23	6/25-7/15	7/9-15
2/15-4/15	2/28-3/12, 3/29-4/10	3/7-4/7	3/7-12, 3/29-4/7	5/15-31	5/27-31	6/1-25	6/1-9, 6/25
2/15-3/7	2/15-27	3/1-31	3/13-28	5/15-6/30	5/15-26, 6/10-24	6/1-30	6/10-24
3/15-4/7	3/15-28	4/15-5/7	4/15-26	5/15-6/30	5/15-26, 6/10-24	6/1-30	6/10-24
4/15-6/1	4/15-26, 5/11-26	5/25-6/15	5/25-26, 6/10-15	6/15-7/10	6/15-24, 7/9-10	6/15-7/7	6/15-24
2/1-28	2/1-10, 2/28	3/1-31	3/1-12, 3/29-31	5/15-6/7	5/27-6/7	6/1-25	6/1-9, 6/25
2/20-3/15	2/20-27, 3/13-15	3/1-31	3/13-28	5/15-31	5/15-26	6/1-15	6/10-15
1/15-2/4	1/29-2/4	3/7-31	3/7-12, 3/29-31	4/1-30	4/1-10, 4/27-30	5/10-31	5/10, 5/27-31
1/15-2/7	1/15-28	3/7-31	3/13-28	4/15-5/7	4/15-26	5/15-31	5/15-26
9/15-30	9/15-20	8/7-31	8/8-22	7/15-31	7/15-23	7/10-25	7/10-23
3/1-20	3/13-20	4/1-30	4/11-26	5/15-6/30	5/15-26, 6/10-24	6/1-30	6/10-24
2/10-28	2/10, 2/28	4/1-30	4/1-10, 4/27-30	5/1-31	5/1-10, 5/27-31	6/1-25	6/1-9, 6/25
3/7-20	3/13-20	4/23-5/15	4/23-26, 5/11-15	5/15-31	5/15-26	6/1-30	6/10-24
1/21-3/1	1/29-2/10, 2/28-3/1	3/7-31	3/7-12, 3/29-31	4/15-30	4/27-30	5/15-6/5	5/27-6/5
10/1-21	10/1-5, 10/21	9/7-30	9/21-30	8/15-31	8/23-31	7/10-31	7/24-31
2/7-3/15	2/11-27, 3/13-15	3/15-4/20	3/15-28, 4/11-20	5/15-31	5/15-26	6/1-25	6/10-24
10/1-21	10/6-20	8/1-9/15	8/8-22, 9/6-15	7/17-9/7	7/17-23, 8/8-22, 9/6-7	7/20-8/5	7/20-23
3/15-4/15	3/15-28, 4/11-15	4/15-30	4/15-26	5/15-6/15	5/15-26, 6/10-15	6/1-30	6/10-24
3/23-4/6	3/29-4/6	4/21-5/9	4/27-5/9	5/15-6/15	5/27-6/9	6/1-30	6/1-9, 6/25-30
2/7-3/15	2/11-27, 3/13-15	3/15-4/15	3/15-28, 4/11-15	5/1-31	5/11-26	5/15-31	5/15-26
3/7-20	3/13-20	4/7-30	4/11-26	5/15-31	5/15-26	6/1-15	6/10-15
1/20-2/15	1/29-2/10	3/15-31	3/29-31	4/7-30	4/7-10, 4/27-30	5/10-31	5/10, 5/27-31
9/1-10/15	9/1-5, 9/21-10/5	8/1-20	8/1-7	7/1-8/15	7/1-8, 7/24-8/7	—	—
3/15-4/7	3/15-28	4/15-5/7	4/15-26	5/15-6/30	5/15-26, 6/10-24	6/1-30	6/10-24
2/15-28	2/15-27	3/1-20	3/13-20	4/7-30	4/11-26	5/15-6/10	5/15-26, 6/10
10/15-12/7	10/15-20, 11/4-19, 12/4-7	9/15-10/20	9/15-20, 10/6-20	8/11-9/15	8/11-22, 9/6-15	8/5-30	8/8-22

FROSTS AND GROWING SEASONS

Dates given are normal averages for a light freeze; local weather and topography may cause considerable variations. The possibility of frost occurring after the spring dates and before the fall dates is 30 percent. The classification of freeze temperatures is usually based on their effect on plants. **Light freeze:** 29° to 32°F—tender plants killed. **Moderate freeze:** 25° to 28°F—widely destructive to most plants. **Severe freeze:** 24°F and colder—heavy damage to most plants. –dates courtesy of National Centers for Environmental Information

STATE	CITY	GROWING SEASON (DAYS)	LAST SPRING FROST	FIRST FALL FROST	STATE	CITY	GROWING SEASON (DAYS)	LAST SPRING FROST	FIRST FALL FROST
AK	Juneau	168	Apr. 27	Oct. 13	ND	Bismarck	122	May 19	Sept. 19
AL	Mobile	267	Mar. 6	Nov. 29	NE	Omaha	160	Apr. 27	Oct. 5
AR	Pine Bluff	226	Mar. 26	Nov. 8	NE	North Platte	146	May 6	Sept. 30
AZ	Phoenix	340	Jan. 20	Dec. 27	NH	Concord	127	May 19	Sept. 24
AZ	Tucson	304	Feb. 5	Dec. 7	NJ	Newark	209	Apr. 8	Nov. 4
CA	Eureka	276	Mar. 2	Dec. 4	NM	Carlsbad	209	Apr. 5	Nov. 1
CA	Sacramento	277	Feb. 21	Nov. 26	NM	Los Alamos	146	May 10	Oct. 4
CO	Denver	153	May 4	Oct. 5	NV	Las Vegas	284	Feb. 15	Nov. 27
CO	Grand Junction	162	May 2	Oct. 12	NY	Albany	153	May 4	Oct. 5
CT	Hartford	159	May 1	Oct. 8	NY	Syracuse	156	May 4	Oct. 8
DE	Wilmington	202	Apr. 12	Nov. 1	OH	Akron	165	May 2	Oct. 15
FL	Orlando	336	Jan. 29	Jan. 1	OH	Cincinnati	175	Apr. 23	Oct. 16
FL	Tallahassee	224	Mar. 29	Nov. 9	OK	Lawton	211	Apr. 3	Nov. 1
GA	Athens	214	Apr. 3	Nov. 4	OK	Tulsa	210	Apr. 4	Nov. 1
GA	Savannah	249	Mar. 15	Nov. 20	OR	Pendleton	152	May 2	Oct. 2
IA	Atlantic	136	May 8	Sept. 22	OR	Portland	255	Mar. 11	Nov. 22
IA	Cedar Rapids	157	Apr. 30	Oct. 5	PA	Franklin	156	May 10	Oct. 14
ID	Boise	152	May 7	Oct. 7	PA	Williamsport	164	May 2	Oct. 14
IL	Chicago	193	Apr. 18	Oct. 29	RI	Kingston	142	May 12	Oct. 2
IL	Springfield	168	Apr. 23	Oct. 9	SC	Charleston	298	Feb. 19	Dec. 15
IN	Indianapolis	171	Apr. 25	Oct. 14	SC	Columbia	235	Mar. 23	Nov. 14
IN	South Bend	162	May 3	Oct. 13	SD	Rapid City	146	May 7	Oct. 1
KS	Topeka	173	Apr. 22	Oct. 13	TN	Memphis	225	Mar. 27	Nov. 8
KY	Lexington	183	Apr. 20	Oct. 21	TN	Nashville	198	Apr. 12	Oct. 28
LA	Monroe	223	Mar. 24	Nov. 3	TX	Amarillo	179	Apr. 21	Oct. 18
LA	New Orleans	297	Feb. 17	Dec. 12	TX	Denton	227	Mar. 27	Nov. 10
MA	Worcester	167	Apr. 28	Oct. 13	TX	San Antonio	262	Mar. 5	Nov. 23
MD	Baltimore	234	Mar. 27	Nov. 17	UT	Cedar City	122	May 28	Sept. 28
ME	Portland	152	May 5	Oct. 5	UT	Spanish Fork	158	May 4	Oct. 10
MI	Lansing	147	May 9	Oct. 4	VA	Norfolk	251	Mar. 20	Nov. 27
MI	Marquette	155	May 11	Oct. 14	VA	Richmond	202	Apr. 10	Oct. 30
MN	Duluth	119	May 25	Sept. 22	VT	Burlington	145	May 10	Oct. 3
MN	Willmar	146	May 5	Sept. 29	WA	Seattle	243	Mar. 17	Nov. 16
MO	Jefferson City	189	Apr. 14	Oct. 21	WA	Spokane	146	May 10	Oct. 4
MS	Columbia	234	Mar. 20	Nov. 10	WI	Green Bay	140	May 11	Sept. 29
MS	Tupelo	206	Apr. 5	Oct. 29	WI	Sparta	138	May 12	Sept. 28
MT	Fort Peck	129	May 15	Sept. 22	WV	Parkersburg	179	Apr. 23	Oct. 20
MT	Helena	123	May 19	Sept. 20	WY	Casper	107	May 31	Sept. 16
NC	Fayetteville	208	Apr. 8	Nov. 3	*Frosts do not occur every year.*				

PHENOLOGY: NATURE'S CALENDAR

Study nature, love nature, stay close to nature. It will never fail you.
–Frank Lloyd Wright, American architect (1867–1959)

For centuries, farmers and gardeners have looked to events in nature to tell them when to plant vegetables and flowers and when to expect insects. Making such observations is called "phenology," the study of phenomena. Specifically, this refers to the life cycles of plants and animals as they correlate to weather and temperature, or nature's calendar.

VEGETABLES

- Plant peas when forsythias bloom.
- Plant potatoes when the first dandelion blooms.
- Plant beets, carrots, cole crops (broccoli, brussels sprouts, collards), lettuce, and spinach when lilacs are in first leaf or dandelions are in full bloom.
- Plant corn when oak leaves are the size of a squirrel's ear (about ½ inch in diameter). Or, plant corn when apple blossoms fade and fall.
- Plant bean, cucumber, and squash seeds when lilacs are in full bloom.
- Plant tomatoes when lilies-of-the-valley are in full bloom.
- Transplant eggplants and peppers when bearded irises bloom.
- Plant onions when red maples bloom.

FLOWERS

- Plant morning glories when maple trees have full-size leaves.
- Plant zinnias and marigolds when black locusts are in full bloom.
- Plant pansies, snapdragons, and other hardy annuals when aspens and chokecherries have leafed out.

INSECTS

- When purple lilacs bloom, grasshopper eggs hatch.
- When chicory blooms, beware of squash vine borers.
- When Canada thistles bloom, protect susceptible fruit; apple maggot flies are at peak.
- When foxglove flowers open, expect Mexican beetle larvae.
- When crabapple trees are in bud, eastern tent caterpillars are hatching.
- When morning glory vines begin to climb, Japanese beetles appear.
- When wild rocket blooms, cabbage root maggots appear.

If the signal plants are not growing in your area, notice other coincident events; record them and watch for them in ensuing seasons.

TABLE OF MEASURES

LINEAR
1 hand = 4 inches
1 link = 7.92 inches
1 span = 9 inches
1 foot = 12 inches
1 yard = 3 feet
1 rod = 5½ yards
1 mile = 320 rods = 1,760 yards = 5,280 feet
1 international nautical mile = 6,076.1155 feet
1 knot = 1 nautical mile per hour
1 fathom = 2 yards = 6 feet
1 furlong = ⅛ mile = 660 feet = 220 yards
1 league = 3 miles = 24 furlongs
1 chain = 100 links = 22 yards

SQUARE
1 square foot = 144 square inches
1 square yard = 9 square feet
1 square rod = 30¼ square yards = 272¼ square feet = 625 square links
1 square chain = 16 square rods
1 acre = 10 square chains = 160 square rods = 43,560 square feet
1 square mile = 640 acres = 102,400 square rods

CUBIC
1 cubic foot = 1,728 cubic inches
1 cubic yard = 27 cubic feet
1 cord = 128 cubic feet
1 U.S. liquid gallon = 4 quarts = 231 cubic inches
1 imperial gallon = 1.20 U.S. gallons = 0.16 cubic foot
1 board foot = 144 cubic inches

DRY
2 pints = 1 quart
4 quarts = 1 gallon
2 gallons = 1 peck
4 pecks = 1 bushel

LIQUID
4 gills = 1 pint
63 gallons = 1 hogshead
2 hogsheads = 1 pipe or butt
2 pipes = 1 tun

KITCHEN
3 teaspoons = 1 tablespoon
16 tablespoons = 1 cup
1 cup = 8 ounces
2 cups = 1 pint
2 pints = 1 quart
4 quarts = 1 gallon

AVOIRDUPOIS
(for general use)
1 ounce = 16 drams
1 pound = 16 ounces
1 short hundredweight = 100 pounds
1 ton = 2,000 pounds
1 long ton = 2,240 pounds

APOTHECARIES'
(for pharmaceutical use)
1 scruple = 20 grains
1 dram = 3 scruples
1 ounce = 8 drams
1 pound = 12 ounces

METRIC CONVERSIONS

LINEAR
1 inch = 2.54 centimeters
1 centimeter = 0.39 inch
1 meter = 39.37 inches
1 yard = 0.914 meter
1 mile = 1.61 kilometers
1 kilometer = 0.62 mile

SQUARE
1 square inch = 6.45 square centimeters
1 square yard = 0.84 square meter
1 square mile = 2.59 square kilometers
1 square kilometer = 0.386 square mile
1 acre = 0.40 hectare
1 hectare = 2.47 acres

CUBIC
1 cubic yard = 0.76 cubic meter
1 cubic meter = 1.31 cubic yards

HOUSEHOLD
½ teaspoon = 2 mL
1 teaspoon = 5 mL
1 tablespoon = 15 mL
¼ cup = 60 mL
⅓ cup = 75 mL
½ cup = 125 mL
⅔ cup = 150 mL
¾ cup = 175 mL
1 cup = 250 mL
1 liter = 1.057 U.S. liquid quarts
1 U.S. liquid quart = 0.946 liter
1 U.S. liquid gallon = 3.78 liters
1 gram = 0.035 ounce
1 ounce = 28.349 grams
1 kilogram = 2.2 pounds
1 pound = 0.45 kilogram

TO CONVERT CELSIUS AND FAHRENHEIT: $°C = (°F - 32)/1.8$; $°F = (°C × 1.8) + 32$

TIDAL GLOSSARY

APOGEAN TIDE: A monthly tide of decreased range that occurs when the Moon is at apogee (farthest from Earth).

CURRENT: Generally, a horizontal movement of water. Currents may be classified as tidal and nontidal. Tidal currents are caused by gravitational interactions between the Sun, Moon, and Earth and are part of the same general movement of the sea that is manifested in the vertical rise and fall, called tide. Nontidal currents include the permanent currents in the general circulatory systems of the sea as well as temporary currents arising from more pronounced meteorological variability.

DIURNAL TIDE: A tide with one high water and one low water in a tidal day of approximately 24 hours.

MEAN LOWER LOW WATER: The arithmetic mean of the lesser of a daily pair of low waters, observed over a specific 19-year cycle called the National Tidal Datum Epoch.

NEAP TIDE: A tide of decreased range that occurs twice a month, when the Moon is in quadrature (during its first and last quarters, when the Sun and the Moon are at right angles to each other relative to Earth).

PERIGEAN TIDE: A monthly tide of increased range that occurs when the Moon is at perigee (closest to Earth).

RED TIDE: Toxic algal blooms caused by several genera of dinoflagellates that usually turn the sea red or brown. These pose a serious threat to marine life and may be harmful to humans.

RIP CURRENT: A potentially dangerous, narrow, intense, surf-zone current flowing outward from shore.

SEMIDIURNAL TIDE: A tide with one high water and one low water every half-day. East Coast tides, for example, are semidiurnal, with two highs and two lows during a tidal day of approximately 24 hours.

SLACK WATER (SLACK): The state of a tidal current when its speed is near zero, especially the moment when a reversing current changes direction and its speed is zero.

SPRING TIDE: A tide of increased range that occurs at times of syzygy each month. Named not for the season of spring but from the German *springen* ("to leap up"), a spring tide also brings a lower low water.

STORM SURGE: The local change in the elevation of the ocean along a shore due to a storm, measured by subtracting the astronomic tidal elevation from the total elevation. It typically has a duration of a few hours and is potentially catastrophic, especially on low-lying coasts with gently sloping offshore topography.

SYZYGY: The nearly straight-line configuration that occurs twice a month, when the Sun and the Moon are in conjunction (on the same side of Earth, at the new Moon) and when they are in opposition (on opposite sides of Earth, at the full Moon). In both cases, the gravitational effects of the Sun and the Moon reinforce each other, and tidal range is increased.

TIDAL BORE: A tide-induced wave that propagates up a relatively shallow and sloping estuary or river with a steep wave front.

TSUNAMI: Commonly called a tidal wave, a tsunami is a series of long-period waves caused by an underwater earthquake or volcanic eruption. In open ocean, the waves are small and travel at high speed; as they near shore, some may build to more than 30 feet high, becoming a threat to life and property.

VANISHING TIDE: A mixed tide of considerable inequality in the two highs and two lows, so that the lower high (or higher low) may appear to vanish. ∎

TIDE CORRECTIONS

Many factors affect tides, including the shoreline, time of the Moon's southing (crossing the meridian), and the Moon's phase. The High Tide Times column on the **Left-Hand Calendar Pages, 120–146,** lists the times of high tide at Commonwealth Pier in Boston (MA) Harbor. The heights of some of these tides, reckoned from Mean Lower Low Water, are given on the **Right-Hand Calendar Pages, 121–147.** Use the table below to calculate the approximate times and heights of high tide at the places shown. Apply the time difference to the times of high tide at Boston and the height difference to the heights at Boston. A more detailed and accurate tide calculator for the United States and Canada can be found at **Almanac.com/Tides.**

TIDAL SITE	TIME (H. M.)	HEIGHT (FT.)	TIDAL SITE	TIME (H. M.)	HEIGHT (FT.)
CANADA			Cape Cod Canal		
Alberton, PE	*–5 45	–7.5	East Entrance	–0 01	–0.8
Charlottetown, PE	*–0 45	–3.5	West Entrance	–2 16	–5.9
Halifax, NS	–3 23	–4.5	Chatham Outer Coast	+0 30	–2.8
North Sydney, NS	–3 15	–6.5	Inside	+1 54	**0.4
Saint John, NB	+0 30	+15.0	Cohasset	+0 02	–0.07
St. John's, NL	–4 00	–6.5	Cotuit Highlands	+1 15	**0.3
Yarmouth, NS	–0 40	+3.0	Dennis Port	+1 01	**0.4
MAINE			Duxbury–Gurnet Point	+0 02	–0.3
Bar Harbor	–0 34	+0.9	Fall River	–3 03	–5.0
Belfast	–0 20	+0.4	Gloucester	–0 03	–0.8
Boothbay Harbor	–0 18	–0.8	Hingham	+0 07	0.0
Chebeague Island	–0 16	–0.6	Hull	+0 03	–0.2
Eastport	–0 28	+8.4	Hyannis Port	+1 01	**0.3
Kennebunkport	+0 04	–1.0	Magnolia–Manchester	–0 02	–0.7
Machias	–0 28	+2.8	Marblehead	–0 02	–0.4
Monhegan Island	–0 25	–0.8	Marion	–3 22	–5.4
Old Orchard	0 00	–0.8	Monument Beach	–3 08	–5.4
Portland	–0 12	–0.6	Nahant	–0 01	–0.5
Rockland	–0 28	+0.1	Nantasket	+0 04	–0.1
Stonington	–0 30	+0.1	Nantucket	+0 56	**0.3
York	–0 09	–1.0	Nauset Beach	+0 30	**0.6
NEW HAMPSHIRE			New Bedford	–3 24	–5.7
Hampton	+0 02	–1.3	Newburyport	+0 19	–1.8
Portsmouth	+0 11	–1.5	Oak Bluffs	+0 30	**0.2
Rye Beach	–0 09	–0.9	Onset–R.R. Bridge	–2 16	–5.9
MASSACHUSETTS			Plymouth	+0 05	0.0
Annisquam	–0 02	–1.1	Provincetown	+0 14	–0.4
Beverly Farms	0 00	–0.5	Revere Beach	–0 01	–0.3

TIDAL SITE	TIME (H. M.)	HEIGHT (FT.)	TIDAL SITE	TIME (H. M.)	HEIGHT (FT.)
Rockport	–0 08	–1.0	**PENNSYLVANIA**		
Salem	0 00	–0.5	Philadelphia	+2 40	–3.5
Scituate	–0 05	–0.7	**DELAWARE**		
Wareham	–3 09	–5.3	Cape Henlopen	–2 48	–5.3
Wellfleet	+0 12	+0.5	Rehoboth Beach	–3 37	–5.7
West Falmouth	–3 10	–5.4	Wilmington	+1 56	–3.8
Westport Harbor	–3 22	–6.4	**MARYLAND**		
Woods Hole			Annapolis	+6 23	–8.5
Little Harbor	–2 50	**0.2	Baltimore	+7 59	–8.3
Oceanographic			Cambridge	+5 05	–7.8
Institute	–3 07	**0.2	Havre de Grace	+11 21	–7.7
RHODE ISLAND			Point No Point	+2 28	–8.1
Bristol	–3 24	–5.3	Prince Frederick–		
Narragansett Pier	–3 42	–6.2	Plum Point	+4 25	–8.5
Newport	–3 34	–5.9	**VIRGINIA**		
Point Judith	–3 41	–6.3	Cape Charles	–2 20	–7.0
Providence	–3 20	–4.8	Hampton Roads	–2 02	–6.9
Sakonnet	–3 44	–5.6	Norfolk	–2 06	–6.6
Watch Hill	–2 50	–6.8	Virginia Beach	–4 00	–6.0
CONNECTICUT			Yorktown	–2 13	–7.0
Bridgeport	+0 01	–2.6	**NORTH CAROLINA**		
Madison	–0 22	–2.3	Cape Fear	–3 55	–5.0
New Haven	–0 11	–3.2	Cape Lookout	–4 28	–5.7
New London	–1 54	–6.7	Currituck	–4 10	–5.8
Norwalk	+0 01	–2.2	Hatteras		
Old Lyme–			Inlet	–4 03	–7.4
Highway Bridge	–0 30	–6.2	Kitty Hawk	–4 14	–6.2
Stamford	+0 01	–2.2	Ocean	–4 26	–6.0
Stonington	–2 27	–6.6	**SOUTH CAROLINA**		
NEW YORK			Charleston	–3 22	–4.3
Coney Island	–3 33	–4.9	Georgetown	–1 48	**0.36
Fire Island Light	–2 43	**0.1	Hilton Head	–3 22	–2.9
Long Beach	–3 11	–5.7	Myrtle Beach	–3 49	–4.4
Montauk Harbor	–2 19	–7.4	St. Helena–		
New York City–Battery	–2 43	–5.0	Harbor Entrance	–3 15	–3.4
Oyster Bay	+0 04	–1.8	**GEORGIA**		
Port Chester	–0 09	–2.2	Jekyll Island	–3 46	–2.9
Port Washington	–0 01	–2.1	St. Simon's Island	–2 50	–2.9
Sag Harbor	–0 55	–6.8	Savannah Beach		
Southampton–			River Entrance	–3 14	–5.5
Shinnecock Inlet	–4 20	**0.2	Tybee Light	–3 22	–2.7
Willets Point	0 00	–2.3	**FLORIDA**		
NEW JERSEY			Cape Canaveral	–3 59	–6.0
Asbury Park	–4 04	–5.3	Daytona Beach	–3 28	–5.3
Atlantic City	–3 56	–5.5	Fort Lauderdale	–2 50	–7.2
Bay Head–Sea Girt	–4 04	–5.3	Fort Pierce Inlet	–3 32	–6.9
Beach Haven	–1 43	**0.24	Jacksonville–		
Cape May	–3 28	–5.3	Railroad Bridge	–6 55	**0.1
Ocean City	–3 06	–5.9	Miami Harbor Entrance	–3 18	–7.0
Sandy Hook	–3 30	–5.0	St. Augustine	–2 55	–4.9
Seaside Park	–4 03	–5.4			

*VARIES WIDELY; ACCURATE ONLY TO WITHIN 1½ HOURS. CONSULT LOCAL TIDE TABLES FOR PRECISE TIMES AND HEIGHTS.
**WHERE THE DIFFERENCE IN THE HEIGHT COLUMN IS SO MARKED, THE HEIGHT AT BOSTON SHOULD BE MULTIPLIED BY THIS RATIO.

TIME CORRECTIONS

Astronomical data for Boston (42°22' N, 71°3' W) is given on **pages 104, 106, 108–109, and 120–146.** Use the Key Letters shown on those pages with this table to find the number of minutes that you must add to or subtract from Boston time to get the correct time for your city. (Times are approximate.) For more information on the use of Key Letters, see **How to Use This Almanac, page 116.**

GET TIMES SIMPLY AND SPECIFICALLY: Download astronomical times calculated for your zip code and presented as Left-Hand Calendar Pages at **Almanac.com/Access.**

TIME ZONES CODES represent standard time. Atlantic is –1, Eastern is 0, Central is 1, Mountain is 2, Pacific is 3, Alaska is 4, and Hawaii-Aleutian is 5.

STATE	CITY	NORTH LATITUDE °	'	WEST LONGITUDE °	'	TIME ZONE CODE	KEY LETTERS (MINUTES) A	B	C	D	E
AK	Anchorage	61	10	149	59	4	–46	+27	+71	+122	+171
AK	Cordova	60	33	145	45	4	–55	+13	+55	+103	+149
AK	Fairbanks	64	48	147	51	4	–127	+2	+61	+131	+205
AK	Juneau	58	18	134	25	4	–76	–23	+10	+49	+86
AK	Ketchikan	55	21	131	39	4	–62	–25	0	+29	+56
AK	Kodiak	57	47	152	24	4	0	+49	+82	+120	+154
AL	Birmingham	33	31	86	49	1	+30	+15	+3	–10	–20
AL	Decatur	34	36	86	59	1	+27	+14	+4	–7	–17
AL	Mobile	30	42	88	3	1	+42	+23	+8	–8	–22
AL	Montgomery	32	23	86	19	1	+31	+14	+1	–13	–25
AR	Fort Smith	35	23	94	25	1	+55	+43	+33	+22	+14
AR	Little Rock	34	45	92	17	1	+48	+35	+25	+13	+4
AR	Texarkana	33	26	94	3	1	+59	+44	+32	+18	+8
AZ	Flagstaff	35	12	111	39	2	+64	+52	+42	+31	+22
AZ	Phoenix	33	27	112	4	2	+71	+56	+44	+30	+20
AZ	Tucson	32	13	110	58	2	+70	+53	+40	+24	+12
AZ	Yuma	32	43	114	37	2	+83	+67	+54	+40	+28
CA	Bakersfield	35	23	119	1	3	+33	+21	+12	+1	–7
CA	Barstow	34	54	117	1	3	+27	+14	+4	–7	–16
CA	Fresno	36	44	119	47	3	+32	+22	+15	+6	0
CA	Los Angeles-Pasadena-Santa Monica	34	3	118	14	3	+34	+20	+9	–3	–13
CA	Palm Springs	33	49	116	32	3	+28	+13	+1	–12	–22
CA	Redding	40	35	122	24	3	+31	+27	+25	+22	+19
CA	Sacramento	38	35	121	30	3	+34	+27	+21	+15	+10
CA	San Diego	32	43	117	9	3	+33	+17	+4	–9	–21
CA	San Francisco-Oakland-San Jose	37	47	122	25	3	+40	+31	+25	+18	+12
CO	Craig	40	31	107	33	2	+32	+28	+25	+22	+20
CO	Denver-Boulder	39	44	104	59	2	+24	+19	+15	+11	+7
CO	Grand Junction	39	4	108	33	2	+40	+34	+29	+24	+20
CO	Pueblo	38	16	104	37	2	+27	+20	+14	+7	+2
CO	Trinidad	37	10	104	31	2	+30	+21	+13	+5	0
CT	Bridgeport	41	11	73	11	0	+12	+10	+8	+6	+4
CT	Hartford-New Britain	41	46	72	41	0	+8	+7	+6	+5	+4
CT	New Haven	41	18	72	56	0	+11	+8	+7	+5	+4
CT	New London	41	22	72	6	0	+7	+5	+4	+2	+1
CT	Norwalk-Stamford	41	7	73	22	0	+13	+10	+9	+7	+5
CT	Waterbury-Meriden	41	33	73	3	0	+10	+9	+7	+6	+5
DC	Washington	38	54	77	1	0	+35	+28	+23	+18	+13
DE	Wilmington	39	45	75	33	0	+26	+21	+18	+13	+10

STATE	CITY	NORTH LATITUDE °	′	WEST LONGITUDE °	′	TIME ZONE CODE	KEY LETTERS (MINUTES) A	B	C	D	E
FL	Fort Myers	26	38	81	52	0	+87	+63	+44	+21	+4
FL	Jacksonville	30	20	81	40	0	+77	+58	+43	+25	+11
FL	Miami	25	47	80	12	0	+88	+57	+37	+14	−3
FL	Orlando	28	32	81	22	0	+80	+59	+42	+22	+6
FL	Pensacola	30	25	87	13	1	+39	+20	+5	−12	−26
FL	St. Petersburg	27	46	82	39	0	+87	+65	+47	+26	+10
FL	Tallahassee	30	27	84	17	0	+87	+68	+53	+35	+22
FL	Tampa	27	57	82	27	0	+86	+64	+46	+25	+9
FL	West Palm Beach	26	43	80	3	0	+79	+55	+36	+14	−2
GA	Atlanta	33	45	84	24	0	+79	+65	+53	+40	+30
GA	Augusta	33	28	81	58	0	+70	+55	+44	+30	+19
GA	Macon	32	50	83	38	0	+79	+63	+50	+36	+24
GA	Savannah	32	5	81	6	0	+70	+54	+40	+25	+13
HI	Hilo	19	44	155	5	5	+94	+62	+37	+7	−15
HI	Honolulu	21	18	157	52	5	+102	+72	+48	+19	−1
HI	Lanai City	20	50	156	55	5	+99	+69	+44	+15	−6
HI	Lihue	21	59	159	23	5	+107	+77	+54	+26	+5
IA	Davenport	41	32	90	35	1	+20	+19	+17	+16	+15
IA	Des Moines	41	35	93	37	1	+32	+31	+30	+28	+27
IA	Dubuque	42	30	90	41	1	+17	+18	+18	+18	+18
IA	Waterloo	42	30	92	20	1	+24	+24	+24	+25	+25
ID	Boise	43	37	116	12	2	+55	+58	+60	+62	+64
ID	Lewiston	46	25	117	1	3	−12	−3	+2	+10	+17
ID	Pocatello	42	52	112	27	2	+43	+44	+45	+46	+46
IL	Cairo	37	0	89	11	1	+29	+20	+12	+4	−2
IL	Chicago-Oak Park	41	52	87	38	1	+7	+6	+6	+5	+4
IL	Danville	40	8	87	37	1	+13	+9	+6	+2	0
IL	Decatur	39	51	88	57	1	+19	+15	+11	+7	+4
IL	Peoria	40	42	89	36	1	+19	+16	+14	+11	+9
IL	Springfield	39	48	89	39	1	+22	+18	+14	+10	+6
IN	Fort Wayne	41	4	85	9	0	+60	+58	+56	+54	+52
IN	Gary	41	36	87	20	1	+7	+6	+4	+3	+2
IN	Indianapolis	39	46	86	10	0	+69	+64	+60	+56	+52
IN	Muncie	40	12	85	23	0	+64	+60	+57	+53	+50
IN	South Bend	41	41	86	15	0	+62	+61	+60	+59	+58
IN	Terre Haute	39	28	87	24	0	+74	+69	+65	+60	+56
KS	Fort Scott	37	50	94	42	1	+49	+41	+34	+27	+21
KS	Liberal	37	3	100	55	1	+76	+66	+59	+51	+44
KS	Oakley	39	8	100	51	1	+69	+63	+59	+53	+49
KS	Salina	38	50	97	37	1	+57	+51	+46	+40	+35
KS	Topeka	39	3	95	40	1	+49	+43	+38	+32	+28
KS	Wichita	37	42	97	20	1	+60	+51	+45	+37	+31
KY	Lexington-Frankfort	38	3	84	30	0	+67	+59	+53	+46	+41
KY	Louisville	38	15	85	46	0	+72	+64	+58	+52	+46
LA	Alexandria	31	18	92	27	1	+58	+40	+26	+9	−3
LA	Baton Rouge	30	27	91	11	1	+55	+36	+21	+3	−10
LA	Lake Charles	30	14	93	13	1	+64	+44	+29	+11	−2
LA	Monroe	32	30	92	7	1	+53	+37	+24	+9	−1
LA	New Orleans	29	57	90	4	1	+52	+32	+16	−1	−15
LA	Shreveport	32	31	93	45	1	+60	+44	+31	+16	+4
MA	Brockton	42	5	71	1	0	0	0	0	0	−1
MA	Fall River-New Bedford	41	42	71	9	0	+2	+1	0	0	−1
MA	Lawrence-Lowell	42	42	71	10	0	0	0	0	0	+1
MA	Pittsfield	42	27	73	15	0	+8	+8	+8	+8	+8
MA	Springfield-Holyoke	42	6	72	36	0	+6	+6	+6	+5	+5
MA	Worcester	42	16	71	48	0	+3	+2	+2	+2	+2

STATE	CITY	NORTH LATITUDE		WEST LONGITUDE		TIME ZONE CODE	KEY LETTERS (MINUTES)				
		°	′	°	′		A	B	C	D	E
MD	Baltimore	39	17	76	37	0	+32	+26	+22	+17	+13
MD	Hagerstown	39	39	77	43	0	+35	+30	+26	+22	+18
MD	Salisbury	38	22	75	36	0	+31	+23	+18	+11	+6
ME	Augusta	44	19	69	46	0	−12	−8	−5	−1	0
ME	Bangor	44	48	68	46	0	−18	−13	−9	−5	−1
ME	Eastport	44	54	67	0	0	−26	−20	−16	−11	−8
ME	Ellsworth	44	33	68	25	0	−18	−14	−10	−6	−3
ME	Portland	43	40	70	15	0	−8	−5	−3	−1	0
ME	Presque Isle	46	41	68	1	0	−29	−19	−12	−4	+2
MI	Cheboygan	45	39	84	29	0	+40	+47	+53	+59	+64
MI	Detroit-Dearborn	42	20	83	3	0	+47	+47	+47	+47	+47
MI	Flint	43	1	83	41	0	+47	+49	+50	+51	+52
MI	Ironwood	46	27	90	9	1	0	+9	+15	+23	+29
MI	Jackson	42	15	84	24	0	+53	+53	+53	+52	+52
MI	Kalamazoo	42	17	85	35	0	+58	+57	+57	+57	+57
MI	Lansing	42	44	84	33	0	+52	+53	+53	+54	+54
MI	St. Joseph	42	5	86	26	0	+61	+61	+60	+60	+59
MI	Traverse City	44	46	85	38	0	+49	+54	+57	+62	+65
MN	Albert Lea	43	39	93	22	1	+24	+26	+28	+31	+33
MN	Bemidji	47	28	94	53	1	+14	+26	+34	+44	+52
MN	Duluth	46	47	92	6	1	+6	+16	+23	+31	+38
MN	Minneapolis-St. Paul	44	59	93	16	1	+18	+24	+28	+33	+37
MN	Ortonville	45	19	96	27	1	+30	+36	+40	+46	+51
MO	Jefferson City	38	34	92	10	1	+36	+29	+24	+18	+13
MO	Joplin	37	6	94	30	1	+50	+41	+33	+25	+18
MO	Kansas City	39	1	94	20	1	+44	+37	+33	+27	+23
MO	Poplar Bluff	36	46	90	24	1	+35	+25	+17	+8	+1
MO	St. Joseph	39	46	94	50	1	+43	+38	+35	+30	+27
MO	St. Louis	38	37	90	12	1	+28	+21	+16	+10	+5
MO	Springfield	37	13	93	18	1	+45	+36	+29	+20	+14
MS	Biloxi	30	24	88	53	1	+46	+27	+11	−5	−19
MS	Jackson	32	18	90	11	1	+46	+30	+17	+1	−10
MS	Meridian	32	22	88	42	1	+40	+24	+11	−4	−15
MS	Tupelo	34	16	88	34	1	+35	+21	+10	−2	−11
MT	Billings	45	47	108	30	2	+16	+23	+29	+35	+40
MT	Butte	46	1	112	32	2	+31	+39	+45	+52	+57
MT	Glasgow	48	12	106	38	2	−1	+11	+21	+32	+42
MT	Great Falls	47	30	111	17	2	+20	+31	+39	+49	+58
MT	Helena	46	36	112	2	2	+27	+36	+43	+51	+57
MT	Miles City	46	25	105	51	2	+3	+11	+18	+26	+32
NC	Asheville	35	36	82	33	0	+67	+55	+46	+35	+27
NC	Charlotte	35	14	80	51	0	+61	+49	+39	+28	+19
NC	Durham	36	0	78	55	0	+51	+40	+31	+21	+13
NC	Greensboro	36	4	79	47	0	+54	+43	+35	+25	+17
NC	Raleigh	35	47	78	38	0	+51	+39	+30	+20	+12
NC	Wilmington	34	14	77	55	0	+52	+38	+27	+15	+5
ND	Bismarck	46	48	100	47	1	+41	+50	+58	+66	+73
ND	Fargo	46	53	96	47	1	+24	+34	+42	+50	+57
ND	Grand Forks	47	55	97	3	1	+21	+33	+43	+53	+62
ND	Minot	48	14	101	18	1	+36	+50	+59	+71	+81
ND	Williston	48	9	103	37	1	+46	+59	+69	+80	+90
NE	Grand Island	40	55	98	21	1	+53	+51	+49	+46	+44
NE	Lincoln	40	49	96	41	1	+47	+44	+42	+39	+37
NE	North Platte	41	8	100	46	1	+62	+60	+58	+56	+54
NE	Omaha	41	16	95	56	1	+43	+40	+39	+37	+36
NH	Berlin	44	28	71	11	0	−7	−3	0	+3	+7
NH	Keene	42	56	72	17	0	+2	+3	+4	+5	+6

STATE	CITY	NORTH LATITUDE °	NORTH LATITUDE ′	WEST LONGITUDE °	WEST LONGITUDE ′	TIME ZONE CODE	KEY LETTERS (MINUTES) A	B	C	D	E
NH	Manchester-Concord	42	59	71	28	0	0	0	+1	+2	+3
NH	Portsmouth	43	5	70	45	0	−4	−2	−1	0	0
NJ	Atlantic City	39	22	74	26	0	+23	+17	+13	+8	+4
NJ	Camden	39	57	75	7	0	+24	+19	+16	+12	+9
NJ	Cape May	38	56	74	56	0	+26	+20	+15	+9	+5
NJ	Newark-East Orange	40	44	74	10	0	+17	+14	+12	+9	+7
NJ	Paterson	40	55	74	10	0	+17	+14	+12	+9	+7
NJ	Trenton	40	13	74	46	0	+21	+17	+14	+11	+8
NM	Albuquerque	35	5	106	39	2	+45	+32	+22	+11	+2
NM	Gallup	35	32	108	45	2	+52	+40	+31	+20	+11
NM	Las Cruces	32	19	106	47	2	+53	+36	+23	+8	−3
NM	Roswell	33	24	104	32	2	+41	+26	+14	0	−10
NM	Santa Fe	35	41	105	56	2	+40	+28	+19	+9	0
NV	Carson City-Reno	39	10	119	46	3	+25	+19	+14	+9	+5
NV	Elko	40	50	115	46	3	+3	0	−1	−3	−5
NV	Las Vegas	36	10	115	9	3	+16	+4	−3	−13	−20
NY	Albany	42	39	73	45	0	+9	+10	+10	+11	+11
NY	Binghamton	42	6	75	55	0	+20	+19	+19	+18	+18
NY	Buffalo	42	53	78	52	0	+29	+30	+30	+31	+32
NY	New York	40	45	74	0	0	+17	+14	+11	+9	+6
NY	Ogdensburg	44	42	75	30	0	+8	+13	+17	+21	+25
NY	Syracuse	43	3	76	9	0	+17	+19	+20	+21	+22
OH	Akron	41	5	81	31	0	+46	+43	+41	+39	+37
OH	Canton	40	48	81	23	0	+46	+43	+41	+38	+36
OH	Cincinnati-Hamilton	39	6	84	31	0	+64	+58	+53	+48	+44
OH	Cleveland-Lakewood	41	30	81	42	0	+45	+43	+42	+40	+39
OH	Columbus	39	57	83	1	0	+55	+51	+47	+43	+40
OH	Dayton	39	45	84	10	0	+61	+56	+52	+48	+44
OH	Toledo	41	39	83	33	0	+52	+50	+49	+48	+47
OH	Youngstown	41	6	80	39	0	+42	+40	+38	+36	+34
OK	Oklahoma City	35	28	97	31	1	+67	+55	+46	+35	+26
OK	Tulsa	36	9	95	60	1	+59	+48	+40	+30	+22
OR	Eugene	44	3	123	6	3	+21	+24	+27	+30	+33
OR	Pendleton	45	40	118	47	3	−1	+4	+10	+16	+21
OR	Portland	45	31	122	41	3	+14	+20	+25	+31	+36
OR	Salem	44	57	123	1	3	+17	+23	+27	+31	+35
PA	Allentown-Bethlehem	40	36	75	28	0	+23	+20	+17	+14	+12
PA	Erie	42	7	80	5	0	+36	+36	+35	+35	+35
PA	Harrisburg	40	16	76	53	0	+30	+26	+23	+19	+16
PA	Lancaster	40	2	76	18	0	+28	+24	+20	+17	+13
PA	Philadelphia-Chester	39	57	75	9	0	+24	+19	+16	+12	+9
PA	Pittsburgh-McKeesport	40	26	80	0	0	+42	+38	+35	+32	+29
PA	Reading	40	20	75	56	0	+26	+22	+19	+16	+13
PA	Scranton-Wilkes-Barre	41	25	75	40	0	+21	+19	+18	+16	+15
PA	York	39	58	76	43	0	+30	+26	+22	+18	+15
RI	Providence	41	50	71	25	0	+3	+2	+1	0	0
SC	Charleston	32	47	79	56	0	+64	+48	+36	+21	+10
SC	Columbia	34	0	81	2	0	+65	+51	+40	+27	+17
SC	Spartanburg	34	56	81	57	0	+66	+53	+43	+32	+23
SD	Aberdeen	45	28	98	29	1	+37	+44	+49	+54	+59
SD	Pierre	44	22	100	21	1	+49	+53	+56	+60	+63
SD	Rapid City	44	5	103	14	2	+2	+5	+8	+11	+13
SD	Sioux Falls	43	33	96	44	1	+38	+40	+42	+44	+46
TN	Chattanooga	35	3	85	19	0	+79	+67	+57	+45	+36
TN	Knoxville	35	58	83	55	0	+71	+60	+51	+41	+33
TN	Memphis	35	9	90	3	1	+38	+26	+16	+5	−3
TN	Nashville	36	10	86	47	1	+22	+11	+3	−6	−14

STATE/PROVINCE	CITY	NORTH LATITUDE °	'	WEST LONGITUDE °	'	TIME ZONE CODE	KEY LETTERS (MINUTES) A	B	C	D	E
TX	Amarillo	35	12	101	50	1	+85	+73	+63	+52	+43
TX	Austin	30	16	97	45	1	+82	+62	+47	+29	+15
TX	Beaumont	30	5	94	6	1	+67	+48	+32	+14	0
TX	Brownsville	25	54	97	30	1	+91	+66	+46	+23	+5
TX	Corpus Christi	27	48	97	24	1	+86	+64	+46	+25	+9
TX	Dallas–Fort Worth	32	47	96	48	1	+71	+55	+43	+28	+17
TX	El Paso	31	45	106	29	2	+53	+35	+22	+6	−6
TX	Galveston	29	18	94	48	1	+72	+52	+35	+16	+1
TX	Houston	29	45	95	22	1	+73	+53	+37	+19	+5
TX	McAllen	26	12	98	14	1	+93	+69	+49	+26	+9
TX	San Antonio	29	25	98	30	1	+87	+66	+50	+31	+16
UT	Kanab	37	3	112	32	2	+62	+53	+46	+37	+30
UT	Moab	38	35	109	33	2	+46	+39	+33	+27	+22
UT	Ogden	41	13	111	58	2	+47	+45	+43	+41	+40
UT	Salt Lake City	40	45	111	53	2	+48	+45	+43	+40	+38
UT	Vernal	40	27	109	32	2	+40	+36	+33	+30	+28
VA	Charlottesville	38	2	78	30	0	+43	+35	+29	+22	+17
VA	Danville	36	36	79	23	0	+51	+41	+33	+24	+17
VA	Norfolk	36	51	76	17	0	+38	+28	+21	+12	+5
VA	Richmond	37	32	77	26	0	+41	+32	+25	+17	+11
VA	Roanoke	37	16	79	57	0	+51	+42	+35	+27	+21
VA	Winchester	39	11	78	10	0	+38	+33	+28	+23	+19
VT	Brattleboro	42	51	72	34	0	+4	+5	+5	+6	+7
VT	Burlington	44	29	73	13	0	0	+4	+8	+12	+15
VT	Rutland	43	37	72	58	0	+2	+5	+7	+9	+11
VT	St. Johnsbury	44	25	72	1	0	−4	0	+3	+7	+10
WA	Bellingham	48	45	122	29	3	0	+13	+24	+37	+47
WA	Seattle-Tacoma-Olympia	47	37	122	20	3	+3	+15	+24	+34	+42
WA	Spokane	47	40	117	24	3	−16	−4	+4	+14	+23
WA	Walla Walla	46	4	118	20	3	−5	+2	+8	+15	+21
WI	Eau Claire	44	49	91	30	1	+12	+17	+21	+25	+29
WI	Green Bay	44	31	88	0	1	0	+3	+7	+11	+14
WI	La Crosse	43	48	91	15	1	+15	+18	+20	+22	+25
WI	Madison	43	4	89	23	1	+10	+11	+12	+14	+15
WI	Milwaukee	43	2	87	54	1	+4	+6	+7	+8	+9
WI	Oshkosh	44	1	88	33	1	+3	+6	+9	+12	+15
WI	Wausau	44	58	89	38	1	+4	+9	+13	+18	+22
WV	Charleston	38	21	81	38	0	+55	+48	+42	+35	+30
WV	Parkersburg	39	16	81	34	0	+52	+46	+42	+36	+32
WY	Casper	42	51	106	19	2	+19	+19	+20	+21	+22
WY	Cheyenne	41	8	104	49	2	+19	+16	+14	+12	+11
WY	Sheridan	44	48	106	58	2	+14	+19	+23	+27	+31
CANADA											
AB	Calgary	51	5	114	5	2	+13	+35	+50	+68	+84
AB	Edmonton	53	34	113	25	2	−3	+26	+47	+72	+93
BC	Vancouver	49	13	123	6	3	0	+15	+26	+40	+52
MB	Winnipeg	49	53	97	10	1	+12	+30	+43	+58	+71
NB	Saint John	45	16	66	3	−1	+28	+34	+39	+44	+49
NS	Halifax	44	38	63	35	−1	+21	+26	+29	+33	+37
NS	Sydney	46	10	60	10	−1	+1	+9	+15	+23	+28
ON	Ottawa	45	25	75	43	0	+6	+13	+18	+23	+28
ON	Peterborough	44	18	78	19	0	+21	+25	+28	+32	+35
ON	Thunder Bay	48	27	89	12	0	+47	+61	+71	+83	+93
ON	Toronto	43	39	79	23	0	+28	+30	+32	+35	+37
QC	Montreal	45	28	73	39	0	−1	+4	+9	+15	+20
SK	Saskatoon	52	10	106	40	1	+37	+63	+80	+101	+119

Good News for Americans, Bad News for Pain Drugs

Millions are expected to benefit from a new technology that could relieve years of severe joint discomfort; reprograms the body to block slow burning inflammation instead of creating it

By Casey Law
Health News Correspondent

NATION — Several of the major drug companies behind popular pain relievers may take a financial hit as manufacturing of a new pill is now complete.

Using a new technology, the pill could be safer and more effective than many store bought brands.

The pill, VeraFlex, was developed in May of this year by a private company in Seattle.

The Science Behind Relief

Research shows that the joint stiffness, soreness and discomfort associated with arthritis is caused by inflammation which attacks healthy cartilage and protective tissue.

And according to leading medical scientists, this inflammation is caused by two inflammatory enzymes released by the body's immune system.

Remarkably, the active ingredients in VeraFlex help to block the production of both these enzymes, resulting in a dramatic decreasing in swelling, inflammation, and discomfort.

Right now, the leading over-the-counter pills are only able to block one of these enzymes!

"VeraFlex users can generally expect more flexibility in three days...their joint pain alleviated in five days...and in just seven days, a tremendous improvement in overall joint function that may help them move like they did years prior" explains Dr. Liza Leal, developer and spokesperson for VeraFlex.

"It's an incredibly powerful little pill. And with the addition of a patented absorption enhancer, it packs an even greater punch. That's why I'm so excited to be the first to share these results. It's giving sufferers their life back."

A Safer Avenue to Amazing Relief

It's widely accepted through the medical community that inflammatory enzymes are the primary cause of pain and suffering in millions of Americans. It's why most prescriptions and even nonprescription pills are designed to block them.

However, what most people don't know is that even the most advanced ones can't block both!

"Top pharma companies have struggled to create a drug that blocks COX and LOX; the medical names for the two inflammatory enzymes in the body. Consider the top seller Celebrex, it only blocks one variation of the COX enzyme" explains Leal.

"Every VeraFlex capsule contains an ultra-high dose of a patented plant extract which has been clinically shown to block both enzymes, bringing relief to every joint that hurts!

Piling on the Clinical Research

Remarkably, the key ingredient in VeraFlex is protected by 8 patents that spread from the US into Canada. And as would one guess, it's backed by an enormous amount of research, including two patient clinical trials.

In the first, 60 participants with rheumatoid arthritis and/or osteoarthritis were randomly placed into four groups.

Two groups were given the patented ingredient in VeraFlex, one was given the drug Celecoxib, and the last group a placebo. The results were monitored at 30, 60, and 90 days and were stunning.

The groups taking the VeraFlex ingredient saw staggering improvements in arthritis symptoms such as flexibility, discomfort and function.

And even more astonishing they experienced a dramatic reduction in pain by the 30-day mark that was even better than Celecoxib, a powerful drug!

A second study was conducted to ensure the data was accurate and again the results participants experienced taking the VeraFlex compound blew away researchers.

This time it beat out the drug Naproxen. Shockingly, both men and women experienced a reduction in joint stiffness two days faster than when using Naproxen.

Faster Delivery, Maximum Absorption

VeraFlex is mainly comprised of two patented ingredients: Univestin, a powerful immune modulator which blocks the enzymes which cause your joints to hurt and BiAloe, an absorption enhancer (accelerator) that ensures maximum potency.

Research shows that severe joint discomfort arises when the immune system goes haywire and releases COX and LOX into your blood stream, two enzymes that cause tremendous swelling and inflammation around cartilage and protective tissue.

Unfortunately, modern day pain pills are only able to block one of these enzymes, resulting in marginal relief and continued suffering.

The Univestin in VeraFlex is one of the only known substances which has been proven successful in blocking both enzymes, resulting in phenomenal relief from the worst kinds of discomfort.

The addition of BiAloe, a unique aloe vera extra, maximizes the delivery of the plant based Univestin extract to every joint in the body because it is proven to improve nutrient absorption for maximum results.

Claim a Free 3-Month Supply

This is the official nationwide release of VeraFlex, so the company is offering our readers up to 3 FREE bottles with their order.

All you have to do is call toll free 1-800-997-5967 and provide the operator with the Free Bottle Approval Code: VF350.

GENERAL STORE CLASSIFIEDS

For advertising information and rates, go to Almanac.com/Advertising
or call RJ Media at 212-986-0016. The 2022 edition closes on April 30, 2021.

ASTROLOGY

REV. BROWN. Removes bad luck, Ritual work, Sickness, Lost nature. Brings back loved ones. 252-366-4078.

SEEKING LUCK, LOVE, MONEY? With Spiritual Cleansing, achieve goals! FREE Tarot Reading! 811 Saluda Street, Rockville, SC 29730. 803-371-7711.

SOPHIA GREEN. Don't tell me, I'll tell you! Helps all problems—Reunites lovers. Guaranteed! 956-878-7053.

FAITH HEALER LYNN. Worried? Suffering? Solves all problems! Specializes: Love, Health, Finances. Call today! 704-550-5975.

GOD-GIFTED HEALTH INTUITIVE. Detox and Rejuvenation. Call now! 310-651-1801.

MADAM SYLVIA. Love & Relationship Expert. Helps all problems. Call for One Free Reading. 864-809-5563.

ATTENTION: SISTER LIGHT
Spartanburg, South Carolina
One FREE READING when you call.
I will help you with all problems.
Call: 864-576-9397

**ANGEL PSYCHIC
MEDIUM CLAIRVOYANT**
Spiritual ~ Positive Energy
*Accurate *Honest *Healing
Call: 323-466-3684
www.TruePsychicReader.com

FREE 10-MINUTE READING
Rev. Grace. God-Gifted Indian Spiritualist.
Solves impossible problems!
Reunites lovers fast!
Removes negative energy. Immediate help!
Guaranteed Results! Call: 316-573-6127

ASTROLOGY cont.

**MYSTERIO, TAROT READER
& ASTROLOGER**
One FREE READING when you call.
I can draw and interpret birth charts
for a small fee.
Call Today: 513-500-1973

PSYCHIC SPIRITUALIST ROSELLA
I don't judge, I solve all love problems.
Helps stop break-ups & divorce.
Reunites loved ones.
Tells past, present, & future.
Spiritual Soul Cleansing
Call: 586-215-3838

BOOKS, MAGAZINES, CATALOGS

$14. *Voyage of the Pink Rowboat
& Philosophy of Flight of the Arrow*
Amazon, Kindle, eBook.
Armadillo Astronomy Theory.
3 Eastern Lane
West Gardiner, ME 04345

BUSINESS OPPORTUNITIES

$800 WEEKLY POTENTIAL! Process HUD/FHA refunds from home. Free information available. Call: 860-357-1599.

HEALTH

**HOW TO REVERSE
MACULAR DEGENERATION,
STARGARDT, RP**
This Program Works, If You Do It.
No need to travel!
Call Dr. Miller: 650-780-9900
support@bettereyehealth.com

JEWELRY

WWW.AZUREGREEN.NET Jewelry, Amulets, Incense, Oils, Statuary, Gifts, Herbs, Candles, Gemstones. 8,000 Items. Wholesale inquiries welcome.

The Old Farmer's Almanac has no liability whatsoever for any third-party claims arising in connection with such advertisements or any products or services mentioned therein.

2020 ESSAY CONTEST WINNERS
"What worn-out possession is dearest to you, and why?"

First Prize: $300

When I was 6, I had major leg surgery. Finally, the day came to get the casts that stretched from the tips of my toes to the top of my hips removed. The sound of the cast saw coming from the other room was as loud as that of any lumberjack to a little girl. The buzzing, whirring, and whining got louder with every passing moment, until I broke out in tears. As the tears spread down my face, I noticed a woman coming to my side. With delicate fingers, she opened her purse and removed a white hanky and placed it in my hand. She said, "This is my Hanky of Courage. Sometimes things come along in our lives that call for a little more courage. I can see that you are a brave girl, but please keep this and let it give you a boost of courage to face your fears." I held on to that wonderful hanky and made it through that tough day, and it has been a treasure that I have kept with me for 52 years.

–Vickie L. Sargent-Kler, Zephyrhills, Florida

Second Prize: $200

In 1941, my father served in the U.S. Army in Tunis, North Africa. While there, he fashioned a ring from the aluminum of a downed enemy plane. He came home alive and wore the shiny ring until his death in 1962. As a family, we were lost in blinding grief that slowly faded but never really passed. Ma trusted me with his ring, which became my touchstone, the band wrapped in white adhesive to fit a boy's slight finger. Over the years, people would ask about it, and I would take a breath and recall his short life.

I lost the ring on the Appalachian Trail and could not forgive myself. It found me a few years later from a deep pocket in my pack. We celebrated like father and son. But, like everything, possessions wear down with use. The script "Tunis, North Africa, 1941" became barely legible.

The ring now stays in a box on the bureau. I open it up from time to time and remember and settle. This possession never lets me down.

–Michael Wing, West Gardiner, Maine

Third Prize: $100

A handmade 12x16-inch quilt of once-colorful homespun squares neatly blanket-stitched is my most cherished possession. Quilted for me by our beloved babysitter, Mrs. Jean Howard, it has frayed edges and is faded in spots. The formerly white squares are now a golden ecru, and bright colors are now much paler than when new 60 years ago.

Even at a young age, my sisters and I were deeply touched by Mrs. Howard's sad memories of losing her young soldier husband in World War I and then, a year later, her darling baby girl to the dreaded influenza epidemic.

A young widow, she became a governess growing deeply attached to the young ones in her charge. Mrs. Howard revealed that she made little quilts for each youngster in loving remembrance of her own little girl. She tried to give these children all of the love that she might have given her own daughter.

From lovely milk-and-cookie doll tea parties to helping us snugly tuck in our dolls for the night, Mrs. Howard gave us her kind and patient attention. A woman who truly understood little girls and their cherished dolls knew that a miniature quilt was indeed a very special gift.

–Roseann Gulla-Devaney, Winchester, Massachusetts

Honorable Mention

The year 1963 was a difficult time for the United States and the world. I was 10 years old and didn't really understand adult issues. I came from a small island republic called Trinidad & Tobago. My grandmother gave me the Little Brown Suitcase to travel. I was heading to Michigan to meet my father for the first time. My mother passed when I was 13 months old. So, as my journey began, it wasn't a happy one. Lots of moving, but I always had my Little Brown Suitcase to remind me of the place I came from and how things had changed. It holds memories that you can't see and words that you can't hear. The years have gotten better and some memories fade, but my suitcase still holds treasured memories.

–Patricia Hoffman, Taylor, Michigan ■

ANNOUNCING THE 2021 ESSAY CONTEST TOPIC:
A KINDNESS I WILL ALWAYS REMEMBER
SEE CONTEST RULES ON PAGE 251.

MADDENING MIND-MANGLERS

Another Tennessee Teaser

Write the numbers from 1 through 9 in a vertical column. Now add 1 plus 2 and write the sum (3) to the right of 2. Then add that sum to the next number (3) and write its sum to the right, and so on. To start:

1
2 = 3
3 = 6
4 = 10
Etc.

1. How many sums (right-hand numbers) are not divisible by 2?

2. How many sums are not divisible by 3?

3. How many sums are prime numbers?

4. How many sums are in the Fibonacci Sequence (see right)?

Fun Fact: The Fibonacci Sequence is a fascinating numerical series found repeatedly in nature, such as in the logarithmic spirals of a nautilus shell. "Fibonacci" was the nickname of Italian mathematician Leonardo Pisano Bogollo (1170–c. 1250), who first referenced the series that occurs when each new number is the sum of the previous two (0, 1, 1, 2, 3, 5, etc.). Fibonacci was also instrumental in helping to spread the use of Hindu-Arabic digits (1, 2, 3) throughout Europe in place of Roman numerals (I, II, III), in addition to many other mathematical accomplishments.

–courtesy of Morris Bowles, Cane Ridge, Tennessee

Down at the Well

5. Cy had a 5-gallon pail, a 3-gallon bucket, and a full well. His wife needed exactly 7 gallons of water—no more, no less. How could he oblige?

Seeing the Light

6. How long would it take a ½-mile-long train to go completely through a ½-mile-long tunnel at 30 miles per hour?

–courtesy of Roger Dutcher, Overland Park, Kansas

Half an Orchard Is Better Than None

7. How can a farmer plant 10 apple trees in five rows with four trees in each row?

–courtesy of Al Pattarozzi, Sarasota, Florida

What Am I?

8. *I'm in the fire but not in the flame.*

I'm in the master but not in the dame.

I'm in the courtier but not in the clown.

I'm in the country but not in the town.

What am I?

–courtesy of Chauncey Attleboro, Toronto, Ontario

ANSWERS:

1. Four. **2.** Two. **3.** One (3). **4.** Two (3, 21). **5.** Fill 5 and give to her. Fill 5 and pour into 3, leaving 2 in 5. Give her 2 from 5. **6.** 2 minutes. A train going 30 mph travels ½ mile in 1 minute. It takes 1 minute for the train to enter and begin to emerge from the tunnel and then another minute for the caboose to finally be out of it. **7.** By planting in the shape of a star. Draw a pentagon (five-sided figure) and "plant" one tree at each point. To each side of the pentagon, add a triangle with a tree at its tip. You now have five "rows" that intersect to form a five-point star. **8.** The letter "r".

ESSAY AND RECIPE CONTEST RULES

ANECDOTES & PLEASANTRIES

*A sampling from the thousands of letters, clippings,
articles, and emails sent to us during the past year by our
Almanac family all over the United States and Canada.*

ILLUSTRATIONS BY TIM ROBINSON

"One Large Pizza to Go, With Peppers, Onions, and Band-Aids"

Who knew?

According to the Consumer Product Safety Commission, pizza-related injuries are now up to around 4,000 a year and range from pizza-cutter wounds and roof-of-the-mouth fork stabbings to delivery people tripping on stairs and a young woman overzealously swallowing her tongue ring amidst the mushrooms.

–courtesy of H. O., Shelby, North Carolina

DEPT. OF READY-MADE EXCUSES

Feeling guilty about not getting your exercise or being late? Not to worry!

Researchers now report that watching movies can equate to a light workout because our hearts beat faster when we get immersed in a film. Plus, trying to figure out the plot is good for our brains. Plus, the hearts of moviegoers watching the same flick begin to beat in sync, bringing on a feeling of togetherness. (And, yes: This study was funded by the film industry.)

–courtesy of L. P., Antigonish, Nova Scotia

A new study indicates that late arrivers are generally happier and live longer due to an innate sense of calm. This is often tied to optimism, which seems to protect the heart and circulation. (If you try this at work, let us know how it goes.)

–courtesy of M. B., Snyder, Texas

Why We See Faces in Clouds and Elvis in a Potato Chip

When you see your Aunt Harriet in a cloud, it's not because you're fixated on her (we hope). According to University of Illinois scientist Kara Federmeier, this all has to do with the way your brain processes visual information.

You see a cloud. It looks like whipped cream. But your brain says, "No, that can't be whipped cream up there," so it keeps on searching your lifetime image slide show for some other object/outline/texture package that resembles the cloud but is not so commonplace that it has been discounted before.

Then it says, "Stop! That time at the picnic 3 years ago when Aunt Harriet looked over at you. That's it! That's a match!"—and you see Aunt Harriet in the cloud.

Your brain passes over images that often look like clouds but have been determined not to be and searches to see if it can find a more unique image that fits. Because facial recognition has been so important in human evolution (e.g., to identify your enemy), your brain is genetically disposed to retain a huge stockpile of facial images. This means that a face might be its first choice, but the best match could also be a horse or a frog or a tugboat.

This is also why you see Elvis in a potato chip.

–courtesy of D. G., Palatine, Illinois

THE MEANING OF A MOLE

A mole on . . .	Means . . .
A woman's or man's neck	a long and happy life, wealth, fame
The right side of a woman's or man's upper lip	good fortune
The right side of a man's forehead	wonderful luck
The left side of a woman's forehead	two husbands and a life of exile
The left side of a man's forehead	a long term in prison

–The Sunny Side of Life, 1916

Life Lessons

Thanks, Mom, for teaching me about . . .

APPRECIATING A JOB WELL DONE: "If you're going to kill each other, do it outside. I just finished cleaning."

TIME TRAVEL: "If you don't straighten up, I'm going to send you into the middle of next week!"

STAMINA: "You'll sit there until all of that spinach is gone!"

PLANNING AHEAD: "Make sure you wear clean underwear, in case you're in an accident."

IRONY: "Keep crying, and I'll give you something to cry about."

OSMOSIS: "Close your mouth and eat your supper."

CONTORTIONISM: "Look at that dirt on the back of your neck!"

RELIGION: "You'd better pray that this comes out of the carpet."

LOGIC: "If you fall out of that swing and break your leg, you're not going to the store with me."

ADVANCED LOGIC: "Because I said so, that's why."

–courtesy of T. T., Nipigon, Ontario

TECH TIME

A Real Head Trip: A multinational team of investigators has found that using GPS might be harmful to your mind because it bypasses and thus atrophies your brain's hippocampus, which is key to many everyday tasks as well as remembering the past and envisioning the future. In other words, GPS can get you to Grandma's house but not to tomorrow.

–courtesy of J. D., Napoleon, Ohio

The Devil's Device: Researchers in Australia have observed small, hornlike bone spurs on the heads of some teenage cellphone users, perhaps because excessive use in the forward-tilted position causes changes in the growth dynamics of the skull. The study has a number of flaws, but millions of parents are saying, "We told you so!"

–courtesy of A. B., Tuscaloosa, Alabama

GOING TO THE DOGS?

Dogs can do math, such as understanding ratios and making simple approximations, according to an English study. No kidding. Like: "You have about 10 treats, so give me about 10 treats."

–courtesy of M. R.., Winooski, Vermont

Trapped in a running car that his owner had locked himself out of, a dog named Max seized the opportunity to put the vehicle in reverse and do doughnuts for an hour around a Port St. Lucie, Florida, cul-de-sac until it finally stopped. "They should give that dog a license," said a neighbor. "He drives better than some people I've seen on the roads here."

–G. T., Jensen Beach, Florida, from the
South Florida Sun-Sentinel

A study in *Frontiers in Zoology* has shown that dogs prefer to poop in alignment with Earth's magnetic field, or when they're facing either north or south. (That's all we're saying about this.)

–courtesy of W. Y., Grand Junction, Colorado

Predicting Weather With a Hole

Might be worth a try . . .

According to the late Prof. Elmar Reiter, esteemed atmospheric scientist at Colorado State University, you can predict rainfall patterns months in advance by using a hole. Just dig one 40 inches deep and take the ground's temperature. Nine times out of 10 . . .

- Warm winter soil means a wet spring.
- Cool summer soil means a dry fall.
- Warm fall soil means a wet winter.
- Cool fall soil means a dry winter.
  –The Old Farmer's Almanac, *1986*

Send your contribution for
The 2022 Old Farmer's Almanac
by January 22, 2021, to "A & P,"
The Old Farmer's Almanac,
P.O. Box 520, Dublin, NH 03444, or email
it to AlmanacEditors@yankeepub.com
(subject: A & P).

NEW PROSTATE PILL HELPS RELIEVE SYMPTOMS WITHOUT DRUGS OR SURGERY

Combats all-night bathroom urges and embarrassment... *Yet most doctors don't even know about it!*

By Health Writer, Peter Metler

Thanks to a brand new discovery made from a rare prostate relief plant; thousands of men across America are taking their lives back from "prostate hell". This remarkable new natural supplement helps you:

- **MINIMIZE** constant urges to urinate
- **END** embarrassing sexual "let-downs"
- **SUPPORT** a strong, healthy urine flow
- **GET** a restful night of uninterrupted sleep
- **STOP** false alarms, dribbles
- **ENJOY** a truly empty bladder

More men than ever before are dealing with prostate problems that range from annoying to downright EMBARRASSING! But now, research has discovered a new solution so remarkable that helps alleviate symptoms associated with an enlarged prostate (sexual failure, lost sleep, bladder discomfort and urgent runs to the bathroom). Like nothing before!

Yet 9 out of 10 doctors don't know about it! Here's why: Due to strict managed health care constrictions, many MD's are struggling to keep their practices afloat. "Unfortunately, there's no money in prescribing natural products. They aren't nearly as profitable," says a confidential source. Instead, doctors rely on toxic drugs that help, but could leave you sexually "powerless" (or a lot worse)!

On a CNN Special, Medical Correspondent Dr. Steve Salvatore shocked America by quoting a statistic from the prestigious Journal of American Medical Association that stated, "... about 60% of men who go under the knife for a prostatectomy are left UNABLE to perform sexually!"

PROSTATE PROBLEM SOLVED!

But now you can now beat the odds. And enjoy better sleep, a powerful urine stream and a long and healthy love life. The secret? You need to load your diet with essential Phyto-Nutrients, (traditionally found in certain fruits, vegetables and grains).

The problem is, most Phyto-Nutrients never get into your bloodstream. They're destroyed

HERE ARE 6 WARNING SIGNS YOU BETTER NOT IGNORE

- ✓ Waking up 2 to 6 times a night to urinate
- ✓ A constant feeling that you have to "go"... but can't
- ✓ A burning sensation when you do go
- ✓ A weak urine stream
- ✓ A feeling that your bladder is never completely empty
- ✓ Embarrassing sputtering, dripping & staining

by today's food preparation methods (cooking, long storage times and food additives).

YEARS OF RESEARCH

Thankfully, a small company (Wellness Logix™) out of Maine, is on a mission to change that. They've created a product that arms men who suffer with prostate inflammation with new hope. And it's fast becoming the #1 Prostate formula in America.

Prostate IQ™ gives men the super-concentrated dose of Phyto-Nutrients they need to beat prostate symptoms. "You just can't get them from your regular diet" say Daniel. It's taken a long time to understand how to capture the prostate relieving power of this amazing botanical. But their hard work paid off. *Prostate IQ*™ is different than any other prostate supplement on the market...

DON'T BE FOOLED BY CHEAP FORMULATIONS!

Many hope you won't notice, but a lot of prostate supplements fall embarrassingly short with their dosages. The formulas may be okay, but they won't do a darn thing for you unless you take 10 or more tablets a day. *Prostate IQ*™ contains a whopping 300mg of this special "Smart Prostate Plant". So it's loaded with Phyto-Nutrients. Plus, it gets into your bloodstream faster and stays inside for maximum results!

TRY IT RISK-FREE

SPECIAL OPPORTUNITY

Get a risk-free trial supply of *Prostate IQ*™ today - just for asking. But you must act now, supplies are limited!

Call Now, Toll-Free at:

1-800-380-0925

A Reference Compendium

CALENDAR

Phases of the Moon 258
When Will the Moon Rise? 258
Full Moon Names. 258
The Origin of Full Moon Names . . .259
Meanings of Full Moon Names 259
The Origin of Month Names 260
Easter Dates (2021–24) 260
Friggatriskaidekaphobia Trivia . . 260
The Origin of Day Names. 261
How to Find the Day of the Week
    for Any Given Date 261
Animal Signs of the Chinese Zodiac . .262

WEATHER

A Table Foretelling the Weather
    Through All the Lunations of Each
    Year, or Forever. 263
Safe Ice Thickness. 263
Heat Index °F (°C) 264
The UV Index for Measuring
    Ultraviolet Radiation Risk 264
What Are Cooling/Heating
    Degree Days? 265
How to Measure Hail. 265
How to Measure Wind Speed 266
Retired Atlantic Hurricane Names. .266
Atlantic Tropical (and Subtropical)
    Storm Names for 2021. 267
Eastern North-Pacific Tropical
    (and Subtropical) Storm Names
    for 2021. .267
How to Measure Hurricane
    Strength. .267
How to Measure a Tornado 268
Wind/Barometer Table 268
Windchill Table 269
How to Measure Earthquakes 269

IN THE GARDEN

A Gardener's Worst Phobias. 270
Plants for Lawns 270
Lawn-Growing Tips. 270
Flowers and Herbs That Attract
    Butterflies 271
Flowers That Attract
    Hummingbirds 271
pH Preferences of Trees, Shrubs,
    Flowers, and Vegetables. 272
Produce Weights and Measures. . .273
Sowing Vegetable Seeds 274
A Beginner's Vegetable Garden . . .274
Soil Fixes 274
When to Fertilize and Water. 275
How to Grow Herbs. 276
Drying Herbs 277
Storing Herbs and Spices 277
Cooking With Herbs 277
How to Grow Bulbs 278

AROUND THE HOUSE

Substitutions for Common
    Ingredients 280
Types of Fat 282
Calorie-Burning Comparisons 282
Freezer Storage Time. 283
Freezing Hints 283
Plastics. 284
How Much Do You Need?
    Wallpaper 285
    Interior Paint 285
Metric Conversion. 286
Where Do You Fit in Your
    Family Tree?. 287
The Golden Rule. 288
Famous Last Words 288

REFERENCE

PHASES OF THE MOON

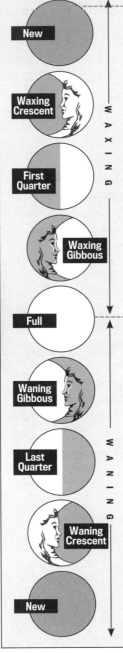

WHEN WILL THE MOON RISE?

Use the following saying to remember the time of moonrise on a day when a Moon phase occurs. Keep in mind that the phase itself may happen earlier or later that day, depending on location.

The new Moon always rises near sunrise;

The first quarter, near noon;

The full Moon always rises near sunset;

The last quarter, near midnight.

Moonrise occurs about 50 minutes later each day.

FULL MOON NAMES

NAME	MONTH	VARIATIONS
Full Wolf Moon	JANUARY	Full Greetings Moon
Full Snow Moon	FEBRUARY	Full Hunger Moon
Full Worm Moon	MARCH	Full Eagle Moon Full Sore Eye Moon Full Sugar Moon Full Wind Strong Moon
Full Pink Moon	APRIL	Full Budding Moon Moon When the Geese Lay Eggs
Full Flower Moon	MAY	Full Corn Planting Moon Full Frog Moon
Full Strawberry Moon	JUNE	Full Hoeing Moon Full Hot Moon
Full Buck Moon	JULY	Full Raspberry Moon Full Salmon Moon
Full Sturgeon Moon	AUGUST	Full Black Cherries Moon Full Flying Up Moon
Full Harvest Moon*	SEPTEMBER	Full Corn Moon Full Yellow Leaf Moon
Full Hunter's Moon	OCTOBER	Full Falling Leaves Moon Full Migrating Moon
Full Beaver Moon	NOVEMBER	Full Frost Moon
Full Cold Moon	DECEMBER	Full Long Nights Moon

*The Harvest Moon is always the full Moon closest to the autumnal equinox. If the Harvest Moon occurs in October, the September full Moon is usually called the Corn Moon.

REFERENCE

THE ORIGIN OF FULL MOON NAMES

Historically, some Native Americans who lived in the area that is now the United States kept track of the seasons by giving a distinctive name to each recurring full Moon. (This name was applied to the entire month in which it occurred.) The names were used by various tribes and/or by colonial Americans, who also brought their own traditions.

Meanings of Full Moon Names

JANUARY'S full Moon was called the **Wolf Moon** because wolves were more often heard at this time.

FEBRUARY'S full Moon was called the **Snow Moon** because it was a time of heavy snow. It was also called the **Hunger Moon** because hunting was difficult and hunger often resulted.

MARCH'S full Moon was called the **Worm Moon** because, as the weather warmed, wormlike insect larvae emerged from the bark of trees, and other winter homes.

APRIL'S full Moon was called the **Pink Moon** because it heralded the appearance of the moss pink, or wild ground phlox—one of the first spring flowers.

MAY'S full Moon was called the **Flower Moon** because blossoms were abundant everywhere at this time.

JUNE'S full Moon was called the **Strawberry Moon** because it appeared when the strawberry harvest took place.

JULY'S full Moon was called the **Buck Moon;** it arrived when a male deer's antlers were in full growth mode.

AUGUST'S full Moon was called the **Sturgeon Moon** because this large fish, which is found in the Great Lakes and Lake Champlain, was caught easily at this time.

SEPTEMBER'S full Moon was called the **Corn Moon** because this was the time to harvest corn.

The **Harvest Moon** is the full Moon that occurs closest to the autumnal equinox. It can occur in either September or October. Around this time, the Moon rises only about 30 minutes later each night, providing extra light after sunset for harvesting.

OCTOBER'S full Moon was called the **Hunter's Moon** because this was the time to hunt in preparation for winter.

NOVEMBER'S full Moon was called the **Beaver Moon** because it was the time when beavers finished preparations for winter and retreated to their lodges.

DECEMBER'S full Moon was called the **Cold Moon.** It was also called the **Long Nights Moon** because nights at this time of year were the longest.

REFERENCE

THE ORIGIN OF MONTH NAMES

JANUARY. For the Roman god Janus, protector of gates and doorways. Janus is depicted with two faces, one looking into the past, the other into the future.

FEBRUARY. From the Latin *februa,* "to cleanse." The Roman Februalia was a festival of purification and atonement that took place during this time of year.

MARCH. For the Roman god of war, Mars. This was the time of year to resume military campaigns that had been interrupted by winter.

APRIL. From the Latin *aperio,* "to open (bud)," because plants begin to grow now.

MAY. For the Roman goddess Maia, who oversaw the growth of plants. Also from the Latin *maiores,* "elders," who were celebrated now.

JUNE. For the Roman goddess Juno, patroness of marriage and the well-being of women. Also from the Latin *juvenis,* "young people."

JULY. To honor Roman dictator Julius Caesar (100 B.C.–44 B.C.). In 46 B.C., with the help of Sosigenes, he developed the Julian calendar.

AUGUST. To honor the first Roman emperor (and grandnephew of Julius Caesar), Augustus Caesar (63 B.C.–A.D. 14).

SEPTEMBER. From the Latin *septem,* "seven," because this was the seventh month of the early Roman calendar.

OCTOBER. From the Latin *octo,* "eight," because this was the eighth month of the early Roman calendar.

NOVEMBER. From the Latin *novem,* "nine," because this was the ninth month of the early Roman calendar.

DECEMBER. From the Latin *decem,* "ten," because this was the tenth month of the early Roman calendar.

Easter Dates (2021–24)

Christian churches that follow the Gregorian calendar celebrate Easter on the first Sunday after the paschal full Moon on or just after the vernal equinox.

YEAR	EASTER
2021	April 4
2022	April 17
2023	April 9
2024	March 31

The Julian calendar is used by some churches, including many Eastern Orthodox. The dates below are Julian calendar dates for Easter converted to Gregorian dates.

YEAR	EASTER
2021	May 2
2022	April 24
2023	April 16
2024	May 5

FRIGGATRISKAIDEKAPHOBIA TRIVIA

Here are a few facts about Friday the 13th:

In the 14 possible configurations for the annual calendar (see any perpetual calendar), the occurrence of Friday the 13th is this:

6 of 14 years have one Friday the 13th.
6 of 14 years have two Fridays the 13th.
2 of 14 years have three Fridays the 13th.

No year is without one Friday the 13th, and no year has more than three.

Months that have a Friday the 13th begin on a Sunday.

2021 has a Friday the 13th in August.

REFERENCE

THE ORIGIN OF DAY NAMES

The days of the week were named by ancient Romans with the Latin words for the Sun, the Moon, and the five known planets. These names have survived in European languages, but English names also reflect Anglo-Saxon and Norse influences.

ENGLISH	LATIN	FRENCH	ITALIAN	SPANISH	ANGLO-SAXON AND NORSE
SUNDAY	dies Solis (Sol's day)	dimanche	domenica	domingo	Sunnandaeg (Sun's day)
		from the Latin for "Lord's day"			
MONDAY	dies Lunae (Luna's day)	lundi	lunedì	lunes	Monandaeg (Moon's day)
TUESDAY	dies Martis (Mars's day)	mardi	martedì	martes	Tiwesdaeg (Tiw's day)
WEDNESDAY	dies Mercurii (Mercury's day)	mercredi	mercoledì	miércoles	Wodnesdaeg (Woden's day)
THURSDAY	dies Jovis (Jupiter's day)	jeudi	giovedì	jueves	Thursdaeg (Thor's day)
FRIDAY	dies Veneris (Venus's day)	vendredi	venerdì	viernes	Frigedaeg (Frigga's day)
SATURDAY	dies Saturni (Saturn's day)	samedi	sabato	sábado	Saeterndaeg (Saturn's day)
		from the Latin for "Sabbath"			

How to Find the Day of the Week for Any Given Date

To compute the day of the week for any given date as far back as the mid–18th century, proceed as follows:

Add the last two digits of the year to one-quarter of the last two digits (discard any remainder), the day of the month, and the month key from the key box below. Divide the sum by 7; the remainder is the day of the week (1 is Sunday, 2 is Monday, and so on). If there is no remainder, the day is Saturday. If you're searching for a weekday prior to 1900, add 2 to the sum before dividing; prior to 1800, add 4. The formula doesn't work for days prior to 1753. From 2000 through 2099, subtract 1 from the sum before dividing.

Example:

THE DAYTON FLOOD WAS ON MARCH 25, 1913.

Last two digits of year:	13
One-quarter of these two digits:	3
Given day of month:	25
Key number for March:	4
Sum:	45

45 ÷ 7 = 6, with a remainder of 3. The flood took place on Tuesday, the third day of the week.

KEY

JANUARY	1
LEAP YEAR	0
FEBRUARY	4
LEAP YEAR	3
MARCH	4
APRIL	0
MAY	2
JUNE	5
JULY	0
AUGUST	3
SEPTEMBER	6
OCTOBER	1
NOVEMBER	4
DECEMBER	6

REFERENCE

ANIMAL SIGNS OF THE CHINESE ZODIAC

The animal designations of the Chinese zodiac follow a 12-year cycle and are always used in the same sequence. The Chinese year of 354 days begins 3 to 7 weeks into the western 365-day year, so the animal designation changes at that time, rather than on January 1. This year, the Chinese New Year starts on February 12.

RAT

Ambitious and sincere, you can be generous with your money. Compatible with the dragon and the monkey. Your opposite is the horse.

1924	1936	1948
1960	1972	1984
1996	2008	2020

OX OR BUFFALO

A leader, you are bright, patient, and cheerful. Compatible with the snake and the rooster. Your opposite is the sheep.

1925	1937	1949
1961	1973	1985
1997	2009	2021

TIGER

Forthright and sensitive, you possess great courage. Compatible with the horse and the dog. Your opposite is the monkey.

1926	1938	1950
1962	1974	1986
1998	2010	2022

RABBIT OR HARE

Talented and affectionate, you are a seeker of tranquility. Compatible with the sheep and the pig. Your opposite is the rooster.

1927	1939	1951
1963	1975	1987
1999	2011	2023

DRAGON

Robust and passionate, your life is filled with complexity. Compatible with the monkey and the rat. Your opposite is the dog.

1928	1940	1952
1964	1976	1988
2000	2012	2024

SNAKE

Strong-willed and intense, you display great wisdom. Compatible with the rooster and the ox. Your opposite is the pig.

1929	1941	1953
1965	1977	1989
2001	2013	2025

HORSE

Physically attractive and popular, you like the company of others. Compatible with the tiger and the dog. Your opposite is the rat.

1930	1942	1954
1966	1978	1990
2002	2014	2026

SHEEP OR GOAT

Aesthetic and stylish, you enjoy being a private person. Compatible with the pig and the rabbit. Your opposite is the ox.

1931	1943	1955
1967	1979	1991
2003	2015	2027

MONKEY

Persuasive, skillful, and intelligent, you strive to excel. Compatible with the dragon and the rat. Your opposite is the tiger.

1932	1944	1956
1968	1980	1992
2004	2016	2028

ROOSTER OR COCK

Seeking wisdom and truth, you have a pioneering spirit. Compatible with the snake and the ox. Your opposite is the rabbit.

1933	1945	1957
1969	1981	1993
2005	2017	2029

DOG

Generous and loyal, you have the ability to work well with others. Compatible with the horse and the tiger. Your opposite is the dragon.

1934	1946	1958
1970	1982	1994
2006	2018	2030

PIG OR BOAR

Gallant and noble, your friends will remain at your side. Compatible with the rabbit and the sheep. Your opposite is the snake.

1935	1947	1959
1971	1983	1995
2007	2019	2031

REFERENCE

A Table Foretelling the Weather Through All the Lunations of Each Year, or Forever

This table is the result of many years of actual observation and shows what sort of weather will probably follow the Moon's entrance into any of its quarters. For example, the table shows that the week following January 6, 2021, will have rain, because the Moon enters the last quarter on that day at 4:37 A.M. EST. (See the **Left-Hand Calendar Pages, 120–146,** for Moon phases.)

EDITOR'S NOTE: Although the data in this table is taken into consideration in the year-long process of compiling the annual long-range weather forecasts for *The Old Farmer's Almanac,* we rely far more on our projections of solar activity.

TIME OF CHANGE	SUMMER	WINTER
Midnight to 2 A.M.	Fair	Hard frost, unless wind is south or west
2 A.M. to 4 A.M.	Cold, with frequent showers	Snow and stormy
4 A.M. to 6 A.M.	Rain	Rain
6 A.M. to 8 A.M.	Wind and rain	Stormy
8 A.M. to 10 A.M.	Changeable	Cold rain if wind is west; snow, if east
10 A.M. to noon	Frequent showers	Cold with high winds
Noon to 2 P.M.	Very rainy	Snow or rain
2 P.M. to 4 P.M.	Changeable	Fair and mild
4 P.M. to 6 P.M.	Fair	Fair
6 P.M. to 10 P.M.	Fair if wind is northwest; rain if wind is south or southwest	Fair and frosty if wind is north or northeast; rain or snow if wind is south or southwest
10 P.M. to midnight	Fair	Fair and frosty

This table was created more than 180 years ago by Dr. Herschell for the Boston Courier; *it first appeared in* The Old Farmer's Almanac *in 1834.*

SAFE ICE THICKNESS*

ICE THICKNESS	PERMISSIBLE LOAD	ICE THICKNESS	PERMISSIBLE LOAD
3 inches	Single person on foot	12 inches	Heavy truck (8-ton gross)
4 inches	Group in single file	15 inches	10 tons
7½ inches	Passenger car (2-ton gross)	20 inches	25 tons
8 inches	Light truck (2½-ton gross)	30 inches	70 tons
10 inches	Medium truck (3½-ton gross)	36 inches	110 tons

*Solid, clear, blue/black pond and lake ice

The strength value of river ice is 15 percent less. Slush ice has only half the strength of blue ice.

REFERENCE

HEAT INDEX °F (°C)

TEMP. °F (°C)	RELATIVE HUMIDITY (%)								
	40	45	50	55	60	65	70	75	80
100 (38)	109 (43)	114 (46)	118 (48)	124 (51)	129 (54)	136 (58)			
98 (37)	105 (41)	109 (43)	113 (45)	117 (47)	123 (51)	128 (53)	134 (57)		
96 (36)	101 (38)	104 (40)	108 (42)	112 (44)	116 (47)	121 (49)	126 (52)	132 (56)	
94 (34)	97 (36)	100 (38)	103 (39)	106 (41)	110 (43)	114 (46)	119 (48)	124 (51)	129 (54)
92 (33)	94 (34)	96 (36)	99 (37)	101 (38)	105 (41)	108 (42)	112 (44)	116 (47)	121 (49)
90 (32)	91 (33)	93 (34)	95 (35)	97 (36)	100 (38)	103 (39)	105 (41)	109 (43)	113 (45)
88 (31)	88 (31)	89 (32)	91 (33)	93 (34)	95 (35)	98 (37)	100 (38)	103 (39)	106 (41)
86 (30)	85 (29)	87 (31)	88 (31)	89 (32)	91 (33)	93 (34)	95 (35)	97 (36)	100 (38)
84 (29)	83 (28)	84 (29)	85 (29)	86 (30)	88 (31)	89 (32)	90 (32)	92 (33)	94 (34)
82 (28)	81 (27)	82 (28)	83 (28)	84 (29)	84 (29)	85 (29)	86 (30)	88 (31)	89 (32)
80 (27)	80 (27)	80 (27)	81 (27)	81 (27)	82 (28)	82 (28)	83 (28)	84 (29)	84 (29)

RISK LEVEL FOR HEAT DISORDERS: CAUTION EXTREME CAUTION DANGER

EXAMPLE: *When the temperature is 88°F (31°C) and the relative humidity is 60 percent, the heat index, or how hot it feels, is 95°F (35°C).*

THE UV INDEX FOR MEASURING ULTRAVIOLET RADIATION RISK

The U.S. National Weather Service's daily forecasts of ultraviolet levels use these numbers for various exposure levels:

UV INDEX NUMBER	EXPOSURE LEVEL	ACTIONS TO TAKE
0, 1, 2	Low	Wear UV-blocking sunglasses on bright days. In winter, reflection off snow can nearly double UV strength. If you burn easily, cover up and apply SPF 30+ sunscreen.
3, 4, 5	Moderate	Apply SPF 30+ sunscreen; wear a hat and sunglasses. Stay in shade when sun is strongest.
6, 7	High	Apply SPF 30+ sunscreen; wear a hat, sunglasses, and protective clothing; limit midday exposure.
8, 9, 10	Very High	Apply SPF 30+ sunscreen; wear a hat, sunglasses, and protective clothing; limit midday exposure. Seek shade. Unprotected skin will be damaged and can burn quickly.
11 or higher	Extreme	Apply SPF 30+ sunscreen; wear a hat, sunglasses, and protective clothing; avoid midday exposure; seek shade. Unprotected skin can burn in minutes.

REFERENCE

85	90	95	100
135 (57)			
126 (52)	131 (55)		
117 (47)	122 (50)	127 (53)	132 (56)
110 (43)	113 (45)	117 (47)	121 (49)
102 (39)	105 (41)	108 (42)	112 (44)
96 (36)	98 (37)	100 (38)	103 (39)
90 (32)	91 (33)	93 (34)	95 (35)
85 (29)	86 (30)	86 (30)	87 (31)

HOW TO MEASURE HAIL

The **TORRO HAILSTORM INTENSITY SCALE** was introduced by Jonathan Webb of Oxford, England, in 1986 as a means of categorizing hailstorms. The name derives from the private and mostly British research body named the TORnado and storm Research Organisation.

What Are Cooling/Heating Degree Days?

In an attempt to measure the need for air-conditioning, each degree of a day's mean temperature that is above a base temperature, such as 65°F (U.S.) or 18°C (Canada), is considered one cooling degree day. If the daily mean temperature is 75°F, for example, that's 10 cooling degree days.

Similarly, to measure the need for heating fuel consumption, each degree of a day's mean temperature that is below 65°F (18°C) is considered one heating degree. For example, a day with a high of 60°F and low of 40°F results in a mean of 50°, or 15 degrees less than 65°. Hence, that day had 15 heating degree days.

INTENSITY/DESCRIPTION OF HAIL DAMAGE	
H0	True hail of pea size causes no damage
H1	Leaves and flower petals are punctured and torn
H2	Leaves are stripped from trees and plants
H3	Panes of glass are broken; auto bodies are dented
H4	Some house windows are broken; small tree branches are broken off; birds are killed
H5	Many windows are smashed; small animals are injured; large tree branches are broken off
H6	Shingle roofs are breached; metal roofs are scored; wooden window frames are broken away
H7	Roofs are shattered to expose rafters; autos are seriously damaged
H8	Shingle and tile roofs are destroyed; small tree trunks are split; people are seriously injured
H9	Concrete roofs are broken; large tree trunks are split and knocked down; people are at risk of fatal injuries
H10	Brick houses are damaged; people are at risk of fatal injuries

REFERENCE

WEATHER

HOW TO MEASURE WIND SPEED

The **BEAUFORT WIND FORCE SCALE** is a common way of estimating wind speed. It was developed in 1805 by Admiral Sir Francis Beaufort of the British Navy to measure wind at sea. We can also use it to measure wind on land.

Admiral Beaufort arranged the numbers 0 to 12 to indicate the strength of the wind from calm, force 0, to hurricane, force 12. Here's a scale adapted to land.

"Used Mostly at Sea but of Help to All Who Are Interested in the Weather"

BEAUFORT FORCE	DESCRIPTION	WHEN YOU SEE OR FEEL THIS EFFECT	WIND SPEED (mph)	(km/h)
0	CALM	Smoke goes straight up	less than 1	less than 2
1	LIGHT AIR	Wind direction is shown by smoke drift but not by wind vane	1–3	2–5
2	LIGHT BREEZE	Wind is felt on the face; leaves rustle; wind vanes move	4–7	6–11
3	GENTLE BREEZE	Leaves and small twigs move steadily; wind extends small flags straight out	8–12	12–19
4	MODERATE BREEZE	Wind raises dust and loose paper; small branches move	13–18	20–29
5	FRESH BREEZE	Small trees sway; waves form on lakes	19–24	30–39
6	STRONG BREEZE	Large branches move; wires whistle; umbrellas are difficult to use	25–31	40–50
7	NEAR GALE	Whole trees are in motion; walking against the wind is difficult	32–38	51–61
8	GALE	Twigs break from trees; walking against the wind is very difficult	39–46	62–74
9	STRONG GALE	Buildings suffer minimal damage; roof shingles are removed	47–54	75–87
10	STORM	Trees are uprooted	55–63	88–101
11	VIOLENT STORM	Widespread damage	64–72	102–116
12	HURRICANE	Widespread destruction	73+	117+

REFERENCE

RETIRED ATLANTIC HURRICANE NAMES
These storms have been some of the most destructive and costly.

NAME	YEAR	NAME	YEAR	NAME	YEAR	NAME	YEAR
Rita	2005	Gustav	2008	Sandy	2012	Harvey	2017
Stan	2005	Ike	2008	Ingrid	2013	Irma	2017
Wilma	2005	Paloma	2008	Erika	2015	Maria	2017
Dean	2007	Igor	2010	Joaquin	2015	Nate	2017
Felix	2007	Tomas	2010	Matthew	2016	Florence	2018
Noel	2007	Irene	2011	Otto	2016	Michael	2018

WEATHER

ATLANTIC TROPICAL (AND SUBTROPICAL) STORM NAMES FOR 2021			EASTERN NORTH-PACIFIC TROPICAL (AND SUBTROPICAL) STORM NAMES FOR 2021		
Ana	Henri	Odette	Andres	Ignacio	Rick
Bill	Ida	Peter	Blanca	Jimena	Sandra
Claudette	Julian	Rose	Carlos	Kevin	Terry
Danny	Kate	Sam	Dolores	Linda	Vivian
Elsa	Larry	Teresa	Enrique	Marty	Waldo
Fred	Mindy	Victor	Felicia	Nora	Xina
Grace	Nicholas	Wanda	Guillermo	Olaf	York
			Hilda	Pamela	Zelda

The lists above are used in rotation and recycled every 6 years, e.g., the 2021 list will be used again in 2027.

How to Measure Hurricane Strength

The **SAFFIR-SIMPSON HURRICANE WIND SCALE** assigns a rating from 1 to 5 based on a hurricane's intensity. It is used to give an estimate of the potential property damage from a hurricane landfall. Wind speed is the determining factor in the scale, as storm surge values are highly dependent on the slope of the continental shelf in the landfall region. Wind speeds are measured at a height of 33 feet (10 meters) using a 1-minute average.

CATEGORY ONE. Average wind: 74–95 mph. Significant damage to mobile homes. Some damage to roofing and siding of well-built frame homes. Large tree branches snap and shallow-rooted trees may topple. Power outages may last a few to several days.

CATEGORY TWO. Average wind: 96–110 mph. Mobile homes may be destroyed. Major roof and siding damage to frame homes. Many shallow-rooted trees snap or topple, blocking roads. Widespread power outages could last from several days to weeks. Potable water may be scarce.

CATEGORY THREE. Average wind: 111–129 mph. Most mobile homes destroyed.

Frame homes may sustain major roof damage. Many trees snap or topple, blocking numerous roads. Electricity and water may be unavailable for several days to weeks.

CATEGORY FOUR. Average wind: 130–156 mph. Mobile homes destroyed. Frame homes severely damaged or destroyed. Windborne debris may penetrate protected windows. Most trees snap or topple. Residential areas isolated by fallen trees and power poles. Most of the area uninhabitable for weeks to months.

CATEGORY FIVE. Average wind: 157+ mph. Most homes destroyed. Nearly all windows blown out of high-rises. Most of the area uninhabitable for weeks to months.

REFERENCE

HOW TO MEASURE A TORNADO

The original **FUJITA SCALE** (or F Scale) was developed by Dr. Theodore Fujita to classify tornadoes based on wind damage. All tornadoes, and other severe local windstorms, were assigned a number according to the most intense damage caused by the storm. An enhanced F (EF) scale was implemented in the United States on February 1, 2007. The EF scale uses 3-second gust estimates based on a more detailed system for assessing damage, taking into account different building materials.

F SCALE		EF SCALE (U.S.)
F0 · 40-72 mph (64-116 km/h)	LIGHT DAMAGE	EF0 · 65-85 mph (105-137 km/h)
F1 · 73-112 mph (117-180 km/h)	MODERATE DAMAGE	EF1 · 86-110 mph (138-178 km/h)
F2 · 113-157 mph (181-253 km/h)	CONSIDERABLE DAMAGE	EF2 · 111-135 mph (179-218 km/h)
F3 · 158-207 mph (254-332 km/h)	SEVERE DAMAGE	EF3 · 136-165 mph (219-266 km/h)
F4 · 208-260 mph (333-419 km/h)	DEVASTATING DAMAGE	EF4 · 166-200 mph (267-322 km/h)
F5 · 261-318 mph (420-512 km/h)	INCREDIBLE DAMAGE	EF5 · over 200 mph (over 322 km/h)

Wind/Barometer Table

BAROMETER (REDUCED TO SEA LEVEL)	WIND DIRECTION	CHARACTER OF WEATHER INDICATED
30.00 to 30.20, and steady	WESTERLY	Fair, with slight changes in temperature, for one to two days
30.00 to 30.20, and rising rapidly	WESTERLY	Fair, followed within two days by warmer and rain
30.00 to 30.20, and falling rapidly	SOUTH TO EAST	Warmer, and rain within 24 hours
30.20 or above, and falling rapidly	SOUTH TO EAST	Warmer, and rain within 36 hours
30.20 or above, and falling rapidly	WEST TO NORTH	Cold and clear, quickly followed by warmer and rain
30.20 or above, and steady	VARIABLE	No early change
30.00 or below, and falling slowly	SOUTH TO EAST	Rain within 18 hours that will continue a day or two
30.00 or below, and falling rapidly	SOUTHEAST TO NORTHEAST	Rain, with high wind, followed within two days by clearing, colder
30.00 or below, and rising	SOUTH TO WEST	Clearing and colder within 12 hours
29.80 or below, and falling rapidly	SOUTH TO EAST	Severe storm of wind and rain imminent; in winter, snow or cold wave within 24 hours
29.80 or below, and falling rapidly	EAST TO NORTH	Severe northeast gales and heavy rain or snow, followed in winter by cold wave
29.80 or below, and rising rapidly	GOING TO WEST	Clearing and colder

NOTE: *A barometer should be adjusted to show equivalent sea-level pressure for the altitude at which it is to be used. A change of 100 feet in elevation will cause a decrease of 1/10 inch in the reading.*

WINDCHILL TABLE

As wind speed increases, your body loses heat more rapidly, making the air feel colder than it really is. The combination of cold temperature and high wind can create a cooling effect so severe that exposed flesh can freeze.

	TEMPERATURE (°F)														
Calm	**35**	**30**	**25**	**20**	**15**	**10**	**5**	**0**	**–5**	**–10**	**–15**	**–20**	**–25**	**–30**	**–35**
5	31	25	19	13	7	1	–5	–11	–16	–22	–28	–34	–40	–46	–52
10	27	21	15	9	3	–4	–10	–16	–22	–28	–35	–41	–47	–53	–59
15	25	19	13	6	0	–7	–13	–19	–26	–32	–39	–45	–51	–58	–64
20	24	17	11	4	–2	–9	–15	22	–29	–35	–42	–48	–55	–61	–68
25	23	16	9	3	–4	–11	–17	–24	–31	–37	–44	–51	–58	–64	–71
30	22	15	8	1	–5	–12	–19	–26	–33	–39	–46	–53	–60	–67	–73
35	21	14	7	0	–7	–14	–21	–27	–34	–41	–48	–55	–62	–69	–76
40	20	13	6	–1	–8	–15	–22	–29	–36	–43	–50	–57	–64	–71	–78
45	19	12	5	–2	–9	–16	–23	–30	–37	–44	–51	–58	–65	–72	–79
50	19	12	4	–3	–10	–17	–24	–31	–38	–45	–52	–60	–67	–74	–81
55	18	11	4	–3	–11	–18	–25	–32	–39	–46	–54	–61	–68	–75	–82
60	17	10	3	–4	–11	–19	–26	–33	–40	–48	–55	–62	–69	–76	–84

WIND SPEED (mph)

FROSTBITE OCCURS IN　　30 MINUTES　　10 MINUTES　　5 MINUTES

EXAMPLE: *When the temperature is 15°F and the wind speed is 30 miles per hour, the windchill, or how cold it feels, is –5°F. For a Celsius version of this table, visit Almanac.com/WindchillCelsius.*

–courtesy of National Weather Service

REFERENCE

HOW TO MEASURE EARTHQUAKES

In 1979, seismologists developed a measurement of earthquake size called **MOMENT MAGNITUDE.** It is more accurate than the previously used Richter scale, which is precise only for earthquakes of a certain size and at a certain distance from a seismometer. All earthquakes can now be compared on the same magnitude scale.

MAGNITUDE	DESCRIPTION	EFFECT
LESS THAN 3	MICRO	GENERALLY NOT FELT
3-3.9	MINOR	OFTEN FELT, LITTLE DAMAGE
4-4.9	LIGHT	SHAKING, SOME DAMAGE
5-5.9	MODERATE	SLIGHT TO MAJOR DAMAGE
6-6.9	STRONG	DESTRUCTIVE
7-7.9	MAJOR	SEVERE DAMAGE
8 OR MORE	GREAT	SERIOUS DAMAGE

A GARDENER'S WORST PHOBIAS

NAME OF FEAR	OBJECT FEARED
Alliumphobia	Garlic
Anthophobia	Flowers
Apiphobia	Bees
Arachnophobia	Spiders
Batonophobia	Plants
Bufonophobia	Toads
Dendrophobia	Trees
Entomophobia	Insects
Lachanophobia	Vegetables
Melissophobia	Bees
Mottephobia	Moths
Myrmecophobia	Ants
Ornithophobia	Birds
Ranidaphobia	Frogs
Rupophobia	Dirt
Scoleciphobia	Worms
Spheksophobia	Wasps

PLANTS FOR LAWNS

Choose varieties that suit your soil and your climate. All of these can withstand mowing and considerable foot traffic.

Ajuga or bugleweed (*Ajuga reptans*)
Corsican mint (*Mentha requienii*)
Dwarf cinquefoil (*Potentilla tabernaemontani*)
English pennyroyal (*Mentha pulegium*)
Green Irish moss (*Sagina subulata*)
Pearly everlasting (*Anaphalis margaritacea*)
Roman chamomile (*Chamaemelum nobile*)
Rupturewort (*Herniaria glabra*)
Speedwell (*Veronica officinalis*)
Stonecrop (*Sedum ternatum*)
Sweet violets (*Viola odorata* or *V. tricolor*)
Thyme (*Thymus serpyllum*)
White clover (*Trifolium repens*)
Wild strawberries (*Fragaria virginiana*)
Wintergreen or partridgeberry (*Mitchella repens*)

Lawn-Growing Tips

• Test your soil: The pH balance should be 7.0 or more; 6.2 to 6.7 puts your lawn at risk for fungal diseases. If the pH is too low, correct it with liming, best done in the fall.

• The best time to apply fertilizer is just before it rains.

• If you put lime and fertilizer on your lawn, spread half of it as you walk north to south, the other half as you walk east to west to cut down on missed areas.

• Any feeding of lawns in the fall should be done with a low-nitrogen, slow-acting fertilizer.

• In areas of your lawn where tree roots compete with the grass, apply some extra fertilizer to benefit both.

• Moss and sorrel in lawns usually means poor soil, poor aeration or drainage, or excessive acidity.

• Control weeds by promoting healthy lawn growth with natural fertilizers in spring and early fall.

• Raise the level of your lawn-mower blades during the hot summer days. Taller grass resists drought better than short.

• You can reduce mowing time by redesigning your lawn, reducing sharp corners and adding sweeping curves.

• During a drought, let the grass grow longer between mowings and reduce fertilizer.

• Water your lawn early in the morning or in the evening.

REFERENCE

Flowers and Herbs That Attract Butterflies

Allium	*Allium*
Aster	*Aster*
Bee balm	*Monarda*
Butterfly bush	*Buddleia*
Catmint	*Nepeta*
Clove pink	*Dianthus*
Cornflower	*Centaurea*
Creeping thyme	*Thymus serpyllum*
Daylily	*Hemerocallis*
Dill	*Anethum graveolens*
False indigo	*Baptisia*
Fleabane	*Erigeron*
Floss flower	*Ageratum*
Globe thistle	*Echinops*
Goldenrod	*Solidago*
Helen's flower	*Helenium*
Hollyhock	*Alcea*
Honeysuckle	*Lonicera*
Lavender	*Lavandula*
Lilac	*Syringa*
Lupine	*Lupinus*
Lychnis	*Lychnis*
Mallow	*Malva*
Mealycup sage	*Salvia farinacea*
Milkweed	*Asclepias*
Mint	*Mentha*
Oregano	*Origanum vulgare*
Pansy	*Viola*
Parsley	*Petroselinum crispum*
Phlox	*Phlox*
Privet	*Ligustrum*
Purple coneflower	*Echinacea purpurea*
Rock cress	*Arabis*
Sea holly	*Eryngium*
Shasta daisy	*Chrysanthemum*
Snapdragon	*Antirrhinum*
Stonecrop	*Sedum*
Sweet alyssum	*Lobularia*
Sweet marjoram	*Origanum majorana*
Sweet rocket	*Hesperis*
Tickseed	*Coreopsis*
Verbena	*Verbena*
Zinnia	*Zinnia*

FLOWERS* THAT ATTRACT HUMMINGBIRDS

Beard tongue	*Penstemon*
Bee balm	*Monarda*
Butterfly bush	*Buddleia*
Catmint	*Nepeta*
Clove pink	*Dianthus*
Columbine	*Aquilegia*
Coral bells	*Heuchera*
Daylily	*Hemerocallis*
Desert candle	*Yucca*
Flag iris	*Iris*
Flowering tobacco	*Nicotiana alata*
Foxglove	*Digitalis*
Larkspur	*Delphinium*
Lily	*Lilium*
Lupine	*Lupinus*
Petunia	*Petunia*
Pincushion flower	*Scabiosa*
Red-hot poker	*Kniphofia*
Scarlet sage	*Salvia splendens*
Soapwort	*Saponaria*
Summer phlox	*Phlox paniculata*
Trumpet honeysuckle	*Lonicera sempervirens*
Verbena	*Verbena*
Weigela	*Weigela*

*NOTE: *Choose varieties in red and orange shades, if available.*

pH PREFERENCES OF TREES, SHRUBS, FLOWERS, AND VEGETABLES

An accurate soil test will indicate your soil pH and will specify the amount of lime or sulfur that is needed to bring it up or down to the appropriate level. A pH of 6.5 is just about right for most home gardens, since most plants thrive in the 6.0 to 7.0 (slightly acidic to neutral) range. Some plants (azaleas, blueberries) prefer more strongly acidic soil in the 4.0 to 6.0 range, while a few (asparagus, plums) do best in soil that is neutral to slightly alkaline. Acidic, or sour, soil (below 7.0) is counteracted by applying finely ground limestone, and alkaline, or sweet, soil (above 7.0) is treated with ground sulfur.

COMMON NAME	OPTIMUM pH RANGE	COMMON NAME	OPTIMUM pH RANGE	COMMON NAME	OPTIMUM pH RANGE
TREES AND SHRUBS		Bee balm	6.0–7.5	Snapdragon	5.5–7.0
Apple	5.0–6.5	Begonia	5.5–7.0	Sunflower	6.0–7.5
Azalea	4.5–6.0	Black-eyed Susan	5.5–7.0	Tulip	6.0–7.0
Beautybush	6.0–7.5	Bleeding heart	6.0–7.5	Zinnia	5.5–7.0
Birch	5.0–6.5	Canna	6.0–8.0		
Blackberry	5.0–6.0	Carnation	6.0–7.0	**VEGETABLES**	
Blueberry	4.0–5.0	Chrysanthemum	6.0–7.5	Asparagus	6.0–8.0
Boxwood	6.0–7.5	Clematis	5.5–7.0	Bean	6.0–7.5
Cherry, sour	6.0–7.0	Coleus	6.0–7.0	Beet	6.0–7.5
Crab apple	6.0–7.5	Coneflower, purple	5.0–7.5	Broccoli	6.0–7.0
Dogwood	5.0–7.0	Cosmos	5.0–8.0	Brussels sprout	6.0–7.5
Fir, balsam	5.0–6.0	Crocus	6.0–8.0	Cabbage	6.0–7.5
Hemlock	5.0–6.0	Daffodil	6.0–6.5	Carrot	5.5–7.0
Hydrangea, blue-flowered	4.0–5.0	Dahlia	6.0–7.5	Cauliflower	5.5–7.5
Hydrangea, pink-flowered	6.0–7.0	Daisy, Shasta	6.0–8.0	Celery	5.8–7.0
		Daylily	6.0–8.0	Chive	6.0–7.0
Juniper	5.0–6.0	Delphinium	6.0–7.5	Collard	6.5–7.5
Laurel, mountain	4.5–6.0	Foxglove	6.0–7.5	Corn	5.5–7.0
Lemon	6.0–7.5	Geranium	6.0–8.0	Cucumber	5.5–7.0
Lilac	6.0–7.5	Gladiolus	5.0–7.0	Eggplant	6.0–7.0
Maple, sugar	6.0–7.5	Hibiscus	6.0–8.0	Garlic	5.5–8.0
Oak, white	5.0–6.5	Hollyhock	6.0–8.0	Kale	6.0–7.5
Orange	6.0–7.5	Hyacinth	6.5–7.5	Leek	6.0–8.0
Peach	6.0–7.0	Iris, blue flag	5.0–7.5	Lettuce	6.0–7.0
Pear	6.0–7.5	Lily-of-the-valley	4.5–6.0	Okra	6.0–7.0
Pecan	6.4–8.0	Lupine	5.0–6.5	Onion	6.0–7.0
Plum	6.0–8.0	Marigold	5.5–7.5	Pea	6.0–7.5
Raspberry, red	5.5–7.0	Morning glory	6.0–7.5	Pepper, sweet	5.5–7.0
Rhododendron	4.5–6.0	Narcissus, trumpet	5.5–6.5	Potato	4.8–6.5
Willow	6.0–8.0	Nasturtium	5.5–7.5	Pumpkin	5.5–7.5
		Pansy	5.5–6.5	Radish	6.0–7.0
FLOWERS		Peony	6.0–7.5	Spinach	6.0–7.5
Alyssum	6.0–7.5	Petunia	6.0–7.5	Squash, crookneck	6.0–7.5
Aster, New England	6.0–8.0	Phlox, summer	6.0–8.0	Squash, Hubbard	5.5–7.0
Baby's breath	6.0–7.0	Poppy, oriental	6.0–7.5	Swiss chard	6.0–7.0
Bachelor's button	6.0–7.5	Rose, hybrid tea	5.5–7.0	Tomato	5.5–7.5
		Rose, rugosa	6.0–7.0	Watermelon	5.5–6.5

REFERENCE

PRODUCE WEIGHTS AND MEASURES

VEGETABLES

ASPARAGUS: 1 pound = 3 cups chopped

BEANS (STRING): 1 pound = 4 cups chopped

BEETS: 1 pound (5 medium) = 2½ cups chopped

BROCCOLI: 1 pound = 6 cups chopped

CABBAGE: 1 pound = 4½ cups shredded

CARROTS: 1 pound = 3½ cups sliced or grated

CELERY: 1 pound = 4 cups chopped

CUCUMBERS: 1 pound (2 medium) = 4 cups sliced

EGGPLANT: 1 pound = 4 cups chopped = 2 cups cooked

GARLIC: 1 clove = 1 teaspoon chopped

LEEKS: 1 pound = 4 cups chopped = 2 cups cooked

MUSHROOMS: 1 pound = 5 to 6 cups sliced = 2 cups cooked

ONIONS: 1 pound = 4 cups sliced = 2 cups cooked

PARSNIPS: 1 pound = 1½ cups cooked, puréed

PEAS: 1 pound whole = 1 to 1½ cups shelled

POTATOES: 1 pound (3 medium) sliced = 2 cups mashed

PUMPKIN: 1 pound = 4 cups chopped = 2 cups cooked and drained

SPINACH: 1 pound = ¾ to 1 cup cooked

SQUASHES (SUMMER): 1 pound = 4 cups grated = 2 cups sliced and cooked

SQUASHES (WINTER): 2 pounds = 2½ cups cooked, puréed

SWEET POTATOES: 1 pound = 4 cups grated = 1 cup cooked, puréed

SWISS CHARD: 1 pound = 5 to 6 cups packed leaves = 1 to 1½ cups cooked

TOMATOES: 1 pound (3 or 4 medium) = 1½ cups seeded pulp

TURNIPS: 1 pound = 4 cups chopped = 2 cups cooked, mashed

FRUIT

APPLES: 1 pound (3 or 4 medium) = 3 cups sliced

BANANAS: 1 pound (3 or 4 medium) = 1¾ cups mashed

BERRIES: 1 quart = 3½ cups

DATES: 1 pound = 2½ cups pitted

LEMON: 1 whole = 1 to 3 tablespoons juice; 1 to 1½ teaspoons grated rind

LIME: 1 whole = 1½ to 2 tablespoons juice

ORANGE: 1 medium = 6 to 8 tablespoons juice; 2 to 3 tablespoons grated rind

PEACHES: 1 pound (4 medium) = 3 cups sliced

PEARS: 1 pound (4 medium) = 2 cups sliced

RHUBARB: 1 pound = 2 cups cooked

STRAWBERRIES: 1 quart = 4 cups sliced

REFERENCE

SOWING VEGETABLE SEEDS

SOW OR PLANT IN COOL WEATHER	Beets, broccoli, brussels sprouts, cabbage, lettuce, onions, parsley, peas, radishes, spinach, Swiss chard, turnips
SOW OR PLANT IN WARM WEATHER	Beans, carrots, corn, cucumbers, eggplant, melons, okra, peppers, squashes, tomatoes
SOW OR PLANT FOR ONE CROP PER SEASON	Corn, eggplant, leeks, melons, peppers, potatoes, spinach (New Zealand), squashes, tomatoes
RESOW FOR ADDITIONAL CROPS	Beans, beets, cabbage, carrots, kohlrabi, lettuce, radishes, rutabagas, spinach, turnips

A Beginner's Vegetable Garden

The vegetables suggested below are common, easy-to-grow crops. Make 11 rows, 10 feet long, with at least 18 inches between them. Ideally, the rows should run north and south to take full advantage of the sun. This garden, planted as suggested, can feed a family of four for one summer, with a little extra for canning and freezing or giving away.

ROW

1 Zucchini (4 plants)
2 Tomatoes (5 plants, staked)
3 Peppers (6 plants)
4 Cabbage

ROW

5 Bush beans
6 Lettuce
7 Beets
8 Carrots
9 Swiss chard
10 Radishes
11 Marigolds
(to discourage rabbits!)

SOIL FIXES

If you have **sandy** soil, amend with compost; humus; aged manure; sawdust with extra nitrogen; heavy, clay-rich soil.

If your soil contains a lot of **silt**, amend with coarse sand (not beach sand) or gravel and compost, or aged horse manure mixed with fresh straw.

If your soil is dense with **clay**, amend with coarse sand (not beach sand) and compost.

TO IMPROVE YOUR SOIL, ADD THE PROPER AMENDMENT(S) . . .

bark, ground: made from various tree barks; improves soil structure

compost: an excellent conditioner

leaf mold: decomposed leaves, which add nutrients and structure to soil

lime: raises the pH of acidic soil and helps to loosen clay soil.

manure: best if composted; never add fresh ("hot") manure; is a good conditioner

coarse sand (not beach sand): improves drainage in clay soil

topsoil: usually used with another amendment; replaces existing soil

REFERENCE

IMPORTANT TIMES TO . . .

	. . . FERTILIZE:	. . . WATER:
BEANS	After heavy bloom and set of pods	When flowers form and during pod-forming and picking
BEETS	At time of planting	Before soil gets bone dry
BROCCOLI	3 weeks after transplanting	Continuously for 4 weeks after transplanting
BRUSSELS SPROUTS	3 weeks after transplanting	Continuously for 4 weeks after transplanting
CABBAGE	2 weeks after transplanting	Frequently in dry weather
CARROTS	5 to 6 weeks after sowing	Before soil gets bone-dry
CAULIFLOWER	3 to 4 weeks after transplanting	Frequently
CELERY	At time of transplanting, and after 2 months	Frequently
CORN	When 8 to 10 inches tall, and when first silk appears	When tassels form and when cobs swell
CUCUMBERS	1 week after bloom, and every 3 weeks thereafter	Frequently
LETTUCE	3 weeks after transplanting	Frequently
MELONS	1 week after bloom, and again 3 weeks later	Once a week
ONION SETS	At time of planting, and then every 2 weeks until bulbing begins	In early stage to get plants going
PARSNIPS	1 year before planting	Before soil gets bone-dry
PEAS	After heavy bloom and set of pods	When flowers form and during pod-forming and picking
PEPPERS	At time of planting, and after first fruit-set	Need a steady supply
POTATO TUBERS	At bloom time or time of second hilling	When the size of marbles
PUMPKINS	Just before vines start to run, when plants are about 1 foot tall	Only during drought conditions
RADISHES	Before spring planting	Need plentiful, consistent moisture
SPINACH	When plants are one-third grown	Frequently
SQUASHES, SUMMER & WINTER	When first blooms appear	Frequently
TOMATOES	When fruit are 1 inch in diameter, and then every 2 weeks	For 3 to 4 weeks after transplanting and when flowers and fruit form

REFERENCE

HOW TO GROW HERBS

HERB	START SEEDS INDOORS (WEEKS BEFORE LAST SPRING FROST)	START SEEDS OUTDOORS (WEEKS BEFORE/AFTER LAST SPRING FROST)	HEIGHT/ SPREAD (INCHES)	SOIL	LIGHT**
BASIL*	6–8	Anytime after	12–24/12	Rich, moist	○
BORAGE*	Not recommended	Anytime after	12–36/12	Rich, well-drained, dry	○
CHERVIL	Not recommended	3–4 before	12–24/8	Rich, moist	◑
CHIVES	8–10	3–4 before	12–18/18	Rich, moist	○
CILANTRO/ CORIANDER	Not recommended	Anytime after	12–36/6	Light	○◑
DILL	Not recommended	4–5 before	36–48/12	Rich	○
FENNEL	4–6	Anytime after	48–80/18	Rich	○
LAVENDER, ENGLISH*	8–12	1–2 before	18–36/24	Moderately fertile, well-drained	○
LAVENDER, FRENCH	Not recommended	Not recommended	18–36/24	Moderately fertile, well-drained	○
LEMON BALM*	6–10	2–3 before	12–24/18	Rich, well-drained	○◑
LOVAGE*	6–8	2–3 before	36–72/36	Fertile, sandy	○◑
MINT	Not recommended	Not recommended	12–24/18	Rich, moist	◑
OREGANO*	6–10	Anytime after	12–24/18	Poor	○
PARSLEY*	10–12	3–4 before	18–24/6–8	Medium-rich	◑
ROSEMARY*	8–10	Anytime after	48–72/48	Not too acidic	○
SAGE	6–10	1–2 before	12–48/30	Well-drained	○
SORREL	6–10	2–3 after	20–48/12–14	Rich, organic	○
SUMMER SAVORY	4–6	Anytime after	4–15/6	Medium-rich	○
SWEET CICELY	6–8	2–3 after	36–72/36	Moderately fertile, well-drained	○◑
TARRAGON, FRENCH	Not recommended	Not recommended	24–36/12	Well-drained	○◑
THYME, COMMON*	6–10	2–3 before	2–12/7–12	Fertile, well-drained	○◑

*Recommend minimum soil temperature of 70°F to germinate

** ○ FULL SUN ◑ PARTIAL SHADE

REFERENCE

GROWTH TYPE
Annual
Annual, biennial
Annual, biennial
Perennial
Annual
Annual
Annual
Perennial
Tender perennial
Perennial
Perennial
Perennial
Tender perennial
Biennial
Tender perennial
Perennial
Perennial
Annual
Perennial
Perennial
Perennial

DRYING HERBS

Before drying, remove any dead or diseased leaves or stems. Wash under cool water, shake off excess water, and put on a towel to dry completely. Air drying preserves an herb's essential oils; use for sturdy herbs. A microwave dries herbs more quickly, so mold is less likely to develop; use for moist, tender herbs.

HANGING METHOD: Gather four to six stems of fresh herbs in a bunch and tie with string, leaving a loop for hanging. Or, use a rubber band with a paper clip attached to it. Hang the herbs in a warm, well-ventilated area, out of direct sunlight, until dry. For herbs that have full seed heads, such as dill or coriander, use a paper bag. Punch holes in the bag for ventilation, label it, and put the herb bunch into the bag before you tie a string around the top of the bag. The average drying time is 1 to 3 weeks.

MICROWAVE METHOD: This is better for small quantities, such as a cup or two at a time. Arrange a single layer of herbs between two paper towels and put them in the microwave for 1 to 2 minutes on high power. Let the leaves cool. If they are not dry, reheat for 30 seconds and check again. Repeat as needed. Let cool. Do not overcook, or the herbs will lose their flavor.

STORING HERBS AND SPICES

FRESH HERBS: Dill and parsley will keep for about 2 weeks with stems immersed in a glass of water tented with a plastic bag. Most other fresh herbs (and greens) will keep for short periods unwashed and refrigerated in tightly sealed plastic bags with just enough moisture to prevent wilting. For longer storage, use moisture- and gas-permeable paper and cellophane. Plastic cuts off oxygen to the plants and promotes spoilage.

SPICES AND DRIED HERBS: Store in a cool, dry place.

COOKING WITH HERBS

A **BOUQUET GARNI** is usually made with bay leaves, thyme, and parsley tied with string or wrapped in cheesecloth. Use to flavor casseroles and soups. Remove after cooking.

FINES HERBES use equal amounts of fresh parsley, tarragon, chives, and chervil chopped fine. Commonly used in French cooking, they make a fine omelet or add zest to soups and sauces. Add to salads and butter sauces or sprinkle on noodles, soups, and stews.

HOW TO GROW BULBS

SPRING-PLANTED BULBS

COMMON NAME	LATIN NAME	HARDINESS ZONE	SOIL	LIGHT*	SPACING (INCHES)
ALLIUM	*Allium*	3–10	Well-drained/moist	○	12
BEGONIA, TUBEROUS	*Begonia*	10–11	Well-drained/moist	◑●	12–15
BLAZING STAR/ GAYFEATHER	*Liatris*	7–10	Well-drained	○	6
CALADIUM	*Caladium*	10–11	Well-drained/moist	◑●	8–12
CALLA LILY	*Zantedeschia*	8–10	Well-drained/moist	○◑	8–24
CANNA	*Canna*	8–11	Well-drained/moist	○	12–24
CYCLAMEN	*Cyclamen*	7–9	Well-drained/moist	◑	4
DAHLIA	*Dahlia*	9–11	Well-drained/fertile	○	12–36
DAYLILY	*Hemerocallis*	3–10	Adaptable to most soils	○◑	12–24
FREESIA	*Freesia*	9–11	Well-drained/moist/sandy	○◑	2–4
GARDEN GLOXINIA	*Incarvillea*	4–8	Well-drained/moist	○	12
GLADIOLUS	*Gladiolus*	4–11	Well-drained/fertile	○◑	4–9
IRIS	*Iris*	3–10	Well-drained/sandy	○	3–6
LILY, ASIATIC/ORIENTAL	*Lilium*	3–8	Well-drained	○◑	8–12
PEACOCK FLOWER	*Tigridia*	8–10	Well-drained	○	5–6
SHAMROCK/SORREL	*Oxalis*	5–9	Well-drained	○◑	4–6
WINDFLOWER	*Anemone*	3–9	Well-drained/moist	○◑	3–6

FALL-PLANTED BULBS

COMMON NAME	LATIN NAME	HARDINESS ZONE	SOIL	LIGHT*	SPACING (INCHES)
BLUEBELL	*Hyacinthoides*	4–9	Well-drained/fertile	○◑	4
CHRISTMAS ROSE/ HELLEBORE	*Helleborus*	4–8	Neutral–alkaline	○◑	18
CROCUS	*Crocus*	3–8	Well-drained/moist/fertile	○◑	4
DAFFODIL	*Narcissus*	3–10	Well-drained/moist/fertile	○◑	6
FRITILLARY	*Fritillaria*	3–9	Well-drained/sandy	○◑	3
GLORY OF THE SNOW	*Chionodoxa*	3–9	Well-drained/moist	○◑	3
GRAPE HYACINTH	*Muscari*	4–10	Well-drained/moist/fertile	○◑	3–4
IRIS, BEARDED	*Iris*	3–9	Well-drained	○◑	4
IRIS, SIBERIAN	*Iris*	4–9	Well-drained	○◑	4
ORNAMENTAL ONION	*Allium*	3–10	Well-drained/moist/fertile	○	12
SNOWDROP	*Galanthus*	3–9	Well-drained/moist/fertile	○◑	3
SNOWFLAKE	*Leucojum*	5–9	Well-drained/moist/sandy	○◑	4
SPRING STARFLOWER	*Ipheion uniflorum*	6–9	Well-drained loam	○◑	3–6
STAR OF BETHLEHEM	*Ornithogalum*	5–10	Well-drained/moist	○◑	2–5
STRIPED SQUILL	*Puschkinia scilloides*	3–9	Well-drained	○◑	6
TULIP	*Tulipa*	4–8	Well-drained/fertile	○◑	3–6
WINTER ACONITE	*Eranthis*	4–9	Well-drained/moist/fertile	○◑	3

REFERENCE

DEPTH (INCHES)	BLOOMING SEASON	HEIGHT (INCHES)	NOTES
3–4	Spring to summer	6–60	Usually pest-free; a great cut flower
1–2	Summer to fall	8–18	North of Zone 10, lift in fall
4	Summer to fall	8–20	An excellent flower for drying; north of Zone 7, plant in spring, lift in fall
2	Summer	8–24	North of Zone 10, plant in spring, lift in fall
1–4	Summer	24–36	Fragrant; north of Zone 8, plant in spring, lift in fall
Level	Summer	18–60	North of Zone 8, plant in spring, lift in fall
1–2	Spring to fall	3–12	Naturalizes well in warm areas; north of Zone 7, lift in fall
4–6	Late summer	12–60	North of Zone 9, lift in fall
2	Summer	12–36	Mulch in winter in Zones 3 to 6
2	Summer	12–24	Fragrant; can be grown outdoors in warm climates
3–4	Summer	6–20	Does well in woodland settings
3–6	Early summer to early fall	12–80	North of Zone 10, lift in fall
4	Spring to late summer	3–72	Divide and replant rhizomes every two to five years
4–6	Early summer	36	Fragrant; self-sows; requires excellent drainage
4	Summer	18–24	North of Zone 8, lift in fall
2	Summer	2–12	Plant in confined area to control
2	Early summer	3–18	North of Zone 6, lift in fall
3–4	Spring	8–20	Excellent for borders, rock gardens and naturalizing
1–2	Spring	12	Hardy, but requires shelter from strong, cold winds
3	Early spring	5	Naturalizes well in grass
6	Early spring	14–24	Plant under shrubs or in a border
3	Midspring	6–30	Different species can be planted in rock gardens, woodland gardens, or borders
3	Spring	4–10	Self-sows easily; plant in rock gardens, raised beds, or under shrubs
2–3	Late winter to spring	6–12	Use as a border plant or in wildflower and rock gardens; self-sows easily
4	Early spring to early summer	3–48	Naturalizes well; a good cut flower
4	Early spring to midsummer	18–48	An excellent cut flower
3–4	Late spring to early summer	6–60	Usually pest-free; a great cut flower
3	Spring	6–12	Best when clustered and planted in an area that will not dry out in summer
4	Spring	6–18	Naturalizes well
3	Spring	4–6	Fragrant; naturalizes easily
4	Spring to summer	6–24	North of Zone 5, plant in spring, lift in fall
3	Spring	4–6	Naturalizes easily; makes an attractive edging
4–6	Early to late spring	8–30	Excellent for borders, rock gardens, and naturalizing
2–3	Late winter to spring	2–4	Self-sows and naturalizes easily

REFERENCE

SUBSTITUTIONS FOR COMMON INGREDIENTS

ITEM	QUANTITY	SUBSTITUTION
BAKING POWDER	1 teaspoon	¼ teaspoon baking soda plus ¼ teaspoon cornstarch plus ½ teaspoon cream of tartar
BUTTERMILK	1 cup	1 tablespoon lemon juice or vinegar plus milk to equal 1 cup; or 1 cup plain yogurt
CHOCOLATE, UNSWEETENED	1 ounce	3 tablespoons cocoa plus 1 tablespoon unsalted butter, shortening, or vegetable oil
CRACKER CRUMBS	¾ cup	1 cup dry bread crumbs; or 1 tablespoon quick-cooking oats (for thickening)
CREAM, HEAVY	1 cup	¾ cup milk plus ⅓ cup melted unsalted butter (this will not whip)
CREAM, LIGHT	1 cup	⅞ cup milk plus 3 tablespoons melted, unsalted butter
CREAM, SOUR	1 cup	⅞ cup buttermilk or plain yogurt plus 3 tablespoons melted, unsalted butter
CREAM, WHIPPING	1 cup	⅔ cup well-chilled evaporated milk, whipped; or 1 cup nonfat dry milk powder whipped with 1 cup ice water
EGG	1 whole	2 yolks plus 1 tablespoon cold water; or 3 tablespoons vegetable oil plus 1 tablespoon water (for baking); or 2 to 3 tablespoons mayonnaise (for cakes)
EGG WHITE	1 white	2 teaspoons meringue powder plus 3 tablespoons water, combined
FLOUR, ALL-PURPOSE	1 cup	1 cup plus 3 tablespoons cake flour (not advised for cookies or quick breads); or 1 cup self-rising flour (omit baking powder and salt from recipe)
FLOUR, CAKE	1 cup	1 cup minus 3 tablespoons sifted all-purpose flour plus 3 tablespoons cornstarch
FLOUR, SELF-RISING	1 cup	1 cup all-purpose flour plus 1½ teaspoons baking powder plus ¼ teaspoon salt
HERBS, DRIED	1 teaspoon	1 tablespoon fresh, minced and packed
HONEY	1 cup	1¼ cups sugar plus ½ cup liquid called for in recipe (such as water or oil); or 1 cup pure maple syrup
KETCHUP	1 cup	1 cup tomato sauce plus ¼ cup sugar plus 3 tablespoons apple-cider vinegar plus ½ teaspoon salt plus pinch of ground cloves combined; or 1 cup chili sauce
LEMON JUICE	1 teaspoon	½ teaspoon vinegar
MAYONNAISE	1 cup	1 cup sour cream or plain yogurt; or 1 cup cottage cheese (puréed)
MILK, SKIM	1 cup	⅓ cup instant nonfat dry milk plus ¾ cup water

ITEM	QUANTITY	SUBSTITUTION
MILK, TO SOUR	1 cup	1 tablespoon vinegar or lemon juice plus milk to equal 1 cup. Stir and let stand 5 minutes.
MILK, WHOLE	1 cup	½ cup evaporated whole milk plus ½ cup water; or ¾ cup 2 percent milk plus ¼ cup half-and-half
MOLASSES	1 cup	1 cup honey or dark corn syrup
MUSTARD, DRY	1 teaspoon	1 tablespoon prepared mustard less 1 teaspoon liquid from recipe
OAT BRAN	1 cup	1 cup wheat bran or rice bran or wheat germ
OATS, OLD-FASHIONED	1 cup	1 cup steel-cut Irish or Scotch oats
QUINOA	1 cup	1 cup millet or couscous (whole wheat cooks faster) or bulgur
SUGAR, DARK-BROWN	1 cup	1 cup light-brown sugar, packed; or 1 cup granulated sugar plus 2 to 3 tablespoons molasses
SUGAR, GRANULATED	1 cup	1 cup firmly packed brown sugar; or 1¾ cups confectioners' sugar (makes baked goods less crisp); or 1 cup superfine sugar
SUGAR, LIGHT-BROWN	1 cup	1 cup granulated sugar plus 1 to 2 tablespoons molasses; or ½ cup dark-brown sugar plus ½ cup granulated sugar
SWEETENED CONDENSED MILK	1 can (14 oz.)	1 cup evaporated milk plus 1¼ cups granulated sugar. Combine and heat until sugar dissolves.
VANILLA BEAN	1-inch bean	1 teaspoon vanilla extract
VINEGAR, APPLE-CIDER	—	malt, white-wine, or rice vinegar
VINEGAR, BALSAMIC	1 tablespoon	1 tablespoon red- or white-wine vinegar plus ½ teaspoon sugar
VINEGAR, RED-WINE	—	white-wine, sherry, champagne, or balsamic vinegar
VINEGAR, RICE	—	apple-cider, champagne, or white-wine vinegar
VINEGAR, WHITE-WINE	—	apple-cider, champagne, fruit (raspberry), rice, or red-wine vinegar
YEAST	1 cake (⅗ oz.)	1 package (¼ ounce) or 1 scant tablespoon active dried yeast
YOGURT, PLAIN	1 cup	1 cup sour cream (thicker; less tart) or buttermilk (thinner; use in baking, dressings, sauces)

TYPES OF FAT

One way to minimize your total blood cholesterol is to manage the amount and types of fat in your diet. Aim for monounsaturated and polyunsaturated fats; avoid saturated and trans fats.

MONOUNSATURATED FAT lowers LDL (bad cholesterol) and may raise HDL (good cholesterol) or leave it unchanged; found in almonds, avocados, canola oil, cashews, olive oil, peanut oil, and peanuts.

POLYUNSATURATED FAT lowers LDL and may lower HDL; includes omega-3 and omega-6 fatty acids; found in corn oil, cottonseed oil, fish such as salmon and tuna, safflower oil, sesame seeds, soybeans, and sunflower oil.

SATURATED FAT raises both LDL and HDL; found in chocolate, cocoa butter, coconut oil, dairy products (milk, butter, cheese, ice cream), egg yolks, palm oil, and red meat.

TRANS FAT raises LDL and lowers HDL; a type of fat common in many processed foods, such as most margarines (especially stick), vegetable shortening, partially hydrogenated vegetable oil, many commercial fried foods (doughnuts, french fries), and commercial baked goods (cookies, crackers, cakes).

Calorie-Burning Comparisons

If you hustle through your chores to get to the fitness center, relax. You're getting a great workout already. The left-hand column lists "chore" exercises, the middle column shows the number of calories burned per minute per pound of body weight, and the right-hand column lists comparable "recreational" exercises. For example, a 150-pound person forking straw bales burns 9.45 calories per minute, the same workout he or she would get playing basketball.

Chopping with an ax, fast	0.135	Skiing, cross country, uphill
Climbing hills, with 44-pound load	0.066	Swimming, crawl, fast
Digging trenches	0.065	Skiing, cross country, steady walk
Forking straw bales	0.063	Basketball
Chopping down trees	0.060	Football
Climbing hills, with 9-pound load	0.058	Swimming, crawl, slow
Sawing by hand	0.055	Skiing, cross country, moderate
Mowing lawns	0.051	Horseback riding, trotting
Scrubbing floors	0.049	Tennis
Shoveling coal	0.049	Aerobic dance, medium
Hoeing	0.041	Weight training, circuit training
Stacking firewood	0.040	Weight lifting, free weights
Shoveling grain	0.038	Golf
Painting houses	0.035	Walking, normal pace, asphalt road
Weeding	0.033	Table tennis
Shopping for food	0.028	Cycling, 5.5 mph
Mopping floors	0.028	Fishing
Washing windows	0.026	Croquet
Raking	0.025	Dancing, ballroom
Driving a tractor	0.016	Drawing, standing position

REFERENCE

FREEZER STORAGE TIME
(freezer temperature 0°F or colder)

PRODUCT	MONTHS IN FREEZER

FRESH MEAT

Beef . . . . 6 to 12
Lamb . . . . 6 to 9
Veal . . . . 6 to 9
Pork . . . . 4 to 6
Ground beef, veal, lamb, pork . . . . 3 to 4
Frankfurters . . . . 1 to 2
Sausage, fresh pork . . . . 1 to 2
Cold cuts . . . . Not recommended

FRESH POULTRY

Chicken, turkey (whole) 12
Chicken, turkey (pieces) . . . . 6 to 9
Cornish game hen, game birds . . . 6 to 9
Giblets . . . . 3 to 4

COOKED POULTRY

Breaded, fried 4
Pieces, plain 4
Pieces covered with broth, gravy 6

FRESH FISH AND SEAFOOD

Clams, mussels, oysters, scallops,
  shrimp . . . . 3 to 6
Fatty fish (bluefish, mackerel, perch,
  salmon) . . . . 2 to 3
Lean fish (flounder, haddock, sole) 6

FRESH FRUIT (PREPARED FOR FREEZING)

All fruit except those
  listed below . . . . 10 to 12
Avocados, bananas, plantains 3
Lemons, limes, oranges . . . . 4 to 6

FRESH VEGETABLES (PREPARED FOR FREEZING)

Beans, beets, bok choy, broccoli,
  brussels sprouts, cabbage, carrots,
  cauliflower, celery, corn, greens,
  kohlrabi, leeks, mushrooms, okra,
  onions, peas, peppers, soybeans,
  spinach, summer squashes . . .10 to 12
Asparagus, rutabagas, turnips . . 8 to 10
Artichokes, eggplant . . . . 6 to 8
Tomatoes (overripe or sliced) 2
Bamboo shoots, cucumbers, endive,
  lettuce, radishes, watercress . . . .
  . . . . Not recommended

PRODUCT	MONTHS IN FREEZER

CHEESE (except those listed below) . . . 6
Cottage cheese, cream cheese, feta,
  goat, fresh mozzarella, Neufchâtel,
  Parmesan, processed cheese (opened)
  . . . . Not recommended

DAIRY PRODUCTS

Margarine (not diet) 12
Butter . . . . 6 to 9
Cream, half-and-half 4
Milk 3
Ice cream . . . . 1 to 2

FREEZING HINTS

FOR MEALS, remember that a quart container holds four servings, and a pint container holds two servings.

TO PREVENT STICKING, spread the food to be frozen (berries, hamburgers, cookies, etc.) on a cookie sheet and freeze until solid. Then place in plastic bags and freeze.

LABEL FOODS for easy identification. Write the name of the food, number of servings, and date of freezing on containers or bags.

FREEZE FOODS as quickly as possible by placing them directly against the sides of the freezer.

ARRANGE FREEZER into sections for each food category.

IF POWER IS INTERRUPTED, or if the freezer is not operating normally, do not open the freezer door. Food in a loaded freezer will usually stay frozen for 2 days if the freezer door remains closed during that time period.

PLASTICS

In your quest to go green, use this guide to use and sort plastic. The number, usually found with a triangle symbol on a container, indicates the type of resin used to produce the plastic. Visit **EARTH911.COM** for recycling information in your state.

NUMBER 1 · *PETE or PET (polyethylene terephthalate)*

PETE

IS USED IN . . . . microwavable food trays; salad dressing, soft drink, water, and juice bottles

STATUS . . . . hard to clean; absorbs bacteria and flavors; avoid reusing

IS RECYCLED TO MAKE. . . carpet, furniture, new containers, Polar fleece

---

NUMBER 2 · *HDPE (high-density polyethylene)*

HDPE

IS USED IN . . . . household cleaner and shampoo bottles, milk jugs, yogurt tubs

STATUS . . . . transmits no known chemicals into food

IS RECYCLED TO MAKE. . . detergent bottles, fencing, floor tiles, pens

---

NUMBER 3 · *V or PVC (vinyl)*

V

IS USED IN . . . . cooking oil bottles, clear food packaging, mouthwash bottles

STATUS . . . . is believed to contain phalates that interfere with hormonal development; avoid

IS RECYCLED TO MAKE. . . cables, mudflaps, paneling, roadway gutters

---

NUMBER 4 · *LDPE (low-density polyethylene)*

LDPE

IS USED IN . . . . bread and shopping bags, carpet, clothing, furniture

STATUS . . . . transmits no known chemicals into food

IS RECYCLED TO MAKE. . . envelopes, floor tiles, lumber, trash-can liners

---

NUMBER 5 · *PP (polypropylene)*

PP

IS USED IN . . . . .ketchup bottles, medicine and syrup bottles, drinking straws

STATUS . . . . transmits no known chemicals into food

IS RECYCLED TO MAKE. . . battery cables, brooms, ice scrapers, rakes

---

NUMBER 6 · *PS (polystyrene)*

PS

IS USED IN . . . . disposable cups and plates, egg cartons, take-out containers

STATUS . . . . .is believed to leach styrene, a possible human carcinogen, into food; avoid

IS RECYCLED TO MAKE. . . foam packaging, insulation, light switchplates, rulers

---

NUMBER 7 · *Other (miscellaneous)*

OTHER

IS USED IN . . . . .3- and 5-gallon water jugs, nylon, some food containers

STATUS . . . . .contains bisphenol A, which has been linked to heart disease and obesity; avoid

IS RECYCLED TO MAKE. . . .custom-made products

HOW MUCH DO YOU NEED?

WALLPAPER

Before choosing your wallpaper, keep in mind that wallpaper with little or no pattern to match at the seams and the ceiling will be the easiest to apply, thus resulting in the least amount of wasted wallpaper. If you choose a patterned wallpaper, a small repeating pattern will result in less waste than a large repeating pattern. And a pattern that is aligned horizontally (matching on each column of paper) will waste less than one that drops or alternates its pattern (matching on every other column).

TO DETERMINE THE AMOUNT OF WALL SPACE YOU'RE COVERING:

• Measure the length of each wall, add these figures together, and multiply by the height of the walls to get the area (square footage) of the room's walls.

• Calculate the square footage of each door, window, and other opening in the room. Add these figures together and subtract the total from the area of the room's walls.

• Take that figure and multiply by 1.15, to account for a waste rate of about 15 percent in your wallpaper project. You'll end up with a target amount to purchase when you shop.

• Wallpaper is sold in single, double, and triple rolls. Coverage can vary, so be sure to refer to the roll's label for the proper square footage. (The average coverage for a double roll, for example, is 56 square feet.) After choosing a paper, divide the coverage figure (from the label) into the total square footage of the walls of the room you're papering. Round the answer up to the nearest whole number. This is the number of rolls you need to buy.

• Save leftover wallpaper rolls, carefully wrapped to keep clean.

INTERIOR PAINT

Estimate your room size and paint needs before you go to the store. Running out of a custom color halfway through the job could mean disaster. For the sake of the following exercise, assume that you have a 10x15-foot room with an 8-foot ceiling. The room has two doors and two windows.

FOR WALLS

Measure the total distance (perimeter) around the room:

(10 ft. + 15 ft.) x 2 = 50 ft.

Multiply the perimeter by the ceiling height to get the total wall area:

50 ft. x 8 ft. = 400 sq. ft.

Doors are usually 21 square feet (there are two in this exercise):

21 sq. ft. x 2 = 42 sq. ft.

Windows average 15 square feet (there are two in this exercise):

15 sq. ft. x 2 = 30 sq. ft.

Take the total wall area and subtract the area for the doors and windows to get the wall surface to be painted:

$$\begin{array}{l} \textbf{400 sq. ft. (wall area)} \\ \textbf{- 42 sq. ft. (doors)} \\ \underline{\textbf{- 30 sq. ft. (windows)}} \\ \textbf{328 sq. ft.} \end{array}$$

As a rule of thumb, one gallon of quality paint will usually cover 400 square feet. One quart will cover 100 square feet. Because you need to cover 328 square feet in this example, one gallon will be adequate to give one coat of paint to the walls. (Coverage will be affected by the porosity and texture of the surface. In addition, bright colors may require a minimum of two coats.)

REFERENCE

METRIC CONVERSION

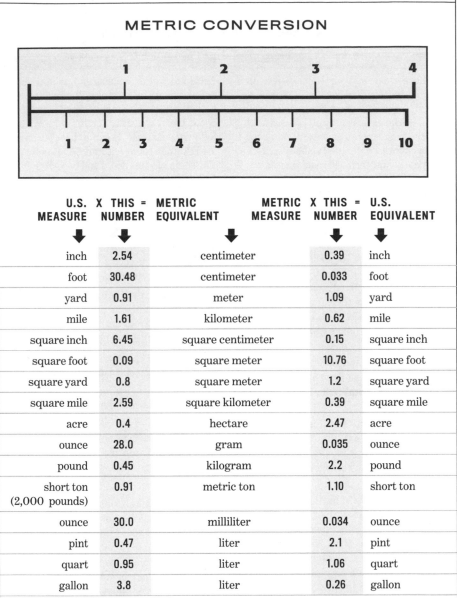

U.S. MEASURE	X THIS = NUMBER	METRIC EQUIVALENT	METRIC MEASURE	X THIS = NUMBER	U.S. EQUIVALENT
inch	2.54	centimeter		0.39	inch
foot	30.48	centimeter		0.033	foot
yard	0.91	meter		1.09	yard
mile	1.61	kilometer		0.62	mile
square inch	6.45	square centimeter		0.15	square inch
square foot	0.09	square meter		10.76	square foot
square yard	0.8	square meter		1.2	square yard
square mile	2.59	square kilometer		0.39	square mile
acre	0.4	hectare		2.47	acre
ounce	28.0	gram		0.035	ounce
pound	0.45	kilogram		2.2	pound
short ton (2,000 pounds)	0.91	metric ton		1.10	short ton
ounce	30.0	milliliter		0.034	ounce
pint	0.47	liter		2.1	pint
quart	0.95	liter		1.06	quart
gallon	3.8	liter		0.26	gallon

If you know the U.S. measurement and want to convert it to metric, multiply it by the number in the left shaded column (example: 1 inch equals 2.54 centimeters). If you know the metric measurement, multiply it by the number in the right shaded column (example: 2 meters equals 2.18 yards).

Where Do You Fit in Your Family Tree?

Technically it's known as consanguinity; that is, the quality or state of being related by blood or descended from a common ancestor. These relationships are shown below for the genealogy of six generations of one family. *–family tree information courtesy of Frederick H. Rohles*

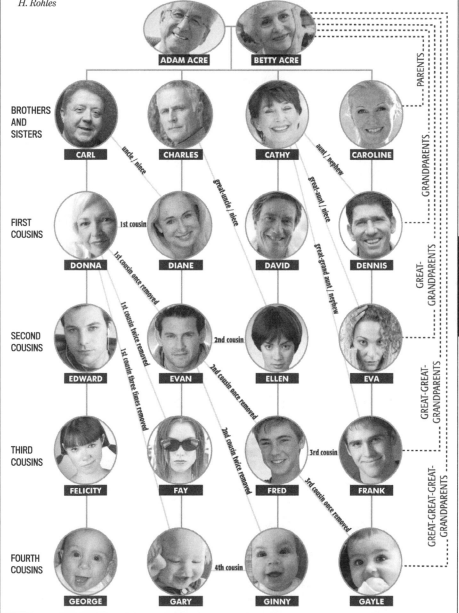

The Golden Rule
(It's true in all faiths.)

BRAHMANISM:
This is the sum of duty: Do naught unto others which would cause you pain if done to you.
Mahabharata 5:1517

BUDDHISM:
Hurt not others in ways that you yourself would find hurtful.
Udana-Varga 5:18

CHRISTIANITY:
All things whatsoever ye would that men should do to you, do ye even so to them; for this is the law and the prophets.
Matthew 7:12

CONFUCIANISM:
Surely it is the maxim of loving-kindness: Do not unto others what you would not have them do unto you.
Analects 15:23

ISLAM:
No one of you is a believer until he desires for his brother that which he desires for himself.
Sunnah

JUDAISM:
What is hateful to you, do not to your fellow man. That is the entire Law; all the rest is commentary.
Talmud, Shabbat 31a

TAOISM:
Regard your neighbor's gain as your own gain and your neighbor's loss as your own loss.
T'ai Shang Kan Ying P'ien

ZOROASTRIANISM:
That nature alone is good which refrains from doing unto another whatsoever is not good for itself.
Dadistan-i-dinik 94:5
–courtesy of Elizabeth Pool

FAMOUS LAST WORDS

Waiting, are they? Waiting, are they? Well–let 'em wait.
(To an attending doctor who attempted to comfort him by saying, "General, I fear the angels are waiting for you.")
–Ethan Allen, American Revolutionary general, d. February 12, 1789

A dying man can do nothing easy.
–Benjamin Franklin, American statesman, d. April 17, 1790

Now I shall go to sleep. Good night.
–Lord George Byron, English writer, d. April 19, 1824

Is it the Fourth?
–Thomas Jefferson, 3rd U.S. president, d. July 4, 1826

Thomas Jefferson–still survives . . .
(Actually, Jefferson had died earlier that same day.)
–John Adams, 2nd U.S. president, d. July 4, 1826

Friends, applaud. The comedy is finished.
–Ludwig van Beethoven, German-Austrian composer, d. March 26, 1827

Moose . . . Indian . . .
–Henry David Thoreau, American writer, d. May 6, 1862

Go on, get out–last words are for fools who haven't said enough.
(To his housekeeper, who urged him to tell her his last words so she could write them down for posterity.)
–Karl Marx, German political philosopher, d. March 14, 1883

Is it not meningitis?
–Louisa M. Alcott, American writer, d. March 6, 1888

How were the receipts today at Madison Square Garden?
–P. T. Barnum, American entrepreneur, d. April 7, 1891

Turn up the lights, I don't want to go home in the dark.
–O. Henry (William Sidney Porter), American writer, d. June 4, 1910

Get my swan costume ready.
–Anna Pavlova, Russian ballerina, d. January 23, 1931

Is everybody happy? I want everybody to be happy. I know I'm happy.
–Ethel Barrymore, American actress, d. June 18, 1959

I'm bored with it all.
(Before slipping into a coma. He died 9 days later.)
–Winston Churchill, English statesman, d. January 24, 1965

You be good. You'll be in tomorrow. I love you.
–Alex, highly intelligent African Gray parrot, d. September 6, 2007